sunday suppers at lucques

sunday suppers at lucques

suzanne goin

WITH TERI GELBER

PHOTOGRAPHS BY SHIMON AND TAMMAR

Alfred A. Knopf   New York   2005

this is a borzoi book
published by alfred a. knopf

www.aaknopf.com

Knopf, Borzoi Books, and the colophon are registered trademarks of Random
House, Inc.

Library of Congress Cataloging-in-Publication Data

Goin, Suzanne, [date]
    Sunday suppers at Lucques / Suzanne Goin with Teri Gelber.—1st ed.
      p. cm.
    "This is a Borzoi book."
    Includes index.
    ISBN 1-4000-4215-1
      1. Cookery, French. 2. Lucques (Restaurant) I. Gelber, Teri. II. Title.

TX719.G623 2005
641.5944—dc22   2004058604

Manufactured in Singapore
Designed by Peter A. Andersen
First Edition

For my parents, John and Marcia Goin,
who brought me into the food world at an early age
and taught me that I could do anything I put my mind to

contents

spring

summer

fall

winter

foreword

In thirty-three years, a great many cooks have come through the kitchen at Chez Panisse, but even among those who moved on to start successful restaurants of their own, Suzanne Goin is a standout. When Suzanne started working at Chez Panisse, we all knew right away that one day she would have a restaurant of her own and that other cooks would be coming to *her* for kitchen wisdom and a warm welcome.

From her first day on the line in the Chez Panisse kitchen, Suzanne looked you right in the eye—but modestly!—and she was always beautifully immaculate, whether in starched whites, or jeans and a T-shirt. She was the perfect line cook in the open café kitchen—charming, friendly, and funny. She had the sunny sarcasm of a young Rosalind Russell, and her sophistication and timing—in and out of the kitchen—left the other young cooks behind. Always thirsty for more knowledge and with a gift for learning, she had figured out which European restaurants would take her as a *stagière* and chosen the ones where she knew she would learn the most. Best of all, she already knew exactly what she liked, and she had the two indispensable characteristics of a great restaurateur: impeccable taste and irrepressible generosity.

Every time I visit her restaurant I'm amazed by her perfect calibration of good cooking and atmospheric joie de vivre. Sometimes when I go to a restaurant where I'm known, the establishment tries too hard to show off its range and goes too far out of its way to impress with too much service and too many dishes in a dizzy display of artistry that becomes an unappetizing embarrassment of riches. They never do that at Suzanne's. There, discernment is folded deftly into the hospitality. They stay focused on the diner and know just what to send out, in the right combinations and with the right balance and restraint, so that the emphasis is always on the purity of the raw materials, not on the kitchen's dazzling technique. When I take friends there, it's like giving them a wonderful gift. The ingredients they use at Lucques are supremely well chosen and appropriate but never utterly obvious, which is what makes Suzanne's creativity of a sort we ought to prize. Recipe names such as Dungeness Crab Salad with Avocado, Beets, Crème Fraîche, and Lime; or Barbara's Apples and Asian Pears with Radicchio, Mint, and Buttermilk Dressing should tell you something about what you'll find in these pages: recipes for food that is truly a creation, in the best sense of the word, but lacks any haughtiness.

It's no surprise that Suzanne has thrived as a down-to-earth chef in a city that often seems so up-in-the-air. Her way of cooking and thinking about food is firmly rooted in the age-old but still lively tradition of real food. Suzanne shares this tradition with everyone she cooks for. Now she shares it with her readers. Her book, which I'm proud to introduce, is ultimately about simple food and pure ingredients.

Suzanne's commitment to organic food of the highest quality—including everything from her tomatoes to her pasta to her oysters—is a vitally important part of her cooking, both the process and the results. She goes above and beyond to find the ultimate examples of beautiful produce (which doesn't necessarily mean a perfectly round apple or a perfectly smooth-skinned tomato), and she is committed to supporting local farmers and food purveyors. Naturally, Suzanne shops at the farmers' market. It's important that you do the same. Find ingredients that are in season, ripe, and organic, because they are the essence of Suzanne's recipes. And the beauty of recipes like these is that they seduce those who make them into a happy awareness of how making the right choices about food makes our world a more sustainable and, at the same time, more meaningful place to live.

—alice waters

acknowledgments

First of all I would like to say a few thank-yous to this book's immediate family:

To my cowriter, Teri Gelber, who, over many gallons of green tea and late-afternoon slivers of bittersweet chocolate, helped to put my thoughts into words.

To my agent, Janis Donnaud, for her professional yet big-sisterly guidance. Thanks for supporting me at the right times and putting me in my place when I needed it.

To Shimon and Tammar Rothstein for coming into my life and giving me the most gorgeous photographs ever.

To the team at Knopf, especially Paul Bogaards and Sarah Robinson, for their unending patience as we turned this into the book I've always dreamed of.

There would be no Lucques and certainly no Sunday suppers without all of our generous investors, the incredible staff from the past seven years, and our loyal, enthusiastic, and trusting customers. Thank you all so very much.

I would like to thank Lucques's other parent, whom I often refer to as my "restaurant wife," Caroline Styne, for sharing the burden and joy of restaurant ownership with me. Thank you for your passion for wine, food, and service, and for always trusting and believing in me.

A huge thank-you to my sister and Lucques general manager, Jessica Goin Norton, who is the reigning queen of Sunday suppers. She's the one joyously "performing" the menu on the phone week after week, the one who knows every Sunday regular customer by name, face, and table and server preference, and the one who convinced me not to give up early on when I was on the verge of tears in the back alley after another slow Sunday. (I was sure that no one was ever going to get the concept and that I would have to throw in the towel and serve the regular menu on Sundays.) Jessica took Sunday suppers as her personal cause and somehow turned Sunday into one of the busiest nights of the week. Thank you for your dedication and devotion to me, to Sunday suppers, and to your beloved regulars!

To Lucques's chef de cuisine, Brian Wolff, who passionately and wholeheartedly embraced the Sunday supper concept as a customer long before he ever worked for us. I am indebted to you for keeping the joy and excitement of Sundays alive, especially while I was locked up in my house testing recipes. You are extraordinarily talented and a joy to work with. Similarly, thanks to chef de cuisine Daniel Mattern, who held down the fort at A.O.C., carrying out my vision but also bringing his own creative ideas and commitment to the restaurant. Without the two of you I could never have taken the time to write this book.

Two spectacular pastry chefs, Roxana Jullapat and Kimberly Sklar Kidder, worked tirelessly to develop and adapt these sweet recipes for the home cook. Breanne Varela and Maria Santos were quick to test and retest recipes for me, and always with smiles on their faces (at least when I was looking).

Corina Weibel, Julie Robles, Robert Chalmers, and Sara Lauren were there in the early days to help me figure out how to make the restaurant and Sunday suppers what I wanted them to be. Sous-chefs John Sadao, Rodolfo Aguado, Molly McCook, and Nathan Allen helped me test recipes and organize the madness of running two restaurants and writing a book simultaneously. Cooks Colleen Hennessey, Jonathan Baltazar, and Javier Espinoza worked meticulously on the recipes and helped me keep it real: "Yes, we really *do* use that much olive oil!" A special thanks to Ian Chang, who, along with testing recipes, pulled a couple of old-school all-nighters, putting his MFA to use with last minute editing and rewriting. The mad dash to the airport FedEx was way beyond "above and beyond." Thank you all for giving so much of yourselves to the restaurants and to me.

Our first employee at Lucques, now general manager of A.O.C., Cynthia Mendoza, has been there for me from day one, consistently going way beyond the call of duty. In the midst of taming the beast that is A.O.C., she manages to call back all the people I'm afraid to call and even run out for an emergency bag of kitty litter. I count on you more than you know, as much for your friendship as for your errand-running skills. When we lost Cynthia to A.O.C., Wendy Gardner took on my oddball requests at Lucques with a vengeance and a smile. And of course, thank you to Ralf Kindler, whose title is server, but whose role at Lucques defies description; he is recipe tester, impromptu translator, event coordinator, service adviser, and all-around know-it-all (really, he does know it all!).

Jesse Lomeli, Juan Avila, Eli Chavez, Flavio Vasquez, Manuel Hernandez, Jesus Morales, Victor Rodriguez, Arturo Kambray, and Miguel "Miggy" Gonzales are the backbone of the restaurant and make coming to work a pleasure. Thank you for your hard work, dedication, and, maybe most important, your sense of humor. James Anderson, Zach Hangauer, Aaron Cook, Eric Durrschmidt, Luis Banuelos, Colleen Duggan, Louise Montoya, and Lucia Tarantino are the servers extraordinaires. Thank you for believing in Sunday suppers and for spreading the word and the love.

The food I make each day relies on our incredible local farmers—Peter Schaner, the Colemans, Phil McGrath, Maryanne Carpenter, Dede and John

Thogmartin, James Birch, Suncoast Farm, Fairview Gardens, Jerry Rutiz, Weizer Family Farm, Scott Peacock, and the Spencers of Windrose Farm. I can't thank you all enough for your commitment, hard work, and all of the beautiful treasures you bring us from the fields.

Thank you also to Niman Ranch and Ocean Jewels for helping me find meat and fish worthy of the produce!

Sunday supper acknowledgments wouldn't be complete without a big thank-you to Cliff Meyer, Cathy Root, Shirlee and Sid Davis, Dan Blow, Karen and Abe Witteles, and Darla and Jack Feldman, who come to Lucques *every single* Sunday. You make it all worthwhile!

Last, but certainly not least, thank you to my husband, David Lentz, who gives me unbelievable love and support in spite of my crazy hours, mangled hands, and obsessive-compulsive behavior. You bring laughter, joy, and encouragement to my everyday life. I love you.

sunday suppers at lucques

introduction

Food was an absurdly large part of my childhood. My parents planned vacations around their dining options; they scoured cookbooks for dinner-party recipes; they even developed a complex and rigid "preferential voting" system to determine which restaurant we would eat at on Friday nights. But my favorite of these culinary obsessions played itself out at home on Sunday mornings, when my dad stood up from the breakfast table and put on his apron. That's when I knew we were in for some fun.

Though my father usually opted for dining at fancy French restaurants, when cooking at home he suddenly became an Italian peasant. His hearty rustic stews involved a lot of work, so I naturally took on the role of his prep cook. I would cut the bacon with scissors, peel the garlic, snip the parsley, and grate the Parmesan. By the time our creation was ready to eat, lunchtime had passed, but it was still too early for dinner. On Sundays, it seemed, traditional mealtimes went out the window. Hungry nonetheless, we'd carry our steaming bowls out to the backyard and indulge in Dad's latest culinary endeavor. When I think about it now, we must have been a funny sight—sitting around the patio table in the 90-degree Southern California heat, hunched over our hot country stew with sweat rolling off our foreheads. As delicious as those late lunches were, the best part was the company: in the kitchen with my dad, and later sitting down at the table with my mother and sister.

As I grew into my teens, I took on a bigger role in the family kitchen. My mother loved to cook and entertain, but felt she missed a lot of the party while tending to dinner in the kitchen. So she enlisted my sister and me to help out. I was the cook, and my sister, Jessica, was the waitress and dishwasher. We loved it. Cooking gave me an excuse to stay in the kitchen (I was shy) while my more outgoing sister socialized with the grown-ups. It was fun to see our parents laugh and go a little wild, to watch a guest dancing on the table; once, my father had one too many glasses of wine and gave away my mother's favorite Limoges ashtray. Being an integral part of the evening's festivities was thrilling. But best of all were the contented looks of my parents' friends at the end of the meal.

My parents' passion for food dovetailed with a passion for travel. I can remember sitting in the living room with my father, a map of France spread out on the floor, as he pinpointed the Michelin-starred restaurants he wanted to visit. He'd assess the most convenient starting point for his eating itinerary, and then find a nearby house for us to rent. Once we'd arrived at our destination my sister and I were charged with gathering provisions from local *boulangeries, boucheries,* and *pâtisseries.* We loved our walks into town, where we encountered fascinating and foreign things, such as sheep farms, pétanque courts, and cute French boys. I was in heaven and happily took on the culinary duties of our temporary French "home."

And then there were the restaurants. My father and I were obsessed with studying the Michelin guide, and together we rated our favorites as we ate our way through the countryside. For every starred Michelin restaurant we went to, there were many other, less formal meals. We would head to the local cafés and bistros for comforting suppers of soft omelettes and simple salads, or grilled *steak frites.* As I grew more adventuresome, I would sometimes choose the set menu—a three-course meal that the chef had proposed for the evening. The main course was usually a country-style stew, or perhaps slices of grilled leg of lamb with flageolet beans. In smaller towns, sometimes the menu wasn't even posted; customers ordered it on faith. Those homey, casual dinners were just as exciting to me as the more elaborate meals at elegant restaurants.

Over the next few years, as I made my way through junior high and high school, I couldn't stop thinking about cooking. The summer before going away to college, while my friends were interning at law offices and candy-striping in hospitals, I did a *stage* at Ma Maison, the most acclaimed French restaurant in Los Angeles at the time. After spending eight hours on my feet in the pastry kitchen, I would come home each day and practice my newfound skills, re-creating the Ma Maison pastry department at home. I should've known I was hooked. But, when fall came around, I followed the traditional path and packed my bags for college. Even there, it didn't take long for the restaurant world to draw me back in. Soon enough I was working three nights a week in the kitchen of Al Forno, the best restaurant in Providence, Rhode Island.

After finishing my degree at Brown University, I chose the route of a self-taught chef. Over the next fifteen years, I worked my way up the ladder, from restaurant to restaurant, learning as much as I possibly could. From Providence to Berkeley to Paris, as I advanced from salad girl to executive chef, those childhood memories of outdoor family meals, luxurious starred restaurants, and humble bistro menus simmered in the back of my mind.

When I opened Lucques in 1998, my partner, Caroline Styne, and I envisioned a place where food would be the catalyst for so much more. We wanted the restaurant to be part of the community—a meeting place where friends could gather, relax, escape, celebrate, and, of course, eat. From the

beginning, I decided that Sundays would be special, with an ambience reminiscent of those late-afternoon family feasts of my childhood and the intimate informal menus I enjoyed in France. A fixed-price menu offering an appetizer, a choice of two main courses (usually a meat and a fish), and dessert would encourage a social environment where everyone shared a similar food experience in a relaxed atmosphere.

Week to week, different factors determine what I cook on Sundays. Sometimes a particular ingredient inspires me. Weather and the mood it brings are also a consideration. Cool, cloudy days call for a comforting stew of braised meat. But on a warm balmy evening, a platter of sliced heirloom tomatoes with burrata cheese dressed in an oregano vinaigrette seems just right. Ethnic holidays like St. Patrick's Day or Bastille Day spur fun, thematic meals. And when I can't find time for a vacation, Moroccan and Spanish ingredients mysteriously find their way onto the Sunday supper menu. As you use the ideas in this book, I encourage you to let your own moods, cravings, and whims inspire your own Sunday suppers.

More than anything, I'm inspired by the beautiful produce grown by our local farmers. The spring crop of sugar snap peas, the last-of-the-season Indian peaches, or bright and shiny Meyer lemons are all cause for a Sunday celebration. Fortunately, today farmers' markets are popping up everywhere from country hamlets to inner cities. Seek out your own regional sources, whether they be farmers' markets, farm stands, or the neighborhood grocer. Always look for what's best at the moment, and let the produce itself guide you. For me, produce starts the creative process and is the ultimate inspiration.

Every twist and turn you take on your cooking path makes you the cook that you are. Cooks I've worked with over the years, faraway jobs arranged by airmail, and other happenstances have provided me with unexpected and valuable lessons and shaped me into the cook I am today.

The lessons I learned at Al Forno in Rhode Island during my college years have stayed with me ever since. There, George Germon and Johanne Killeen's approach to cooking proved eye-opening. Because they were self-taught, they weren't boxed in by culinary conventions and rules; they were making food they liked to eat, using fresh and seasonal ingredients and giving them an Italian twist. It was a revelation to me that great food didn't have to be French.

At Chez Panisse I learned how to cook locally, from the market and by the seasons. Every other day, one of the cooks would drive up to Sonoma to load up the truck with whatever farmer Bob Cannard had picked for us that morning.

Our daily challenge was to create a menu that would showcase the sometimes odd combination of produce that showed up. Each day was a surprise that taught me how to cook with the ingredients that were available.

Everywhere I worked, from Boston to Paris and back to L.A., I saw different styles and approaches, and I learned not just from the chefs but from all the cooks working around me. Over time, all the various lessons at the stovetop become part of a cook's unconscious. Eventually, as his or her personal style begins to take shape, a cook gains the freedom to create without thinking about *how* to create. It wasn't until I started writing this book that I noticed some of my own patterns and habits in the kitchen. I realized that almost every savory dish I make starts with a seasoning foundation of olive oil, rosemary, chile, and onion. It's a flavor base that I resort to instinctively. In the end, you barely taste the rosemary and chile specifically, but they lend an aromatic depth to the dish.

As you cook your way through these recipes, you'll come upon my ingredient fixations. I use lots of shallots, thyme, sherry vinegar, and opal basil. I love bacon, breadcrumbs, feta cheese, Mexican chorizo, toasted nuts, pecorino, fresh herbs, and copious amounts of olive oil.

Great ingredients are the foundation of cooking. But to be a great cook you must be an interactive cook. Using all of your senses throughout the entire process is key. Watch, smell, listen to, and most of all taste the dish as you go along. Cooking isn't an assembly line or a chemistry project—adding A to B to C and then stirring 10 minutes. When food is cooking properly it's "happy" and "dancing" in the pan, glistening and sizzling along the way. By watching what's happening in the pan, you'll know what the food is "asking" for. Be on the lookout at all times. If your spot prawns are seizing up and drying out, add more olive oil. If a braise appears to be boiling too hard, it probably is, so lower the heat a little. Taste your salad as you dress it, asking yourself "Does it need more lemon or salt?" and "Are the leaves sufficiently glazed with vinaigrette?" You'll come to realize that this way of cooking isn't burdensome but that the pleasure of creation is in the process.

In this creative process, one of the most important skills you'll need to develop is seasoning. It's a fundamental part of being a good cook, and a skill you'll acquire by practicing and tasting as you go. One of my first lessons in seasoning came at an early age, in a funny, roundabout way. My father considered my sister and me built-in waitresses; if, partway through dinner, he wanted seconds, it was my job to replenish his plate. On my way to the kitchen, I'd always sneak a bite of whatever was left on his plate, and for some reason, his food always tasted better than mine. Over time, I began to realize the connection

between my father's liberal use of sea salt, fresh black pepper, and butter and the deliciousness of his food. Thoughtful seasoning is the key to great-tasting food.

When I started this book, there was a lot of debate about whether or not to give exact measurements for salt or simply tell the reader to "season to taste." As I thought about it, I realized that a lot of people don't know how to "season to taste" and might end up being disappointed with the results of the recipes. So I changed my mind and decided to give measurements after all. Think of these salt and pepper measurements as guidelines to coach you through the "seasoning to taste" process. Once you develop your seasoning palate, you'll most likely find those measuring spoons awkward and no longer necessary. You'll notice that in the recipe ingredient lists I sometimes simply call for kosher salt and freshly ground pepper without any particular measurement, while other times I specify exactly how much to add in the text of the recipe. No matter what, you should

always be tasting and seasoning throughout the cooking process. The same is true for lemons: I usually call for ½ lemon or 1 lemon, which doesn't mean you will need all of it, but it's nice to have it in case you do. If the recipe says "a generous squeeze of lemon juice," squeeze it in, taste, and add more if you like. I don't know any cooks who measure lemon juice or salt as they cook.

So much of cooking can't be taught from a book, but as you make these dishes you'll begin to learn the steps and skills that will enable you to cook with your own intuition. Eventually you'll get to a point where you have a built-in battery of skills to create something of your own, the way I did over time.

The upcoming recipes are all meant for a gathering of six people. That's not a large number for a restaurant chef, but at home, preparing food for that many requires some forethought. Start each recipe by preparing your *mise en place,* prepping your ingredients ahead of time, the way we do at the restaurant. Read through the recipe to find out what needs to be done before you begin cooking. Often there are onions to be chopped, spices to be toasted and ground, garlic to be minced, flour to be measured, and herbs to be picked. Tackling these tasks ahead of time makes cooking more pleasurable and satisfying.

My Sunday supper menus are meant to inspire you and to lead you from season to season. Part of the fun of planning a meal is that you get to cook what you're in the mood to eat. Feel free to mix and match the dishes according to your own tastes and cravings. And if you're not cooking for six, you could cut the recipes in half or just have leftovers for lunch or dinner the next day.

Some of the recipes are simpler than others. If you don't have much experience, start with the salads and less demanding grilled dishes. Once you've made your way through a few of those, go ahead and try your hand at the Leg of Lamb with Chorizo Stuffing, Romesco Potatoes, and Black Olives or the Grilled Pork Confit with Braised Rice Soubise and Roasted Figs. These recipes take longer, but if you set aside some extra time, they will be worth the effort. If you come across a technique that isn't familiar, refer to the section at the beginning of the book where I explain in detail cooking techniques such as braising, grilling, and sautéing.

Before you begin cooking, take a quick glance at the pantry section, where I list the ingredients I find myself reaching for time and time again. Stock your pantry with some of these items so you'll be prepared for what's to come. In addition to the year-round produce list in the beginning of the book, you'll also find helpful market sections preceding each seasonal chapter. Use these market lists as guides to shopping for fresh fruits and vegetables. Don't obsess about finding exactly the same ingredients that I use here in Southern California; the beauty of local produce is that it's specific to your region, so, when you're cooking, highlight what's best in your area. And if you can't find a specific ingredient, feel free to improvise and make substitutions. When I'm going on and on about Elgin Marble apricots, don't panic. Realize that you may find an equally delicious apricot variety that I've never heard of. Most important, choose the most pristine ingredients available to you. If the rapini at your market isn't looking so good, you're better off substituting broccoli or mustard greens if they look fresher and more lively.

Above all else, when you're cooking, remember to enjoy the process. Give yourself enough time, and forgive yourself if you make a mistake. I hope that you will follow the guidelines of these recipes, and that as you do, you will watch, listen, and learn what is going on in the pan, taking that knowledge on to the next dish you make.

year-round produce

arugula

This spicy green is related to radishes and watercress, and you'll taste a hint of both in the pungent deep green leaves. Although the prime time for arugula is during the cooler months, fortunately for me there's always a local farmer growing arugula year-round. Some chefs remove the stems, but I prefer to leave some of them on because they add texture and an extra-peppery note. There are quite a few different types of arugula—some have smooth, flat leaves like spinach; others are more elongated, with jagged edges and a crinkly texture. Small baby leaves are more delicate and tend to be milder in flavor. Wild arugula is harder to find and much more pungent than its cultivated cousin.

Arugula is great in salads, by itself, or mixed with other greens like frisée and radicchio. In a salad with fruit, arugula balances the sweetness with its spice. Don't think of arugula strictly for first courses; I love to dress the heartier, more strongly flavored large leaves in lemon juice and olive oil and serve them on the plate with grilled steak. The spicy greens provide a counterpoint to the rich meat, and the steak juices run into the salad, further dressing the greens and wilting them slightly. When serving family-style, I often place the starch or vegetable on the platter first and then scatter some arugula leaves over it before arranging the fish, meat, or poultry on top.

Wash arugula the same way you would other greens, by submerging it in a large bowl of water and swirling it with your hands to release any sand. Gently lift the greens out of the water, and dry them in a salad spinner. The arugula sold in bags at the supermarket doesn't have the same texture and sharp distinct flavor that the fresher bunched greens have.

beets

When I was growing up, beets were just a crinkle-cut curiosity out of a can. Years later, when I tasted my first fresh beet, it was a revelation. Whether in a salad dressed with cumin or horseradish, or in a gingered salsa to accompany fish, beets' sweet, earthy flavor adds a bright note to many dishes. Their rainbow assortment of colors—red, pink, yellow, white, and candy-striped—are fun to show off in a salad or an antipasto. Beets pair wonderfully with nuts or cheese, and in the winter make a refreshing first course with citrus fruit.

To roast beets, cut off the greens (save them), leaving a few inches of the stems still attached. Wash the beets and toss them with olive oil, salt, and pepper. Place them in a shallow pan with a little bit of water, cover tightly with foil, and roast in the oven until tender when pierced. When the beets have cooled, slip off the skin with your fingers.

Choose rock-hard beets with bright, perky greens. These delicious green tops are a bonus. If the leaves are small and tender, steam or sauté them lightly and add them to your beet salad. Larger beet greens are delicious sautéed and served by themselves, in a vegetable ragoût, or with pasta.

carrots

Carrots are often taken for granted in the kitchen. When freshly picked with verdant, dirt-covered stems, carrots are something to get excited about. They are delicious, sweet, and filled with intense flavor. At the market, I buy the large, sometimes knobby and odd-shaped carrots to make juices, soups, and purées. Slender and delicate baby carrots come in a variety of

Arturo Reyes of McGrath Family Farms

colors—crimson red, pale yellow, and of course orange. To prepare the smaller carrots, I peel them carefully, leaving some of the stem attached, and roast them in the oven or sauté them with a little butter and water. Look for carrots that feel very firm with bright, lively tops still attached.

fennel

I never tire of fennel. Its anise aroma and taste are intoxicating, and I'm continually amazed at how few home cooks have fennel in their repertoires. To me, it's almost as essential as onions and thyme. Though fennel is available year-round, I especially love the sweet, tender bulbs of spring.

I like fennel both raw and cooked and can never resist crunching on a juicy piece when I'm working with it. It's delicious tossed into salads or served on an antipasto plate with prosciutto. And when making a mirepoix, that classic flavoring base normally made with onions, carrots, and celery, I frequently replace the celery with fennel. When seared and braised in olive oil, fennel tastes like a completely different vegetable, rich and luscious, soft and sweet.

To prepare raw fennel, remove the outer leaves and stalks and cut in half lengthwise. Use a mandoline or sharp knife, and leave the root end intact so you can cut the bulb into pretty wispy slices. Sometimes when cooking fennel, it's fun to reinforce its anise flavor by adding a few fennel seeds, some fennel fronds, or a dash of Pernod. When buying fennel, choose firm bulbs that feel heavy for their size and still have their long, feathery green tops attached.

garlic

Garlic is a member of the lily family, as are onions, shallots, and leeks. In its raw state, garlic can be hot and pungent, so remember that a little goes a long way. Pounded with a mortar and pestle, it's the first step to making aïoli, salsa verde, and pesto. When cooking garlic, I prefer to slice it lengthwise and stew it gently in olive oil. The flavors mellow and become sweet, while still imparting that unmistakable garlic flavor to your cooking. Stay away from peeled garlic sold in jars. To keep it from oxidizing, peel and slice garlic just before cooking. When buying garlic, look for firm, tight bulbs without green sprouts. If you find a sprout running through a clove after you peel it, cut the clove in half lengthwise and remove the sprout with a paring knife.

herbs

Fresh herbs, with their bright, intense flavors, are essential to great cooking. I divide herbs into two categories: soft and hearty. Some of my favorite soft herbs are tarragon, chives, chervil, parsley, basil, and cilantro. Soft herbs are usually best in their raw state, torn or sliced into salads, ground in the mortar to make salsas or vinaigrettes, and sprinkled over dishes just before serving. When I make an herb salad, I leave the smaller leaves whole to show off their shapes. Hearty herbs, like rosemary, thyme, oregano, marjoram, savory, and sage, are usually added earlier in the cooking process, to season dishes and add depth and aroma. Unless otherwise stated, all herbs used in the upcoming recipes are fresh rather than dried.

leeks

Leeks come in all sizes, from slender baby leeks to the larger, chunky stalks topped with dark-green shoots. Baby leeks are delicious grilled and served with fish or on an antipasto plate. I like to sear and braise the bigger leeks in olive oil, white wine, and stock, or slice them on the diagonal and add them to soups, sauces, or vegetable ragoûts. Large or small, leeks impart an elegant, delicate flavor.

Because leeks' many layers tend to hold dirt and sand, it's important to wash them carefully. If you're keeping the leeks intact to braise or grill, cut them in half lengthwise and trim the roots carefully, leaving the root end attached. Soak the stalks in a bowl of water, shaking them to release the sand hidden in between the layers. You may need to repeat this process in a clean bowl of water if the leeks are very dirty. When sliced leeks are called for, slice them first and then clean them in a bowl of water. Though they are available year-round, the peak seasons for leeks are fall and spring. Choose leeks that have some flexibility in their lower portion (avoid those with hard, woody cores) and have crisp, unblemished green tops.

lettuces

Salad mixes sold in the supermarket are convenient, but if you can buy directly from farmers or grow your own lettuces, you'll develop a new appreciation for the "simple" green salad. Some of my favorite lettuces are Little Gems, Baby Romaine, Butter, and Red or Green Oak. Rather than seeking out one particular variety, let the market guide you and choose the perkiest, most appealing greens.

Lettuce heads and leaves should be tight and crisp. When you wash the leaves, fill the sink or a large bowl with cold water and place the leaves in, pushing them around gently to free the dirt and sand. Lift the leaves out carefully and dry the lettuce thoroughly in a salad spinner before dressing it, so the vinaigrette doesn't get watered down.

onions

There isn't a cook that I know of who could exist without onions. So many savory dishes rely on their deep, rich flavor. For cooked dishes, I usually call for yellow or Spanish onions, but you can substitute milder-flavored white onions in a pinch. Red onions are often sweeter than yellow onions and are delicious raw. I like to use them for relishes and salsas and sliced into tomato salads. To mellow their pungency and to crisp them up a bit, I soak sliced red onions briefly in ice water before adding them to salads. Choose firm, unsprouted onions, and store them in a cool, dark place away from other root vegetabes.

potatoes

Not all potatoes are created equal. With farmers growing such a great variety—like French fingerlings, Banana, Purple Peruvian, Bintje, and Yellow Finn—there are more potatoes to choose from today than ever before. I love the various yellow-fleshed types, which are usually richer in flavor and have a denser, creamier flesh than others. Fingerlings, named for their long fingerlike shape, are another favorite; they come in red, yellow, purple, and white. Experiment with some of the varieties grown in your area. Except for mashing or making French fries, Russet potatoes are a little too dry and mealy for my taste.

Choose potatoes that are very firm, not discolored or bruised, and avoid any that have a green tint to them. Store them in a cool, dark place, separate from onions, which will cause them to sprout. Despite what my mother may have done, it's best not to store potatoes for more than a few weeks. (See Spring Market Report, page 32, for information on new potatoes.)

shallots

I can't imagine cooking without shallots. A milder, more nuanced member of the onion family, shallots have less heat than onions and can be used raw or cooked. I start most vinaigrettes with diced shallots, both to season the dressing and to add a burst of flavor and texture to the final salad. When cooked, shallots add both sweet and savory background notes. (See Techniques, pages 23–24, for how to dice or slice shallots.) Choose firm, unbruised shallots that aren't sprouting.

watercress

You'll find this zesty green throughout the year, though it's best when the air is still cool, keeping the fragile leaves crisp and upright. Tossed with other greens into a salad or used on its own as a bed for grilled meat or fish, watercress surprises with peppery brightness. Watercress also makes a wonderful soup when lightly cooked and puréed.

Be sure the watercress you buy has been picked recently and smells fresh. Avoid wilted bunches. The leaves should be a deep green without any discoloration or yellowing. The hothouse-grown variety is flimsier and doesn't have the same spicy deliciousness as field-grown watercress. Wash the watercress, dry it, and store it wrapped in paper towels for a very short time, to retain the crispness of the leaves. Trim the coarse stems from the watercress just before using.

pantry

anchovies

Anchovies are one of those funny foods that gourmets love and "regular" people fear. Used in small amounts, anchovies are a great seasoning agent, giving many dishes a mysterious layer of flavor that doesn't taste fishy or salty. You'll find that oftentimes people who "hate" anchovies love Caesar salad! I prefer anchovies packed in salt. They hold their shape and taste better than oil-packed anchovies. Before using salt-packed anchovies soak them in a few changes of water and carefully remove the fins and bones.

bacon and pancetta

Bacon is side pork that is cured and then smoked; Pancetta is an Italian-style bacon that is cured in salt and spices but not smoked. I like to think of bacon and pancetta as seasoning agents as much as ingredients on their own, adding savory, salty, and, in the case of bacon, smoky flavor. I tend to use bacon for salads and with roasted vegetables, but choose pancetta for dishes that are long cooked, like stuffings or braises. The smokiness of bacon can be overpowering when it cooks for a long time.

I prefer bacon in slabs rather than precut slices, so I can slice it however I like. Often I cut bacon into classic French *lardons,* chunky rectangles. To get even-shaped *lardons,* place the slab of bacon on a cutting board and cut it lengthwise into ⅜-inch-thick slices. Stack a few of the slices and cut crosswise into ⅜-inch-wide rectangles. Pancetta is rolled and usually sold in slices. To use it for wrapping fish, ask your butcher to slice it thinly; for dicing, ask for a thicker-cut slice.

Nueske's bacon from Wisconsin is an excellent choice and can be mail ordered (see Sources). If you really get into the bacon swing of things I highly recommend the Grateful Palate's Bacon of the Month Club (see Sources).

black pepper

Most of the recipes in this book call for freshly ground black pepper. Its store-bought counterpart, pre-ground and aged for who knows how long on the supermarket shelf, should be avoided. If you don't own a pepper mill, run out to the store right now! Look for Tellicherry black peppercorns from India. Remember that, as with all spices, freshness counts.

black rice

Grown in the salty marshes of the Veneto region in Italy, this deep-purple rice has a mild, salty, oceany essence and, once cooked, results in tender and chewy midnight-colored grains. The Asian version, often sold under the name "forbidden rice," is an adequate substitute although it doesn't have the same intense aroma and flavor as the Italian variety (see Sources).

breadcrumbs and croutons

Save leftover pieces of country-style artisanal bread for breadcrumbs or croutons. Never throw them away! To make breadcrumbs, remove the crust from the bread, tear it into 2-inch pieces, and grind the bread in a food processor. Store the breadcrumbs in a ziplock bag or airtight plastic container in the freezer for up to a month. I toss breadcrumbs with olive oil and toast them in the oven until crispy before sprinkling them on pastas, stews, and other dishes.

To make croutons, remove the crust and tear the bread into uneven, rustic-looking 1-inch pieces. Toss them with olive oil and squeeze them gently to help them absorb the oil. Bake the croutons in the oven, turning them a couple of times so they brown evenly. Toasted croutons are delicious in salads and for stuffings.

capers

Capers are the buds from thorny caper bushes that populate the craggly hillsides of the Mediterranean. Once picked, they're brined and packed in either salt or vinegar. I prefer salt-packed capers, because they taste more like their pungent caper selves than their vinegar-saturated counterparts. Capers come in different sizes. The larger ones are meaty and have a floral aspect, making them excellent for pounding into salsa verde. Smaller capers require no chopping or pounding, and add the distinctive piquant effect only a caper can contribute. Before using capers, soak only as many as you need for a few minutes in two or three changes of water to remove the salt (or vinegar). Drain well and pat dry before using.

chiles

When used with care, dried red chiles de árbol add a hint of heat and flavor without overwhelming a dish. Many of my savory dishes begin with a sofrito, a flavor base of sautéed onions, dried chile, and a fresh rosemary sprig sizzled together in olive oil. You'll find chiles de árbol in the ethnic section of the supermarket or in most spice shops. You can substitute another small dried red chile if you like (see Sources).

Barbara Spencer of Windrose Farm

chorizo

Chorizo is a spicy Mexican pork sausage seasoned with cumin, paprika, garlic, and chiles. Don't confuse fresh Mexican chorizo with the harder, salami-like Spanish chorizo (which is also delicious). The recipes in this book call for the fresh Mexican sausage, available in many supermarkets and Hispanic groceries. If you buy it in the casing, you'll need to slit the casing with a paring knife, remove it, and discard it.

crème fraîche

Crème fraîche is a thickened cultured cream with a tangy, rich flavor. Although you can buy it in most supermarkets, it's really easy to make at home. To make your own crème fraîche, heat 1 cup heavy cream to body temperature. Stir in 2 tablespoons buttermilk, pour into a glass container, and cover with plastic wrap. Leave at room temperature overnight or up to 24 hours, until thickened. Crème fraîche will keep in the refrigerator for a few weeks. To make more crème fraîche, follow the above recipe, substituting your homemade crème fraîche for the buttermilk. If you continue in this way, as time goes on your homemade crème fraîche will become thicker, stickier, and even more delicious.

extra-virgin olive oil

Extra-virgin olive oil comes from the first cold pressing and must have an acidity level of 1 percent or less. I always have at least two kinds of extra-virgin olive oil in the pantry—one less-expensive basic oil with a fairly neutral flavor that I use for cooking, and another, more special oil for finishing dishes. There are many different finishing oils to choose from. Like wine, each one reflects where it came from, the type of olives used, and the person who made it. Some of these oils are fruity, some are more acidic, and others have a peppery bite.

Remember that olive oil is affected by heat and light and can turn rancid quickly, so don't buy more than you need. At home I keep my good oils in the refrigerator since I don't get a chance to use them as often as I'd like. Take the oil out of the refrigerator to come to room temperature 15 minutes before using it.

farro

Farro, also known as spelt, is probably my all-time favorite grain. It resembles barley or wheat berries and has a deep, nutty flavor with an addictive, chewy texture. Its popularity is on the rise here in the States, making it easier to find in quality markets and Italian specialty shops (see Sources).

nut oils

Look for oils made from stone-milled toasted nuts. These full-flavored oils should taste intensely of the nut they are made from and have a brown hue to them. (Avoid clear nut oils, which are fine for cooking but lack rich nut flavors.) Artisanal nut oils have a short shelf life, but will keep a few months if stored in the refrigerator. Use them in vinaigrettes, sauces, and compound butters, or drizzle a few drops over a finished dish. I love to toss toasted nuts with a little of their matching nut oil right when they come out of the oven. Huilerie Leblanc of France makes excellent artisanal almond, walnut, pistachio, and pine nut oils (see Sources).

olives

Lucques olives are the namesake of my restaurant and considered the Rolls-Royce of olives—deep green, buttery, slightly briny, with a firm, irresistible texture. Picholines, also from the south of France, are a similarly flavored green olive, but to me don't have the same buttery elegance as Lucques olives. For black olives, I love

Niçoises, those little gems from the region around Nice, in the south of France, as well as dry-cured and brined olives called Nyons. They're intense and meaty, with an assertive flavor that makes them great for slicing and adding to pastas or salads. If you can't find Nyons, a good substitute is an oil-cured olive from Morocco or Greece (see Sources).

parmigiano-reggiano

Beware of imitators; seek out true Parmigiano-Reggiano from Italy. Monitored under very strict standards set by the *consorzio* there, the six hundred or so dairies that produce this tangy and sweet cheese are located in and around Parma, Modena, and Reggio Emilia. Made from cow's milk, the giant wheels of cheese spend anywhere from 1 to 3½ years in aging rooms. A word of advice: keep a hunk of Parmesan on hand at all times. It has saved me on numerous occasions when I have found myself hungry for dinner, with a practically empty pantry and almost bare refrigerator at home. Grated over pasta with butter or olive oil, or shaved over a simple arugula salad, Parmesan turns mere scraps into a last-minute supper.

pastas

I prefer artisanal and handmade Italian pastas to their industrially made counterparts (see Sources). Their firmer texture holds up better after cooking, giving them a toothier bite. More than just a vehicle for the sauce, these authentic pastas have more flavor and character than machine-produced noodles. You'll also find many more interesting shapes to try from the smaller pasta-producers in Italy. The artisanal pastas are more expensive, but if you think about how far they go compared with other ingredients, they're worth the money. I'd rather splurge on a great pasta bathed in sweet butter and Parmigiano-Reggiano cheese, than have a mediocre pasta sauced with lots of fancy ingredients.

polenta

I have two different polentas in my pantry. The first is a stone-ground cornmeal from Bob's Red Mill in Oregon (see Sources). It's coarser than most polentas and has an old-fashioned quality and sweet, rich corn flavor. My other favorite is from Anson Mills in South Carolina. This is a finer-ground polenta that's milled to order and cooks to a soft and creamy consistency. Depending on grind, dryness, and age, polentas will vary, requiring different amounts of water and time. Watch your polenta as it cooks; pay attention to its texture as you stir, adding water when needed. When making a soft-style polenta, the goal is a loose consistency, like that of porridge. Remember as you're adding water that the butter added at the end will thin it further. If you have leftover polenta, spread it on a baking sheet and cool in the refrigerator. The next day, you can cut it into rectangles to grill or sauté.

prosciutto

There are several areas in Italy that produce prosciutto. Consult your butcher or read the label carefully so you don't end up with something from Canada curiously labeled "Parma Ham." The three types of prosciutto I like come from Parma, Carpegna, and San Daniele in Italy. Each region has its own rules and style of curing the famous pork legs. The prosciutto from Carpegna is cured on the coast, where the salty air and longer curing times make the meat slightly saltier. Whichever type of prosciutto you choose, don't be afraid of the fat; it's an essential aspect of the cured meat. When prosciutto is thinly sliced, the rich fat balances the salty and sweet cured pork. In Italy, the fat is considered the best part of the prosciutto.

puff pastry

Unless you have lots of time on your hands and are in the mood to make your own, you can find good puff pastry in the freezer section of most supermarkets. Seek out an all-butter puff pastry. It usually comes in 8-by-12- or 9½-by-9½-inch sheets. The dimensions don't really matter, as long as you have enough pastry for six servings, which is what these recipes call for. Be sure the puff pastry is defrosted before you unroll it. Puff pastry bakes best when very cold or frozen, so, in between the steps of assembling a tart, return the pastry to the freezer for 5 to 10 minutes to chill. That way, you're sure to get a crust with flaky, delicate layers.

salt

fleur de sel   In the coastal French regions of Brittany and the Camargue, sea salt is harvested from narrow marsh basins flooded by gravity. Evaporation brings to the surface natural salt with complex marine flavor, which is collected by artisans called *paludiers* armed with specialized rakes. The season's harvest is mostly *sel gris,* or gray salt, whose color comes from the natural clay of the local soil and whose robust oceanic flavor makes it wonderful for baking whole fish or potatoes or for seasoning soups. But on those rare summer days when conditions are just right—a warm, brisk wind and no rain at all—a fine, snow white layer of purest salt forms at the top of these basins, untouched by the impurities below. This is the prized *fleur de sel,* or "flower of the salt," and salt farms yield only about one pound of it for every eighty pounds of *sel gris. Fleur de sel* has a distinctive, intense flavor and a lively, fleeting crunch. I recently discovered the Portuguese equivalent, *flor da sal,* which is just as delicious and much more affordable. Use this special salt to finish dishes, season larger pieces of meat, and pass at the table.

kosher salt   All measurements in this book are based on kosher salt, so if you use the finer-grained table variety, you'll need to cut the amount of salt called for in the recipe in half. (Because of its larger grains, kosher salt has twice the volume of fine-grained salt.) I like kosher salt for its clean, neutral flavor and coarse texture.

san marzano tomatoes

When tomatoes are out of season, you're much better off using a good-quality canned tomato than pink, mealy Romas from the supermarket. Obviously, you wouldn't want to eat them in a salad, but for cooking stews and sauces, they're a practical and delicious option. Vine-ripened and picked at the peak of their sweetness, San Marzano canned tomatoes are the pride of southern Italy. If you can't find San Marzanos, look for other canned tomatoes imported from Italy.

spices

Purchase your spices whole and in small amounts. Their shelf life is about a year; after that, they lose their depth and distinctive aromas. If you buy them in small quantities, you'll be able to use them before they lose their luster. There are many online sources for great spices (see Sources). For information about toasting and grinding spices, see Techniques, page 24.

vinegar

I use an assortment of vinegars when cooking. I love balsamic vinegar for its slightly fruity sweetness. When shopping for balsamic vinegar, look for one from Modena. Don't confuse regular balsamic vinegar with the pricier, aged vinegars labeled "Aceto Balsamico Tradizionale," sold in small, shapely bottles. These aged balsamics are used more as a condiment than a vinegar.

Thick, syrupy, and rich, they're delicious drizzled over cured and grilled meats, antipasti, and even ice cream and strawberries.

Sherry vinegar is my favorite vinegar to cook with. Its nutty, complex flavor is more subtle than other vinegars. It is neither too acidic nor cloyingly sweet. I reach for it all the time to dress salads and finish sauces. It works particularly well with fruit, roasted vegetables, and bitter greens. Look for a quality sherry vinegar from Spain made in the traditional manner, slowly aged in oak barrels.

Red wine vinegar adds sharp, straightforward acid without any of the sweetness you get from balsamic or sherry vinegars. Rice vinegar is a mellow white vinegar, perfect for dishes that need a lighter touch. I use it in some fruit-based vinaigrettes to add a little acid and balance out the sweetness of the fruit. Rice vinegar also works well in charmoula, a spicy North African condiment. Avoid "seasoned" rice vinegar, which has sweeteners, salt, or other additives. Champagne vinegar is another mild option, best on delicately flavored foods like cucumbers and seafood.

techniques

blanching

Blanching is a method of quickly cooking raw vegetables by immersing them in heavily salted, rapidly boiling water until just tender. Before blanching, cut the vegetables into pieces that are approximately the same size, so they will cook evenly. Many cooks use an ice bath to stop the cooking after blanching; however, I prefer to drain the vegetables in a colander and spread them out on a baking sheet to cool. This prevents the vegetables from becoming waterlogged.

braising

Braising is an inventive way to transform tough cuts of meat into tender and satisfying meals. Braising always starts on the stovetop, where the meat is seared, the vegetables are caramelized, and the wine and stock are reduced. Then all the ingredients are cooked together slowly in the oven until the meat is meltingly tender. After years of braising, I've developed a few tips to pass along.

First, bring the meat to room temperature, and then season it well with salt and pepper. Let the meat sit out another ½ hour to absorb the seasoning. Choose a large wide-bottomed pot that will accommodate all the meat in one layer. If you don't have a big enough pot, use two smaller pots.

Sear the meat very well on all sides in a very hot heavy-bottomed pan. If the meat is in pieces, add them one at a time, placing them flat side down. The meat should never be crowded, so it is usually necessary to sear it in batches or in two pans. I like to use the same pan for searing and braising—that way I have one less pan to clean and all the yummy brown bits left from searing go straight into the braising liquid. Watch the meat as it sears to be sure it's browning evenly. Let the meat brown completely on one side before moving or turning it.

Braise the meat according to the directions in the recipe, making sure the meat is almost completely covered by liquid. I like to braise meats the day before, so my work is minimal the next day, when I want to serve it. If you make the braise the day before, let the meat cool in the juices for 20 to 30 minutes at room temperature. Place the cooled pan (both the meat and the juices) in the refrigerator, allowing the fat to come to the surface and solidify. Once it does, remove the fat and discard it, being careful not to lose any of the precious braising juices.

The next day, about an hour before you're ready to serve dinner, preheat the oven to 350°F. Remove the meat and juices from the refrigerator well ahead of time, so it's not ice-cold going into the oven. Reheat the meat and juices, covered, for about 30 minutes. Uncover, pour a third of the braising juices into a pot, turn the heat up to 400°F, and return the meat to the oven to brown on top, for about 15 minutes. If the braising liquid in the pot seems thin, reduce it on the stove over medium-high heat.

browning butter

Brown butter is a magical ingredient that is equally wonderful spooned over fish, tossed with roasted sweet potatoes, or, of course, used in desserts. When butter is cooked to a deep golden brown, its familiar creaminess is transformed into something rich, nutty, and spectacular.

To make brown butter, heat a small pan over

medium-high heat for a minute. Add the butter and cook a few minutes, swirling the pan occasionally, until the butter browns and smells nutty. The small brown flecks in the melted brown butter are filled with flavor, so be sure to get them, too. Finally, be careful if you're adding another ingredient to the brown butter while it's still hot—it may foam up and possibly overflow.

grilling

Part of the fun of grilling is the fire—working with it, standing over it, and smelling it. I prefer to grill over hot coals, ideally from wood or natural charcoal. Grilling over gas is convenient but doesn't lend any smoky flavor to the food. If you have a gas grill, check the instructions to see if you can add some mesquite or hardwood charcoal over the gas plate. When using an old-school charcoal grill, the coals should be glowing red before you cook. If the coals have cooled to a white color before you're done grilling, throw some more fuel on top and wait for them to glow red before you continue.

In order to get a nice sear on any fish, fowl, or meat, and to ensure the food doesn't stick, the grill needs to be very hot. Before cooking, scrub the grill rigorously with a metal brush and rub the grates down with an oiled towel (any cooking oil will suffice). Place the meat on the hot grill, being careful not to crowd pieces too close together. When you place the meat on the grill you should hear an instant sizzle, signifying the grill is hot and the meat is beginning to cook. If not, move the meat to a hotter spot if there is one, or take it off and wait for the grill to heat up, adding more fuel if necessary.

Let the meat cook a few minutes before trying to move it. Don't rush it; once a nice sear has been achieved, the meat will release itself from the grill. To get even more surface caramelization, turn the meat 45 degrees and let it cook a little longer on the first side.

When you are cooking larger pieces of meat, there will be time to make a few 45-degree turns throughout the cooking process for maximum caramelization. With fish you will need to work more quickly; a 5- to 6-ounce fillet takes about 3 to 5 minutes per side, depending on how thick the piece is.

How do you know when it's done? Some cooks follow the touch method. When you press a finger to the meat and it's soft to the touch, it's rare. As the meat becomes firmer, this is a signal that it's becoming more well done. When beef is cooked to the medium stage, the juices begin running to the surface. When you're cooking fish, use either the touch method, or find an opening or a seam in the flesh and peek inside. The fish should be slightly translucent at the center. Take into account that the food will continue to cook a little more once it comes off the grill.

Plan ahead when you're grilling. Take advantage of those great coals by grilling some extra things. If you're grilling quail for a Sunday supper, put on a slab of tri-tip (see page 185) for tomorrow night's dinner. In the summer, slice some eggplant, zucchini, and peppers, slather them in olive oil, and grill them a few minutes on each side. And if you're having bread for dinner, why not grill it? There's nothing tastier than olive-oil-grilled bread rubbed lightly with a garlic clove.

In California, the grill never goes out of season. But if you've already packed yours away for the winter, don't worry: many grilled dishes can be made indoors with heavy cast-iron pans. They won't have that serious, smoky essence from a hot fire, but they'll still be delicious.

making mayonnaise

Making mayonnaise at home is easy, once you learn the technique. Before you start, place a damp kitchen towel on the countertop. Center a medium-sized pot over the towel. Place another small towel over the pot, and fit a stainless steel bowl (snugly) into the towel-lined pot. This will keep your bowl from shifting and slipping on the counter as you whisk your mayonnaise.

In making a mayonnaise, the goal is to add the oil to the egg as slowly as possible at first, to create an emulsion. Whisk the egg yolk in the stainless bowl, and slowly drizzle the oil, drop by drop, into the yolk, whisking the entire time. Once you've added about ¼ cup of the oil, and the mixture is starting to emulsify, add the remaining oil a little more quickly, in a steady stream, increasing the amount as the mayonnaise thickens. Add a few drops of water or lemon juice if the mixture gets too thick.

If the mixture looks like it's separating and you notice little isolated flecks, your mayonnaise is "broken" and you'll need to start over. Get a clean bowl and another egg yolk, keeping that first, "broken" mixture on the side. Start the process again, adding small amounts of oil, drop by drop, to the new egg yolk. Once it's emulsified, begin to add the "broken" mixture, spoonful by spoonful. Continue whisking until you have a thick, "unbroken" mayonnaise.

plating and arranging

The way food is presented on the plate is almost as important as how it tastes. The visual aspect of a dish will form your guests' first impression of your efforts and color the remainder of their experience with your food. The food should be arranged in a natural manner to show off the beauty of the ingredients, never appearing forced or overworked. George Germon and Johanne Killeen, the chef-owners of Al Forno, said it best. They used to tell us that the food "should look like it was born on the plate." When plating a dish, be careful not to crowd the individual ingredients. Layer and nestle them to create a unified yet elegant composition on the plate.

resting

Letting meat or poultry rest after it's cooked is essential. Resting allows time for all of the juices to redistribute throughout the meat. A cake-cooling rack placed over a baking sheet (to collect all those delicious juices) makes an excellent resting rack. If you don't have a cooling rack, invert a saucer onto a large plate and prop the meat up against it. Instead of simply placing the meat on a plate, where it would steam from underneath, this makeshift cooling rack allows air to circulate around the entire piece of meat. Once the meat has rested—5 to 10 minutes for a smaller cut, and 12 to 15 minutes for a larger roast—slice it and finish by pouring the juices left under the cooling rack over the top. These juices provide an instant sauce.

roasting

For tender, succulent results, try slow-roasting. Start by searing the meat on the grill or in a hot cast-iron pan to get nice caramelization on the outside, then place the seared meat on a rack set in a roasting pan. I like to top the meat with lots of big sprigs of herbs and slabs of butter. As the meat cooks slowly and evenly in a 325°F oven, the butter melts and marries with the meat's natural juices and the herbs, creating a delicious basting liquid.

sautéing

The French meaning of *sauter* is literally "to jump," and that's what your ingredients should be doing as they sauté over high heat in the pan. Start by heating the pan for a minute or two, then swirl in the oil or butter, and once it's hot add your ingredients. It's important not to load your pan too full, or the ingredients won't have room to jump. Cramming too many ingredients together will also cause the pan to lose its heat, and you'll end up stewing the ingredients instead of sautéing them. Watch carefully as you sauté and stay involved in the process. Use all of your senses, and listen for that happy sizzle. If it looks like the oil or butter has been totally absorbed, add a touch more. And if your ingredients aren't active and jumping in the pan, turn up the heat.

searing

Searing meat or fish creates a layer of caramelization that tastes delicious and provides textural contrast. To get a good sear, it's crucial to have your pan hot before you add any ingredients to it. This is why you'll find that most of the recipes start with "heat your pan over high heat for 2 minutes." The hot pan will ensure that the cooking process starts immediately and that your meat or fish doesn't stick. Once the pan is hot, swirl in the olive oil or butter and give it a moment to heat up before adding anything else to the pan. If you don't hear an instant sizzle when you place your meat or fish in the pan, take it out and let the pan heat up further. Once you begin to sear, don't shake the pan or try to move the meat or fish until you have a good crust and the surface is well browned. Remember not to crowd the meat or fish in the pan, or it won't sear properly.

seasoning and marinating

Seasoning and marinating beforehand can enhance even the simplest of dishes. Most of my recipes for fish, chicken, and meat tell you to season ahead to add flavor and depth. It's best if you can do this the night before, but if not, seasoning even a few hours before cooking will make a difference.

When deciding which spices or seasonings to use, think about the end goal. Choose seasonings that complement other flavors in the dish, or ones that reinforce the regional cuisine that influences the dish. I often

season fish with a simple combination of lemon zest, thyme leaves, and parsley. For a more exotic, spicy result, I sometimes add garlic, toasted ground cumin, and sliced chile. When the meat or fish is ready to go on the grill, into a sauté pan, or into the oven, I brush a little olive oil on it, leaving the seasonings in place, so they cook into the flesh. When creating seasoning or marinades, think of combining herbs, spices, garlic, citrus zest, pepper, shallots, chiles, juices, wine, and spirits.

slicing and dicing

Knowing the proper technique for slicing and dicing onions and shallots will make life in the kitchen a lot easier. A word to the wise—a sharp knife makes all this slicing and dicing much faster and more pleasant, not to mention safer.

When slices are called for, cut the onion in half lengthwise, through the root, and peel the halves. Place one half, cut side down, on a cutting board. Holding your knife at a 20-degree angle, remove the root end. Then, starting on one side, begin slicing the onion lengthwise at a 20-degree angle. As you slice, adjust the angle of your knife, working your way over the top of the onion half and down the other side, slicing along the full radius of the onion. This will give you consistent slices, instead of the rounded pieces you would get if you were to cut straight down (without adjusting your knife).

To dice an onion, cut it in half through the root end, and peel as above. Place one half cut side down on a cutting board, leaving the root end intact. (The root end holds the onion together while you make all of your cuts.) Carefully make two evenly spaced horizontal slices (i.e., parallel to the board) into the onion all the way up to, but not through, the root end. Next, make vertical slices straight down, spaced ¼ inch apart. Finally, make crosswise cuts through the onion, again straight down, to make small diced pieces.

These same techniques can be used to slice or dice fennel, shallots, and other vegetables.

soup

Making soup from scratch is a cinch. There are no super kitchen skills required. If you follow these few guidelines and easy techniques, your homemade soup will be exceptional.

The first step for building flavor in soups is to sauté lots of onions in olive oil or butter until they're soft and translucent. Stir in dried chile, spices, and herbs and cook a little longer, until the onions begin to caramelize. Add the vegetables called for, stirring to coat them with the onions, spices, and herbs. Sautéing the vegetables in these flavorful aromatics gives the soup more depth. Add the liquid, and cook until the vegetables are tender but not mushy. Remember to taste and season with salt along the way. Soup will always taste better if it's seasoned while it cooks, rather than at the very end.

Now that your soup is seasoned and flavored, the next step in making great soup is getting the right consistency. When the vegetables are tender, strain the soup to separate them from the liquid. I find a blender works best to achieve a smooth and creamy texture. It's important not to add too much liquid in the beginning of the blending process. Start by puréeing the vegetables with a small amount of the liquid. This will result in a smoother consistency than if you were to add all the liquid at one time. Once the vegetables are puréed, then you can begin to add more liquid slowly, until the soup has the consistency of heavy cream. This technique guarantees a soup that tastes creamy, without actually containing any cream. When using a blender, be careful not to burn yourself. Always start on low speed and hold the lid in place firmly, using a towel to protect your hand. If you're not careful, the pressure can sometimes cause the top to come loose and spray scalding soup everywhere.

toasting and grinding spices

Toasting whole spices brings out their flavors and nuances. Heat them in a small pan over medium heat, shaking the pan often, until you smell their aroma and they just begin to color. Keep an eye on the spices as they toast; they can go from being perfectly toasted to burned in a matter of seconds. Grind the spices by hand with a mortar and pestle, or in a small spice grinder or electric coffee grinder reserved strictly for spices.

vinaigrettes

Most of my vinaigrettes start with finely diced shallots that are macerated in vinegar or lemon juice and kosher salt for about 5 minutes. This softens the pungency of the shallots, dissolves the salt, and lets the flavors meld. Next, I whisk in the oil and taste for balance and seasoning. I choose particular oils and vinegars according to the flavors of the final dish. If I'm making a salad with sweet Kabocha squash, I'll use sherry vinegar to add a nutty, sharper note. For a salad with figs, I like to mash some of the soft fruit into the vinaigrette. If a salad has a particular nut in it, I like to reinforce that flavor by adding some of that nut's oil to the vinaigrette.

washing greens

Fill a large bowl with cold water, then add the greens. Don't do the reverse: lots of water running over the greens will bruise them. Gently submerge the greens in the water with your hands, running your fingers through them to loosen any sand or dirt clinging to the leaves. The dirt will fall to the bottom of the bowl. If the greens are very sandy, wash them in a few changes of water until they're clean. Lift the greens from the water and place them in a colander to drain. Dry them in a salad spinner, in batches. It's best to wash greens just before you use them, but if you want to do it ahead of time, once they're dry, cover them with a paper towel and store them loosely in a container in the refrigerator.

working with fresh herbs

If you have the luxury of growing fresh herbs in your garden, on your balcony, or in your windowsill, you'll be grateful they're at arm's length while you cook. Thyme is my favorite herb and I use it in most of my cooked dishes to add an indescribable savory and aromatic flavor. I like to use the whole leaves rather than chop it. Rosemary is another herb I couldn't live without. I use small amounts to sizzle in olive oil and cook with onions. And could you imagine summer without basil? I particularly love deep purple–colored opal basil, which, like its green counterpart, is easy to grow in a pot during the summer.

Besides parsley, there are very few herbs I chop. I think you get prettier, more elegant-looking shapes when you slice or tear, instead of chopping the delicate leaves. To slice basil or parsley, I stack the leaves and then carefully cut them lengthwise or on the diagonal into ribbons. When slicing herbs, it's particularly important to use a sharp knife, since a dull one will bruise the herbs and cause their edges to brown. Softer herbs, such as tarragon, chervil, and chives, are delicate and fragile. I like to pick the leaves and tiny sprigs right before using them, keeping them whole, to toss into salads or to garnish dishes.

Fresh herbs make great salsas and condiments. For salsa verde, pesto, and charmoula, I prefer to crush the herbs with a mortar and pestle, rather than using a blender or food processor. The mortar and pestle extract more of their flavors without bruising them and result in a deep green rustic sauce.

spring

’m a vegetable fanatic. I always joke that I could be a vegetarian, as long as I were allowed a little steak and bacon every now and then. When I dine out, while others are torn between the veal chop and the salmon, my main concern is "What vegetables do they come with?" And when I get hungry at work, with all the choices that abound in our kitchen, what I crave and reach for most are vegetables. Every season offers its vegetal specialties, but if I had to choose a favorite, it would be spring.

Spring, however, is a moody season: its lingering cold spells and sudden warm stretches can make for temperamental dining. I've tried to provide for such climatic whims by offering a variety of choices in my spring menus. Pick and choose as you like; mix and match according to what's available. Don't banish braised meats and creamy pastas just yet. Instead, give them a spring flourish.

When the sky is threatening showers, I head to the kitchen to make a nourishing stew. Veal Osso Buco with Saffron Risotto, English Peas, and Pea Shoots will warm you up, and with all of those bright spring vegetables, you'll know that winter is finally at an end. When a warm spring day hits, it's the perfect time to make a lighter main course and eat alfresco. Halibut with Fingerlings, Fava Beans, Meyer Lemon, and Savory Crème Fraîche will satisfy the heartiest of appetites, while letting you know that the green season has arrived.

The spring collection of menus calls for simpler cooking techniques that do not blunt the brightness of young, fresh spring ingredients. A quick blanch or brief sauté is often all that's needed for certain vegetables. A bowl of English peas cooked a few minutes in a pool of sweet butter is perfection. Whereas summer finds me reaching mostly for olive oil, in the spring I still yearn for butter. Saffron Chicken with Parmesan Pudding, Spring Onions, and Sugar Snap Peas needs butter to add depth and dimension to the crunchy green vegetables. And a Sauté of White Asparagus, Morels, and Ramps over Polenta cries for the richness only butter can provide.

And oh, spring fruit! Not that winter fruit doesn't have its charms, but after months of relying on dried and cooked fruits for variety, nothing feels more welcome than the advent of the season's first ripe strawberries, apricots, and cherries—eaten out of hand they taste like relief itself. But don't be fooled; it's not summer yet. Certain spring arrivals, like rhubarb, require a little manipulation. Even those cherries can stand some cooking: simmered in vanilla caramel, they make an exquisite burgundy-colored compote. Many spring fruits, in fact, are delicious both raw and cooked, and I would never want to choose. Fortunately, as with most of this transitional season's bounty, I don't have to.

spring market

apricots

Enjoy these lovely golden stone fruit as much as possible during their season. Starting in mid-May, apricots appear at the market, and by mid-June, they've all but disappeared. Castlebrites, Pattersons, and Elgin Marbles are some of my favorite varieties. The smaller, old-fashioned Blenheims are also delicious and have an intense apricot flavor. Apricots won't continue to ripen once they're picked, so avoid greenish-tinted fruit. Look for apricots that have a little red blush on their skin; brown markings or blemishes often indicate a sweeter specimen. Apricots are great eaten out of hand as well as baked into tarts or poached in sweet wine.

artichokes

Plucked from a large, prehistoric-looking bush, the artichoke is an intriguing edible bud. Large artichokes range from 4 to 6 inches in diameter and conceal meaty, flavorful hearts beneath layers and layers of fibrous leaves. Baby artichokes, as they're called, are actually not babies at all. These mature chokes are smaller-sized buds that grow on the lower portion of the same plant that produces the larger buds.

Though their flavors are similar, small and large artichokes should be treated differently. The larger buds, above the woody stem, have three discrete parts: the leaves, the heart, and the fuzzy and inedible "choke." The traditional method for eating large artichokes is to steam them whole and eat the leaves one by one, dipping them in butter and scraping off (with your teeth) the bit of meat. The payoff for this low-yield (but delicious) work is arriving at the heart—all meaty, edible goodness. If you want to dispense with the extra work, however, you can tear the leaves away, scrape out the choke (a spoon works well for removing all the hairy bits), and steam, sauté, or roast the hearts. Sometimes I simply shave raw artichoke hearts into thin slices and dress them in a lemony vinaigrette for a quick artichoke salad.

To prepare baby artichokes, which never really form a choke, you can simply remove the toughest outer leaves, cut about a third off the top of the buds, trim the stems, and then halve or quarter them lengthwise. I like to sear baby artichokes in olive oil, then pan-braise them with a little white wine.

When choosing artichokes, look for unblemished, compact buds with a thick, firm stem still attached. If the stem appears thin or withered, it's an indication that the artichoke was picked more than a few days ago and may be drying out or losing flavor. While preparing artichokes for cooking, you may wish to put the ones you've cut in water with a squeeze of lemon juice to prevent discoloration.

asparagus

When it comes to asparagus, I'm frequently asked which is better—the fat ones or the skinny ones. I like both. Jumbo asparagus is juicier and has a meaty texture. The skinnier spears are more delicate in flavor and usually require no peeling.

To prepare asparagus, start by snapping off the ends. The stalk will break at the point where tough meets tender. Visually, I prefer unpeeled asparagus, but sometimes peeling is unavoidable. After you've discarded the ends, cut off a small piece of a spear and taste it. If the skin of the asparagus seems unpleasantly stringy, use a vegetable peeler to peel the lower section of the stalk, usually about 2 inches' worth.

Big asparagus is delicious steamed and then sautéed in olive oil and topped with a fried egg and shavings of Parmesan. Thinner spears are great cut on the diagonal and sautéed in a spring vegetable ragoût.

If you've traveled to certain areas of Germany, Austria, or eastern France in spring, you may have experienced their annual white asparagus craze. Most restaurants display prominent signs announcing the long-awaited arrival of *Weisser Spargel*. They usually serve the asparagus simply, with a little hollandaise sauce and a slice of Black Forest ham.

Pearly and rich, white asparagus tastes very different from its green counterpart. Grown in complete darkness under a mound of sandy soil, it produces no chlorophyll during its development. Its flavor is nuttier than that of green asparagus, with hints of artichoke and heart of palm.

White asparagus needs to be cooked longer than green; it should be tender and soft rather than al dente. White spears can also be woodier than green, so be sure to snap off the ends and discard them. You'll just have to grin and bear the pain of throwing away a large portion of this expensive delicacy. You'll also want to peel the lower portion of the stalks to remove the fibrous skin.

When choosing asparagus, look for firm spears and smooth, unbroken tips. Store it, standing upright in a few inches of water, in the refrigerator.

cherries

Cherry-picking begins in early May, depending on the variety, and lasts until late June or sometimes even July. Eaten out of hand or cooked into a compote, cherries are among my favorite stone fruits. The cherries that grow around Southern California are all sweet cherries; sour cherries dominate the markets east of the Rockies. A few of the sweet varieties I love are Burlats, Lapins, and of course the classic Bing cherries. The paler Rainiers are delicious for eating, but lose some of their intensity when cooked. When choosing cherries, look for unbruised, plump fruit, and, of course, taste them!

fava beans

Fava beans' slippery texture and unusual marshy flavor make them unique among shell beans. You can't always judge a fava bean by its cover; check inside the pod and inspect the beans themselves. They should be firm, plump, and unblemished. If you can, taste one for sweetness and flavor.

To prepare them, remove the beans from their pods and blanch them in salted boiling water for about 2 minutes. Plunge them into ice water to cool them, then slip off their little jackets. At this point, they can be tossed into ragoûts or salads or made into a purée.

green garlic

This green-and-white shoot is the immature precursor to head garlic. Its shape resembles a scallion and its size is similar to a baby leek. Green garlic is easily mistaken for these other members of the onion family, and every new, young cook at Lucques confuses them. I'll tell you the same thing I tell the cooks: use your senses. Smell the stalk. If you detect a garlicky scent, you know it's green garlic. Milder than a garlic clove, green garlic isn't hot or pungent, but it's unmistakably related. To prepare green garlic, trim off the root end and slice the stalks on the diagonal, including some of the flavorful green stems.

I'm a devout fan of green garlic and use it constantly when it's in season. When June rolls around and it disappears from the market, I'm at a loss. Nothing can replace its herbal garlic flavor and slightly chewy texture. If I'm desperate, though, I substitute sliced garlic cloves sautéed in olive oil and tossed with a handful of sliced scallions.

morels

Morels are the quintessential mushroom of spring. These cone-shaped fungi have a honeycombed surface and a nutty, woodsy perfume. Smell them to check for that deep, earthy aroma. Store them in the refrigerator in an open paper bag or basket to allow them to breathe.

In a perfect world, you would never submerge a morel in water to clean it, for fear of ruining its beautiful texture. Unfortunately, the only thing worse than eating a waterlogged morel is eating a mouthful of sand hidden within one. You can't always see the sand in the honeycombed exterior or deep inside the cavity of the mushroom. The best way to find out if morels are sandy is to sauté a few and taste them. If they're gritty, wash them by filling a large bowl with lukewarm water. Place the morels in the water and gently press down to immerse them. Let the mushrooms sit for a few minutes, occasionally stirring them with your hands, until the dirt loosens and falls to the bottom of the bowl. Carefully lift the morels out of the water and place them on paper towels to dry. If you see a lot of dirt or sand on the bottom of the bowl, repeat the soaking process until the water is clean. If your morels are large, cut them in half lengthwise, maintaining their original conical shape.

In order not to mask their intense, meaty flavor, I like to prepare morels very simply, sautéing them in butter with thyme and shallots. They're delicious with pasta, in omelettes, or in a ragoût spooned over toasted brioche.

new potatoes

All year long, my cooking depends on potatoes in some form or another. But in spring, freshly dug new potatoes appear at the farmers' markets, causing potatomania. A new potato is dug from a live plant that still has green leaves attached aboveground. Regular or mature potatoes remain underground longer, allowing them to become larger in size and develop tougher skins; by the time they're harvested, the leaves have long since turned brown and withered away.

Swathed in practically sheer, papery skin, new potatoes are usually on the small side. Europeans have long had a fondness for this preemie-potato, called early-crop potatoes in England and *primeurs* in France. They have a relatively low starch content, allowing flavor subtleties to come forward, and they require very little dressing up. I love new potatoes steamed and lightly crushed with butter and *fleur de sel*. Choose potatoes that feel very solid and firm and have no discoloration or sprouts. Store them in a dark, cool cupboard and keep them no longer than a week or two. If you're shopping for new potatoes, be wary: some supermarkets label small red potatoes as new potatoes when they're not new at all.

peas

Peas demand precise growing conditions, which nature, along with a learned and lucky farmer, can only sometimes achieve. From the minute they're picked, peas begin to lose their flavor. Crack open a pod and sample one. It should pop with super-sweet pea flavor. If they taste a little bitter or seem starchy, hold out for better ones. Store peas in the refrigerator, and keep them in their pods to shuck just before cooking.

As for cooking peas, the less you do to them, the better. I cook them in a little water, butter, and salt, and sometimes a pinch of saffron. And remember, fresh peas cook very quickly; watch them carefully so you don't end up with those dreaded mushy peas of childhood.

pea shoots

Also called pea tendrils, pea vines, pea leaves, or pea tenders, these delicate leafy sprigs hold the essence of spring. Their small-to-medium-sized emerald green leaves string together to make the curly knotted vines of the common pea plant. Because they're fragile, it's best to use pea shoots within a few days of purchasing them. Store them in an open plastic bag, surrounding them loosely in paper towels to prevent them from getting wet and mushy. If they smell of old mowed grass, toss them out. If they feel very wet when you buy them, dry them in a salad spinner, cover with a dry towel, and be sure their own weight doesn't compress and mash them. If you buy pea shoots when they're mature and close to the end of their life cycle, trim off the long, tough, stringy tendrils. If you can't find pea shoots at your local farmers' markets, try an Asian market.

Pea shoots are delicious when quickly sautéed with shallots and garlic. In spring, I find myself tossing handfuls of them into many dishes, letting them wilt for just a few seconds. If they're really young and tender, you can eat them raw in salads.

ramps

Also called wild leeks, these pungent, garlicky roots are scallionlike, with elegant, wide leaves protruding from their slender purplish white bulbs. Choose ramps that have unwilted bright green leaves.

To cook the bulbs yet preserve the beautiful leaves, I have a special technique, which the cooks at Lucques call my copyrighted ramp technique. I wrap the green tops together loosely in tinfoil and carefully lower the bulb ends into salted boiling water, leaning them against the side of the pot and keeping the tinfoil-wrapped leaves protected from the water. Cook a few minutes or so, until the bulbs are tender. Carefully remove the ramps from the water, then unwrap the tinfoil and dip the leaves in the boiling water for just a few seconds. This guarantees fully cooked, tender bulbs and bright-green leaves that are barely blanched. Once they're blanched, I like to brush them with olive oil, grill or sauté them in a little butter, and eat the entire ramp, leaves and all.

rhubarb

Though it's actually a vegetable, rhubarb is treated as a fruit in most American kitchens. The celerylike ruby red stalks should be sturdy and crisp when you buy them. Because rhubarb requires a cold winter, not many Southern California farmers grow it, so I usually resort to a hothouse variety. If you live in a cooler area, look for field-grown rhubarb, which has thinner, more brightly colored stalks.

Rhubarb's sour taste and fibrous texture make it a little tricky to work with; often it's overcooked into a mushy one-dimensional pulp, and there's a temptation to add too much sugar to compensate for the rhubarb's inherent tartness. Rhubarb should be tender and just cooked through, not too soft. Remember to taste it as it cooks; you can always add more sugar, but if you add too much at the beginning, you can't take it out. Made into a

compote, rhubarb is delicious served with vanilla semi-freddo or a simple pound cake.

spring onions

Spring onions are young onions with long green tops still attached. The spring onions themselves can be bulbous or long like a scallion. They impart a milder, fresher flavor to food than ordinary onions, and you don't have to cook them nearly as long.

I love spring onions as much for their shape as their flavor. To show off their sexy curves, trim the roots from the bulb, being careful to leave the root end intact to hold the layers of onion together. When you cut the greens from the onion, be sure to leave a few inches still attached to the bulb; they add a green, piquant flavor that refreshes the dish. Be thoughtful as you cut, slicing the onion lengthwise into beautiful, slender pieces.

Now that you've gone to the trouble of cutting your onions so carefully, be sure to cook them with love and attention over even heat (not too hot, not too low), without crowding too many into the pan. Spring onions are also delicious grilled or roasted. In most cases, if you can't find spring onions, you can substitute scallions.

strawberries

Buy strawberries just before you want to eat them, store them on your kitchen counter or in a cool place, and give them a quick rinse just before eating. Of all the varieties grown here in Southern California, my favorites are Chandlers and Gaviotas. When shopping for straw-berries, try to taste when you can, and discover your own favorite varieties.

sugar snap peas

Aptly named, a sugar snap pea is a bright green pod that bursts with candy-sweet juice when you bite into it. I love them raw in salads as well as cooked.

When you're buying sugar snap peas, choose bright, firm, and unbruised pods. Snap off the stem and pull it down to remove the stringlike green fiber. Sugar snap peas cook quickly; watch them closely or they will lose their crisp, irresistible crunch.

endive salad with meyer lemon, fava beans, and oil-cured olives

Certain foods taste better when you eat them with your hands, like barbecued ribs and corn on the cob. This salad is the perfect way to indulge that primal urge. Use the endive leaves as scoops to gather up some olive shards, a fava bean or two, and a slice of lemon. The crisp spears explode with flavor, and before you've finished the first your hand will be reaching for another.

Hand out forks if you must, and make sure to tell your friends that the Meyer lemon slices are for eating. They're sweet and delicious, peel and all. Slice the olives thinly, so their intense taste doesn't overwhelm the other ingredients. As for the dressing, gently stir (don't whisk) in the cream to incorporate it without whipping it.

Place the lemon on its side on a cutting board. Holding it with one hand, cut off the pithy end and slice the lemon into paper-thin pinwheels. Pick out the seeds.

Place the endive spears in a large bowl and pour the Meyer lemon cream over them. Add the fava beans, lemon slices, and sliced shallots. Season with salt and pepper and toss gently to coat the endive with the dressing. Taste for seasoning, and arrange on a large chilled platter. Scatter the olives and herbs over the salad.

1 Meyer lemon

5 Belgian endives, cores removed, separated into spears

Meyer lemon cream (recipe follows)

¾ cup shucked fava beans

¼ cup thinly sliced shallots

⅓ cup oil-cured black olives, pitted and thinly sliced lengthwise

2 tablespoons flat-leaf parsley leaves

1 tablespoon ½-inch-snipped chives

Kosher salt and freshly ground black pepper

meyer lemon cream

Place the shallot, lemon juice, and ¼ teaspoon salt in a bowl and let sit for 5 minutes. Whisk in the olive oil. Gently stir in the cream, add a few grinds of pepper, and taste for balance and seasoning.

2 tablespoons finely diced shallot

¼ cup Meyer lemon juice

½ cup plus 2 tablespoons extra-virgin olive oil

¼ cup plus 1 tablespoon heavy cream

Kosher salt and freshly ground black pepper

hawaiian snapper with green rice and cucumbers in crème fraîche

Part Indian, somewhat Moroccan, a little bit French, and vaguely Slavic, this dish is a true mutt. Arranged on a bed of vibrant herbed rice and topped with spiced cucumbers, this snapper takes you into a world where hot, sour, sweet, and salty exist harmoniously.

NOTE Season the fish with the lemon zest and herbs at least 4 hours before serving. You can make the green rice ahead and rewarm it in the oven. For the cucumbers in crème fraîche, you can mix the crème fraîche with all the seasonings except the mint ahead of time. Just before serving, salt the cucumbers and toss them with the crème fraîche mixture and mint.

6 Hawaiian snapper fillets, 5 to 6 ounces each, skin on

1 lemon, zested

1 tablespoon thyme leaves

2 tablespoons sliced flat-leaf parsley

3 or 4 Persian cucumbers, just under 1 pound total

½ teaspoon cumin seeds

¾ cup crème fraîche

½ teaspoon minced garlic

2 tablespoons finely diced shallot

3 tablespoons finely diced preserved lemon (see Sources)

½ teaspoon preserved lemon juice

A healthy pinch cayenne pepper

2 tablespoons sliced mint leaves

2 tablespoons extra-virgin olive oil

Green rice (recipe follows)

1 bunch watercress, cleaned, tough stems removed

A drizzle super-good extra-virgin olive oil

6 sprigs cilantro

Kosher salt and freshly ground black pepper

Season the fish with the lemon zest, thyme, and parsley. Cover, and refrigerate for at least 4 hours.

Take the fish out of the refrigerator 15 minutes before cooking to bring it to room temperature.

Cut a small piece of cucumber, taste it, and decide if it needs to be peeled and seeded (see Summer Market Report, page 119). If necessary, slice the cucumbers in half lengthwise and scoop out the seeds. Cut the cucumbers into thin crosswise slices, on the diagonal. Toss the cucumbers with 1 teaspoon salt, and let sit 10 minutes.

Toast the cumin seeds in a small pan over medium heat 2 to 3 minutes, until the seeds release their aroma and darken slightly. Use a mortar and pestle to crush them coarsely.

Drain the cucumbers for a few minutes, and then pat them dry with paper towels. Toss the cucumbers in a bowl with the crème fraîche, garlic, shallot, preserved lemon and juice, cumin, cayenne, and a pinch of pepper. Taste for balance and seasoning. The sauce should be assertive and have a nice kick to it. If not, add more cayenne. Gently stir in the mint.

Heat a large sauté pan over high heat for 2 minutes. (Depending on the size of your pan, you may need to cook the fish in batches.) Season the fish with salt and pepper on both sides. Swirl in the olive oil and wait 1 minute. Carefully lay the fish in the pan, skin side down, and cook 3 to 4 minutes, until the skin is crispy. Turn the fish over, lower the heat to medium-low, and cook a couple more minutes, until the snapper is just cooked through. Be careful not to overcook the fish. When it's done, the fish will begin to flake and separate a little; the center will still be slightly translucent. Remember, the fish will continue to cook a little more when you take it out of the pan.

Transfer the hot rice to a large warm platter. Spoon two-thirds of the cucumbers over the rice, and scatter the watercress over both. Arrange the fish on top, and season with lots of lemon juice and a drizzle of super-good olive oil. Spoon the remaining cucumbers over the fish, and garnish with the cilantro sprigs.

green rice

1 cup chicken stock

½ cup packed flat-leaf parsley leaves

¼ cup packed mint leaves

2 tablespoons minced chives

¼ cup packed cilantro leaves

2 teaspoons fennel seeds

¼ cup plus 1 tablespoon extra-virgin olive oil

¾ cup finely diced fennel

¾ cup finely diced red onion

1 chile de árbol

1½ cups white basmati rice

1 tablespoon unsalted butter

Kosher salt and freshly ground black pepper

To make this exotic green rice, simmer basmati rice in a broth of mint, chives, parsley, and cilantro perfumed with sautéed red onion, fennel, and fennel seeds. When you prepare the herbs, don't waste too much time on fastidious herb-picking. They all get puréed into an emerald green broth, so no one will ever know if you cheated a little and left some of the stems on.

Bring the chicken stock and 1¼ cups water to a boil in a medium pot, and then turn off the heat.

Place the parsley, mint, chives, and cilantro in a blender. Add 1 cup of the hot liquid, and purée the herbs on medium speed. Pour in the rest of the liquid slowly, and purée on high speed for almost 2 minutes, until you have a very smooth, very green broth.

Toast the fennel seeds in a small pan over medium heat for 2 to 3 minutes, until they release their aroma and turn light golden brown. Pound them with a mortar and pestle.

Quickly rinse out the chicken stock pot and heat it over high heat for 2 minutes. Add the olive oil, diced fennel and onion, toasted fennel seeds, chile, and ½ teaspoon salt. Cook over medium-high heat for about 5 minutes, stirring often, until the onion and fennel are translucent. Add the rice, 1 teaspoon salt, and a pinch of pepper. Stir well to coat the rice with the oil and vegetables. Add the herb broth and ½ teaspoon salt. Bring to a boil, and reduce the heat to a low simmer. Add the butter, cover, and cook the rice 15 to 20 minutes, until tender. Turn off the heat, and leave the rice covered for 5 minutes. Fluff the rice with a fork and taste for seasoning.

leg of lamb with chorizo stuffing, romesco potatoes, and black olives

This gutsy lamb dish pays homage to two camps of Latin cooking: Mexico and Spain. The lamb is stuffed with a mixture of toasted breadcrumbs and a fresh, spicy Mexican sausage called chorizo. Traditionally stirred into scrambled eggs or used as a filling for gorditas, the chorizo infuses the stuffing with its piquant character. The Spanish accents come from the olives and the romesco, a classic Catalan sauce of puréed chiles, garlic, tomatoes, nuts, and fried bread. Just as the lamb absorbs the spiciness of the chorizo stuffing while it roasts in the oven, the robust romesco saturates the potatoes as they sauté.

NOTE   This is one of the most involved recipes in the book, so plan ahead and set yourself up. Both the chorizo stuffing and the romesco can be made up to 2 days ahead. You can roast the potatoes in the morning, waiting to crumble and brown them until just before serving. And if you like, stuff the lamb the morning of your supper. But remember to take it out of the refrigerator 45 minutes before roasting to bring it to room temperature. Start the romesco potatoes after the lamb has been in the oven for about 30 minutes.

One 2½-pound boneless leg of lamb, butterflied

6 cloves garlic, smashed

¼ cup rosemary leaves

¼ cup chopped flat-leaf parsley, plus ¼ cup whole parsley leaves

2 teaspoons freshly cracked black pepper

Chorizo stuffing (recipe follows)

½ cup sliced pitted Nyons or other oil-cured black olives

¼ cup small mint leaves (or torn larger leaves)

1 teaspoon super-good extra-virgin olive oil

½ lemon, for juicing

Romesco potatoes (recipe follows)

Kosher salt and freshly ground black pepper

Place the lamb in a baking dish and coat it well on all sides with the smashed garlic, rosemary, chopped parsley, and cracked black pepper. Cover, and refrigerate overnight.

Take the lamb out of the refrigerator 30 minutes before stuffing it, to bring it to room temperature. Reserve the marinade.

Preheat the oven to 350°F.

Season the lamb on both sides with salt and a little freshly ground black pepper. Lay the meat on a cutting board, fat side down, and open like a book. Spoon as much of the chorizo stuffing as you can (about half, or a little more) on the right side of the lamb. Fold the left side over the stuffing, as if you're closing the "book." If some of the stuffing falls out, stuff what you can back in. Tie the lamb with butcher string at 2-inch intervals to hold it together while roasting. Carefully place the lamb on a roasting rack set in a roasting pan. Drizzle the leftover marinade over the lamb. Put the remaining chorizo stuffing into a small baking dish and set aside.

Roast the lamb about 1¼ hours, until a meat thermometer inserted into the center (of the meat, not the stuffing) reads 120°F. Remove the lamb from the oven, and let it rest 15 minutes before slicing.

While the lamb is resting, heat the extra stuffing in the oven until it's hot, about 10 minutes.

Toss the olives, parsley leaves, and mint leaves with a drizzle of the super-good olive oil and a squeeze of lemon. Taste for seasoning. (The herb salad might not need salt, because the olives are rather salty.) Arrange the hot romesco potatoes on a large warm platter.

Slice the lamb into ¼-inch-thick slices, removing the butcher string as you go. Using a spatula and spoon (so you don't lose too much of the stuffing), arrange the meat over the potatoes. Scatter the herb salad over the top, and serve the extra stuffing and romesco on the side.

chorizo stuffing

Preheat the oven to 375°F.

Toss the breadcrumbs with 2 tablespoons olive oil. Spread them on a baking sheet and toast 6 to 8 minutes, stirring once or twice, until they are golden brown.

Heat a medium pot over high heat for 1 minute. Add the remaining 6 tablespoons olive oil, the rosemary sprig, and the chile; let them sizzle in the oil about 1 minute. Stir in the onions, garlic, and thyme, and season with salt and pepper. Turn the heat down to medium and cook about 10 minutes, until the onions are translucent. Transfer the mixture to a large bowl and discard the rosemary and chile.

While the onions are cooking, heat a medium sauté pan over high heat for 2 minutes. Crumble the chorizo into the pan, and sauté about 8 minutes, until the sausage is crisp and cooked through. Drain the chorizo of excess oil and add it to the bowl with the onions. Stir in the breadcrumbs, mint, and parsley, and combine well. Taste for seasoning.

2 cups fresh breadcrumbs

½ cup extra-virgin olive oil

1 large sprig rosemary

1 chile de árbol, broken in half

2 cups finely diced onions

2 teaspoons minced garlic

1 teaspoon thyme leaves

¾ pound fresh Mexican chorizo, casing removed

3 tablespoons chopped mint

3 tablespoons chopped flat-leaf parsley

Kosher salt and freshly ground black pepper

romesco potatoes

Preheat the oven to 400°F.

Place the potatoes in a roasting pan and toss well with 2 tablespoons olive oil, the garlic, bay leaves, thyme sprigs, and a heaping teaspoon salt. Cover tightly with aluminum foil and roast the potatoes about 50 minutes, until tender when pierced (the time will really depend on size, age, and variety of potatoes). When the potatoes have cooled, reserve the garlic, discard the bay and thyme, and crumble the potatoes into chunky pieces with your hands. Squeeze the garlic out of its skin and set aside.

Heat a large sauté pan over high heat for 2 minutes. (To get the potatoes nicely browned and crisp, don't overcrowd them. You may have to use two pans or brown them in batches.) Pour in the remaining 2 tablespoons olive oil, turn the heat to medium-high, and wait 1 minute more. Add the crumbled potatoes, and season with the thyme leaves, salt, and pepper. Sauté the potatoes 6 to 8 minutes until they are crispy on one side. (Don't try to move them or turn them if they are stuck to the pan; they will eventually release themselves—just be patient.) After they've browned nicely on the first side, turn them to let them

1½ pounds Yukon Gold potatoes

¼ cup extra-virgin olive oil

4 to 5 cloves garlic, unpeeled

2 bay leaves

6 sprigs thyme, plus 2 teaspoons thyme leaves

1 cup romesco (recipe follows)

2 tablespoons chopped flat-leaf parsley

Kosher salt and freshly ground black pepper

color on all sides. Once they're nicely browned on all sides, spoon the romesco and reserved garlic into the hot potatoes. Toss and stir to coat them well. Taste for seasoning. Toss in the parsley. Or, if you're not ready to serve the dish yet, turn off the heat and leave the potatoes in the pan; then, just before serving, reheat for a few minutes and toss in the parsley at the last moment.

romesco

5 ancho chiles

2 tablespoons raw almonds

2 tablespoons blanched hazelnuts

1¼ cups extra-virgin olive oil

1 slice country bread, about 1 inch thick

⅓ cup San Marzano canned tomatoes

1 clove garlic, chopped

1 tablespoon chopped flat-leaf parsley

½ lemon, for juicing

Kosher salt

This sauce will keep for 2 weeks in the refrigerator. Try it on sandwiches and with cheese, eggs, grilled fish, and roasted meats.

Preheat the oven to 375°F.

Remove and discard the stems and seeds from the chiles, and then soak them in warm water for 15 minutes to soften. Strain the chiles, and pat dry with paper towels.

Meanwhile, spread the nuts on a baking sheet and toast for 8 to 10 minutes, until they smell nutty and are golden brown.

Heat a large sauté pan over high heat for 2 minutes. Add 2 tablespoons olive oil and wait a minute. Fry the slice of bread on both sides until golden brown. Remove the bread from the pan and cool. Cut it into 1-inch cubes and set aside.

Return the pan to the stove over high heat. Add 2 tablespoons olive oil and the chiles and sauté for a minute or two. Add the tomatoes. Season with ½ teaspoon salt and cook 2 to 3 minutes, stirring often, until the tomato juices have evaporated and the tomato starts to color slightly. Turn off the heat, and leave the mixture in the pan.

In a food processor, pulse together the toasted nuts, garlic, and fried bread until the bread and nuts are coarsely ground. Add the chile-tomato mixture, and process for 1 minute more.

With the machine running, slowly pour in the remaining 1 cup olive oil and process until you have a smooth purée. Don't worry, the romesco will "break" or separate into solids and oil; this is normal. Add the parsley, and season to taste with lemon juice and more salt if you like.

vanilla semifreddo with rhubarb compote

In Italy, there are many variations of semifreddo, which, literally translated, means "partially frozen." Sometimes a semifreddo is made from sponge cake layered with slightly frozen cream; other times it's cake-free, simply a lighter version of ice cream. At Lucques, we make this semifreddo from an uncooked "custard" base that has beaten egg whites (to make it buoyant and light) and whipped cream (to prevent it from freezing completely) folded into it. The result is a creamy frozen dessert that doesn't require an ice cream maker or a true custard cooked at the stovetop.

Strawberry and rhubarb are a classic combination, but though it's tempting to temper the sourness of the rhubarb with sweet strawberries, I prefer the intense mouth-puckering quality of rhubarb on its own. This is a great party dessert since you can prepare all the components ahead of time.

NOTE The semifreddo needs to be made at least 4 hours ahead (preferably the day before), so it has time to set completely.

About 1 teaspoon flavorless oil for greasing the pan

1⅓ cups heavy cream

½ vanilla bean

3 extra-large eggs, separated

¼ teaspoon pure vanilla extract

⅔ cup granulated sugar

Rhubarb compote (recipe follows)

Lightly oil a 9-inch round cake pan and line it with plastic wrap, tucking the wrap into the corners and smoothing it out completely with your hands. Let the excess plastic drape over the sides of the pan.

In a stand mixer fitted with the whisk attachment, whip the cream at medium speed, until it forms stiff peaks. Transfer the whipped cream to another bowl, cover, and chill while you make the rest of the dessert. Wash and dry the mixing bowl and whisk attachment.

Split the vanilla bean in half lengthwise. Use a paring knife to scrape the seeds and pulp into the mixing bowl. Add the egg yolks, vanilla extract, and half of the sugar, and mix at high speed with the whisk attachment about 3 minutes, until the mixture is thick and light-colored and has doubled in volume. Transfer to a large bowl and set aside. Wash and dry the mixing bowl and whisk attachment.

Whip the egg whites at medium speed about 1 minute, until frothy. Turn the speed up to high, and slowly pour in the remaining ⅓ cup sugar. Whip on high speed about 4 minutes, until stiff peaks have formed.

Fold the chilled whipped cream into the yolk mixture. Then gently fold in the egg whites, a third at a time. Pour the mixture into the prepared cake pan and tap the pan on the counter three times. Place a piece of plastic wrap over the surface, smoothing it with your hands (wrinkles in the plastic wrap will leave lines on the semifreddo). Fold the draping plastic wrap over the edges, and freeze for at least 4 hours.

Take the semifreddo out of the freezer 10 minutes before serving. Spoon a little rhubarb compote onto six plates. Cut six slices from the semifreddo and place them on the plates over the compote. Spoon a little more compote over the top of each slice of the semifreddo. Pass the remaining compote at the table.

rhubarb compote

1 pound rhubarb
½ vanilla bean
½ cup granulated sugar
¼ cup white wine
¾ teaspoon cornstarch

Cut the rhubarb stalks in half lengthwise, and slice crosswise into ½-inch-long pieces.

Split the vanilla bean in half lengthwise, and use a paring knife to scrape the seeds and pulp into a medium pan. Add the vanilla pod, sugar, and 2 tablespoons water. Without stirring, bring the ingredients to a boil over medium heat. Continue cooking for about 8 minutes, swirling the pan once in a while, until you have a deep golden brown caramel. *Immediately* toss in half the rhubarb and all the wine. The caramel will seize up and harden slightly. Turn the heat down to medium and stir constantly with a wooden spoon, breaking up the rhubarb, until it's jammy. Stir in the rest of the rhubarb and ½ cup water. Cook a few minutes until the rhubarb is tender but not mushy. Remove the pan from the heat, and strain the rhubarb over a bowl. Return the liquid to the pan, and bring it to a boil over medium-high heat.

Meanwhile, stir 1 tablespoon water into the cornstarch (this is called a "slurry" and will help thicken the fruit juices). Whisk the slurry into the liquid, and let it come back to a boil, stirring continuously. Cook over medium heat a few minutes, until the liquid is shiny and thickened. Pour the liquid back into the bowl, and stir in the rhubarb. Chill before serving.

mcgrath farms' watercress soup with gentleman's relish toast

Super-green watercress makes the perfect starter to a St. Patrick's Day dinner. One St. Patrick's Day at Lucques, in order not to lose the bright, vivid green color and fresh lively taste of the watercress, I decided to make the soup to order. Rather than cooking the watercress, I planned to wilt it with hot vegetable stock and then purée it with tarragon, parsley, chives, and a touch of cream. As that night approached, the restaurant was booked solid, and I began to worry about my made-to-order soup scheme, but Daniel Mattern, my equally obsessive sous-chef, insisted we go for it in spite of the anticipated 180 reservations. He recruited the waitstaff to bring their blenders from home, and organized his newfound equipment into a lean, mean soup station as if it were business as usual. That night, all 180 bowls of soup were made to order and managed to arrive at the tables piping-hot. Dan must have had the luck of the Irish because he pulled it off without a hitch. Served with an anchovy toast, this "*à la minute*" soup is great any day of the year.

7 tablespoons unsalted butter

1 cup sliced white onion plus 2 cups diced white onions

2 leeks, whites only, sliced

1 carrot, peeled and sliced

2 stalks celery, sliced

1 chile de árbol, crumbled

¼ bunch thyme

¼ bunch flat-leaf parsley, plus 2 tablespoons chopped flat-leaf parsley

A pinch cayenne pepper

5 cups chopped watercress (about 2 bunches)

2 tablespoons minced chives

1 tablespoon chopped tarragon

1 cup heavy cream

1 lemon

Gentleman's relish on toasts (recipe follows)

Kosher salt and freshly ground black pepper

Heat a large pot over medium heat for 2 minutes. Add 4 tablespoons butter, and when it foams, add the sliced onion, leeks, carrot, and celery. Stir to coat with the butter, and season with 1 tablespoon salt and some pepper. Cook 5 minutes and add the chile, thyme, and parsley sprigs. Cook over medium heat about 5 minutes, until the vegetables are just starting to caramelize.

Add 10 cups of water and bring to a boil over high heat. Turn the heat down and simmer 30 minutes. Strain the stock, discard the vegetables, and set the stock aside.

Return the pot to medium heat for 2 minutes. Add 3 tablespoons butter, and when it foams, add the diced onions, cayenne, 1 teaspoon salt, and a healthy grind of pepper. Cook the onions about 5 minutes, stirring often, until they're translucent and tender. Add the vegetable stock, turn the heat up to high, and bring to a boil.

You will need to purée the soup in batches. Place 2½ cups of the watercress, 1 tablespoon chives, 1 tablespoon chopped parsley, and 1½ teaspoons tarragon in the blender. Ladle 1½ cups of the hot stock over the greens. Cover tightly, and carefully start the blender at the lowest possible speed. When the mixture is puréed, add another cup of stock and turn the blender up to high. Add more stock, until the soup is a little thicker than heavy cream. Run the blender at high for 1 minute to ensure the soup is very smooth and creamy. With the motor running, pour in ½ cup of cream and taste for seasoning. Add a little squeeze of lemon juice if you like. At this point, the soup's consistency should be that of heavy cream.

Set the first batch of soup aside, and repeat the process with the remaining watercress, herbs, stock, and cream.

Pour the hot soup into a large tureen or soup bowl and pass the toasts on the side, so they remain crunchy. Tell your guests to float the toasts in their soup.

gentleman's relish on toasts

1 baguette

¼ cup extra-virgin olive oil

6 tablespoons unsalted butter, softened

1 teaspoon minced anchovy

2 teaspoons finely diced shallot

1 teaspoon lemon juice

¼ teaspoon lemon zest

Healthy pinch cayenne pepper

1 teaspoon minced flat-leaf parsley

1 teaspoon minced chives

Kosher salt and freshly ground black pepper

This Irish condiment, sold in jars under the name *Patum Peperium*, was created in 1828 and is still made by only one company, from a secret blend of anchovy, butter, herbs, and spices. The story goes that the man who created it presumed that ladies' taste buds were too delicate for this hearty anchovy spread. As my version demonstrates, I disagree.

Preheat the oven to 375°F.

Cut the baguette on the diagonal into twelve ¼-inch-thick slices. (You may have leftover bread.) Brush both sides of each slice generously with olive oil, about ¼ cup in all. Arrange the slices on a baking sheet and toast them in the oven 10 to 12 minutes, until golden and crispy but still tender in the center. Let cool.

Combine the butter, anchovy, shallot, lemon juice, zest, cayenne pepper, parsley, and chives in a bowl. Season with salt and pepper to taste.

When the toasts have cooled, spread them with gentleman's relish.

buttered cockles with peas, pea shoots, green garlic champ, and brown scones

One year while researching ideas for our St. Patrick's Sunday supper, I discovered that the Irish obsession with potatoes is not a myth. Page after page of old Irish "cookery books" reveal numerous formulas for the tuber, with whimsical names for each. I fell for champ, an Irish version of mashed potatoes flavored with a handful of finely sliced scallions. Since it was spring, I skipped the scallions and used lots of sliced green garlic instead.

But the Irish don't live on potatoes alone; seafood is actually the backbone of their diet. So I decided to celebrate their patron saint with something from the sea. I found lots of recipes for fish as well as tiny clams known as cockles. Trying to bring these Irish specialties together, I steamed the cockles with white wine and butter and then spooned them over the creamy green garlic champ. And what more Irish way to sop up those briny juices than with a savory brown scone?

NOTE Most of the cooking for this dish needs to be done right before serving. You can boil and smash the potatoes earlier in the day, but don't make the champ ahead or your green garlic will turn brown. Also, do not add the cream until just before serving. Of course you can slice the spring onions and green garlic, wash the cockles, and prep the herbs ahead of time. The scones can be made earlier in the day but are best right out of the oven! (If you must make them earlier, warm them in the oven just before serving.)

To release any bits of sand from the cockles, soak them in milk and water with a handful of cornmeal for 10 minutes or so and then rinse them in cold water.

¼ cup extra-virgin olive oil

1½ cups thinly sliced spring onions plus 1 cup thinly sliced spring onion tops

1 tablespoon thyme leaves

3 pounds cockles, or small Manila clams, well scrubbed

½ cup white wine

1 cup chicken stock

1¾ cups peas (from 2 pounds in the pod)

6 tablespoons unsalted butter, cut into small pieces

½ lemon, for juicing

¼ cup chopped flat-leaf parsley

4 ounces pea shoots

Green garlic champ (recipe follows)

Brown scones (recipe follows)

Kosher salt and freshly ground black pepper

Heat a large wide-bottomed sauté pan or Dutch oven over high heat for 2 minutes. Swirl in the olive oil and wait 1 minute. Add the spring onions, thyme, ½ teaspoon salt, and ¼ teaspoon pepper. Cook about 2 minutes, stirring often, until the onions are just wilted. Add the cockles to the pan, and stir well to coat them with the onions and oil. Cook 2 minutes, add the white wine, and cover the pan.

Steam the cockles 3 to 4 minutes, until they open. Remove the lid and pour in the stock. When the stock comes to a boil, add the peas. Cook 1 minute and then add the butter, stirring to incorporate. Season with a squeeze of lemon juice and taste for seasoning. Discard any unopened cockles.

Quickly toss the parsley, pea shoots, and spring onion tops into the pot. Stir just until the greens begin to wilt, and transfer to a warm large shallow bowl.

Serve with the green garlic champ, and pass around the warm brown scones.

green garlic champ

Cook the potatoes in a large pot of heavily salted boiling water for about 15 minutes, until tender. (The cooking time will depend on the size and type of potato.) When the potatoes have just cooled, crush them slightly on a cutting board with the heel of your hand or the back of a large spoon.

Heat a medium pot over high heat for 1 minute. Add the butter, and when it foams, add the green garlic, thyme, ½ teaspoon salt, and a pinch of pepper. Cook 3 to 4 minutes, stirring with a wooden spoon, until the green garlic has softened.

Add the potatoes, stirring and mashing them to incorporate all of the ingredients. Season with ¾ teaspoon salt and cook another 2 to 3 minutes. Turn off the heat, cover, and leave the pot on the stove. When you are ready to serve the champ, make sure it's hot, and then stir in the cream. Taste for seasoning.

1½ pounds fingerling or small yellow potatoes

4 tablespoons unsalted butter

1½ cups thinly sliced green garlic

½ teaspoon thyme leaves

¼ cup heavy cream

Kosher salt and freshly ground black pepper

brown scones

MAKES 12 SCONES

Preheat the oven to 375°F.

Place the flours, sugar, salt, and baking powder in a food processor, and process 30 seconds, until well combined.

Add the butter and pulse about ten times, until the mixture is a coarse meal.

With the machine running, quickly pour in 1 cup of the buttermilk. Stop the machine as soon as the dough comes together. It's important not to overwork the dough.

Turn the dough onto a lightly floured work surface and bring it together with your hands into a large ball. Divide the dough into three pieces, and shape each of them into a 5-inch-wide disc. Cut each disc into quarters.

Brush the tops of the scones with a little buttermilk. Place on a lightly buttered baking sheet and bake 25 minutes, until the scones are golden brown.

2¼ cups all-purpose flour

¾ cup whole-wheat flour

3 tablespoons granulated sugar

1 teaspoon kosher salt

2 tablespoons plus 2 teaspoons baking powder

9 tablespoons unsalted butter, chilled and cut into small cubes

1 cup plus 2 tablespoons buttermilk

corned beef and cabbage with parsley-mustard sauce

One 6-pound corned-beef brisket

2 onions

4 whole cloves

2 bay leaves, preferably fresh

½ bunch thyme

2 chiles de árbol

6 small carrots

9 golf ball–sized turnips

1¼ pounds yellow potatoes, peeled

1 medium green cabbage (about 2 pounds)

Parsley-mustard sauce (recipe follows)

Since both my parents worked full-time, when I was 2 weeks old they hired a seemingly proper English lady to take care of me. But Ammie was not the mild-mannered woman she appeared to be. In fact, she turned out to be the quirkiest third parent you could ever imagine. She fed us forbidden chocolate (despite her belief that chocolate actually "made your blood boil"), and she let us watch TV when my parents were out of town (very illegal).

Ammie was nothing if not opinionated. She displayed the nationalist zeal of an expatriate and was completely obsessed with the royal family. She was so pro-British and anti-Irish that every March 17 she would thumb her nose at her enemy by sending my sister and me off to school dressed completely in orange, in honor of the British monarchy.

Needless to say, corned beef and cabbage was not a food ritual in our household. I didn't discover it until I moved back east to college, where I sampled it at the homes of many of my Irish-American friends. The Lucques version is an updated rendition of that classic one-pot Irish meal. Traditionally, the vegetables are cooked alongside the meat for hours, producing dull, mushy carrots and sad, gray turnips. To keep the vegetables bright, I cook them separately in the beef broth. The parsley-mustard sauce (great for sandwiches the next day) cuts the richness of the corned beef and perks up the entire dish.

NOTE Timing is an important aspect of this meal. While the meat is resting, finish cooking the vegetables. Though you can prep the vegetables in advance, it's best to wait and cook them at the last moment. You could also cook the corned beef a day or two ahead, slice it when it's cold, and then reheat and crisp the slices in the broth.

In most non-Irish neighborhoods, this large, brined hunk of meat is a special-occasion item and not always kept in stock. Call your butcher ahead to make sure you can get one.

Preheat the oven to 325°F.

Place the corned beef in a large deep pot and cover with cold water by 6 inches. Bring to a boil over medium heat.

Cut the onions in half lengthwise, peel them, and poke one clove into each half.

When the water comes to a boil, turn off the heat and add the onions, bay leaves, thyme, and chiles. Cover the pot with plastic wrap (yes, it can go in the oven), aluminum foil, and a tight-fitting lid if you have one.

Cook the corned beef in the oven 4 to 4½ hours, until it's fork-tender. (Carefully remove the foil and plastic and pierce the meat with a fork. If the fork doesn't penetrate easily, the corned beef is not ready.)

While the beef is cooking, peel the carrots, leaving ½ inch of stem. Cut the carrots in half lengthwise. Trim the turnip tops, leaving ½ inch of stem attached. Cut the turnips in half through the stems. Cut the potatoes into 1-inch chunks. Remove any tough outer leaves from the cabbage and slice it in half through the core. Cut each cabbage half into three wedges, leaving the core intact to hold the leaves together.

When it's done, remove the meat from the oven, let it cool a few minutes, and transfer it to a baking sheet.

Turn the oven up to 375°F.

Return the meat to the oven for about 15 minutes, until it browns and crisps on top. Let the corned beef rest 10 to 15 minutes before slicing it.

Meanwhile, skim the fat from the broth. (There probably won't be very much.) Taste the broth. If it tastes good—not too salty but nicely seasoned and meaty—set half of the liquid aside in a medium saucepan. If the broth is salty, add a little water before setting half of it aside.

Add water to the broth in the large corned-beef cooking pot until you have enough liquid to poach the vegetables. Bring to a boil over high heat, then turn the heat down to medium, and add the potatoes to the pot. Simmer 5 minutes and then add the cabbage, turnips, and carrots. (If your pot is not big enough, divide the broth into two pots, adding more water if needed.) Simmer over low heat 15 to 20 minutes, until the vegetables are very tender. Test each type of vegetable occasionally, and if one is ready before the others, use tongs or a slotted spoon to take the vegetables out of the broth.

Taste the reserved broth and the vegetable-cooking broth. Combine them to your taste. If the vegetable broth tastes best, use it for the finished broth. If the vegetable broth is watery but has good flavor, add a little of it to the reserved broth, to your liking. Or, if you like the meat broth best, use it by itself.

Place the cabbage on a large warm platter. Slice the corned beef against the grain into ¼-inch-thick slices. Arrange the meat over the cabbage. Scatter the other vegetables over and around the platter. Pour over a good quantity of your chosen broth, and drizzle with the parsley-mustard sauce. Pass the extra broth and sauce at the table.

parsley-mustard sauce

¼ cup plus 2 tablespoons finely diced shallots

¼ cup red wine vinegar

¾ cup chopped flat-leaf parsley

1 tablespoon whole grain mustard

½ cup plus 2 tablespoons extra-virgin olive oil

½ lemon, for juicing

Kosher salt and freshly ground black pepper

This delicious salsa is great on corned-beef sandwiches as well as on grilled lamb, veal, or even a melted-Gruyère sandwich.

Place the shallots, vinegar, and ¼ teaspoon salt in a small bowl, and let sit 5 minutes. Pound the parsley with a mortar and pestle and add it to the shallots. Whisk in the mustard and olive oil, and season with a squeeze of lemon juice, a pinch of pepper and a pinch more salt, if you like. Be careful not to overseason, since the corned beef may be on the salty side.

chocolate-stout cake
with guinness ice cream

Only on St. Patrick's Day is it imperative that both your ice cream and your cake contain beer. Not your typical chocolate cake, and definitely not as intensely rich as the 1970s Moms' Double-Chocolate Bundt Cake (page 112), this chocolate-stout cake has an unexpected kick to it. The addition of molasses, cloves, cinnamon, and nutmeg steers it into the spice cake category, with chocolate undertones and an indefinable depth from the dark, full-bodied stout.

For me, the biggest surprise of this dessert is the Guinness ice cream. I'm a vanilla girl all the way, and when chefs use weird ingredients just for the sake of being different, I usually pass. But here the dark beer flavor really works in the ice cream to complement the cake. A touch spicy, it might just cure a hangover.

2 cups all-purpose flour

¾ cup unsweetened cocoa powder

1½ teaspoons baking powder

½ teaspoon ground cloves

½ teaspoon ground cinnamon

½ teaspoon freshly ground nutmeg

1 cup Guinness stout

1 cup molasses

1½ teaspoons baking soda

3 extra-large eggs

½ cup dark-brown sugar

½ cup granulated sugar

1 cup vegetable oil

1 teaspoon unsalted butter, softened

Guinness ice cream (recipe follows)

Preheat the oven to 350°F.

Sift the flour, cocoa powder, baking powder, cloves, cinnamon, and nutmeg together into a large mixing bowl.

Pour the beer and molasses into a medium pot, whisk together, and bring to a boil over medium-high heat. Remove from the heat, and whisk in the baking soda. Don't be surprised when it foams up.

In another bowl, whisk together the eggs and both sugars, mixing well to combine. Whisk in the oil, and then the beer mixture.

Make a well in the center of the dry ingredients. Pour in the liquid ingredients, whisking slowly until just incorporated. Be careful not to overmix or the cake will be tough.

Pour the batter into a lightly buttered Bundt pan and bake 30 minutes. The cake is done when it begins to pull away from the sides of the pan and the top surface is just starting to crack. When you insert a skewer into the center, it should come out mostly clean. To keep the cake moist, cover it with a dry kitchen towel as it cools. After 30 minutes, invert the cake onto a platter.

Serve slices of the cake with scoops of the Guinness ice cream.

guinness ice cream

½ vanilla bean

1 cup whole milk

1 cup heavy cream

⅔ cup Guinness stout

2 tablespoons plus 2 teaspoons
    molasses

3 extra-large egg yolks

⅓ cup granulated sugar

½ teaspoon pure vanilla extract

Split the vanilla bean in half lengthwise. Using a paring knife, scrape the seeds and pulp into a medium saucepan. Add the vanilla pod, milk, and cream, and bring to a boil over medium heat. Turn off the heat, cover, and allow the flavors to infuse for 30 minutes.

While the cream is infusing, whisk the beer and molasses together in a small saucepan, bring to a boil, and then turn off the heat.

Whisk the egg yolks, sugar, and vanilla extract together in a bowl. Whisk a few tablespoons of the warm cream mixture into the yolks to temper them. Slowly, add another ¼ cup or so of the warm cream, whisking continuously. At this point you can add the rest of the cream mixture in a slow, steady stream, whisking continuously. Pour the mixture back into the pot, and return to the stove.

Stir the beer mixture into the cream and cook the custard over medium heat, 6 to 8 minutes, stirring frequently with a rubber spatula and scraping the bottom and sides of the pan. The custard will thicken and when it's done will coat the back of the spatula. Strain the mixture, and chill at least 2 hours in the refrigerator. When the custard is very cold, process it in an ice cream maker according to the manufacturer's instructions.

swiss chard tart with goat cheese, currants, and pine nuts

Look in any Sicilian cookbook and you'll find a recipe for the popular side dish, or *contorno*, of cooked greens with currants and pine nuts. I make Swiss chard the main attraction of this dish, layering it onto a savory tart with rich and tangy goat cheese, then topping it with sweet currants and toasted pine nuts.

Use a crumbly, slightly aged goat cheese, such as Bûcheron, Rodin Affiné, or the domestically produced Laura Chanel aged chèvre. Feel free to substitute any other tender greens, such as the tops of beets or turnips, or a bunch of young mustard greens for the Swiss chard.

NOTE Assemble the tart in the morning, cover, and refrigerate. Bake just before you're ready to serve. You can make the currant–pine nut relish in the morning.

Preheat the oven to 400°F.

Defrost the puff pastry slightly and unroll it on a parchment-lined baking sheet. Use a paring knife to score a ¼-inch border around the edge of the pastry. Make an egg wash by whisking one egg yolk with ½ teaspoon water, and brush the egg wash along the border. (You will not need all of the egg wash.) Chill the puff pastry in the freezer until ready to use.

Tear the chard into large pieces.

Heat a large sauté pan over high heat for 2 minutes. Add 2 tablespoons olive oil, the shallots, and the thyme. Sauté a few minutes, and add half the Swiss chard. Cook a minute or two, tossing the greens in the oil to help them wilt. Add the second half of the greens, and season with a heaping ¼ teaspoon salt and a pinch of black pepper. Cook for a few more minutes, stirring frequently, until the greens are tender.

Spread the greens on a baking sheet or platter to cool. (You may want to put them in the refrigerator, so they cool more quickly.) When they've cooled, squeeze the excess water out with your hands.

Place the ricotta, remaining egg yolk, and remaining 1 tablespoon olive oil in the bowl of a food processor. Purée until smooth, and remove to a mixing bowl.

1 frozen sheet all-butter puff pastry (8 by 12 inches or equivalent)

2 extra-large egg yolks

1 large bunch Swiss chard, cleaned, center ribs removed

3 tablespoons extra-virgin olive oil

¼ cup sliced shallots

1 teaspoon thyme leaves

½ cup whole milk ricotta, drained if wet

¼ cup crème fraîche

6 ounces semi-aged goat cheese

Currant–pine nut relish (recipe follows)

Kosher salt and freshly ground black pepper

Gently fold in the crème fraîche, and season with a healthy pinch of salt and freshly ground black pepper.

Spread the ricotta mixture on the puff pastry inside the scored border. Crumble half the goat cheese over the ricotta, arrange the greens on top, and sprinkle the remaining goat cheese over the tart. If you aren't ready to bake, cover the tart with plastic and chill.

Bake the tart for 20 to 25 minutes, rotating the baking sheet halfway through, until the cheese is bubbling and the crust is golden brown. Check underneath the tart to make sure the crust is really cooked through (if you underbake the tart, it will be soggy).

Cool a few minutes, and then transfer the tart to a cutting board. Spoon some of the currant–pine nut relish over the tart and serve it on the cutting board at the table. Pass the remaining currant–pine nut relish in a small bowl for anyone who would like a little more.

currant–pine nut relish

½ cup pine nuts

⅓ cup extra-virgin olive oil

½ sprig rosemary

1 chile de árbol

¾ cup finely diced red onion

⅓ cup dried currants

¼ cup balsamic vinegar

2 tablespoons chopped flat-leaf parsley

Kosher salt and freshly ground black pepper

Preheat the oven to 375°F.

Toast the pine nuts for about 8 minutes, stirring once or twice, until they're golden brown and smell nutty.

Heat a small sauté pan over high heat for 2 minutes. Turn down the heat to medium, and add the olive oil, rosemary, and chile. When the rosemary and chile start to sizzle, add the onion and season with ½ teaspoon salt. Turn the heat down to low, and let the onions stew gently for about 10 minutes, until tender. Transfer to a small bowl to cool and discard the rosemary sprig and chile.

While the onion is cooking, place the currants in a small bowl and cover with hot water. Let the currants soak for 10 minutes, and then drain well.

Add the balsamic vinegar to the pan the onions were in, and reduce it over medium-high heat to a scant 1 tablespoon. Stir the reduced vinegar into the onion mixture.

Add the toasted pine nuts, currants, and parsley to the onion mixture, and stir to combine. Taste for balance and seasoning.

wild striped bass with farro, black rice, green garlic, and tangerine

The first incarnation of this dish did not include rice. Tasting it over and over again, I knew it needed a final element that would bring its flavors into harmony: nutty farro, meaty bass, pungent green garlic, sweet pea shoots, tart tangerines. I racked my brain for just the right thing, then remembered a sample of black rice I had stashed in my desk drawer weeks before.

I had little experience with black rice—varieties of rice whose kernels are covered by extremely dark bran. The black rice I found was grown in the salt marshes of the Veneto, so I cooked it in an Italian style. As I would for risotto, I sautéed the rice in olive oil to seal the outer layer and toast it slightly. Then I deglazed with white wine, added water, and let it simmer away. When the rice was done, I found it solved my problem perfectly. The rice's marshy origins gave it a subtle oceany taste, complementing the fresh fish and giving the entire dish a springtime-by-the-sea coherence. What's more, there was a visual bonus: the black rice was gorgeous to behold, coated in its own deep purple sauce.

> NOTE Season the fish with the zest and herbs at least 4 hours before cooking. You can cook the farro and black rice ahead of time and sauté them together when you're ready to serve. If you are not comfortable cooking the grains and the fish at the same time, sauté the grains, and hold them in the oven until the fish is cooked. Add the pea shoots to the grains at the last minute.

Season the fish with the tangerine zest, thyme, and parsley. Cover, and refrigerate for at least 4 hours.

Remove the fish from the refrigerator 15 minutes before cooking, to bring it to room temperature.

Slice the stem and bottom ends from the tangerines. Stand the tangerines on one end and, following the contour of the fruit with a sharp knife, remove the cottony white pith. Work from top to bottom and rotate the fruit as you go. Then hold each tangerine over a bowl and carefully slice between the membranes and the fruit to release the segments in between. Discard all the seeds. You should have about ⅓ cup tangerine segments.

Heat a large sauté pan over high heat for 2 minutes. (Depending on the size of your pan, you may need to cook the fish in batches.) Season the fish with salt

---

6 wild striped bass fillets, 5 to 6 ounces each, skin on

3 tangerines, zested, plus 1½ cups fresh juice

1 tablespoon thyme leaves

2 tablespoons chopped flat-leaf parsley

2 tablespoons extra-virgin olive oil

1 teaspoon granulated sugar

4 tablespoons unsalted butter

Farro and black rice with green garlic and pea shoots (recipe follows)

Kosher salt and freshly ground black pepper

and pepper on both sides. Swirl in the olive oil and wait 1 minute. Carefully lay the fish in the pan, skin side down, and cook 3 to 4 minutes, until the skin is crisp. Turn the fish over, lower the heat to medium-low, and cook a few more minutes, until the bass is almost cooked through. Be careful not to overcook the fish. When it's done, the fish will begin to flake and separate a little, and the center will still be slightly translucent. Remember, the fish will continue to cook a bit more once you take it out of the pan.

Wipe out the pan and return it to the stove over medium-high heat. Add the tangerine juice and sugar and bring to a boil. When the juice has reduced by half, turn the heat down to low and quickly whisk in the butter, ¼ teaspoon salt, and a pinch of freshly ground pepper. Remove from the heat, and stir in the tangerine segments. Taste for seasoning.

Place the farro and black rice with green garlic and pea shoots on a large warm platter. Arrange the bass on top, and spoon the sauce over the fish.

farro and black rice with green garlic and pea shoots

6 tablespoons extra-virgin olive oil

1 cup diced onion

2 chiles de árbol

2 bay leaves

¾ cup black rice (see Sources)

¾ cup white wine

1 tablespoon thyme leaves

1½ cups farro (see Sources)

½ cup thin diagonally sliced green garlic

4 ounces pea shoots

Kosher salt and freshly ground black pepper

Heat a medium saucepan over medium heat for 1 minute. Swirl in 2 tablespoons olive oil, and add ½ cup onion, one chile, and a bay leaf. Cook 3 to 4 minutes, stirring often, until the onion is translucent. Add the rice, stirring to coat it with the oil, and toast it slightly. Pour ¼ cup white wine into the pan and reduce by half. Add 4½ cups water and 1 teaspoon salt, and bring to a boil. Turn the heat to low, and simmer about 40 minutes, stirring occasionally, until the rice is tender but slightly "al dente." When the rice is almost done, stir continuously about 5 more minutes, until all the liquid has evaporated. Season with a few grindings of black pepper, and transfer the rice to a baking sheet to cool. Discard the chile and bay leaf.

Meanwhile, heat a second medium saucepan over medium heat for 1 minute. Swirl in 2 tablespoons olive oil, the remaining ½ cup diced onion, the thyme, and the remaining bay leaf. Cook, stirring often, 3 to 4 minutes, until the onion is translucent. Add the farro, stirring to coat it with the oil and toast it slightly. Pour in the remaining ½ cup wine and reduce by half. Add 8 cups water and 2 teaspoons salt and bring to a boil. Turn the heat to low, and simmer about 30 minutes, until the farro is tender and just cooked through. Strain the farro and transfer it to a baking sheet to cool. Discard the bay leaf.

Heat a large sauté pan over high heat for 1 minute. Slice the remaining chile thinly on the diagonal. Swirl in the remaining 2 tablespoons olive oil, and add the green garlic, sliced chile, and ¼ teaspoon salt, and sauté 2 to 3 minutes. Add the farro, ¼ teaspoon salt, and a few grindings of black pepper. Cook about 5 minutes, stirring constantly with a wooden spoon, scraping the bottom of the pan as the grains crisp slightly. Stir in the rice, and cook another 2 to 3 minutes. Add the pea shoots, and cook until just wilted. Taste for seasoning.

boeuf à la niçoise: braised beef stew with red wine, tomato, olives, and buttered noodles

This robust stew is best in late winter or early spring, when there's still a lingering chill in the air. Tomatoes, olives, and red wine, hallmark flavors of the stew's southern-French provenance, make up its flavorful saucy base. Traditionally, it's made with a chuck roast, but I find that boneless short ribs yield a more succulent result. The tomatoes help thicken the sauce and add a deep sweetness. This time of year, rather than using mealy, out-of-season tomatoes, I opt for canned San Marzanos. If you can't find San Marzanos, look for another brand of Italian canned tomatoes.

Toss the beef in a large bowl with the cracked black pepper, 1 tablespoon thyme, the garlic, and the orange zest. Cover and refrigerate overnight.

Take the meat out of the refrigerator 45 minutes before cooking. After 15 minutes, season it on all sides with 1 tablespoon plus 2 teaspoons salt. Reserve the garlic and orange zest.

Preheat the oven to 325°F.

Heat a large Dutch oven over high heat for 3 minutes. Pour in 3 tablespoons olive oil and wait a minute or two, until the pan is very hot and almost smoking. Place the meat in the pan, being careful not to crowd it. (You will need to do this in batches.) Sear the meat until well browned on all sides. (This step is very important and should not be rushed; it will probably take 15 to 20 minutes.) As the batches of meat are browned, remove them to a baking sheet.

Turn the heat down to medium and add the onion, fennel, and carrot. Stir with a wooden spoon, scraping up all the crusty bits left in the pan. Add the thyme sprigs, bay leaf, and the reserved garlic and orange zest. Cook 6 to 8 minutes, until the vegetables are caramelized.

Add the crushed tomatoes and cook 2 minutes, stirring constantly to coat the vegetables. Add the balsamic vinegar and reduce to a glaze. Pour in the red wine and reduce it by half (about 5 minutes). Add the beef stock and bring to a boil.

Add the meat to the pot. Cover the pan with plastic wrap (yes, it can go in the oven!), aluminum foil, and a tightly fitting lid if you have one. Braise in the oven about 3 hours.

3 pounds boneless beef short ribs, cut into 1½-to-2-inch chunks

1 tablespoon freshly cracked black pepper

1 tablespoon plus ½ teaspoon thyme leaves, plus 6 sprigs

6 cloves garlic, smashed

Zest of ½ orange

5 tablespoons extra-virgin olive oil

1 cup diced onion

½ cup diced fennel

½ cup diced carrot

1 bay leaf, preferably fresh

¾ cup San Marzano canned tomatoes, crushed slightly, plus 8 whole San Marzano tomatoes

¼ cup balsamic vinegar

2½ cups hearty red wine, preferably southern French

4 cups beef or veal stock

½ cup pitted Niçoise olives

¾ pound pappardelle

6 tablespoons unsalted butter

4 ounces young spinach, cleaned

¼ cup plus 2 tablespoons chopped flat-leaf parsley

Kosher salt and freshly ground black pepper

While the meat is in the oven, cut the whole tomatoes in half lengthwise. Pour 2 tablespoons olive oil into a baking dish in which the tomatoes will fit snugly. Place the tomatoes in the dish, cut side up, and season with ¼ teaspoon salt, pepper, and the remaining ½ teaspoon thyme. Roast the tomatoes in the same oven for 1½ hours, until they are shriveled and slightly caramelized on top.

To check the meat for doneness, carefully remove the plastic and foil, being aware of the hot steam. Spoon a piece of meat out of the pan and press it with your thumb or a spoon. If it's done, it will yield easily and almost fall apart. If it's not super-tender, cover again and return the pot to the oven. When in doubt, taste it!

Take the pan out of the oven and uncover completely. Using a ladle, skim off the fat that rises to the top.

Turn the oven up to 400°F.

Bring a large pot of heavily salted water to a boil.

Ladle half the braising juices into a large sauté pan and add the olives. Return the meat to the oven for 15 minutes to caramelize.

When the water boils, cook the pasta to al dente and drain. Transfer the noodles to the pan with the braising juices and olives. Over medium-low heat, toss the noodles in the juices to coat well and bring to a low simmer. Stir in the butter, and season to taste with salt and pepper. Quickly add the spinach and ¼ cup chopped parsley, and toss for just 1 minute, until the spinach begins to wilt.

Transfer the pasta to a large warm platter. Spoon the meat and its juices over the noodles. Tuck the roasted tomatoes in and around the noodles and meat. Sprinkle the remaining 2 tablespoons chopped parsley over the top.

tangelo "creamsicles" with lindsay's sugar cookies

1 recipe vanilla ice cream
(see page 113)

5 to 6 cups fresh-squeezed
tangelo juice

Lindsay's sugar cookies (recipe
follows)

In grade school, my sister and I knew that summer was on its way when Mom carted in a giant bag of tangelos. Those bulbous, loose-skinned citrus fruits with their peculiar protruding stem-ends were a sweet-tart treat after a winter of dull navel oranges. Tangelo season was fast and fleeting, so we ate as many as we could while they lasted.

Local farmer Peter Schaner grows what I consider to be the best tangelos in the world. Several years back, as my pastry chef Kimberly Sklar and I were drinking some of his amazing tangelo juice, Creamsicles (or, depending where you come from, 50-50 bars) came to mind. So, for the next Sunday supper, we poured the fresh juice from pitchers into glass tumblers filled with vanilla ice cream, and this deconstructed Creamsicle was born.

Place two scoops of ice cream into each of six glass tumblers. Pass a pitcher of the tangelo juice around the table for your guests to pour over their ice cream. Serve the cookies on the side.

lindsay's sugar cookies

1 cup (2 sticks) unsalted butter,
softened

¾ cup granulated sugar, plus a
little extra for rolling

1 extra-large egg yolk

1 teaspoon pure vanilla extract

2 cups all-purpose flour

¼ teaspoon kosher salt

6 pieces candied tangelo zest
(recipe follows)

Trying to come up with a new sugar cookie recipe is like trying to reinvent the wheel. Over the years I've tried, but, inevitably, I always come back to this one from *Chez Panisse Desserts* by Lindsay Shere.

Sometimes I like to top the sugar cookies with a little black pepper, fennel seeds, candied ginger, or lavender sugar, but here they're embellished with candied tangelo zest to complement the "Creamsicle."

MAKES ABOUT 40 COOKIES

Preheat the oven to 350°F.

In a stand mixer fitted with the paddle attachment, cream the butter at high speed about 1 minute. Add the sugar, and beat 3 to 4 minutes at medium high, until light and fluffy.

Add the egg yolk and vanilla and beat a few more minutes, until light and fluffy. Slowly add the flour and salt, and mix at low speed until the dough comes together.

Shape the dough into logs about 1½ inches in diameter. Roll the logs in sugar, then wrap each one in plastic and refrigerate until firm.

Julienne the candied tangelo zest.

Slice the logs into ¼-inch-thick rounds and top each one with candied tangelo zest. Bake 10 to 12 minutes, until they're lightly browned on the bottom.

candied tangelo zest

NOTE This recipe will make more than you need for the cookies, but you can use the excess to garnish other citrus-flavored desserts.

Using a peeler, make long strips of zest about ⅓ inch wide. Place them in a small pot, cover with cold water, and bring to a boil. Boil for 1 minute, drain, rinse with cool water, and repeat the process two more times.

4 tangelos
¾ cup granulated sugar

Place the sugar in a pot and add ½ cup water. Add the blanched zest and bring to a boil. Turn the heat to low and cook very slowly, about 30 minutes, until the liquid becomes thick and syrupy.

Store the zest in the syrupy liquid in the refrigerator.

fava bean purée with oil-cured olives, french feta, and garlic toasts

1 baguette

1 cup extra-virgin olive oil

2 cloves garlic

2½ pounds fava beans in the pod

1 small sprig rosemary

1 chile de árbol, crumbled

½ lemon, for juicing

½ cup pitted oil-cured black
   olives, sliced in half

¼ cup sliced flat-leaf parsley
   leaves

¼ pound French feta

Kosher salt and freshly ground
   black pepper

Fava beans have a cult status in my kitchen, and during their short spring season, I use them as much as possible in salads, ragoûts, and salsas.

Here, they are gently stewed in olive oil with garlic and chile and puréed until creamy. This fava bean "hummus" is on my list of perfect foods. Though the classic cheese served with favas in Italy is pecorino, I break with tradition and crumble feta over the purée instead. If you have any leftover purée, make an open-faced sandwich topped with arugula, shallots, a drizzling of olive oil, a squeeze of lemon, and a few shavings of pecorino (or feta). It's the ultimate snack or light lunch.

NOTE I shuck, blanch, and peel the favas ahead of time but wait to cook and purée them until just before serving.

Preheat the oven to 375°F.

Cut the baguette on the diagonal into twelve ¼-inch-thick slices. (You may have leftover bread.) Brush both sides of each slice generously with olive oil (about ¼ cup in all). Arrange the slices on a baking sheet and toast them in the oven 10 to 12 minutes, until golden and crispy but still tender in the center. While the toasts are warm, rub them with one of the garlic cloves.

Mince the remaining garlic clove.

Bring a medium pot of salted water to a boil over high heat.

Meanwhile, remove the beans from their pods.

Blanch the beans for about 2 minutes in the boiling water. Drain the beans in a colander, cool them in the ice water, and then slip them out of their pale green shells with your fingers.

Heat a medium saucepan over low heat. Add the remaining ¾ cup olive oil, the rosemary sprig, and the chile. Let them sizzle in the oil a minute or two, then stir in the minced garlic. Let it sizzle for a minute and stir in the fava beans, ¾ teaspoon salt, and some freshly ground black pepper. Simmer the beans 5 to 7 minutes, stirring occasionally, until they're tender (the exact time will depend on the starchiness of the favas). Strain the beans, reserving the oil. Discard the rosemary and chile.

Transfer the beans into a food processor and purée them. With the motor running, pour in half the reserved oil slowly, until the purée is velvety smooth. Once the purée is smooth, pour in more of the reserved olive oil to taste. Squeeze in some lemon juice, and taste for seasoning. (The amount of oil you will need depends on the starchiness of the beans.)

In a small bowl, toss the olives and parsley with a drizzle of olive oil and a squeeze of lemon juice. Crumble in the feta, tossing gently to combine.

Spoon the warm fava bean purée onto a platter. Place the grilled toasts off to one side, and scatter the feta-olive salad over the purée.

dungeness crab salad with avocado, beets, crème fraîche, and lime

Dungeness crabs are caught off the Pacific coast, from the tip of Alaska to as far south as Baja California, during the cold-water months of November to early June. If you're not on the West Coast or can't find Dungeness crabs, look for stone, peekytoe, or blue crabs. And if you're short on time, purchase the crabs already cooked, cracked, and cleaned from a good fishmonger. If you're feeling less extravagant or can't get to the fish market, a crabless version of this dish makes a pretty good salad, too.

3 bunches small to medium beets

¾ cup extra-virgin olive oil

½ lemon, for juicing

¼ cup finely diced shallots

3 tablespoons seeded, diced jalapeños

⅓ cup lime juice, plus a little extra for seasoning

1 Reed avocado, or 2 large Hass avocados

1 bunch watercress, cleaned, tough stems removed

¾ pound picked-over steamed Dungeness crabmeat

1 tablespoon chopped flat-leaf parsley

1 tablespoon chopped cilantro

½ cup crème fraîche

A healthy pinch of freshly cracked black pepper

Kosher salt and freshly ground black pepper

Preheat the oven to 400°F.

Cut the leaves from the beets, leaving 1 inch of stem still attached. (Save the greens for another dish.) Clean the beets well, and toss them with 1 tablespoon olive oil and 1 teaspoon salt. Place the beets in a roasting pan with a splash of water in the bottom. Cover with foil, and roast 30 to 40 minutes, until tender when pierced. (The roasting time will depend on the size and type of beet.) When the beets are done, carefully remove the foil. Let cool, and peel the beets by slipping off the skins with your fingers. Cut the beets into ½-inch wedges. Toss them in a medium bowl with 1 tablespoon olive oil, a generous squeeze of lemon juice, and a pinch of salt and pepper. Taste for seasoning.

While the beets are in the oven, combine the shallots, jalapeños, lime juice, and ½ teaspoon salt in a small bowl, and let sit 5 minutes. Whisk in ½ cup plus 2 tablespoons olive oil. Taste for balance and seasoning.

Cut the avocados in half lengthwise, remove the pit, and peel. Cut into ¼-inch slices, and season with ½ teaspoon salt and freshly ground black pepper. Fan the avocado slices on one side of a chilled platter. Place the beets on the other side, and arrange the watercress in the center.

Toss the crab gently with two-thirds of the jalapeño-lime vinaigrette, the parsley, and the cilantro in a large bowl. Taste the crab, and season with more salt or lime if you like. Pile the crab on the watercress, and top with the crème fraîche. Sprinkle a little cracked black pepper over the crème fraîche, and drizzle a little more vinaigrette over the avocado.

saffron chicken with parmesan pudding, spring onions, and sugar snap peas

½ teaspoon saffron threads

3 tablespoons unsalted butter, softened

5 tablespoons extra-virgin olive oil

6 boneless chicken breasts, about 5 ounces each, skin on

1 tablespoon thyme leaves

2 tablespoons sliced flat-leaf parsley

1 lemon, zested

¾ pound sugar snap peas, sliced on the diagonal into ¼-inch-thick pieces

1½ cups sliced spring onions plus ½ cup sliced spring onion tops

4 ounces pea shoots

Parmesan pudding (recipe follows)

Kosher salt and freshly ground black pepper

This dish proves my quirky theory that green and orange foods go together. Think about it: peas and carrots, oranges and asparagus, winter squash and arugula. Saffron, a beautiful rusty orange, pairs perfectly with spring's green bounty.

Saffron has been used as a flavoring and coloring agent (even as hair dye!) since ancient Egyptian times. The saffron thread is actually the stigma (part of the female reproductive organ) of the saffron crocus. Each one must be handpicked from the flower, which accounts for saffron's outrageous price. Fortunately, a little goes a long way. Use it with a light hand, as too much saffron can easily overwhelm a dish. Buy whole threads, not powder, and store them in a cool, dark place. Buy only a little saffron at a time, so you'll be able to use all of it while it's still fresh.

NOTE Marinate the chicken the night before serving. You can make and bake the pudding ahead of time and refrigerate it covered. Bring it to room temperature about an hour before serving, and rewarm it in a 400°F oven 15 to 20 minutes, uncovered, until it's hot and begins to brown slightly around the edges.

Toast the saffron in a small pan over medium heat until it just dries and becomes brittle. Pound the saffron to a fine powder in a mortar. Dab a tablespoon of the softened butter into the saffron powder, using the butter to scoop up about half of the powder. Set aside.

Stir 4 tablespoons olive oil into the mortar, scraping with a rubber spatula to incorporate all of the saffron powder.

Toss the chicken breasts gently with the saffron oil, 2 teaspoons thyme, the parsley, and the lemon zest, coating the chicken well. Marinate in the refrigerator at least 4 hours, preferably overnight.

Heat a large sauté pan over high heat for 2 minutes. Season the chicken with salt and pepper on both sides. Swirl in 1 tablespoon olive oil and wait a minute. Place the chicken, skin side down, in the pan (you might need to cook the chicken in batches). Cook for 3 to 4 minutes, until the skin is crispy and golden brown. Turn the breasts over, reduce the heat to medium-low, and cook them a few more minutes, until just cooked through and springy to the touch. Transfer the chicken to a resting rack.

Return the pan to the stove over medium heat for 1 minute. Add the remaining 2 tablespoons butter, and when it foams, add the sliced spring onions, sugar snap peas, ½ teaspoon salt, a pinch of pepper, and the remaining teaspoon thyme. Cook over medium heat 2 to 3 minutes, stirring, until the onions are translucent. Add the saffron butter and 1 tablespoon water. Swirl the pan, and when the liquid comes to a simmer, toss in the pea shoots and onion tops. Immediately remove the pan from the heat, and squeeze a little lemon juice over the vegetables. Taste for seasoning.

Arrange the chicken on a large warm platter and spoon the vegetables over it. Serve with the hot Parmesan pudding.

parmesan pudding

When it finally occurred to me that custards didn't have to be sweet, I went on a savory custard kick, and I've never looked back. Once you learn the technique and feel comfortable with this custard recipe, you can play around with other variations, by adding sliced prosciutto, asparagus, or mushrooms. Be sure to bake it in a pretty dish, such as an old French earthenware or enameled gratin, that will look nice at the table.

Preheat the oven to 350°F.

Heat a medium pot over medium heat for 1 minute. Add the butter, and when it foams, whisk in the flour, 1 tablespoon at a time, and cook for about 5 minutes, being careful not to let the flour brown. Slowly pour in the milk and cream, whisking constantly to incorporate it. The butter and flour will seize up and get pasty at first. Continue whisking vigorously as you add the liquid, and the mixture will become smooth. Cook a few more minutes, until warm to the touch. Remove the pan from the heat.

Whisk the egg and egg yolk together in a small bowl. Slowly drizzle the eggs into the cream mixture, whisking continuously until combined. Stir in the cheese, and season with a heaping ½ teaspoon salt. Pour the mixture into an 8-by-6-inch (or equivalent) baking dish, and cover tightly with foil. Place the baking dish in a roasting pan, and add hot water to the pan until it comes halfway up the outside of the custard dish. Place the pan in the oven, and bake about 1 hour, until the pudding is just set.

3 tablespoons unsalted butter

¼ cup plus 2 tablespoons all-purpose flour

1¾ cups whole milk

⅔ cup heavy cream

1 extra-large egg

1 extra-large egg yolk

1¼ cups grated Parmigiano-Reggiano

Kosher salt

tarte au fromage with lemon cream and blueberry compote

This not-too-sweet tart is the perfect ending to a spring meal. The key to keeping the pastry nice and crisp is to bake it ahead and then scoop out some of the center, to make room for the filling. Don't overmix the ricotta filling or you'll smooth away those luscious natural curds in the cheese. At Lucques, we add dried blueberries to the fresh blueberry compote, giving it an unexpected chewiness.

> NOTE You can make the blueberry compote the day before. The lemon cream can be made ahead up to the point when you fold in the cream, which should be done right before serving.

1 frozen sheet all-butter puff pastry (8 by 12 inches or equivalent)

½ cup plus 1 tablespoon granulated sugar

2 extra-large eggs

1 extra-large egg yolk

¼ cup heavy cream

1 teaspoon pure vanilla extract

Zest of 1 lemon

¼ teaspoon kosher salt

1 pound fresh ricotta cheese

Lemon cream (recipe follows)

Blueberry compote (recipe follows)

Defrost the puff pastry slightly and unfold it onto a parchment-lined baking sheet. Use a paring knife to score a ½-inch border around the edge of the pastry. Brush the border with water and sprinkle with 1 tablespoon sugar. Place the puff pastry (on the baking sheet) back in the freezer for at least 30 minutes.

Preheat the oven to 350°F.

Remove the pastry from the freezer and bake about 30 minutes, until it's golden brown and cooked through (if you underbake the pastry, the ricotta filling will make it soggy). Remove the pastry from the oven and let it cool.

Turn the oven down to 325°F.

Meanwhile, whisk together the eggs, egg yolk, remaining ½ cup sugar, cream, vanilla, lemon zest, and salt in a medium bowl. Add the ricotta, and stir in gently to incorporate, without overworking it.

Remove the top layer of pastry from the area inside the ½-inch border. Press down the remaining pastry with your fingers, to flatten it. Spoon the ricotta mixture into the center of the tart. Use a rubber spatula or the back of a spoon to distribute the filling evenly just up to the ½-inch border.

Bake 30 to 40 minutes, until the ricotta mixture is set (look for "Jell-O motion") and just starting to color on top.

Cut the tart into six squares and garnish with dollops of the lemon cream and blueberry compote.

lemon cream

2 extra-large eggs

1 extra-large egg yolk

½ cup granulated sugar

½ cup lemon juice

2 tablespoons cold unsalted butter, cut into small pieces

A pinch of kosher salt

½ cup heavy cream

Whisk together the eggs, egg yolk, sugar, and lemon juice in a small nonreactive pot. Cook over medium heat about 10 minutes, stirring constantly (alternating between a whisk and a rubber spatula), until the lemon curd has thickened to the consistency of pastry cream. It should coat the back of a spoon, and when you run your finger through the custard on the back of the spoon, it should leave a clean line that holds its shape even when you tilt the spoon. Remove the pot from the heat and whisk in the butter. Season with a pinch of salt, and chill in a nonreactive dish.

When the lemon cream has chilled completely, transfer it to a bowl. Whip the heavy cream until it holds stiff peaks and gently fold it into the lemon cream.

blueberry compote

½ cup granulated sugar

½ vanilla bean

2 teaspoons cornstarch

2 cups fresh blueberries

2 tablespoons brandy

¼ cup dried blueberries

Place the sugar in a medium pot. Split the vanilla bean in half lengthwise, and use a paring knife to scrape out the seeds and pulp into the sugar. Add ⅓ cup water and bring to a boil over medium heat, without stirring. Cook about 10 minutes, swirling the pan occasionally, until the mixture is an amber caramel color.

Meanwhile, stir 1 tablespoon water into the cornstarch (this is called a "slurry" and will help thicken the fruit juices).

When the sugar has reached an amber caramel color, add half the fresh blueberries and the brandy to the pot. The sugar will harden. Cook for a minute or two over low heat, stirring gently, until the berries release their juices and the sugar dissolves.

Strain the mixture over a bowl, and return the liquid to the pan, whisk in the cornstarch slurry, and cook another minute, stirring often, until it comes to a boil. Transfer the cooked berries to the bowl and stir in the remaining fresh and the dried blueberries. Pour the thickened juices over the berries, and stir to combine.

ragoût of morels with crème fraîche, soft herbs, and toasted brioche

Morels are to spring what tomatoes are to summer: they epitomize the season. Their spongy texture and funny pine-cone shape give these wild mushrooms unmistakable personality. In order not to mask their delicious earthy flavor, morels are best when prepared simply. In a French kitchen, morels are often cooked with cream. And as with so many traditional pairings, when you taste the combination you understand why it's a classic. Here the morel ragoût is bound with a little cream, spooned over toasted slices of brioche, and topped with dollops of crème fraîche. The soft herbs are left whole; when you bite into them you get a big burst of flavor.

1 tablespoon tarragon leaves

1 tablespoon chervil sprigs

2 tablespoons flat-leaf parsley leaves

2 tablespoons ½-inch-snipped chives

¾ pound fresh morels, stems trimmed and cleaned (see page 32)

5 tablespoons unsalted butter, softened

1 teaspoon thyme leaves

½ cup sliced shallots

1 cup mushroom, vegetable, or chicken broth

Three ¾-inch-thick slices brioche

½ cup heavy cream

6 tablespoons crème fraîche

Kosher salt and freshly ground black pepper

Toss the tarragon, chervil, parsley leaves, and chives together in a small bowl and set aside, covered with a damp paper towel in the refrigerator. If the morels are large, cut them in half lengthwise.

Heat a large sauté pan over high heat for 2 minutes. Add 3 tablespoons butter, and when it foams, scatter the morels into the pan, being careful not to overcrowd them. Sauté 3 to 4 minutes, stirring often. Turn down the heat to medium, and add the thyme, ½ teaspoon kosher salt, and a few grindings of pepper. Let the mushrooms cook another 6 to 8 minutes, until they're crispy on the outside yet still tender. (The amount of cooking time really depends on the mushrooms; some give off more water than others, which will require a longer cooking time in order for the water to evaporate and the morels to crisp.)

Add 1 tablespoon butter, and stir in the shallots. Cook about 2 minutes, until the shallots are translucent and tender. Turn the heat up to high, add the broth, and reduce by half. Immediately remove from the heat.

Meanwhile, lightly butter the brioche on both sides. Heat a large cast-iron pan over medium-high heat, and toast the slices on both sides until golden brown.

Cut the brioche slices in half on the diagonal, and place them on a platter.

When the brioche is ready, return the mushrooms to medium heat for a minute or two. Swirl in the cream, and taste for seasoning. Spoon the morels over and around the toasts—not completely covering the bread, and spilling onto the platter.

Dollop each toast with crème fraîche and scatter the herbs over the top.

sautéed alaskan black cod with endive and hazelnuts

6 fillets black cod, 5 to 6 ounces each, bones removed if possible

1 lemon, zested

1 tablespoon plus 2 teaspoons thyme leaves

¼ cup sliced flat-leaf parsley

½ cup blanched hazelnuts

6 Belgian endives

10 tablespoons unsalted butter

1 tablespoon plus 1 teaspoon granulated sugar

2 tablespoons extra-virgin olive oil

Kosher salt and freshly ground black pepper

Black cod, despite its name, is not a true cod. Its other names—sablefish and butterfish—suit it better: its texture is as silky as sable, its flavor as rich as butter. I love the Japanese pairing of black cod and miso, but in this recipe, black cod gets a French treatment, a smothering with hazelnut brown butter.

Ask your fishmonger where the black cod is from. It's overfished in California and Oregon so look for black cod from Alaska, where the commercial fishing is better regulated.

Black cod has a single row of bones that is very difficult to remove when the fish is raw. You can ask your fishmonger to remove the bones or cut them out yourself before cooking. Or just cook the fish bones and all; it's easy to spot them and eat around them.

Season the fish with the lemon zest, 1 tablespoon thyme, and 2 tablespoons parsley. Cover, and refrigerate at least 4 hours or overnight.

Remove the fish from the refrigerator 15 minutes before cooking, to bring it to room temperature.

Preheat the oven to 375°F.

Toast the hazelnuts on a baking sheet 10 to 12 minutes, until they're golden brown and smell nutty. When the nuts have cooled, chop them coarsely.

Remove any wilted or brown outer leaves from the endives. Slice off the root ends, and separate the endives into spears. Arrange the endive into stacks of five, and cut each stack in half lengthwise.

Heat a large sauté pan over high heat for 1 minute. Add 3 tablespoons butter, and when it foams, add the endive and remaining 2 teaspoons of thyme. (You may need to do this in two pans or two batches. Divide the ingredients accordingly if so.) Sprinkle in the sugar, 1 teaspoon salt, and ¼ teaspoon pepper. Sauté over medium heat about 4 minutes, until the endive is slightly caramelized and softened. Turn off the heat, and leave the endive in the pan while you cook the fish.

Heat a large sauté pan over high heat for 2 minutes. (Depending on the size of your pan, you may need to cook the fish in batches.) Season the fish with salt and pepper on both sides. Swirl in the olive oil and wait 1 minute. Carefully lay the fish in the pan, skin side down, and cook 3 to 4 minutes, until the skin is crisp. Turn the fish over, lower the heat to medium-low, and cook a few more minutes, until it's just cooked through. Be careful not to overcook the fish. When it's done, the fish will begin to flake and separate a little. Remember, the fish will continue to cook a little more once you take it out of the pan.

Transfer the endive to a warm platter, and wipe out the fish pan with paper towels. Heat the pan over medium-high heat for a minute. Add the remaining 7 tablespoons butter and cook a few minutes, swirling the pan occasionally, until the butter browns and smells nutty. Turn off the heat, wait 30 seconds, and add the hazelnuts. Season with ½ teaspoon salt, a pinch of pepper, and a squeeze of lemon juice. Stir in the remaining 2 tablespoons sliced parsley.

Arrange the fish over the endive. Stir the brown butter, scraping the bottom of the pan to incorporate all the little brown flecks. Spoon the butter over the fish.

orecchiette carbonara with english peas and pea shoots

2 tablespoons extra-virgin olive oil

4 ounces applewood-smoked bacon, diced

6 ounces pancetta, diced

4 extra-large eggs

4 extra-large egg yolks

1½ cups grated Parmigiano-Reggiano

1½ pounds orecchiette pasta (see Sources)

1½ cups finely diced onions

1 tablespoon minced garlic

1 tablespoon thyme leaves

2 cups freshly shucked peas (from 2¼ pounds in the pod)

3 ounces pea shoots

2 tablespoons chopped flat-leaf parsley

Kosher salt and freshly ground black pepper

Spaghetti carbonara was one of the simpler dishes in my dad's weekend repertoire, and it was by far my all-time favorite thing to make with him. After chopping the bacon, snipping the parsley, and grating the cheese, my sister and I would stand back and watch the grand master perform the final act. As he whisked the eggs and tossed in the piping-hot noodles, we marveled at the transformation of our seemingly simple and innocent ingredients into a magnificent bowl of indulgence. It all happened in a matter of seconds; unlike his laborious stews, which took hours to make, this meal was all about instant gratification.

In the spring, I stray from tradition and add lots of sweet peas and pea shoots to Dad's original formula. The shape of orecchiette pasta suits this dish well; the "little ears" capture the sauce inside, ensuring plenty of flavor in every bite. If you can't find orecchiette, use spaghetti or penne.

NOTE When you add the eggs, they should be warmed just enough to thicken them, so they coat the pasta. If you overcook them, the eggs will curdle and scramble. If the sauce is very soupy, then the eggs haven't cooked enough. In that case, I place the bowl of pasta directly over a very low flame, stirring or tossing for a few seconds, to cook the eggs until the sauce just thickens and coats the orecchiette. For this reason, I like to use a stainless steel bowl.

Bring a large pot of heavily salted water to a boil.

Heat a large Dutch oven over high heat for 1 minute. Swirl in the olive oil, and add the bacon and pancetta. Turn the heat down to medium-high and cook about 5 minutes, stirring occasionally, until the bacon and pancetta are slightly crisped but still tender.

Meanwhile, whisk the eggs, egg yolks, and 1¼ cup cheese together in a large stainless steel bowl. Season lightly with salt and pepper.

Drop the pasta into the rapidly boiling water.

Add the onion, garlic, and thyme to the bacon, and cook about 6 minutes, stirring occasionally, until the onion is translucent. Just before the pasta is ready, stir in the peas, coating them well with the onion and bacon.

As the pasta cooks, measure out and reserve about a cup of the hot pasta water. When the pasta is al dente, drain it and immediately add it to the bacon mixture, with 1 teaspoon salt, tossing well. Grind lots of black pepper into the pot, and cook 1 to 2 minutes more, stirring well to incorporate. Add the orecchiette to the eggs, stirring vigorously to "cook" the eggs and coat the pasta in the egg "sauce" (see note). Season with salt and pepper to taste. If the mixture seems too thick, add a little of the reserved pasta water. Toss in the pea shoots and parsley, and transfer to a warm shallow bowl. Sprinkle the remaining ¼ cup cheese over the top.

crème fraîche panna cotta
with strawberries

½ cup cold whole milk

Heaping 3½ teaspoons
    unflavored gelatin, or
    ¼-ounce package

3 cups heavy cream

6 tablespoons granulated sugar

Vegetable oil, for molds

½ cup plus 2 tablespoons crème
    fraîche

1½ pints fresh strawberries

The stated purpose of my junior year abroad was to study at the famous London School of Economics, but the first thing I did when I got to England was land a part-time job at the Roux brothers' (also famous) restaurant, Le Mazarin. Of all the challenges of living abroad, I never thought I'd have a problem finding something decent to eat.

Boy, was I wrong. While the food we served guests at Le Mazarin was top-notch, staff meals were a different story. Stripped chicken carcasses, limp vegetable trimmings, and, if we were lucky, a box of just-add-water mashed-potato flakes were the components of just about every meal. The rest of London wasn't offering many great options either at that time. Fish and chips and heavy pub fare dominated the food scene in the late eighties, before Britain's culinary renaissance. The one thing I found worth eating (and could afford on the £10 a week my job paid) was scones with clotted cream and strawberries. And that's exactly what I ate, for 6 straight months.

After so many meals of strawberries and cream, it's a wonder that I still love that combination. Panna cotta ("cooked cream"), a silken, eggless Italian custard, is an easy-to-make complement to perfectly ripe berries. I've added crème fraîche to the traditional recipe to balance the strawberries' sweetness with some tang. You can make the panna cotta in individual ramekins and unmold them just before serving or make it in a large gratin dish and spoon it out at the table family-style.

Place the milk in a large bowl, sprinkle the gelatin over it, and stir to combine.

In a medium saucepan, bring the cream and 5 tablespoons sugar to a boil. Lightly oil eight 4-ounce ramekins or custard cups (or a large gratin dish if serving family-style).

When the cream mixture comes to a boil, turn off the heat and let it sit a few minutes.

Slowly whisk the cream into the gelatin, and then whisk in the crème fraîche.

Strain the mixture, and pour it into the prepared molds. Chill in the refrigerator for at least 3 hours.

Ten minutes before serving, slice the strawberries, and toss them with a tablespoon or so of sugar, to taste.

Run a hot knife around the edges of the panna cotta and invert it onto a large chilled platter. Surround the custard with the strawberries and their juice.

prosciutto and grilled asparagus with whole grain mustard

When I was growing up, my dad and I had an ongoing asparagus arrangement: I would cut off the tips of my asparagus spears and trade them for his ends. While most asparagus eaters like the tender tips best, to this day I still prefer the fibrous-textured stalk and would happily swap tips for ends if anyone offered. In this simple first course, asparagus is grilled, then layered with prosciutto and dressed with mustard cream. I hope it's delicious enough to disappear before your guests have a chance to debate which end is better.

NOTE You can make the whole grain mustard sauce a few hours ahead. If you don't have a grill, roast the asparagus on a baking sheet for 5 to 7 minutes at 400°F.

1¼ pounds asparagus, pencil-thin variety

2 tablespoons extra-virgin olive oil

3 tablespoons whole grain mustard

½ cup crème fraîche

12 thin slices prosciutto di Parma or San Daniele

½ lemon, for juicing

Kosher salt and freshly ground black pepper

Light the grill 30 to 40 minutes before you're ready to cook.

Snap the ends off the asparagus to remove the tough woody portion. Toss the asparagus on a baking sheet with the olive oil, ½ teaspoon salt, and some pepper.

Stir the mustard and crème fraîche together in a small bowl, and set aside.

When the coals are broken down, red, and glowing, drape the prosciutto over a platter. Grill the asparagus 2 to 3 minutes, until slightly charred and tender.

Arrange the asparagus on the prosciutto and drizzle the mustard crème fraîche over the top.

halibut with fingerlings, fava beans, meyer lemon, and savory crème fraîche

6 filets halibut, 5 to 6 ounces each

1 Meyer lemon, zested

1 tablespoon thyme leaves

2 tablespoons sliced flat-leaf parsley

1¼ pounds small fingerling potatoes

4 tablespoons unsalted butter

1½ cups shucked fava beans, from 2 pounds in the pod

2 tablespoons extra-virgin olive oil

4 ounces pea shoots

Savory crème fraîche (recipe follows)

Meyer lemon salsa (recipe follows)

Kosher salt and freshly ground black pepper

Savory is possibly the most underappreciated herb in this country. I fell in love with it many years back when I was cooking in France. There, it's used in the traditional seasoning mix *herbes de Provence* and added to all types of stews, ragoûts, and sauces. Its aroma—earthy, slightly sweet, and a little bit peppery—reminds me of the brush-covered hillsides where we played growing up. Winter savory, summer savory's seasonal opposite, is more robust in flavor but would be a fine substitute in this recipe. If you can't find either of the savories, substitute a combination of equal amounts of thyme, rosemary, and mint.

This isn't a difficult dish to make, but it does require some last-minute multi-tasking. Have your prepared ingredients—or, as we say in the kitchen, your *mise en place*—ready to go. Be sure that your herbs are chopped, the vinaigrette is made, the crème fraîche is mixed, and your seasonings are in reach.

This dish is a great way to initiate the unconverted to the Church of the Fava Bean. The potatoes and favas are mashed together with butter and finished with pea shoots and a vibrant Meyer lemon salsa. The seared halibut goes on top with a dollop of savory crème fraîche.

NOTE You can make the Meyer lemon salsa and the savory crème fraîche earlier in the day. You could also boil and smash the potatoes ahead of time.

Season the halibut with the lemon zest, thyme, and parsley. Cover and refrigerate at least 4 hours or overnight.

Remove the fish from the refrigerator 15 minutes before cooking to bring it to room temperature.

Place the potatoes in a medium pot, cover with cold water (by at least 4 inches), and add 1 tablespoon salt. Bring to a boil, turn down the heat, and simmer gently for about 15 minutes, until the potatoes are tender when pierced. Reserve a cup of the water and strain the potatoes. When the potatoes have cooled, slightly smash them with the heel of your hand.

Heat a large sauté pan over medium heat for 1 minute. Add the butter, smashed potatoes, and ¾ teaspoon salt. Stir to coat the potatoes with the butter.

Add the fava beans and a few tablespoons of the reserved potato water to the pan. Turn off the heat and cover while you cook the fish.

Heat a large sauté pan over high heat for 2 minutes. (You may need to cook the fish in batches or in two pans.) Swirl in the olive oil and wait 1 minute. Carefully lay the fish in the pan and cook 3 to 4 minutes, until it's lightly browned. Turn the fish over, lower the heat to medium-low, and cook a few more minutes until it's almost cooked through. Be careful not to overcook the fish. When it's done, it will begin to flake and separate a little and the center will still be slightly translucent. Remember, the halibut will continue to cook a bit more once you take it out of the pan.

Turn the heat under the potatoes up to medium, uncover, and heat the potatoes and favas until hot through. Toss in the pea shoots and cook about 1 minute, stirring to combine until the pea shoots are just wilted. Taste for seasoning. Spoon the potatoes onto a large warm platter, dot half the crème fraîche over them, and spoon half the lemon salsa on top. Arrange the halibut over the potatoes and spoon the remaining crème fraîche and lemon salsa over each piece of fish.

savory crème fraîche

Using a mortar and pestle, pound the savory leaves to a paste. Add the crème fraîche and use a rubber spatula to scrape the sides and combine well. Season with ¼ teaspoon salt and a pinch of black pepper.

2 teaspoons savory leaves

¾ cup crème fraîche

Kosher salt and freshly ground black pepper

meyer lemon salsa

Cut both ends off the Meyer lemons. Place the lemons cut side down on a cutting board. Following the contour of the fruit with your knife, remove the peel and white cottony pith, working from top to bottom and rotating the fruit as you go. Then, one at a time, hold each lemon in your hand and carefully slice between the membranes and the fruit to release the segments in between. Discard the seeds and reserve the juice. You should have about ¼ cup of segments and ¼ cup of juice.

Place the lemon juice in a small bowl and add the shallots and ¼ teaspoon salt. Let sit 5 minutes and slowly whisk in the olive oil. Stir in the lemon segments, savory, mint, and parsley. Taste for balance and seasoning.

2 to 3 large Meyer lemons

2 tablespoons finely diced shallots

⅓ cup extra-virgin olive oil

1 teaspoon minced savory

1 tablespoon sliced mint

2 tablespoons chopped flat-leaf parsley

Kosher salt and freshly ground black pepper

veal osso buco with saffron risotto, english peas, and pea shoots

Braised meats are ideal for any large gathering because much of the work can be done the day before. In my opinion, braises actually taste better when the flavors have had time to meld and develop. And in the braising process, not only have you cooked the meat, you've also created a sauce. Osso buco is a classic braised dish of northern Italy, usually garnished with gremolata, a popular condiment made of minced lemon zest, parsley, and garlic. That's fine in the winter, but in spring, I like to add two of my favorite spring ingredients: peas and pea shoots. It's a brighter rendition of the traditional preparation. The risotto, perfumed with saffron, is the perfect starch for spooning up with the braising juices. I'm usually pro-cheese, but in the case of this risotto I find myself torn. Though the Parmesan gives the risotto richness, without it the dish is a little lighter and "more of the season." You decide.

NOTE You can braise the veal shanks a day or two ahead of time; just remember they need to marinate a full day beforehand. Bring the cooked meat to room temperature and then gently reheat it, covered, in the broth. Start the risotto after you take the veal out of the oven the first time (or after you have reheated it) and strain the braising juices. After the risotto has been cooking about 10 minutes, put the shanks in the oven to brown. Recruit a friend to help you by preparing the sauté of peas and pea shoots while you finish the risotto.

6 center-cut veal shanks,
   10 to 12 ounces each

6 cloves garlic, smashed

1 tablespoon lemon zest

1 tablespoon plus 1 teaspoon
   thyme leaves

1 tablespoon rosemary leaves

3 tablespoons extra-virgin olive
   oil

1 cup diced onion

½ cup diced carrot

½ cup diced celery

3 sprigs sage

½ cup chopped San Marzano
   canned tomatoes

1 cup dry vermouth

6 cups veal stock

6 sprigs flat-leaf parsley

2 tablespoons unsalted butter

1½ cups English peas (from
   about 1½ pounds in the pod)

¼ cup sliced shallots

3 ounces pea shoots

Saffron risotto (recipe follows)

Kosher salt and freshly ground
   black pepper

Season the veal shanks with the garlic, lemon zest, 1 tablespoon thyme, and rosemary. Cover, and refrigerate overnight.

Take the veal shanks out of the refrigerator an hour before cooking, to bring them to room temperature. After 30 minutes, season the shanks on all sides with 3 tablespoons salt and 2 teaspoons pepper. Reserve the garlic and any excess herbs.

Preheat the oven to 325°F.

Heat a large sauté pan over high heat for 3 minutes. Pour in the olive oil and wait a minute or two, until the pan is very hot, almost smoking. Place the shanks in the pot, and sear until caramelized and nicely browned on all sides. Depending on the size of your pan, you will probably have to sear the meat in batches. (Do not crowd the meat or get lazy or rushed with this step. It's very important that the meat sear to a deep golden brown on all sides; this will take a good 15 to 20 minutes.) When the shanks are nicely browned, transfer them to a braising pan. They should sit flat, bones standing up, in one layer.

Turn the heat down to medium, and add the onion, carrot, celery, sage sprigs, and reserved garlic and herbs. Stir with a wooden spoon to scrape up all the crusty bits in the pan. Cook 6 to 8 minutes, until the vegetables just begin to caramelize. Stir in the tomatoes and cook a few more minutes. Add the vermouth, turn the heat to high, and reduce the liquid by half.

Add the stock and bring to a boil. Pour the liquid over the shanks, scraping any of the vegetables that fall on the meat back into the liquid. The stock mixture should almost cover the shanks (if not, add a little more stock or water). Tuck the parsley sprigs in the broth around the shanks. Cover tightly with plastic wrap (yes, it can go in the oven), then foil, plus a tight-fitting lid if you have one. Braise in the oven about 3 hours.

To check the meat for doneness, carefully remove the plastic and foil (watch out for the hot steam), and pierce one of the shanks with a paring knife. When the meat is done, it will yield easily. Taste a piece if you are not sure.

Turn the oven up to 400°F.

Carefully transfer the veal shanks to a baking sheet and return them to the oven to brown 10 to 15 minutes.

Strain the broth into a saucepan, pressing down on the vegetables with a ladle to extract all the juices. Skim the fat from the braising juices. If necessary, reduce the broth over medium-high heat about 5 minutes, to thicken slightly. Taste for seasoning.

Heat a large sauté pan over medium heat for 1 minute. Add the butter, and when it foams, add the peas. Turn the heat down to low, and sauté the peas gently about 3 minutes, shaking the pan a few times. Add the shallots, 1 teaspoon thyme, 1 teaspoon salt, and ¼ teaspoon pepper.

Stir to combine, and cook a few minutes, until the shallots are soft and translucent.

Add ½ cup water and turn the heat up to medium. Cook a minute or so, until the peas are just tender. Turn off the heat and toss in the pea shoots.

Arrange the veal shanks on a large warm platter. Ladle lots of the braising juices over the meat. Spoon the sauté of peas and pea shoots on top. Serve a bowl of saffron risotto and the remaining braising juices on the side.

saffron risotto

Toast the saffron threads in a small pan over medium heat, just until they dry and become brittle. Pound the saffron in a mortar to a fine powder. Add half the butter, and use a rubber spatula to incorporate it.

Bring the chicken stock and 3½ cups water to a boil over high heat. Turn off the heat.

Meanwhile, heat a medium heavy-bottomed pot over medium-high heat for

½ teaspoon saffron threads

4 tablespoons unsalted butter, softened

3½ cups chicken stock

1 cup diced white onion

2 teaspoons thyme leaves

1 chile de árbol, crumbled

1½ cups high-quality Arborio rice (see Sources)

¼ cup dry white wine

2 tablespoons chopped flat-leaf parsley

¼ cup grated Parmigiano-Reggiano (optional)

Kosher salt and freshly ground black pepper

2 minutes. Swirl in the saffron butter, and when it foams, add the onion, thyme, chile, ½ teaspoon salt, and a few grindings of black pepper. Sauté about 5 minutes, stirring often, until the onion is translucent. Stir in the rice and 1½ teaspoons salt. Cook about 2 minutes, stirring continuously, until the rice just begins to toast and the grains of rice have a white dot at their center.

Pour in the white wine, and once it has evaporated, quickly add 1 cup of the hot stock and stir continuously. When the stock is completely absorbed, begin adding the liquid in 1 cup batches, stirring all the time, with a wooden spoon, back and forth in a rhythmic motion. Wait for each batch of liquid to be absorbed before adding the next. The rice should be bubbling and quickly absorbing the liquid. After about 15 minutes, taste the rice for tenderness. It should be slightly but not too al dente. The risotto may need more liquid and more time, so keep cooking until it's done. It should be neither soupy nor dry; each grain of rice should be coated in a flavorful starchy "sauce."

When the rice is almost done, turn off the heat. Let the risotto "rest" for a minute or two, then quickly stir in the remaining 2 tablespoons butter and the parsley (and Parmigiano-Reggiano if you are using it). Taste for seasoning. The rice will keep absorbing liquid, so add a little more stock if it seems dry. Spoon the risotto into a serving bowl.

roman cherry tart with almond crust and almond ice cream

In so many American childhoods, cherry pie is a gloppy, cloying, Day-Glo affair. As a chef, I'm expected to disdain such things now, and, officially, I do. But I've always loved cherries. This Italian cherry and almond tart is everything a bad cherry pie is not: flaky, buttery, and sophisticated, with a filling the color of darkest rubies.

But if someday, when cherries are long out of season, you happen to see in a corner booth at DuPar's Coffee Shop someone who looks like me, wolfing down a slice of all-American diner pie, wearing dark sunglasses and a stain that looks suspiciously like Red Dye #40, well, keep it to yourself. Even chefs have fond memories of their misguided youth.

NOTE You can make the crust and line the tart shell the day before, and chill overnight. The sweet cherry compote can also be made the day before.

Heaping ½ cup raw almonds

¼ cup granulated sugar

1 cup plus 5 tablespoons all-purpose flour

¼ teaspoon kosher salt

8 tablespoons (1 stick) unsalted butter, melted and cooled slightly

¼ teaspoon pure almond extract

¼ teaspoon pure vanilla extract

Sweet cherry compote (recipe follows)

Almond ice cream (recipe follows)

Preheat the oven to 375°F.

Toast the almonds on a baking sheet about 10 minutes, until they darken slightly and smell nutty. When the nuts have cooled, place them in a food processor with the sugar and pulse to a coarse meal. Add the flour and salt and pulse again to combine. Transfer to a mixing bowl, and pour in the melted butter, almond and vanilla extracts, and 1 tablespoon ice-cold water. Using a wooden spoon, mix until just combined, adding more ice-cold water if necessary to help bring the dough together.

Use your fingers to press the dough into a buttered 9-inch fluted tart pan, pressing the sides first and then the bottom, to form an even crust. Chill at least an hour, or preferably overnight.

Preheat the oven to 350°F.

Prick the bottom of the tart shell with a fork, and line it with a few coffee filters opened out, or a piece of parchment paper. Fill the lined tart shell with beans or pie weights, and bake 20 minutes, until it begins to brown lightly around the edges. Remove from the oven and cool on a rack. Once it cools, lift the paper and beans out of the tart.

Fill the shell with the sweet cherry compote to just below the level of the rim. Return the tart to the oven and bake 1 hour, until the cherries darken to a deep ruby red. Let the tart cool 15 minutes before cutting.

Slice the tart into wedges, and serve with scoops of almond ice cream.

sweet cherry compote

½ vanilla bean
⅓ cup granulated sugar
1 tablespoon cornstarch
2¼ pounds Bing cherries, pitted
2 tablespoons grappa or brandy

Split the vanilla bean in half lengthwise and, using a paring knife, scrape the seeds and pulp into a medium saucepan. Add the vanilla pod, sugar, and ¼ cup water. Over medium heat, cook the mixture, without stirring, until it's caramelized to an amber color. Once it begins to brown, you can swirl the pot a little to get the caramel to color evenly.

While the sugar is caramelizing, stir 1 tablespoon water into the cornstarch (this is called a "slurry" and will help thicken the fruit juices).

When the sugar is an amber brown, add the cherries, and swirl the pan again. Add the grappa, turn the flame down, and let the cherries simmer a few minutes, until they have softened. (The caramel will seize up and harden at first; don't worry, it will remelt.) Strain the cherries over a bowl, return the liquid to the pot, and bring it to a boil over medium-high heat. Whisk the cornstarch slurry into the liquid and bring it back to a boil once again, stirring often. Cook a few more minutes, until thickened. Transfer the cherries to the bowl, pour the liquid over them, and stir to combine. Let cool completely.

almond ice cream

MAKES 1 QUART

2½ cups raw whole almonds
2 cups whole milk
2 cups heavy cream
4 extra-large egg yolks
½ cup granulated sugar
1 teaspoon pure almond extract

Preheat the oven to 375°F.

Toast the almonds on a baking sheet in the oven 10 to 12 minutes, until they darken slightly and smell nutty. When they've cooled, chop the nuts coarsely.

Place 1½ cups of the chopped almonds in a medium saucepan, and pour in the milk and cream. Bring to a boil over medium heat. Turn off the heat, cover, and let the flavors infuse for about 30 minutes.

Bring the mixture back to a boil over medium heat, stirring occasionally. Turn off the heat.

Whisk the egg yolks and sugar together in a bowl. Whisk a few tablespoons of the warm cream mixture into the yolks to temper them. Slowly, add another ¼ cup or so of the warm cream, whisking to incorporate. At this point, you can add the rest of the cream mixture in a slow, steady stream, whisking constantly. Pour the mixture back into the pot and return to the stove.

Add the almond extract, and cook the custard over medium heat 6 to 8 minutes, stirring frequently with a rubber spatula, scraping the bottom and sides of the pan. The custard will thicken, and when it's done will coat the back of the spatula. Strain the mixture, and chill at least 2 hours in the refrigerator. Process in an ice cream maker according to the manufacturer's instructions and, when it's done, stir in the remaining almonds.

sauté of white asparagus, morels, and ramps over polenta

30 stalks white asparagus, double-pencil-sized (about 2 pounds untrimmed)

12 pencil-thin ramps, leaves attached

6 ounces morels, stems trimmed, cleaned (see page 32)

6 tablespoons unsalted butter

2 teaspoons thyme leaves

Polenta (recipe follows)

1 tablespoon sliced flat-leaf parsley

Kosher salt and freshly ground black pepper

White asparagus, ramps, and morels are the caviar, foie gras, and truffles of the vegetable world. Simply sautéing them together in brown butter and serving them with creamy polenta is one of my favorite ways to enjoy these edible trophies of spring.

NOTE You can blanch the asparagus and ramps a few hours ahead.

Bring a large pot of salted water to a boil over high heat.

Snap off the ends of the asparagus (they will break naturally where their toughness begins), and peel the stalks.

Clean the ramps and prepare the ramps according to the method described on page 33.

Blanch the asparagus in heavily salted boiling water about 5 minutes, until tender. To test for doneness, take a spear out of the water, cut a small piece off the end, and taste it. (Remember, the spears will continue to cook a little as they cool.) Carefully remove the asparagus to a baking sheet to cool.

If the morels are large, cut them in half.

Heat a large sauté pan over high heat for 2 minutes. (If you don't have a pan that's large enough to hold all of the vegetables, heat two pans and divide ingredients accordingly.) Add 4 tablespoons butter to the pan, and when it foams, scatter the morels into the pan, being careful not to overcrowd them. Sauté the mushrooms 3 to 4 minutes, stirring often. Turn down the heat to medium, and add the thyme, ¼ teaspoon kosher salt, and a few grindings of pepper. Let the mushrooms cook another 6 to 8 minutes. They should be crispy on the outside, yet still tender. (The amount of cooking time really depends on the mushrooms; sometimes they give off water, which will require a longer cooking time, to allow the water to evaporate and the morels to crisp.)

Add the remaining 2 tablespoons butter to the mushrooms, and place the blanched asparagus carefully in the pan. Toss to coat the asparagus in all the mushroomy brown butter, and cook over medium heat for 2 minutes. Add the ramps to the pan, season with salt and freshly ground black pepper, and cook another 2 minutes, tossing often so all the flavors meld and everything is coated in the butter. Taste for seasoning.

Spoon the polenta onto a large warm platter. Using tongs, arrange the asparagus and ramps, randomly overlapping them over the polenta. Spoon the morels and all the butter over the top, and scatter the parsley over everything.

polenta

This recipe was perfected by Brian Wolff, our lovably obsessive-compulsive chef de cuisine at Lucques. He developed it using our cornmeal of choice from Bob's Red Mill. If you're using a different polenta, the cooking time and quantities of water might be a little different. The most important thing to learn from this recipe is the technique. Keep adding a little water at a time throughout the cooking process. There are only a few ingredients, so the cook makes all the difference. Watch carefully, and let the polenta tell you when it needs more water. And most of all, stir, stir, stir!

1 cup medium-grain polenta
   (see Sources)

3 tablespoons unsalted butter

Kosher salt

In a heavy-bottomed pot, bring 5½ cups water and 1 tablespoon salt to a boil over high heat. Add the polenta slowly, whisking continuously. Turn the heat down to low, and continue cooking for another 20 minutes, whisking often. Add another ½ cup water and cook 1 more hour, whisking often and adding ½ cup water as needed, about every 20 minutes. The flame should be low, so that the polenta is barely simmering. As you whisk, make sure that you reach the bottom of the pan to prevent the polenta from scorching. I like to use a rubber spatula to scrape the bottom and sides of the pot.

Whisk in the butter, and taste for seasoning. Even when the polenta is finished, you might sense it thickening up a little. If so, add a little more water and whisk to get the right consistency. If you're not serving right away, cover the pan with plastic wrap to keep the polenta from thickening or losing moisture. If necessary, rewarm over low heat before serving.

wild salmon salad with beets, potato, egg, and mustard vinaigrette

Inspired by main-course salads found in the bistros of France, this dish comprises some of my favorite ingredients—beets, mustard, dandelion, and soft-boiled egg. The salmon is covered in minced herbs, seasoned with *fleur de sel*, and then slow-roasted in a humid oven until it's moist and custardlike at the center.

NOTE Although there are a lot of components to this dish, the herb marinade, beets, potatoes, eggs, and mustard vinaigrette can be prepared ahead of time and dressed at the last minute. Even the salmon can be baked an hour or two before serving, since it's served at room temperature.

3 bunches beets, preferably mixed colors

6 tablespoons extra-virgin olive oil

1 pound very small potatoes

1 teaspoon thyme leaves

2 pounds wild salmon (1 piece), skin on, bones removed

1 lemon

½ cup finely diced shallots

2 tablespoons minced dill

2 teaspoons minced tarragon

¼ cup minced flat-leaf parsley

½ teaspoon *fleur de sel*

3 extra-large eggs

Dijon mustard vinaigrette (recipe follows)

4 ounces young dandelion greens, cleaned and dried

Kosher salt and freshly ground black pepper

Preheat the oven to 400°F.

Cut the greens from the beets, leaving ½ inch of stem still attached. (Save the leaves for sautéing later; they are delicious!) Clean the beets well, and toss them with 2 tablespoons olive oil and 1 teaspoon salt.

Place the beets in a roasting pan with a splash of water. Cover tightly with foil, and roast about 40 minutes, until tender when pierced. (The roasting time will depend on the size and type of beet.) When the beets are done, carefully remove the foil. Let cool, and peel the beets by slipping off the skins with your fingers. Cut the beets into ½-inch wedges.

Once the beets are in the oven, toss the potatoes with 1 tablespoon olive oil, the thyme, and 1 teaspoon salt. Place in a roasting pan, cover with foil, and cook in the oven about 30 minutes, until tender when pierced. When the potatoes have cooled, cut them in half.

Remove the salmon from the refrigerator 30 minutes before cooking, to bring it to room temperature.

Turn the oven down to 250°F and place a shallow pan of water on the bottom rack.

Finely grate the zest of the lemon until you have 1 teaspoon. Combine the lemon zest, shallots, dill, tarragon, and parsley in a small bowl, and stir in 2 tablespoons olive oil.

Place the salmon, skin side down, on a baking sheet, and season with 2 teaspoons kosher salt and some freshly ground black pepper. Smear about a third of the herb mixture on the fish, and turn it over. Slather the skin side of the fish with the remaining herb mixture, and season with the *fleur de sel* and a little more black pepper.

Place the salmon on a wire rack set on a baking sheet, or in a roasting pan. Bake the salmon about 25 minutes, until medium-rare to medium. The center will still be slightly translucent. To check if the salmon is done, peek between the flakes. If it doesn't separate into flakes, it's not ready yet.

Meanwhile, bring a small pot of water to a boil, and carefully lower the eggs into the pot. Turn the heat down to low, and gently simmer exactly 9 minutes. Immediately transfer the eggs to a bowl of ice water to stop the cooking. When they're completely cooled, peel the eggs, and cut them into halves. Season with salt and pepper.

Season the beets with a healthy pinch of salt, a pinch of pepper, the remaining tablespoon olive oil, and a squeeze of lemon juice. Season the potatoes with ½ teaspoon salt and 2 tablespoons Dijon mustard vinaigrette. Taste both for seasoning.

Scatter the dandelion greens on a large platter, and drizzle ¼ cup mustard vinaigrette over them. Nestle the potatoes and beets in and around the greens. Using your hands, pull the salmon into 2-inch chunks, tucking them throughout the salad. Spoon another ¼ cup vinaigrette over the salad, and tuck the eggs in and around the other ingredients. Season the salad with a healthy squeeze of lemon juice, and pass the rest of the vinaigrette at the table.

dijon mustard vinaigrette

1 extra-large egg yolk

1 tablespoon Dijon mustard

1½ tablespoons red wine vinegar

1 tablespoon lemon juice

¾ cup extra-virgin olive oil

Kosher salt and freshly ground
    black pepper

Whisk the egg yolk in a small bowl with the mustard, red wine vinegar, lemon juice, ½ teaspoon salt, and a pinch of pepper. Slowly whisk in the olive oil. Thin the vinaigrette with 1 teaspoon water or more if needed. Taste for balance and seasoning.

glazed duck confit with black rice, mizuna, and cherries

Like a lamb shoulder or veal shank, duck legs require a long, slow braise (in fat in this case, rather than stock) to break down their sinew and make them succulent and tender. Choose an earthenware dish or a roasting pan that will hold the legs snugly (the legs should just fit in the dish, without overlapping). Four cups of duck fat sounds like a lot, but don't worry, most of it is left behind in the pan, and you can use it over and over again, as long as it's strained well and kept chilled or frozen. You can also store the duck legs in the fat.

NOTE Like so many slow-cooked dishes, duck confit tastes better the next day. The savory cherry compote can also be made ahead and rewarmed before serving. Forty-five minutes before you want to put dinner on the table, start the rice. After 30 minutes, put the duck in the oven to crisp.

6 large duck legs, tip of the leg bone trimmed

1 tablespoon thyme leaves

1 cup sliced red onion

1 orange, sliced

3 bay leaves

2 chiles de árbol, crumbled

3 star anise

2 teaspoons freshly cracked black pepper

4 to 5 cups duck fat

Black rice (recipe follows)

Savory cherry compote (recipe follows)

Kosher salt

Trim the excess fat from the duck legs. Season them with the thyme, onion, orange, bay leaves, crumbled chiles, star anise, and cracked black pepper. Cover, and refrigerate overnight.

Preheat the oven to 325°F.

Take the duck out of the refrigerator 45 minutes before cooking to let it come to room temperature. After 15 minutes, scrape off the onion and spices into a 12-by-9-inch (or equivalent) baking dish. Season the duck legs on all sides with 1 tablespoon plus 1 teaspoon salt, let sit 30 minutes, and then place them in the baking dish, skin side up.

Heat the duck fat in a medium saucepan over low heat until it is just warm and has completely melted.

Pour the melted duck fat over the legs, just covering them. Carefully transfer the baking dish to the oven, and cook about 2½ hours, until tender. To check for doneness, insert a paring knife into the meat. When the duck is ready, it will be tender and fall right off the knife.

Remove the duck legs from the fat, and place them on a baking sheet. Turn the oven up to 400°F and return the legs to the oven for 10 to 15 minutes to crisp the skin.

Place the hot rice on a large warm platter. Arrange the duck legs on the rice, and spoon the warm cherry compote over the top.

black rice

2 tablespoons extra-virgin olive oil

1 cup diced onion

2 teaspoons thyme leaves

1 bay leaf

1 chile de árbol

2 cups black rice

½ cup white wine

2 tablespoons unsalted butter

6 ounces mizuna or baby spinach

Kosher salt and freshly ground black pepper

Heat a large saucepan over medium heat for 1 minute. Swirl in the olive oil and add the onion, thyme, bay leaf, chile, and ½ teaspoon salt. Cook, stirring often, 3 to 4 minutes, until the onion is translucent. Add the rice, stirring to coat it in the oil and toast it slightly. Add the white wine, and reduce by half. Add 10 cups water and 2 teaspoons salt and bring to a boil. Turn the heat down to low, and simmer about 40 minutes, stirring occasionally, until the rice is tender but slightly al dente. When the rice is almost done, stir continuously until all the liquid has evaporated. Discard the chile and bay leaf. Season with a few grindings of black pepper. Stir in the butter and taste for seasoning. Quickly stir in the mizuna, until just wilted.

savory cherry compote

Julie Robles, one of the first cooks at Lucques and later the chef de cuisine at A.O.C., came up with this delicious savory (as opposed to sweet) cherry compote. This time of year I go crazy for cherries and also serve this compote on roast pork or with an assertive cheese like Taleggio.

½ bunch thyme

2 bay leaves

2 chiles de árbol

3 star anise

1 cinnamon stick

1 teaspoon black peppercorns

¼ cup granulated sugar

½ cup port

Juice of 2 oranges

1½ cups pitted cherries (about ⅓ pound)

1 tablespoon unsalted butter

Kosher salt and freshly ground black pepper

Make a sachet of cheesecloth and put in it the thyme, bay leaves, chiles, star anise, cinnamon stick, and peppercorns. Place the sugar and 1 cup water in a medium saucepan. Bring to a boil over medium-high heat, and then add the port, the orange juice, and the sachet. Turn down to a simmer, and add the cherries. Poach the cherries 8 to 10 minutes, until just tender. (The cherries should retain their shape; if they've begun to look squashed, you've overcooked them.)

Strain the cherries over a bowl, and return the liquid to the saucepan. Cook the liquid over high heat about 5 minutes, until it has reduced by two-thirds. It should be slightly thickened and have a glossy sheen. Strain the liquid, and cool. Stir in the cherries, and season to taste with salt and a pinch of pepper.

When you are ready to serve the cherry compote, heat it in a saucepan and swirl in the butter.

coconut flan with apricots and beaumes de venise

Call me boring, but I prefer my sweets on the simpler side, and I drive my pastry chefs crazy with my penchant for, well, plain vanilla. When it comes to custards, I'm a particularly staunch traditionalist. So, when pastry chef Roxana Jullapat told me about her coconut flan, I was skeptical. But its elegant and classic presentation charmed me instantly—a snow white cylindrical custard oozing with golden caramel syrup and surrounded by Elgin Marble apricots simmered in Beaumes de Venise, orange juice, and spices. Roxana's coconut flan convinced me that there's life beyond a vanilla pot de crème (which is also delicious! See page 235).

NOTE If apricots are not in season, serve this with fresh sliced peaches, or with a side of sugar cookies (see pages 66–67).

MAKES 8 SERVINGS

1 cup granulated sugar

One 14-ounce can condensed milk

One 12-ounce can evaporated milk

1 teaspoon pure vanilla extract

4 extra-large eggs

1 cup dried unsweetened shredded coconut

Apricots and Beaumes de Venise (recipe follows)

Preheat the oven to 300°F.

Stir together the sugar and ¼ cup water in a very clean medium-sized saucepan. Over medium heat, bring to a boil without stirring. Continue cooking about 10 minutes, until the sugar caramelizes and becomes a deep golden brown. Immediately remove the pot from the heat and pour about 1 teaspoon of the caramel (being very careful, because it's very hot) into each of eight ramekins. Swirl the ramekins, to coat the bottom evenly with the caramel. Allow to cool and harden.

Pour the condensed milk, evaporated milk, vanilla extract, eggs, and coconut into a blender, and mix at high speed for 30 seconds or so, until incorporated.

Pour the mixture into the caramel-coated ramekins—stirring it before you pour, to make sure the coconut is incorporated. Fill each one to about ¼ inch beneath the rim. Place the ramekins in a large baking dish, and then pour water into the baking dish until it comes halfway up the sides of the ramekins. Cover the whole pan tightly with foil, carefully place it in the oven, and bake about 1 hour. The custard should be just set.

When the custards are done, carefully remove the baking dish from the oven (watching that the hot water doesn't splash into the custards), uncover, and allow to cool in the water bath 15 minutes. Refrigerate for at least 2 hours.

Before serving, run a hot paring knife around the edges and turn each custard onto a plate. Let the caramel ooze over the top. Spoon the apricots and their sauce around the flans.

apricots and beaumes de venise

Split the vanilla bean in half lengthwise and, using a paring knife, scrape the seeds and pulp into a large saucepan. Add the orange juice, wine, sugar, honey, cinnamon stick, vanilla pod and cloves. Bring to a boil over medium-high heat. Turn the heat to medium-low and continue cooking the liquid 5 to 7 minutes, to reduce and thicken it slightly.

Turn the heat to low and place the apricot halves in the pan, cut side up. Simmer about 3 minutes, until they just begin to soften. Turn off the heat, and let the apricots cool in the pan of liquid. Keep in mind that the apricots will continue to cook in the warm liquid.

1 vanilla bean

½ cup freshly squeezed orange juice

½ cup Beaumes de Venise or other sweet white wine, such as Sauternes

2 tablespoons granulated sugar

2 tablespoons orange-blossom honey

½ cinnamon stick

5 whole cloves

9 apricots, pits removed, halved

curried english pea soup with crème fraîche

6 tablespoons unsalted butter

1½ cups diced white onion

A heaping ¼ teaspoon curry powder

2 cups thinly sliced butter lettuce

3 cups shucked English peas, from 3 pounds in the pod (or frozen peas out of season)

1 teaspoon granulated sugar

6 large whole mint leaves, plus 2 tablespoons sliced mint

5 cups vegetable stock or water

½ lemon, for juicing

¼ cup plus 2 tablespoons crème fraîche

Kosher salt and freshly ground black pepper

This soup was inspired by Roger Vergé, who, unbeknownst to him, was one of my first cooking teachers. I was lucky enough to dine at his restaurant Moulin de Mougins with my parents when I was in sixth grade.

Set in a restored mill in the hills of Provence, the restaurant was paradise. I remember the thoughtful waiter who spent 15 minutes discussing the cheeses on that beautiful wicker trolley. That summer afternoon, when we finished lunch, my father surprised me with Monsieur Vergé's cookbook. This soup was one of the first recipes I made from the book when we returned home from our trip. My mother loved it, and now, every Mother's Day, I make this pea soup for her, to remind us of that amazing lunch in Mougins.

Heat a large saucepan over high heat for about 1 minute. Add 4 tablespoons butter, and when it foams, stir in the onion, curry powder, and 1 teaspoon salt. Turn the heat down to medium and cook 5 to 7 minutes, until the onion is translucent and just starting to color.

Add the lettuce, peas, 1¼ teaspoons salt, sugar, and remaining butter. Stir to coat well, and cook another 4 to 5 minutes, until the lettuce is wilted. Stir in the whole mint leaves, add the stock, and bring to a boil over high heat. Turn down to a low simmer, and cook until the peas are just tender. (This may happen very quickly. Taste one to check for doneness.)

Strain the soup over a bowl. Put half the pea mixture into a blender with ½ cup of the stock or water. (You will need to purée the soup in batches.) Process on the lowest speed until the mixture is puréed. With the blender running at medium speed, slowly pour in more of the stock, until the soup is the consistency of heavy cream. Turn the speed up to high, and blend for at least a minute, until completely smooth. Set aside, and repeat with the second batch. Add ½ teaspoon lemon juice, and taste for seasoning.

Pour the soup into six bowls, spoon some crème fraîche in the center of each, and scatter the sliced mint over the top. Or serve family-style in a tureen, garnish with mint, and pass the crème fraîche on the side.

lobster chopped salad with fava beans, cherry tomatoes, avocado, corn, and applewood-smoked bacon

When I was growing up, my mom and sister were obsessed with lobster. My father and I just never got it. But on both their birthdays, my father would take us all to the chosen lobster spot of the moment. While Jessica and my mom happily cracked their way through dinner, hardly glancing up from their plates, Dad and I would glumly saw through our landlubber specials. I admit I felt a little envious watching Jessica and Mom picking apart their matching dinners, knowing that I would never have that lobster bond with my mother.

Normally, my mother prefers her lobster plain and simple—steamed and served with lemon and drawn butter. But one Mother's Day, I took liberty, hoping to entice her with this rendition of a classic chopped salad. It worked; while we're still on opposite sides of the table at the lobster shack, we both get excited about this salad.

NOTE You can boil and prepare the lobsters, make the vinaigrette, and sauté the bacon and corn ahead of time. Prepare the avocado and tomatoes just before serving.

Bring a large pot of water to a boil over high heat.

Insert the tip of a large chef knife just below the eyes of each lobster—this will kill them instantly. Add the lobsters to the pot of boiling water, making sure they are completely submerged. Cook the lobsters 10 minutes, and then remove them immediately to a bowl of ice water.

When the lobsters have cooled, twist off the tails and claws from the bodies. Save the bodies for another use, or discard.

Place the tails on their sides, and crush gently with the heel of your hand to break open the shells. Carefully pull out the tails. Cut the tails in half lengthwise, and remove the intestinal tract and any green tomalley. Cut each half crosswise into six or seven pieces.

Use the back of a large not-precious knife to break open the shell on the claws. Remove the claw meat, and cut each claw into three or four pieces. Carefully crack the shells of the knuckles and remove the meat. You should have about 12 ounces of lobster meat total.

2 live Maine lobsters,
    1¾ to 2 pounds each

10-ounce slab applewood-
    smoked bacon

⅓ cup plus 1 tablespoon extra-
    virgin olive oil

1½ cups fresh corn (from
    about 2 ears)

1 teaspoon thyme leaves

2 tablespoons finely diced
    shallots

3 tablespoons lemon juice

Pinch cayenne pepper

2 ripe avocados

¾ pint cherry tomatoes, mixed
    colors if possible

1 large head butter lettuce, leaves
    separated, cleaned, and dried

2 tablespoons chopped flat-leaf
    parsley

2 tablespoons sliced green and
    opal basil

Kosher salt and freshly ground
    black pepper

Slice the bacon into ⅜-inch-thick slices. Arrange the bacon strips in two stacks, then cut the strips crosswise into ⅜-inch even-sided rectangles or *lardons*. Heat a large sauté pan over medium heat for 1 minute. Swirl in 1 tablespoon olive oil, add the bacon, and cook about 5 minutes, stirring frequently, until the bacon is tender and lightly crisped. Using a slotted spoon, remove the bacon to a plate lined with paper towels. Reserve the fat in the pan.

Return the pan to medium-high heat. Add the corn, thyme, ¼ teaspoon salt, and a pinch of black pepper. Sauté over medium heat 3 to 4 minutes, until the corn is just cooked and tender. Remove to a platter or baking sheet to cool.

While the corn is cooling, make the vinaigrette: Place the shallots, lemon juice, and ¼ teaspoon salt in a small bowl, and let sit 5 minutes. Whisk in the ⅓ cup olive oil and a pinch of cayenne. Taste for balance and seasoning.

Cut the avocados in half lengthwise. Remove the pit and peel. Dice the avocados into ½-inch cubes and season with ¼ teaspoon salt. Slice the cherry tomatoes in half, and season with ¼ teaspoon salt.

Place the lobster, corn, avocados, tomatoes, and bacon in a large salad bowl. Toss with 5 tablespoons vinaigrette and taste for seasoning, adding a little more vinaigrette if you like. Place the lettuce leaves on a large chilled platter and spoon a little vinaigrette over them. Toss the parsley into the lobster salad, and arrange it over the lettuce. Scatter the basil over the top.

grilled skirt steak with artichoke-potato hash and black olive aïoli

Skirt steak is among those cuts of beef that a novice cook sometimes avoids, despite their excellent flavor and reasonable price. But few steaks will be more delicious when properly cooked, and I assure you it's not hard to get right. With skirt steak, remember a few key points. Start by caramelizing it well on the hottest part of the grill. Then move it over to a cooler spot to finish cooking just to medium-rare. Any less cooked, and it's chewy; any more than medium, and it becomes leathery, livery, and tough. Be sure to let the skirt steak rest a few minutes before slicing it. The most crucial thing of all is to slice the meat against the grain to ensure that it's tender and not rubbery. Though mayonnaise might sound strange as an accompaniment for steak, the aïoli melts into a creamy sauce, leaving behind a trail of olives.

NOTE Season the steak with the chiles, pepper, and herbs the night before cooking. You can roast the potatoes and sauté the artichokes ahead of time. Sauté them together to make the hash just before serving; the hash can sit in the pan while you finish the steaks. You can make the aïoli a few hours ahead as well.

2 pounds skirt steak

3 chiles de árbol, thinly sliced

2 teaspoons cracked black pepper

1 tablespoon rosemary leaves

1 tablespoon thyme leaves, plus 4 thyme sprigs

1¼ pounds Yukon Gold potatoes

1¼ to 1⅓ cup extra-virgin olive oil

4 cloves garlic, unpeeled

1 bay leaf

12 baby artichokes

⅔ cup sliced shallots

2 tablespoons chopped flat-leaf parsley

1 bunch arugula, cleaned

Black olive aïoli (recipe follows)

Kosher salt and freshly ground black pepper

Trim the skirt steak of excess fat and sinew, if any (it doesn't usually need much trimming). Season the skirt steak with the sliced chiles, cracked black pepper, rosemary, and thyme leaves. Cover, and refrigerate for at least 4 hours or overnight.

Preheat the oven to 400°F.

Toss the potatoes with 2 tablespoons olive oil, the garlic cloves, thyme sprigs, bay leaf, and 1 teaspoon salt. Place in a roasting pan, cover with aluminum foil, and roast about 45 minutes, until tender when pierced. (Depending on the size, age, and variety of potatoes, cooking time will vary.)

While the potatoes are roasting, prepare the artichokes. Cut off the top third of the artichokes, and remove the tough outer leaves, down to the pale yellow-green leaves. Using a paring knife, trim the bottom of the stem and the stalks. Cut each artichoke in half and remove the fuzzy choke if there is one. (If you clean the artichokes ahead of time, immerse them in a bowl of cold water with the juice of one lemon added, to prevent them from turning brown. Be sure to drain and dry them well before cooking.)

Heat a large sauté pan over high heat for 2 minutes. Pour ¼ cup olive oil into the pan, and wait a minute. Add the artichokes, and season with 1 teaspoon thyme, 1 teaspoon salt, and a pinch of pepper. Turn the heat to medium, and sauté about 10 minutes, tossing often, until the artichokes are golden brown. (If the pan seems dry, add another tablespoon or two of olive oil.)

When the potatoes have cooled, crumble them into chunky pieces. Squeeze the roasted garlic out of its skin and set aside.

Wipe out the artichoke pan and return it to the stove over high heat, for 2 minutes. (To get the potatoes nicely browned and crisp, don't overcrowd them. You may have to use two pans or do it in batches.) Swirl in the remaining ¼ cup olive oil and wait a minute. Add the crumbled potatoes, and season with the remaining 2 teaspoons thyme, 1 teaspoon salt, and freshly ground black pepper. Cook until the potatoes are crispy on one side. (Don't try to move them or turn them if they are stuck to the pan; they will eventually release themselves, just be patient.) After about 8 minutes, when they've browned nicely on the first side, turn the potatoes in the oil, letting them color on all sides.

When the potatoes are golden brown, turn the heat down to medium and add the shallots, artichokes, and roasted garlic. Toss well, and sauté the hash together 5 to 6 minutes, until the artichokes are hot and the shallots are translucent. Toss in the chopped parsley just before serving.

Light the grill 30 to 40 minutes before cooking, and remove the steak from the refrigerator so it reaches room temperature by the time you're ready to grill it.

When the coals are broken down, red, and glowing, season the steak generously with salt, and brush it lightly with olive oil. Place the meat on the hottest part of the grill, to get a nice sear on the outside. Cook about 2 minutes, turn the meat a quarter-turn, and cook another minute. Turn the meat over, and move it to a cooler spot on the grill. Cook another minute or two for medium-rare. Rest the steak on a wire rack set over a baking sheet for a few minutes.

Arrange the artichoke-potato hash on a large warm platter, and scatter the arugula leaves over the top. Slice the steak against the grain, and lay the slices over the potatoes and artichokes. Spoon some of the black olive aïoli over the meat, and pass the rest at the table.

black olive aïoli

Place the egg yolk in a stainless steel bowl. Begin whisking in the grapeseed oil drop by drop, as slowly as you can bear. Continue in this manner, following with the olive oil, as the mixture thickens. Once the mayonnaise has emulsified, add the remaining oil in a slow steady stream, whisking all the time. If the mixture gets too thick and is difficult to whisk, add a drop or two of water.

Pound the garlic with ¼ teaspoon salt in a mortar. Add half the olives and pound to a paste. Roughly chop the remaining olives.

Fold the garlic-olive paste and the chopped olives into the mayonnaise. Season with ¼ teaspoon salt, a squeeze of lemon juice, and the cayenne pepper. Taste for balance and seasoning. If the aïoli seems thick and gloppy, thin it with a little water; this will also make it creamier.

1 extra-large egg yolk

½ cup grapeseed oil

½ cup extra-virgin olive oil

1 small clove garlic

¼ cup pitted black oil-cured olives, such as Nyons

½ lemon, for juicing

Pinch cayenne pepper

Kosher salt and freshly ground black pepper

1970s moms'
double-chocolate bundt cake

5 ounces bittersweet chocolate (I like Scharffen Berger 70%), coarsely chopped, plus 2 ounces bittersweet chocolate, cut into small slivers

8 tablespoons (1 stick) unsalted butter, cut into cubes, plus a little more for greasing the pan

2 teaspoons vanilla extract

⅓ cup good-quality unsweetened cocoa powder

1¼ cups unbleached all-purpose flour

2 teaspoons baking soda

1½ teaspoons baking powder

½ teaspoon kosher salt

3 extra-large eggs

3 extra-large egg yolks

1¼ cups granulated sugar

½ cup crème fraîche or sour cream

Vanilla ice cream (recipe follows)

Every Mother's Day, I like to put something on the menu in honor of my own mother. Since my mother's busy career left little time for baking, coming up with a dessert that represents her is sometimes challenging. One Mother's Day, in need of help, I turned to Caroline, my business partner, and pastry chef Kimberly Sklar for inspiration. They both began to reminisce about a moist chocolate-chip Bundt cake their mothers used to make when they were little. As they compared notes other staff joined in, starting a passionate debate about whether it was best made with mayonnaise or sour cream. Soon they had all worked themselves into a Bundt cake frenzy.

With all this emotional attachment to a cake, you'd think that someone out of the group would have a recipe. Alas, no one did, and we were forced to start from scratch. After lots of trial and error with sunken cakes, soggy cakes, and just plain bad cakes, Kim and I managed to re-create a stellar version of the dessert, using only the very best chocolate and substituting rich crème fraîche for sour cream.

Even if this decadent dessert wasn't part of your childhood, once you taste it, it could become a favorite, maybe even something worthy of being passed down to your own children.

NOTE The only tricky part about baking this cake is deciding when it's done. Unlike most cakes, the top won't bounce back and the clean-toothpick test doesn't apply. Press gently on the top to see if the inside is still soupy: though it will be very soft, it should not be liquidy or shifting from side to side when you move it. In truth, this cake sinks every time. While it's not the glamourpuss of the pastry kitchen, it's so rich and delicious you won't care!

Preheat the oven to 350°F.

Lightly butter a Bundt pan.

Place the 5 ounces of coarsely chopped chocolate, butter, and vanilla extract in a small saucepan. Put the pan in the oven to melt the ingredients as the oven preheats. When melted, remove from the oven, and stir to combine.

Meanwhile, whisk together ¾ cup water and the cocoa powder in a saucepan.

Bring it to a boil over medium heat, whisking constantly to avoid burning the cocoa. Remove from the heat, and set aside to cool.

Sift together the flour, baking soda and baking powder. Stir in the salt.

In a stand mixer fitted with the whisk attachment, beat the eggs and yolks together for a few seconds to combine. Pour in the sugar and whip at high speed, 5 to 6 minutes, until very pale yellow and thick enough to hold a ribbon when you lift the whisk away from the bowl.

Meanwhile, add the cocoa powder mixture to the melted chocolate (using a rubber spatula to be sure to get all of the cocoa). Transfer the egg mixture to a large bowl, and fold in the melted chocolate and then the crème fraîche.

Gently fold the dry ingredients into the batter in thirds, being careful not to deflate it, but making sure to combine them well.

Pour half the batter into the Bundt pan and sprinkle the chocolate slivers on top. Pour in the remaining batter and bake 25 minutes, until the cake is just set but still very moist. Cool for 30 minutes, and invert onto a plate. Serve with vanilla ice cream.

vanilla ice cream

MAKES 1 QUART

Split the vanilla bean in half lengthwise, and, using a paring knife, scrape the seeds and pulp into a medium saucepan. Add the vanilla pod, milk, and cream, and bring to a boil over medium heat. Turn off the heat, cover, and allow the flavors to infuse about 30 minutes.

Return the mixture to the stove, and bring it back to a boil over medium heat, stirring occasionally. When it boils, turn off the heat.

Whisk the egg yolks and sugar together in a bowl. Whisk a few tablespoons of the warm cream mixture into the yolks to temper them. Slowly, add another ¼ cup or so of the warm cream, whisking constantly. At this point you can add the rest of the cream mixture in a slow steady stream, whisking all the time. Pour the mixture back into the pot, and return it to the stove.

Cook the custard over medium heat 6 to 8 minutes, stirring frequently with a rubber spatula, scraping the bottom and sides of the pan. The custard will thicken, and when it's done it will coat the back of the spatula. Strain the mixture, and chill at least 2 hours in the refrigerator. Process in an ice cream maker according to the manufacturer's instructions.

1 vanilla bean

2 cups whole milk

2 cups heavy cream

4 extra-large egg yolks

½ cup granulated sugar

summer

t sounds like a cliché, but one summer in the south of France, I spent one of the happiest, sunniest weeks of my life. It was July 1992, and I had just completed a grueling 6-month *stage* at Pain, Adour et Fantaisie, in the southwest of France. The restaurant was open 7 days a week, and the cooks were expected to be there for both lunch and dinner, from 8 a.m. to 1 a.m. We had a short break in the afternoon, which left just enough time to walk to the local bar to recharge with *un café* (or maybe two) and try to get psyched up for dinner service. At one in the morning, we had to scrub down the kitchen from top to bottom, and then, finally, I'd walk home exhausted and reeking of garlic, fish, and duck fat.

After a long winter and spring of hard physical labor and kitchen "hazing," I was ready for a break. The gang at Chez Panisse kindly hooked me up with the wonderful Peyraud family—winemakers in southern France, known for their refreshing rosés and deep, dark Domaine Tempier wines. I arrived at their estate in Provence like a wounded bird, wondering if I would ever recover.

The Peyrauds treated me like family and gave me a whole new perspective on France, and on life. We spent our mornings in the seaside town of Bandol, where Catherine Peyraud and I gathered the day's provisions. After we made our rounds, we'd head back home and spend the afternoon cooking together. When evening rolled around, we'd sit on the stone terrace eating tapenade toasts and sipping glasses of chilled rosé made at the family winery just a few steps away. A few days into the routine, I knew that everything was going to be okay; life was still worth living. It's not surprising that years later I named my restaurant after an olive from the south of France.

That summer of seafood, olives, rosé, and tomatoes made a permanent impression on me. I fell in love with the flavors that characterized the Peyraud family's cooking: capers, garlic, mint, parsley, basil, anchovies, pine nuts, olive oil. They turn up in my own cooking time and time again. Pounded into salsa verde, chopped into a vinaigrette, crushed into tapenade, these bright Provençal ingredients make fresh, uncooked sauces that suit the flavors of summer.

What are these bright flavors? The list begins with tomatoes. And tomatoes and tomatoes. Every summer, tomatoes invade Lucques. They take over the menu, they take over the pantry station, and they even take over the already cramped office. To the dismay of the office staff, in the summer tomatoes have priority over file folders and fax machines.

In these menus you'll find other summer treasures, too, like corn, eggplant, sweet peppers, summer squash, and fresh shell beans. The dessert recipes are simple and highlight the refreshing fruits of summer. I love nectarines and berries tossed with a little sugar and spooned over almond financier. Or plums puréed with honey and frozen into a tart and uplifting sorbet.

These summer recipes reflect the generosity and joie de vivre that so inspired me all those years ago in France. As a chef, I don't get to spend as many evenings as I would like sitting on the patio drinking rosé, but I certainly cherish the ones that I do.

summer market

avocados

This creamy fruit is one of California's state treasures. Indigenous to Mexico, avocados in this country are grown predominantly in California and Florida. California avocados are higher in fat and less watery than their East Coast counterparts. The Hass avocado is the best-known Californian variety, but the prized avocado in our kitchen is the Reed, grown by Peter Schaner on his farm in Vista, near San Diego. Other good varieties to seek out are Bacon and Fuerte.

The avocado's nutty, decadent flesh is delicious paired with a variety of flavors and also tasty on its own with a squeeze of lime juice and a sprinkling of sea salt. Choose unbruised fruit that yield slightly to gentle pressure. If they're very firm, let them ripen on the kitchen counter.

berries

Berries are the jewels of the summer market.

In Southern California, the first summer berry to come along is the boysenberry. Walter Knott, famous for Knott's Berry Farm, an amusement park in Orange County, California, transplanted and started cultivating the vines. His berries gained commercial recognition in the form of Mrs. Knott's preserves. These large dark purple berries have a concentrated, vibrant flavor.

Blackberries are the oldest berry variety known, gathered since prehistoric times. Because they reproduce so readily, there are hundreds of species. Their season is longer than boysenberry season and, depending on the climate, usually begins around midsummer. They should be harvested when they're fully ripe; if they're picked too soon, they will be sour and not as juicy.

The blueberry is native to North America, and it's still best loved at home—the United States produces 90 percent of the world's crop. Here on the West Coast, we're slightly less blueberry crazy than certain more easterly quarters, but we still snap them up with the rest when berry season begins. Good blueberries not only taste great; they're also good for you. Free radicals, watch out; blueberries are high in antioxidants. Look for taut berries that pop with sweet juice when you bite into them.

Raspberries come in four colors: yellow, orange, black, and red. Their flavors vary slightly, from sweet to tart. The Greeks and Romans used them medicinally and made them into wines. Raspberries are delicate and should be handled gingerly. Sometimes soft, misshapen raspberries are the flavorful ones. Perfect, pristine berries can be deceiving, since they may look perfect because they were picked before they were completely ripe. Trust your palate more than your eyes, and taste them. Because of their fragile nature, raspberries should be stored in the refrigerator and used within a few days.

corn

In California, the corn season is longer than in other parts of the country, beginning as early as May and running through late October. In most areas corn is best at the height of its midsummer season.

I buy white, yellow, or calico corn, depending on which tastes best at the moment. The only way to find out how good a particular ear of corn is is by tasting a kernel or two raw. I look for corn that's bursting with juice and has a perfect balance of starch and sweetness. When it's that good, I love it raw and cooked. Remember, the sugars in corn begin to turn to starch just after it's

picked, so the sooner you eat it, the better. If you must store it, keep the cobs in their husks, and refrigerate them wrapped in a damp towel.

cucumbers

There are better cucumbers out in the world than those waxy supermarket types. I prefer Persian cucumbers, also called Armenian or Middle Eastern cucumbers, which have a delicate skin and aren't too seedy inside. Japanese cucumbers are another good alternative. If you can't find any of these varieties, substitute a firm hothouse cucumber.

When it comes to peeling and seeding cucumbers, cooks differ. Some peel them on principle and remove the seeds, whereas others leave them as they are. People want a rule, but you have to use and trust your senses. Taste a slice! If the skin tastes bitter and feels bulky on your tongue, peel your cucumber. If the seeds are large and slimy, deseed it. To do this, cut the cucumber in half lengthwise and use a spoon to scrape out the seeds. When buying cucumbers, pick them up to check that they feel solid and firm.

eggplant

Essential to the cuisines of the Mediterranean and Middle East, these members of the nightshade family are delicious and easy to cook with. At the market we find lots of interesting varieties beyond the common globe. I love white eggplants as well as Rosa Bianca, a medium-sized variety—purple and white, with creamy, sweet flesh. Neons are buttery and sweet, and, true to their name, their skin is a bright, almost fluorescent purple color.

Traditional recipes often call for heavily salting eggplant before cooking it to draw out bitter juices. I find that if you seek out freshly picked eggplant in season, bitterness isn't usually an issue. To prepare eggplant, I slice it, score it, and season the pieces with only as much salt as they need for taste. Let the slices sit for 5 to 10 minutes and then pat them gently with a paper towel, to absorb the water that beads on the surface. Because eggplant acts like a sponge, I never rinse it, lest it become waterlogged. Choose firm, unblemished eggplant that have tight, shiny skin.

figs

Figs are a symbol of fertility and are considered an aphrodisiac in some cultures. They're high in sugar and fiber. Fig season begins in August, when the trees have had enough warm sun to ripen the plump, tear-shaped fruit. Figs are best when they're ripened on the tree

before being picked. When ready to eat, they should be practically bursting from their skin and feel heavy for their size. You'll find both green-skinned figs and purple-skinned figs at the market. Some of my favorite varieties are Adriatic, Honey, and Osbourne.

haricots verts

These thin, elegant French green beans are the first fresh beans of the summer season. A member of the snap-bean family, they're picked when very young and only a few inches long. Because of the labor they demand, haricots verts can be on the pricey side, but they're well worth it. Their texture is fine, almost like noodles, and their sweet flavor tastes of the garden.

It's easy to overcook haricots verts, so don't walk away while they're blanching. Taste them to check if they're done; they should have lost their raw flavor but retain a slight crunch. Depending where you live, haricots verts might be hard to find. At the supermarket, don't be seduced by prepackaged haricots verts. Who knows when they were picked? You're better off substituting a larger variety of green bean that is crisp and fresh.

melons

Melons are available from July through October and can be divided into three categories: smooth-skinned, such as the honeydew; rough and scaly-skinned, like the Charentais; and net-skinned, like the well-known cantaloupe. Some have orange flesh, others pale green. Each variety has a different aroma, texture, and sugar content. Some of my favorite melons are Charentais, Golden Gopher, Champlain, Hollybrook, and Ambrosia.

Melons are difficult to put on the menu at the

(lines on the flesh) and brown, mottled skin, and, whatever you do, don't refrigerate your peaches and nectarines. Of course they are delicious eaten out of hand or in desserts, but peaches and nectarines also work well in savory dishes. I like to slice them and toss them into salads with goat or sheep's milk cheese and toasted nuts. Or I season them with olive oil, salt, pepper, and thyme and roast them in the oven. The roasted fruit offers a surprising and delectable accompaniment to duck or pork.

peppers

Sweet peppers come in a range of colors—white, pale green, yellow, orange, red, purple, and brown. Sweet peppers can be divided into two groups: the thicker-skinned bell and lipstick peppers and the thinner-skinned varieties like gypsy, Hungarian, and Romanian peppers. I like to char thicker-skinned peppers on the grill, then let them steam in a bag before peeling off their blackened skin. Thinner-skinned varieties are best when sliced and sautéed. No matter what variety you're buying, choose firm peppers with a smooth, shiny, and unwrinkled skin.

Then there are the hot peppers, also known as chile peppers. The smaller, spicier varieties like jalapeños and serranos are best added to soups, or finely diced and stirred into salsas and vinaigrettes. The milder, larger varieties, such as poblanos, are great roasted and stuffed. Beware of the small, jewellike, but deadly hot habaneros. Though fruity and deeply flavored, they're considered the hottest chile in the world. Spicy peppers tend to be hotter near the stem end. And, contrary to what you may have heard, it's not the seeds that hold the heat but rather the membranes inside. Be very careful when working with these hot chiles. Use rubber gloves if possible, wash your hands well, and avoid touching your eyes and other sensitive areas.

restaurant, because melon is great only when it's really great—the difference between a mediocre specimen and a sweet and juicy melon is vast. Consistently choosing the latter is more art than science, but fragrance has always been the most reliable method for me. Up close, most melons (watermelons excepted) should smell sweet and floral. Once picked, they don't really ripen or sweeten further. Net-skinned melons should be netted all the way around, and all melons should feel heavy for their size. Some ripe melons will make a quiet slushing sound when gently shaken.

peaches and nectarines

Peaches and nectarines are best when ripened on the tree. Sometimes the first fruit of the season can be disappointing, as they haven't had enough sunshine to coax them into sweet, juicy perfection. Look for fruit that's firm but not hard. You can't tell just by looking; you need to smell the fruit and taste it. Sometimes the imperfect, odd-looking peaches and nectarines are the most intensely flavored. Look for unbruised fruit with seaming

plums

Starting in mid June, an astounding array of plums come to the market, ranging in color from deep purple-blue to red, yellow, and green.

One of the most commonly grown plums is the Santa Rosa, developed from a Japanese variety at the end of the nineteenth century and still considered one of the tastiest of all. Some other great varieties to look for are Elephant Hearts, Casselmans, Mariposas, and Green-gages. And just when you think you have a handle on plums, you'll discover the many varieties of pluot, a cross between a plum and an apricot. Flavorosas are one of my favorite pluot varieties.

Their tart skin and sweet, juicy flesh make plums perfect for cooking. Because their sweetness varies, you'll need to taste them as they cook and add sugar accordingly. When plums abound, I purée them into a refreshing sorbet, or bake them into a plum tarte Tatin. Dried plums, of course, are prunes, which are excellent added to savory stews or cooked down in rich compotes paired with desserts or grilled meats.

Select smooth-skinned plums that are free of spots or bruises and yield slightly when gently pressed. Ideally, plums should ripen on the tree. Although they will get softer as they sit on the counter, their sugar levels will not increase.

shell beans

All those bagged dried beans stacked on supermarket shelves start their lives in the fields as fresh, supple shell beans. Harvested in the middle of summer, each variety has its own shape, color, and flavor. To find a wide variety of shell beans, you'll most likely have to go to a farmers' market or farmstand, unless you grow them yourself. Toward the end of the season, some of the best beans are hidden in what appear to be dried pods. Open

which is also delicious added to soups or vegetable ragoûts.

If you've ever shucked fava beans, you'll be relieved at the ease of shucking summer shell beans. Most of the time—with a little nudge—they fall right out of their shells. If they're too hard to shuck, it might mean that the beans aren't quite ready.

summer squash

In the summer, our markets are full of yellow, dark green, pale green, and even striped summer squash in all shapes and sizes.

Look for smooth, firm, unblemished, and brightly colored summer squash. At the farmers' market, I like to pick them up and smell them; when they're freshly picked, you'll get a whiff of a summer garden—earthy and green. Sometimes just-picked squash even have a layer of peach fuzz on their skin. Their blossoms are a treat stuffed and fried, or torn and tossed into a sauté of summer vegetables. Don't leave summer squash in the refrigerator too long: their high moisture content causes them to perish quickly.

tomatoes

The tomato is the ultimate symbol of summer. The appropriately named Early Girl arrives in late June, and has a mellow, sweet flavor. But what we chefs really get worked up about are those stunning heirloom tomatoes that come midsummer and continue sometimes as late as November in Southern California. There are hundreds of types of heirlooms, all with slightly different colors, markings, flavors, and shapes. The relatively recent explosion of heirloom tomato production and the proliferation of farmers' markets have made it possible for many nongardeners to taste and cook with these incredible tomatoes. I especially love Cherokee Purple, Black

one to check that the beans are moist and fresh (their pods can be deceiving). Like peas, shell beans' flavor is best preserved in their pods, so don't shuck them too long before cooking them.

Lima beans, also called butter beans, come in a vivid green, flattened pod. Cranberry (or borlotti) beans have eccentric speckled red-and-cream-colored pods. Once cooked, they become a brownish pink color. Black-eyed peas, or Southern peas, range in color from purple to pinkish brown to yellow-green. Their pods are very long and narrow, and their flavor is somewhat nutty. Cannellini are white beans inside a yellow pod. Flageolets are smaller and elongated, in pale green pods.

I love to cook a few different types of beans and serve them together. Unlike their dried counterparts, fresh shell beans cook quickly, in about 15 to 20 minutes. Different varieties of shell beans require different cooking times, so don't be tempted to cook them all in the same pot at the same time. Store them in their cooking liquid,

Krim, Georgia Streak, Marizol Purple, Ruby Gold, and Arkansas Traveler.

When choosing heirloom tomatoes, don't be afraid of flaws; many tend to be misshapen and odd-looking. If you see a tomato that has "seaming," or brown dotted lines and indentations on the skin, grab it. Heirloom experts will tell you it's a good sign and the sure mark of a more flavorful specimen. When working with a tomato with lots of seaming, simply cut the seaming out, being careful to lose as little of the tomato as possible. Look for slightly firm tomatoes that are heavy for their size. It can be hard to judge a tomato by its cover, so always ask for a sample. Store tomatoes at room temperature, never in the refrigerator.

green goddess salad with romaine, cucumbers, and avocado

2 large heads romaine lettuce

1 extra-large egg yolk

1 cup grapeseed oil

1¼ cups flat-leaf parsley leaves

1 cup packed watercress, cleaned, tough stems removed

2 tablespoons tarragon leaves

3 tablespoons minced chives, plus 2 tablespoons ½-inch-snipped chives

1 clove garlic, chopped

2 salt-packed anchovies, rinsed, bones removed

Juice of 1 lemon

1 tablespoon plus 1 teaspoon champagne vinegar

2 large ripe avocados, preferably Reed, Hass, or Bacon

3 Persian cucumbers or 1 hot-house cucumber

Kosher salt and freshly ground black pepper

I love dishes with catchy retro names. The Green Goddess salad was invented in the 1920s by the chef of the Palace Hotel in San Francisco, who made it in honor of British actor George Arliss. The actor was a guest at the hotel while starring in a local production of William Archer's The Green Goddess.

The basic components of this classic California dressing are anchovies, mayonnaise, garlic, tarragon, parsley, and chives. I add watercress to the puréed herbs, which turns the dressing a deep emerald green and adds a clean, peppery flavor. Thick and rich, the dressing coats the romaine leaves the same way a Caesar salad dressing does. Once you have this dressing in your repertoire, you'll find yourself using it for all sorts of things. Try a dollop over grilled fish, or spread it on bread instead of mayonnaise when making a sandwich.

Remove the tough outer leaves of the romaine. Trim the root and core and separate the leaves. Tear the larger leaves in half. Clean by submerging in cold water. Spin dry, and chill in the refrigerator.

Place the egg yolk in a stainless steel bowl. Slowly pour ¼ cup of the oil in the bowl, drop by drop, whisking all the time. Continue in this manner as the mixture thickens. Once the mayonnaise has emulsified, whisk in another ¼ cup oil in a slow, steady stream.

Purée 1 cup parsley leaves, the watercress, tarragon, and minced chives in a blender with the garlic, anchovies, lemon juice, and remaining ½ cup oil.

Whisk the herb purée, vinegar, 2 teaspoons salt, and ½ teaspoon pepper into the mayonnaise. If the dressing seems too thick, thin it with a little water. Taste for balance and seasoning.

Cut each avocado in half lengthwise, remove the pit, and peel. Slice into long wedges. Taste the cucumbers and peel and seed them if necessary. Cut the cucumbers in half lengthwise, and cut them on the diagonal into ¼-inch-thick slices. Season the avocado and cucumber generously with salt and pepper.

Place the romaine in a large salad bowl, and toss with 1 cup dressing, ¼ teaspoon salt, and some more black pepper. Gently toss in the avocado and cucumber. Arrange on a large chilled platter, and scatter the remaining ¼ cup parsley leaves and the snipped chives over the top.

soft-shell crabs with lima bean salad, grilled bacon, and cornbread

Every summer when my husband, David, and I visit his parents, we arrive at their house to a feast of peel-and-eat shrimp, Jean's crab salad, and of course enough "softies" to feed the entire neighborhood. On the Eastern Shore of Maryland, soft-shell crabs (blue crabs that have molted their shells) are a grand tradition. The season starts in late spring and continues through the summer. Crabbers must be vigilant: there is only a 4- to 5-hour window during which molting blue crabs are in the "soft-shell" stage, after which their new shells harden if they are not removed from the water.

David keeps his Maryland pride alive while living on the West Coast. Every year when crab season starts, his father ships us a few flats of live crabs, and we throw a decadent soft-shell party. We decided that if our humble castle had a coat of arms, it would be two crossed strips of bacon with a soft-shell crab in the center.

NOTE Fine-milled Wondra flour helps to get a really delicate and crisp crust on the crabs. It is available at most supermarkets. Substitute all-purpose flour if you can't find it. To prepare for this dish you can cut the bacon, cook the lima beans, bake the cornbread, and make the mustard crème fraîche all ahead of time.

½-pound slab applewood-smoked bacon

3 tablespoons whole grain mustard

¾ cup crème fraîche

12 jumbo soft-shell crabs (about 3½ ounces each)

1 cup Wondra or all-purpose flour

Cornbread (recipe follows)

3 tablespoons unsalted butter, softened

1 to 1½ cups vegetable oil

2 ounces small arugula

Lima bean salad (recipe follows)

Kosher salt and freshly ground black pepper

Light the grill 30 to 40 minutes before cooking.

Cut the bacon into ⅜-inch-thick slices, and then cut each slice in half, into 4-inch lengths.

Stir the mustard and crème fraîche together in a small bowl. Taste for seasoning. The mixture usually doesn't need salt.

To clean the crabs, use scissors to remove the gills, then the pouch, and then the eyes. Dredge the crabs in the flour. Season them with some pepper. (In my experience, they don't usually need salt.)

When the coals are broken down, red, and glowing, place the bacon on the grill and cook 2 to 3 minutes on each side, rotating often, until it's tender and a little crisped. If the fire flares up under the bacon, move the slices to the sides of the grill, away from the direct heat. Transfer the bacon to a paper-towel-lined baking sheet. Slice half the cornbread into ½-inch-thick pieces and butter them lightly. (You will not need the other half of the cornbread for this recipe.) Place the cornbread on the grill and cook, rotating a few times, to brown nicely on both sides without burning.

Meanwhile, heat two large sauté pans over high heat for 1 minute. Pour ¼ inch vegetable oil into the pans. Heat the oil until it shimmers and is not quite smoking. Turn the heat down to medium, and carefully lay the crabs in the pan, soft-shell side down. Cook the crabs over medium heat 5 to 7 minutes. Do not shake the pan or move the crabs. When the first sides are crisp, turn the crabs over and cook another 3 minutes or so, until the crabs are cooked through. Peek under the shell to check that the flesh is opaque. Remove the crabs to a paper-towel-lined baking sheet.

Place the grilled cornbread on a large platter. Scatter the arugula over the cornbread, and top with the grilled bacon. Spoon the lima bean salad over and around the cornbread and bacon. Arrange the crabs on top, and dollop each one with mustard crème fraîche.

lima bean salad

7 tablespoons extra-virgin olive oil

¼ cup finely diced onion

1 teaspoon minced garlic

2 teaspoons thyme leaves

2 cups fresh lima beans (from 2 pounds in the pod)

2 tablespoons finely diced shallots

2 tablespoons lemon juice

2 tablespoons sliced opal basil

2 tablespoons sliced flat-leaf parsley

Kosher salt and freshly ground black pepper

to cook the lima beans   Heat a medium saucepan over high heat for 1 minute. Swirl in 2 tablespoons olive oil, and add the onion, garlic, and thyme. Sauté over medium heat 3 to 4 minutes, until the onion is translucent. Add the beans, and cook a few minutes, stirring often to coat the beans with the onion and oil. Season with salt and pepper, and add enough water to cover the beans by a few inches. Simmer 5 to 7 minutes, until the beans are just tender. Cool and store the beans in the cooking liquid.

to make the salad   Combine the shallots, lemon juice, and ¼ teaspoon salt in a small bowl. Let sit 5 minutes. Whisk in 5 tablespoons olive oil. Drain the cooled beans well and toss them with this vinaigrette and a pinch of salt and pepper. Taste for seasoning and stir in the herbs.

cornbread

10 tablespoons unsalted butter

2 cups cornmeal

2 cups all-purpose flour

¼ cup granulated sugar

1 tablespoon baking powder

¼ teaspoon baking soda

1 tablespoon kosher salt

2 extra-large eggs

2½ cups buttermilk

3 tablespoons honey

Preheat the oven to 400°F.

Heat a 10-inch cast-iron pan over medium heat for 1 minute. Add 8 table-spoons (1 stick) butter and cook 4 to 5 minutes, swirling the pan often, until the butter browns and smells nutty. Turn off the heat.

Combine the cornmeal, flour, sugar, baking powder, baking soda, and salt in a large bowl. Make a well in the center of the dry ingredients.

Whisk together the eggs, buttermilk, and honey in another bowl. Pour the liquid into the well, and whisk until just combined. (Don't overwork the batter.) Fold in the brown butter.

Return the cast-iron pan to the stove over medium-high heat. Swirl in the remaining 2 tablespoons butter, and when it foams pour the batter into the pan. Transfer the pan immediately to the oven, and bake 25 to 30 minutes, until golden brown and set.

veal scaloppine with fresh corn polenta and salsa verde–brown butter

One of my favorite dinners growing up was my mother's veal piccata. Her recipe came from an old cookbook called *The Pleasures of Italian Cooking*, by Romeo Salta, a gift to her from my father.

My father had been a devoted fan of Romeo Salta when he was the chef at Chianti in Los Angeles in the fifties. Back then, it was a swinging Italian joint with red-checkered tablecloths, opera 78s blasting, and red wine flowing into the late hours.

My mother's (and Romeo's) veal was pounded thin, sautéed, and drenched in a lemony caper-butter sauce. There's nothing wrong with that classic rendition, but, to add another layer of flavor, I brown the butter and finish it with salsa verde, a pungent purée of capers, anchovies, garlic, oregano, and tons of parsley. To get the finest, crispy crust on the veal, I dredge it in Wondra, a finely milled flour sold at most supermarkets. This dish is home-style Italian comfort food at its best.

NOTE You can pound the veal and prepare the salsa verde a few hours ahead. You can make the polenta and sauté the corn ahead of time, too. Stir the corn into the polenta at the last minute.

1¾ pounds veal top round

1½ cups Wondra or all-purpose flour

¼ to ½ cup extra-virgin olive oil

8 tablespoons (1 stick) unsalted butter

Salsa verde (recipe follows)

Juice of ½ lemon

Fresh corn polenta (recipe follows)

2 ounces dandelion greens or arugula, cleaned and dried

Kosher salt and freshly ground black pepper

Cut the veal against the grain into ½-inch-thick pieces. Cut the slices into eighteen 1½-ounce pieces (or have your butcher do this for you). Pound the veal between sheets of plastic wrap to ⅛-inch thickness. Season the meat with salt and pepper. Dredge the veal in flour, coating well on both sides. Set the floured veal aside on a baking sheet.

Heat two large sauté pans over high heat for 2 minutes. Swirl 2 tablespoons oil in each pan, and wait a minute. Shake the excess flour from the veal, and place a single layer in each pan (make sure the pieces of veal are not crowded or over-lapping). Cook a minute or two on each side, until the veal is nicely browned. Remove the meat to a baking sheet, and finish cooking the remaining veal, adding more oil to the pan, as necessary.

Pour the oil out of one of the pans but don't wipe it clean (those crusty bits are tasty). Return the pan to medium-high heat (you will only need one pan to make the sauce), and add the butter. Cook a few minutes, swirling the pan often, until the butter browns and smells nutty. Turn off the heat and wait a minute. Then stir in ⅓ cup salsa verde, ¼ teaspoon salt, a pinch of freshly ground black pepper, and the juice of ½ lemon. Taste for balance and seasoning. Be careful—the butter will be very hot.

Spoon half the hot polenta onto a large warm platter, and scatter the dandelion greens over the top. Arrange the veal over the greens, allowing some of the polenta and greens to show through. Spoon the salsa verde–brown butter over the veal. Serve the rest of the polenta and remaining salsa verde on the side.

salsa verde

1 teaspoon marjoram or oregano leaves

¼ cup coarsely chopped mint

1 cup coarsely chopped flat-leaf parsley

¾ cup extra-virgin olive oil

1 small clove garlic

1 salt-packed anchovy, rinsed, bones removed

1 tablespoon salt-packed capers, rinsed and drained

½ lemon, for juicing

Freshly ground black pepper

Using a mortar and pestle, pound the herbs to a paste. (You may have to do this in batches.) Work in some of the olive oil, and transfer the mixture to a bowl. Pound the garlic and anchovy, and add them to the herbs.

Gently pound the capers until they're partially crushed, and add them to the herbs. Stir in the remaining oil, a pinch of black pepper, and a squeeze of lemon juice. Taste for balance and seasoning.

fresh corn polenta

2 tablespoons unsalted butter

1½ cups fresh corn (from about 2 ears)

2 teaspoons thyme leaves

1 recipe polenta (see page 97)

Kosher salt and freshly ground black pepper

Heat a large sauté pan over medium heat for 1 minute. Add 2 tablespoons butter and, when it foams, add the corn. Season with the thyme, ¼ teaspoon salt, and a pinch of pepper and sauté 3 to 4 minutes, until the corn is just cooked and tender. Stir the corn into the polenta right before serving.

plum sorbet sandwiches with mary jones
from cleveland's molasses cookies

After a year of 80-hour workweeks cooking in France, I moved to Boston, where I worked a very civilized 40 hours a week. With so much free time on my hands, I focused my attention that summer on making ice cream sandwiches. I sandwiched lemon ice cream with gingersnaps, coconut ice cream with macadamia nut tuiles, and mint ice cream with chocolate chunk cookies. My friends and neighbors could hardly keep up with the frozen cookie–ice cream combos that filled my freezer.

Many summers later at Lucques, local farmer James Birch delivered several unexpected crates of his delicious Santa Rosa plums. We were drowning in summer fruit at the time, and I couldn't imagine what on earth we were going to do with those extra plums. I remembered that hot Boston summer and decided to purée the plums into a sorbet and sandwich them between chewy molasses cookies. If it's a truly lazy summer day, you can skip the sandwiching step and serve the sorbet in bowls with the cookies on the side.

MAKES 1 QUART

1 pound very ripe juicy plums

½ cup granulated sugar

2 tablespoons honey

½ lemon, for juicing

Molasses cookies (recipe follows)

Cut the plums in half, remove the pits, and cut the halves into quarters.

Toss the plums with the sugar and honey, and let sit 30 minutes. Transfer the fruit to a blender, and purée until very smooth. Season with lemon juice, to taste.

Chill at least 1 hour in the refrigerator.

Process the purée in an ice cream maker according to the manufacturer's instructions.

To make each plum sorbet sandwich, scoop up about ¼ cup of the sorbet and place it on the bottom side of one of the cookies. Then place the bottom side of a second cookie over the ice cream and gently press to make a sandwich. Wrap in plastic wrap and freeze.

mary jones from cleveland's molasses cookies

2 cups all-purpose flour

2 teaspoons baking soda

1 teaspoon ground cinnamon

½ teaspoon ground cloves

½ teaspoon ground ginger

½ teaspoon kosher salt

¼ cup molasses

1 cup granulated sugar, plus extra for sprinkling

¾ cup vegetable shortening, melted to equal ½ cup, cooled

1 extra-large egg

Great cookie recipes are to be honored and shared, passed from friend to neighbor to cousin. This recipe was passed down from one of my pastry chefs, Kimberly Sklar, who got it from her best friend's husband's mother, who happens to live in Cleveland.

Preheat the oven to 325°F.

Sift together the flour, baking soda, cinnamon, cloves, and ginger. Stir in the salt.

In a stand mixer fitted with a whisk attachment, beat the molasses, sugar, melted shortening, and egg at medium speed for 3 minutes.

Turn the mixer off and add half of the dry ingredients to the bowl. Turn the mixer to medium-low and mix to incorporate, scraping down the sides of the bowl, as needed. Add the remaining dry ingredients and mix to combine. Chill the dough for about 15 minutes, to make it easier to work with.

On a lightly floured surface, roll half the dough out to ⅛-inch thickness. Use a 3-inch round cutter to cut out the cookies. Place them on a parchment-lined or lightly buttered baking sheet, spaced about 1 inch apart. Sprinkle a little sugar over the tops of the cookies, and bake about 12 minutes, until they puff up slightly and are starting to crack in the middle. The cookies will be crisp on the outside and chewy in the center.

heirloom tomato salad with burrata, torn croutons, and opal basil

As soon we were old enough to fly alone, my sister and I would travel back east for a few weeks every summer to visit our grandmother in Connecticut. Our late-summer arrival always coincided with the peak of her beefsteak tomato crop. Every evening, we'd venture out to the backyard to pick tomatoes for that night's salad. Still warm from the sun, those juicy red slices, sprinkled with salt, left an indelible impression on me.

My next life-changing tomato experience was at Al Forno, in Providence, Rhode Island. The owners, George Germon and Johanne Killeen, would drive 35 miles to a tiny town called Little Compton to pick up crates and crates of big red beefsteak tomatoes from their favorite farmer. Slicing the tomatoes to order, they served them with red onion, salt, basil, oil, and vinegar. Again, so simple, yet one of the best things I'd ever tasted.

I didn't discover heirloom tomatoes until a few years later, when I got a job at Chez Panisse in Berkeley. Amazed by the odd shapes and variety of colors, from white to orange to almost black, I sampled every variety I could get my hands on. At Lucques, our regular customers start asking for this heirloom salad in early June. It's been on the menu every year since we opened and seems to signal that summer is finally here.

⅓ pound country white bread

½ cup extra-virgin olive oil

1 tablespoon oregano leaves

½ clove garlic

1½ tablespoons red wine vinegar

1 tablespoon balsamic vinegar

½ pint cherry tomatoes

3 pounds heirloom tomatoes, assorted sizes, shapes, and colors

1 teaspoon *fleur de sel*

2 tablespoons sliced opal basil

2 tablespoons sliced green basil

1 pound burrata cheese

½ cup thinly sliced shallots

¼ cup flat-leaf parsley leaves

Kosher salt and freshly ground black pepper

Preheat the oven to 375°F.

Cut the crust off the bread and tear the remaining loaf into rustic 1-inch pieces. Using your hands, toss the pieces with 2 tablespoons olive oil, squeezing the bread gently to help it absorb the oil. Toast on a baking sheet 12 to 15 minutes, stirring a few times, until the croutons are golden brown and crispy on the outside but still a little soft and tender inside.

Using a mortar and pestle, pound the oregano, garlic, and a heaping ¼ teaspoon salt to a paste. Transfer to a bowl and stir in the vinegars. Whisk in the remaining 6 tablespoons olive oil and taste for balance and seasoning.

Stem the cherry tomatoes and cut them in half. Core the heirloom tomatoes. Cut half of them into wedges and set them aside. Then one by one, hold the

remaining tomatoes on their sides and cut them into ¼-inch-thick slices. Season the slices with the *fleur de sel* and some pepper. Place the slices overlapping on a large platter, spoon a little of the vinaigrette over them, and scatter a little basil on top.

Cut the burrata into twelve slices, and tuck them in and around the slabs of tomato.

Toss the heirloom wedges and cherry tomatoes gently in a large bowl with the sliced shallots, ½ teaspoon kosher salt, a pinch of pepper, and 3 tablespoons of the vinaigrette. Taste for seasoning, adding more vinaigrette if you like. Gently toss in the croutons.

Arrange the salad on the platter, piling it up in the center, allowing the slices of tomato and cheese to peek through. Scatter the parsley and remaining basil over the top of the salad.

wild salmon à la lutèce with sweet corn, green cabbage, and brown butter vinaigrette

1 cup whole milk

3 ounces diced applewood-smoked bacon

2 extra-large eggs

2¼ cups fresh breadcrumbs

¼ cup chopped flat-leaf parsley

6 wild salmon fillets, 5 to 6 ounces each, skin removed

2 tablespoons extra-virgin olive oil

6 tablespoons unsalted butter

1½ tablespoons red wine vinegar

3 tablespoons finely diced white onion

½ lemon, for juicing

Sweet corn, green cabbage, and bacon (recipe follows)

André Soltner is one of my culinary heroes. I admire his interpretations of regional dishes from his Alsatian homeland, which are refined enough to serve in one of New York City's fanciest French restaurants yet still true to their humble origins. Only a great chef can strike that balance.

I discovered his recipe for salmon sautéed in a bacon-and-egg "batter" and served with a brown butter sauce in the middle of summer, so I added corn to the sautéed cabbage for a sweet seasonal touch. The tart brown butter–vinegar sauce beautifully balances the smoky bacon and rich salmon.

NOTE You can make the base of the batter ahead of time; just wait and add the breadcrumbs and parsley at the last minute. You can also make the brown butter–vinegar sauce ahead of time if you like. Cook the vegetables while you cook the salmon.

In a small saucepan, bring the milk and bacon to a boil over medium-high heat. Cook a few minutes, remove from the heat, and cool 5 minutes. Purée the mixture in a food processor until the bacon is fully incorporated into the milk. Add the eggs, and pulse a few times to combine. Transfer to a baking dish and set aside.

When you are ready to cook the salmon, stir the breadcrumbs and 2 tablespoons chopped parsley into the bacon-milk mixture.

Season the salmon with salt and pepper on both sides. Place the salmon in the batter and turn the fillets with your hands to coat well.

Heat a large sauté pan over medium heat for 2 minutes. (Depending on the size of your pan, you may need to cook the fish in batches.) Swirl in the olive oil and wait a minute. Carefully place the batter-coated fish in the pan. (Some of the batter might fall off; use your hands to pat it back on, making sure each piece is well coated.) Turn the heat to low, and cook for about 3 minutes, until golden brown. Carefully turn each piece over, and cook another 3 to 4 minutes, until it's nicely browned on the second side and still a little rare at the center. Transfer the fish to a resting rack.

Meanwhile, place the butter in a small saucepan and cook 2 to 3 minutes over medium heat, swirling the pan a few times, until it browns and smells nutty. Turn off the heat and wait a minute. Add the red wine vinegar, the onion, and a heaping ¼ teaspoon salt. Return the butter to the stove over low heat, and cook a minute or two, until the onion is just softened but still slightly crunchy. Turn off the heat, and squeeze in lemon juice to taste.

Arrange the sweet corn, green cabbage, and bacon on a large warm platter and top with the salmon. Stir 2 tablespoons chopped parsley into the brown butter vinaigrette and spoon it over the fish.

sweet corn, green cabbage, and bacon

Cut the bacon into ⅜-inch-thick slices. Stack them in two piles, then cut the bacon crosswise into ⅜-inch rectangles or *lardons*.

Heat a large sauté pan over medium heat for 1 minute. Add the bacon *lardons* and cook about 5 minutes, stirring often, until tender and lightly crisped. Using a slotted spoon, transfer the bacon to a paper-towel-lined plate, leaving the fat in the pan.

Swirl in the butter, and, when it foams, add the spring onions, thyme, ½ teaspoon salt, and a pinch of pepper. Sauté over medium heat, about 3 minutes, then add the corn, and continue cooking another 3 minutes, stirring occasionally. Season with ½ teaspoon salt and some freshly ground black pepper. Add the cabbage, and cook 2 minutes, stirring occasionally, until the cabbage just wilts. Taste for seasoning, and toss in the spring onion tops and chopped parsley.

5-ounce slab applewood-smoked bacon

2 tablespoons unsalted butter

1½ cups thinly sliced spring onions plus ¾ cup thin diagonal slices spring onion tops

2 teaspoons thyme leaves

1½ cups fresh corn (from about 2 ears)

½ small green cabbage, about 1 pound, cored, sliced thinly lengthwise

2 tablespoons chopped flat-leaf parsley

Kosher salt and freshly ground black pepper

grilled veal chops with summer squash gratin and salsa verde

6 free-range veal chops, about
   10 ounces each (see Sources)

1 tablespoon rosemary leaves

1 tablespoon thyme leaves

2 cloves garlic, smashed

3 tablespoons extra-virgin
   olive oil

1 bunch arugula, cleaned

Salsa verde (see page 132)

Summer squash gratin with
   salsa verde and Gruyère
   (recipe follows)

Fleur de sel and freshly cracked
   black pepper

Most people have heard horror stories about the conditions under which calves are raised for veal. Fortunately, today there are thoughtful ranchers raising free-range veal without antibiotics. This contemporary veal won't taste or look like the pale, white meat your grandparents were accustomed to. The free-range veal we serve at Lucques is rosy red in color, with more character and flavor than its inhumanely treated counterpart. It's worth pursuing. To keep the chops juicy, grill them medium-rare to medium.

NOTE Season the chops with herbs and garlic overnight. You can make the gratin ahead of time and wait until just before serving to bake it. Light the grill when the gratin goes in the oven. If you like, make the salsa verde a few hours ahead of time. You will need 1½ batches salsa verde for the gratin and the finished dish.

Season the veal chops with the rosemary, thyme, smashed garlic, and olive oil. Cover, and refrigerate for at least 4 hours, preferably overnight.

Light the grill 30 to 40 minutes before cooking, and remove the veal chops from the refrigerator to allow them to come to room temperature.

When the coals are broken down, red, and glowing, season both sides of the veal chops generously with *fleur de sel* and cracked black pepper. Place them on the grill, and cook 4 to 5 minutes per side, rotating a couple of times on each side, to sear nicely. Cook until medium-rare to medium—you can peek inside at the bone to check that the meat is still a little pink.

Scatter the arugula on a large platter, and place the chops on top. Spoon about a tablespoon of salsa verde over each one, and drizzle a little more over the greens. Serve the summer squash gratin and the extra salsa verde on the side.

summer squash gratin with salsa verde and gruyère

Preheat the oven to 400°F.

Cut the squash into ⅛-inch-thick slices. If you're using long zucchini-type summer squash, slice them on the diagonal. Toss the slices in a large bowl with 1 teaspoon kosher salt, and let sit 10 minutes.

Place the breadcrumbs in a bowl.

Heat a small sauté pan over medium heat for 1 minute. Swirl in the butter and cook a few minutes, until it browns and smells nutty. Pour the brown butter over the breadcrumbs (being sure to scrape all the brown bits into the bowl with a rubber spatula). Wait a minute or so for the butter to cool, and toss well.

Drain the squash and transfer it to a large mixing bowl. Add the shallots, minced garlic, thyme, ½ cup salsa verde, and some pepper. Toss to combine, and add the cheese and half the butter-coated breadcrumbs. Toss again, and taste for seasoning. (The raw garlic will taste strong at this point but will be delicious when cooked.)

Place the squash in a pretty 9-by-9-inch (or equivalent) gratin dish. Scatter the remaining breadcrumbs over the top, and bake 35 to 40 minutes, until the squash is tender and the top is crisp.

2 pounds summer squash

1½ cups fresh breadcrumbs

3 tablespoons unsalted butter

¾ cup sliced shallots

1 teaspoon minced garlic

1 tablespoon thyme leaves

½ cup salsa verde (see page 132)

1 cup grated Gruyère cheese

Kosher salt and freshly ground
   black pepper

almond financier with nectarines and berries

1¼ cups plus 2 tablespoons unsalted butter, plus a little extra for the pan

1 vanilla bean

¾ cup all-purpose flour

¾ cup confectioners' sugar

½ cup plus 3 tablespoons granulated sugar

1 cup almond meal (finely ground blanched almonds, available in quality markets or health food stores)

¼ teaspoon kosher salt

1 cup egg whites (from about 6 extra-large eggs)

2 tablespoons honey

3 nectarines

¾ cup heavy whipping cream

¼ cup crème fraîche

1 pint blackberries, raspberries, or both

While living in France, I took some time off from the savory kitchen to explore the sweet side of Paris at Pâtisserie Christian Pottier. Although I was fascinated by the fancy layered creations there, I preferred simpler, homier pastries, like buttery madeleines, crisp millefeuilles, and of course the very French financiers.

Invented in a pastry shop near the Paris Stock Exchange, these one-bite cakes provided a quick sweet fix for bankers on the run. They were originally made in small rectangular molds to resemble gold bricks, but financiers can now be found in myriad shapes and sizes all over France. The easy-to-make batter has ground nuts, egg whites, sugar, and vanilla brown butter. At Lucques, we sometimes bake our financiers into round cakes and serve the slices with sugared summer fruit and whipped cream. Try a slice crisped in the toaster the next morning for breakfast.

Lightly butter the bottom and sides of a round 9-inch cake pan.

Place 1¼ cups plus 2 tablespoons butter in a medium sauté pan. Slice the vanilla bean in half lengthwise, and use a paring knife to scrape the seeds and pulp onto the butter. To make sure not to lose any of the precious seeds, run your vanilla-coated knife through the butter. Add the vanilla pod to the pan, and cook the butter and vanilla over medium heat 8 to 10 minutes, shaking the pan occasionally, until the butter browns and smells nutty. Discard the vanilla pod. Set the butter aside and keep warm.

Sift the flour, confectioners' sugar, and ½ cup granulated sugar into a large mixing bowl. Add the almond meal and salt and stir to combine well.

Beat the egg whites in a medium bowl until frothy. Whisk the whites and the honey into the dry ingredients. Next, whisk the brown butter into the batter, making sure to get all the little brown bits as well.

Let the batter rest in the refrigerator for at least 1 hour.

Preheat the oven to 350°F.

Pour the batter into the prepared cake pan and sprinkle 2 teaspoons of the granulated sugar over the top. Bake about 40 minutes, until the cake is a deep golden brown and pulls away from the sides of the pan. It will be springy to the touch, and a toothpick inserted into the center should come out clean. Cool on a rack.

Cut the nectarines in half and remove the pits. Slice each half into six wedges. Toss the nectarines in a bowl with 2 heaping tablespoons sugar, and let sit 20 minutes to draw out the juices.

While the nectarines are sitting, place the cream and crème fraîche in a mixing bowl. Whip at medium-high speed with the whisk attachment until you have very soft peaks. (You could also whip it by hand.)

Just before serving, gently toss the berries in with the nectarines. Taste and add more sugar if you like. Slice six wedges from the financier. Arrange the slices on six plates, spoon the fruit over each slice, and dollop with whipped cream.

first-of-the-season succotash salad

1 tablespoon finely diced shallot

3 tablespoons lemon juice, plus more to taste

½ cup plus 2 tablespoons extra-virgin olive oil

¾ cup diced red onion

2 teaspoons thyme leaves

2 cups diced summer squash

3 cups fresh corn (from about 4 ears)

½ pint cherry tomatoes, cut in half

1 cup cooked fresh lima beans (see page 128), well-drained

¼ cup sliced basil, opal and green

1 tablespoon sliced parsley

1 tablespoon minced chives

4 ounces mixed salad of watercress and arugula

Kosher salt and freshly ground black pepper

There's a moment in late May when something in the air shifts. Fava beans and other spring treats are still plentiful and the evenings are still cool, but change is coming. The air at the farmers' market is suddenly humid with the scent of basil. Small piles of cherry tomatoes, summer squash, and fresh beans show up on the folding tables beside mounds of fresh corn. It's as if summer is testing the waters, seeing if we're ready, because it can hardly hold back any longer.

Before changing my spring menu to summer, I sample a few beans, checking for crunch. I peel back a cornhusk, bite into the cob—is the corn sweet yet? And finally, I pop a cherry tomato in my mouth to gauge its sugar. If they all pass the test, it's time to make this First-of-the-Season Succotash Salad, dressed with a simple lemon vinaigrette. After waiting all year, what a joy it is to taste all these sunny flavors on one plate.

Place the shallot, 3 tablespoons lemon juice, and ½ teaspoon salt in a bowl, and let sit 5 minutes. Whisk in 5 tablespoons olive oil, and taste for balance and seasoning.

Heat a large sauté pan over high heat for 2 minutes. Add 3 tablespoons olive oil, the red onion, and the thyme. Sauté about 1 minute, and then add the squash. Season with 1 teaspoon salt, and cook another 4 minutes or so, until the squash is tender and has a little color. Cool on a platter or baking sheet.

Wipe the pan out with paper towels, return it to the stove, and heat over high for 2 minutes. Add the remaining 2 tablespoons olive oil, the corn, 1 teaspoon salt, and ¼ teaspoon pepper. Sauté quickly, tossing often, for about 2 minutes, until the corn is just tender. Cool on a platter or baking sheet.

Place the cherry tomatoes in a large salad bowl, and season with ½ teaspoon salt. Add the squash, corn, and lima beans, and toss with half of the dressing. Taste for seasoning, and adjust with more salt and lemon juice if you like. Gently toss the herbs into the succotash.

Toss the watercress and arugula with the remaining dressing, and season with a pinch of salt and pepper. Place the greens on a large chilled platter, and arrange the succotash on top.

bucatini and clams with fennel, white wine, and thyme breadcrumbs

My very first chef position was at a twenty-eight-seat restaurant called Alloro, located in Boston's very Italian North End. At that point in my career, my cooking experience was rooted mostly in French cuisine, but the owner didn't seem to mind. When I asked him if I had to cook strictly Italian food, his answer was, "No, no, no! Cook whatever you want. We'll just give it an Italian name." The French bistro classic salmon with beluga lentils and red wine butter was abbreviated to "Salmone" on the menu, and other quasi-French dishes were likewise masked under short Italian names.

The pasta dishes I made at Alloro also strayed from Italian tradition. For my version of the classic spaghetti alle vongole, I added generous amounts of onion, fennel, and olive oil, and sprinkled breadcrumbs toasted with thyme on top. I also finished the sauce with a spot of butter (the French influence again), which thickened and enriched it. In theory, I'm sure my version of spaghetti with clams would outrage purists in both the Italian and the French camps, but one bite ought to be enough to convince them they have lots to learn from each other.

Though you might not think of it as such, the water in which you cook pasta is a valuable ingredient, in virtually any pasta recipe. Do your noodles seem a little dry once you've tossed them in the sauce? Rather than correcting the problem with stock (which can alter the flavor balance) or oil (which can add greasiness), add a little pasta water instead. Not only will it moisten the dish, but the starch in it (left from the cooking of the pasta) will also help bind the sauce to the noodles. Try it out; it works.

NOTE This pasta needs to be "made to order." Although you can grind and toast your breadcrumbs, dice your vegetables, and clean the clams ahead of time, most of the work is at the last minute.

To clean the clams, soak them in cold water for 10 minutes, tossing them every few minutes or so. If the clams are very sandy, add a small handful of cornmeal or a splash of milk to the water, to encourage them to spit out the sand.

The pot you choose for this dish needs to be large enough to accommodate the clams and the noodles. If you don't have one large enough, make this dish in two pots, splitting the ingredients accordingly.

1½ cups fresh breadcrumbs

½ cup plus 2 tablespoons extra-virgin olive oil

2 tablespoons thyme leaves

½ sprig rosemary

2 chiles de árbol, plus 1 teaspoon sliced

2 cups diced red onion

2 cups diced fennel

2 bay leaves, preferably fresh

¼ cup sliced garlic

1 pound bucatini, spaghetti, or linguine

3½ pounds small Manila clams, cleaned

¾ cup dry white wine

4 tablespoons unsalted butter

1 lemon

½ cup sliced parsley

Kosher salt and freshly ground black pepper

Preheat the oven to 375°F.

Toss the breadcrumbs with 2 tablespoons olive oil and 1 tablespoon thyme. Spread them on a baking sheet, and toast in the oven 8 to 10 minutes, stirring once or twice, until golden brown.

Put a large pot of heavily salted water on to boil.

Heat a very large sauté pan or Dutch oven over high heat for 2 minutes. Pour in the remaining ½ cup olive oil, swirl the pan, and add the rosemary sprig and the chiles, crumbled with your hands. Let them sizzle in the oil about a minute or so, turn the heat down to medium, and add the onion, fennel, bay leaves, and remaining tablespoon thyme. Season with 2 teaspoons kosher salt and ¼ teaspoon pepper.

Cook 3 minutes over medium heat, stirring often. Add the garlic, and continue cooking another 3 to 4 minutes, until the vegetables are translucent and soft.

Drop the pasta in the rapidly boiling water.

Add the clams to the vegetables and toss to coat well. Add the wine and cover the pot. Cook until the clams open, about 5 minutes or so. (After a couple of minutes, lift the lid, gently stir the clams to help distribute the heat, and re-cover the pan.) When all the clams have opened, remove the pan from the heat and use a slotted spoon to transfer the clams to a roasting pan or baking sheet. When they're cool enough to handle, take half of the clams out of their shells and set aside. (If you like, you can skip this step and serve all the clams in their shells.) Discard any unopened clams.

When the pasta is al dente, reserve 1 cup of the cooking water, and then drain the pasta.

Return the pan to medium-high heat, and add the pasta to the vegetables, tossing the noodles well. Cook 3 to 4 minutes, to reduce the juices and coat the pasta. If the noodles seem dry, add some of the reserved pasta water. Add the butter, a big squeeze of lemon juice, the sliced chile, shucked clams, parsley, and ¼ teaspoon salt. Toss well and taste for seasoning.

Arrange the pasta on a large warm platter and spoon the clams still in their shells over the noodles. Sprinkle the breadcrumbs on top.

grilled pork burgers with rob's famous coleslaw

My cooks sometimes refer to Lucques as the "house of pork." I use pork often and in every form I can think of—marinated, brined, grilled, sautéed, confited, braised, ground into sausage or forcemeat, wrapped around fish or poultry, as a seasoning or an appetizer or a complete main course. This recipe is proof: with three kinds of pork packed into one dish, it's a regular porkapalooza. These burgers completely satisfy my frequent pork cravings, and I think they'll take care of yours, too. After all, few cultures appreciate pork better than the Latin ones, and these burgers pay homage to that culinary love. And it's some spicy, decadent homage, too: Mexican chorizo, Spanish romesco, and the coup de grâce, a slice of melted Manchego on top.

Do not be afraid to cook these burgers only until pink in the middle, when they are still juicy and delicious. Not only are all dangerous pork parasites killed at 137°F (long before the last pink disappears), but those organisms have been nearly eliminated from modern pork farming, so the risk is extremely low even from completely raw pork.

> **NOTE** I think these burgers taste best when the flavors have had time to meld. So—mix the meat ingredients together in the morning or the night before. The romesco can be made a day or two ahead of time, if you like. Make the aïoli a few hours before serving.
>
> When you make the burgers, combine the ingredients gently so you don't over-work the meat, which would make a tough burger. Shape it into a loose ball until it just comes together, and flatten slightly to form a patty. To be sure the meat is well seasoned, make a small test burger first.

1½ teaspoons cumin seeds

3 tablespoons extra-virgin olive oil, plus more for grilling

½ cup diced shallots

1 tablespoon minced garlic

1 tablespoon thyme leaves

2 chiles de árbol, thinly sliced on the bias

2 pounds ground pork

¼ pound fresh Mexican chorizo, casing removed

3 ounces applewood-smoked bacon, finely diced

2 tablespoons chopped flat-leaf parsley

6 slices Manchego cheese

6 brioche or other good burger buns

Aïoli (recipe follows)

Romesco (see page 44)

2 ounces arugula

Rob's famous coleslaw (recipe follows)

Kosher salt and freshly ground black pepper

In a medium sauté pan, toast the cumin seeds over medium heat a few minutes, until the seeds release their aroma and darken slightly. Pound the seeds in a mortar or spice grinder until coarsely ground.

Return the pan to the stove over high heat for 1 minute. Add the olive oil and shallots. Turn the heat down to medium-low, and cook a few minutes, stirring once or twice, until the shallots start to soften. Add the garlic, thyme, cumin, and sliced chile. Season with ¼ teaspoon salt and a few grindings of black pepper, and cook 3 to 4 minutes, until the shallots become translucent. Set aside to cool.

In a large bowl, use your hands to combine the ground pork, chorizo, bacon, shallot mixture, and parsley, being careful not to overmix the meat. Season with 1¼ teaspoons salt and lots of freshly ground black pepper. Shape the meat into six 6-ounce patties. Chill in the refrigerator if not using right away.

Light the grill 30 to 40 minutes before cooking, and remove the pork burgers from the refrigerator to come to room temperature (if you made them in advance).

When the coals are broken down, red, and glowing, brush the pork burgers with olive oil, and grill them 3 to 4 minutes on the first side, until they're nicely browned. Turn the burgers over, and place a piece of cheese on each one. Cook another 3 minutes or so, until the pork is just cooked through. (It should still be slightly pink in the center.)

Slice the buns in half, brush them with olive oil, and toast them on the grill, cut side down, for a minute or so, until they're lightly browned.

Spread both sides of the buns with aïoli. Place a burger on the bottom half of each bun, and dollop with a generous amount of romesco. Place some arugula leaves on top, and finish with the top half of the bun.

Serve the burgers on a platter with mounds of Rob's famous coleslaw. For your more indulgent friends, serve extra romesco and aïoli on the side.

aïoli

1 extra-large egg yolk
½ cup grapeseed oil
½ cup extra-virgin olive oil
1 small clove garlic
½ lemon, for juicing
Pinch cayenne pepper
Kosher salt

Place the yolk in a stainless steel bowl. Begin whisking in the grapeseed oil drop by drop. Once the mixture has thickened and emulsified, you can whisk in the remaining grapeseed and olive oils in a slow steady stream. If the mixture gets too thick, add a drop or two of water.

Pound the garlic with ¼ teaspoon salt with a mortar and pestle. Whisk the garlic paste into the aïoli. Season with ¼ teaspoon salt, a squeeze of lemon juice, and the cayenne. Taste for balance and seasoning. If the aïoli seems thick and gloppy, thin it with a little water. In addition to thinning the aïoli, this will also make it creamier.

rob's famous coleslaw

Every year, we celebrate the heart of summer with a Sunday barbecue feast at Lucques. This annual tradition always includes at least four different barbecued meats, baked beans, long-cooked greens, grilled cornbread, and former Lucques chef Rob Chalmers's infamous coleslaw. The first year he made it, he miscalculated "slightly" and made enough for about six hundred people! It became a running joke to tease Rob about his coleslaw, and for about a year after the barbecue, the servers and busboys used to greet every staff meal with the predictable, "What, no coleslaw?" Here is a manageable-sized recipe for Rob's light, crunchy, and always satisfying slaw.

In a small saucepan, reduce the vinegar by half over medium heat. Cool 5 minutes, and then stir in the honey until it dissolves. Combine the cabbages, onion, and carrot in a large bowl. Pour the vinegar-honey mixture over the vegetables, and toss well to combine. Season with salt and pepper, and let sit 15 minutes, tossing occasionally. Add the mayonnaise, cayenne, and herbs, and toss well. Taste for balance and seasoning.

½ cup red wine vinegar

2 teaspoons honey

½ small head red cabbage, about 1 pound, cored and thinly sliced

½ small head green cabbage, about 1 pound, cored and thinly sliced

½ red onion, thinly sliced

1 carrot, peeled and grated

½ cup mayonnaise, preferably homemade

A healthy pinch cayenne pepper

2 tablespoons minced chives

¼ cup chopped flat-leaf parsley

Kosher salt and freshly ground black pepper

cornmeal shortcakes with peaches, mint, and soured cream

While living in Rhode Island and working at Al Forno, I was fascinated by the celebrations that revolved around food (especially in the Italian and Portuguese neighborhoods) and the connection Rhode Islanders felt to certain local produce, like their native tomatoes and homegrown corn.

The most prized dish in tiny Rhode Island is the johnnycake. Originally called journey cakes, these cornmeal griddle cakes, made with locally milled native corn, have been the pride and joy of Rhode Island since the seventeenth century. County competitions are held annually, and there's even a group called the Society for the Propagation of Johnny Cakes that sees to it that their corn-pancake tradition stays alive and well. So it seemed natural at Al Forno to add that famous stone-ground corn to our shortcake biscuit.

Here I've borrowed Al Forno's foolproof recipe and added peaches and my own "soured cream." To get the peaches nice and saucy, I marinate them in simple syrup with mint and then purée a portion of the fruit to spoon over the biscuit. Feel free to make this shortcake with whatever juicy fruit you like, such as nectarines or berries. The biscuit recipe makes about eight in all. So don't worry when you notice one or two mysteriously missing after they're pulled from the hot oven and left to cool on the counter; you'll still have enough to feed six.

1½ cups all-purpose flour

½ cup stone-ground cornmeal

1 tablespoon plus 1 teaspoon baking powder

¼ teaspoon kosher salt

¼ cup granulated sugar

4 tablespoons cold unsalted butter, cut into small cubes

1 cup plus 1 tablespoon heavy cream

Peaches and soured cream (recipe follows)

Preheat the oven to 425°F.

Place the flour, cornmeal, baking powder, salt, and 3 heaping tablespoons of sugar in the bowl of a food processor. Pulse to combine. Add the butter, and pulse about ten times, to a coarse meal. With the machine running, quickly pour in 1 cup cream. Stop the machine immediately when the dough starts to come together. (It is important not to overwork the dough.)

Place the dough on a clean work surface and bring it together with your hands. Shape it into a circle 1¼ inches thick. Cut the circle in half, and then cut each half into four wedges. Place the shortcakes on a buttered baking sheet. Brush them with the remaining tablespoon of cream, and sprinkle a little sugar on top of each one.

Bake about 15 minutes, until the biscuits are set and a light golden brown.

When they have cooled, cut the shortcakes in half horizontally, and place the bottom halves on each of six plates or on a large platter. Place a spoonful of peach purée onto each biscuit. Spoon a large dollop of the soured cream over each, and ladle some of the peaches and their juices over the cream, letting some of the fruit fall onto the plates. Drizzle a little more peach purée, and place the shortcake tops back on.

peaches and soured cream

½ cup granulated sugar

¾ pound mascarpone

1 tablespoon lemon juice plus
    more to taste

4 ripe peaches

16 small mint leaves

NOTE You'll have leftover simple syrup. It keeps in the refrigerator for several weeks and is fun to have around, to sweeten fruit and use for cocktails.

To make the simple syrup, combine the sugar and ½ cup water in a small pot and bring to a boil. Swirl the pan until the sugar has dissolved completely. Pour the simple syrup into a small clean container, and cool in the refrigerator. (If you're in a hurry, put it in the freezer to cool.)

Place the mascarpone in the bowl of a food processor. Add ⅓ cup of the simple syrup, and pulse to combine. Taste for sweetness, and add a little more syrup if you like. Squeeze 1 tablespoon lemon juice into the mascarpone. Pulse to combine, but don't overwork it or it will curdle. Adjust the simple syrup and lemon to your taste. Keep cold in the refrigerator. Clean the bowl of the food processor.

Peel the peaches. Cut each in half, remove the pit, and then cut into slices. Toss the peach slices in a bowl with 3 tablespoons simple syrup. Tear the mint with your hands, add it to the peaches, and toss to combine. Taste the peaches, and add a little more syrup if you like. Let the peaches macerate in the syrup for 10 minutes.

Purée a quarter of the peaches in the food processor and set aside. See main recipe for assembly instructions.

dad's steakhouse salad:
early girl tomatoes, red onion, and roquefort

My father hated salad. I remember him saying, "The only salad worth eating is one with green beans and foie gras, because it's not all mucked up with lettuce." And yet, somehow, I grew to love salads, especially the kind with leafy greens. This lettuce-free, classic steakhouse salad, made with first-of-the-season Early Girl tomatoes, sweet young red onions, and slabs of potent Roquefort, is a tribute to my dad, who I know would approve.

1 tablespoon oregano leaves

½ clove garlic

1½ tablespoons red wine vinegar

1 tablespoon balsamic vinegar

6 tablespoons extra-virgin olive oil

1 large red onion

2½ pounds Early Girl or beefsteak tomatoes

1¾ to 2 teaspoons *fleur de sel*

½ lemon, for juicing

⅓ pound Roquefort or your favorite blue cheese

¼ cup sliced green and opal basil

Kosher salt and freshly ground black pepper

Pound the oregano, garlic, and ¼ teaspoon salt in a mortar to a paste. Remove to a mixing bowl, and stir in the vinegars. Whisk in the olive oil, and taste for balance and seasoning.

Peel the onion, and cut it into ¼-inch-thick rings. Soak the rings in ice water for 5 minutes, to mellow their strong flavor and get them super-crisp.

Core the tomatoes. One by one, hold each tomato on its side and slice into ¼-inch-thick round slices. Spread the slices out on a cutting board or platter, and season them with the *fleur de sel* and some pepper. Drain the onion slices, pat them dry with paper towels, and toss them with a pinch of salt, a squeeze of lemon, and a teaspoon of the vinaigrette.

Slice the cheese into ¼-inch-thick slabs.

Arrange half the tomatoes overlapping on a large chilled platter. Tuck half the onions and half the Roquefort in and around the tomatoes. Spoon half the vinaigrette over the salad, and scatter half the basil over it. Arrange the remaining tomatoes, onions, and Roquefort on top. Spoon the rest of the vinaigrette over the salad, and sprinkle the remaining basil around.

grilled bluefish wrapped in pancetta with yellow tomato sauce and aïoli

6 bluefish fillets, 5 to 6 ounces each, without skin

1 lemon, zested

1 tablespoon thyme leaves

3 tablespoons chopped flat-leaf parsley

6 slices pancetta, ⅛-inch thick

3 heirloom tomatoes, mixed colors if possible

Scant teaspoon *fleur de sel*

2 tablespoons super-good extra-virgin olive oil

1 teaspoon red wine vinegar

2 tablespoons finely diced shallot

2 tablespoons sliced opal basil

1 tablespoon extra-virgin olive oil for brushing the fish

Yellow tomato sauce (recipe follows)

1 recipe aïoli (see page 148)

Kosher salt and freshly ground black pepper

I first discovered bluefish when I was working at Angels, a restaurant in Providence. I was fresh off the boat from California when Jamie, the chef, and Eileen, his sous-chef, began introducing me to all the local food specialties. First they took me to a salumeria on Federal Hill, the Italian district of Providence, where the prosciutto was called "prah-jhute" and ricotta was "rha-got." Then one day they brought in smoked bluefish. We piled it high on crusty Italian rolls, and topped it with sliced red onions, lemon, and way too much crème fraîche. I was in Rhode Island heaven.

In honor of that beguiling and unforgettable fish, here I wrap fresh bluefish in pancetta to give the fish a salty, smoked flavor. Served with a yellow tomato sauce, juicy slices of heirloom tomatoes, and garlicky aïoli, this is my tribute to summer in Rhode Island.

NOTE Season the fish with herbs and wrap it in pancetta in the morning. You can make the tomato sauce earlier in the day and warm it up when you need it. The aïoli can also be prepared a few hours before serving.

Season the fish with the lemon zest, the thyme, and 2 tablespoons chopped parsley. Wrap each fillet with a piece of pancetta, spiraling the meat around the fish like the stripe on a candy cane. Cover, and refrigerate at least 4 hours. Remove the fish from the refrigerator 15 minutes before cooking to bring it back to room temperature.

Light the grill 30 to 40 minutes before cooking.

Cut the heirloom tomatoes horizontally into ⅛-inch-thick slices. Season with the *fleur de sel* and pepper. Drizzle with the super-good olive oil and red wine vinegar. Scatter the shallot, opal basil, and the remaining tablespoon chopped parsley over the tomatoes. Let them marinate while you grill the fish.

When the coals are broken down, red, and glowing, season the bluefish fillets lightly with salt and pepper, and brush them with a little olive oil. Grill the fish 3 to 4 minutes on the first side, rotating once or twice, until the pancetta is crispy. Turn the fish over, and cook another few minutes, until just cooked through.

Spoon the hot yellow tomato sauce onto a large warm platter, and arrange the tomato slices on top, overlapping them slightly. Place the fish on the platter, squeeze lemon juice over the top, and dollop each piece of bluefish with aïoli. Pass the remaining aïoli at the table.

yellow tomato sauce

Blanch the yellow tomatoes in boiling water for 30 seconds. Cool the tomatoes in a bowl of ice water a few minutes, and then use your fingers to slip off their skins. Remove the cores, and cut each tomato in half horizontally. Squeeze the tomato halves, cut side down, over a strainer set in a bowl. Scoop the seeds out with your fingers and discard them. Chop the tomatoes coarsely and reserve the juice.

Heat a medium saucepan over medium-high heat for 1 minute. Swirl in the olive oil, and heat another minute. Add the onion, season with salt and pepper, and sauté 3 to 4 minutes, until the onion is translucent. Add the chopped tomatoes and their juice. Season with 1 teaspoon salt, and cook 6 to 8 minutes over medium-low heat, until the tomatoes are softened but not completely cooked. Remove from the heat, stir in the basil sprigs, and taste for seasoning. Discard the basil sprigs just before serving.

2 pounds ripe yellow tomatoes

3 tablespoons extra-virgin olive oil

1 cup diced onion

4 sprigs basil

Kosher salt and freshly ground black pepper

herb-roasted pork loin with haricots verts, spring onions, and mustard breadcrumbs

Pork loin is a lean, delicate cut of meat compared to, say, a big, fatty chop, and this recipe is all about maximizing its taste and preserving its moisture. Applying the mustard marinade twice and roasting slowly with butter and herbs will simultaneously infuse the meat with complex flavor and help protect its precious internal juices. It's very important to use a roasting rack, which helps the air circulate, resulting in even cooking.

> NOTE Marinate the pork the day before serving. You can blanch the haricots verts and cut the spring onions ahead of time, but cook them while the pork is resting. The mustard breadcrumbs can be made a few hours ahead of time.

Whisk together the mustard, thyme leaves, parsley, and 2 tablespoons olive oil in a shallow baking dish. Stir in the garlic, and slather the pork with this mustard mixture. Cover and refrigerate at least 4 hours, preferably overnight.

Take the pork out of the refrigerator 1 hour before cooking, to bring it to room temperature. After 30 minutes, season the pork generously with salt and pepper. Reserve the marinade.

Preheat the oven to 325°F.

Heat a large sauté pan over high heat for 3 minutes. Swirl in the remaining 2 tablespoons olive oil, and wait a minute or two, until the pan is very hot, almost smoking. Place the pork loin in the pan, and sear it on all sides until well browned and caramelized. Don't turn or move the pork too quickly or all the mustard will be left in the pan and not on the pork. Be patient; this searing process takes 15 to 20 minutes.

Transfer the pork loin to a roasting rack, and slather the reserved marinade over the meat. Reserve the pan. Arrange the rosemary, sage, and thyme sprigs on the roast and top with 3 tablespoons butter.

Roast the pork until a thermometer inserted into the center reads 120°F, about 1¼ hours. Let the pork rest at least 10 minutes before slicing.

While the pork is roasting, return the pork-searing pan to the stove over medium-high heat. Wait 1 to 2 minutes and then deglaze it with the chicken stock

½ cup Dijon mustard

1 tablespoon thyme leaves, plus 6 sprigs

2 tablespoons chopped flat-leaf parsley

¼ cup extra-virgin olive oil

10 cloves garlic, smashed

3 pounds center-cut pork loin

3 sprigs rosemary, broken into 3-inch pieces

3 sprigs sage

6 tablespoons unsalted butter, sliced

Haricots verts and spring onions (recipe follows)

Mustard breadcrumbs (recipe follows)

Kosher salt and freshly ground black pepper

or water. Bring to a boil, whisking and scraping the bottom of the pan to release the crispy bits. Swirl in 3 tablespoons butter and set aside.

Arrange the haricots verts and spring onions on a large warm platter. Slice the pork thinly, about ¼-inch thick, and fan the meat over the beans. Add the buttery pork juices and herbs to the sauce, bring it to a boil, and then spoon it over the pork. Shower the mustard breadcrumbs over the top.

haricots verts and spring onions

1½ pounds haricots verts, stems removed, tails left on

3 bunches spring onions

4 tablespoons extra-virgin olive oil

2 teaspoons thyme leaves

2 tablespoons unsalted butter

10 small sage leaves

Kosher salt and freshly ground black pepper

Blanch the haricots verts in a large pot of salted boiling water 2 to 3 minutes, until tender but still al dente.

Cut the spring onions 1 inch above the bulb, leaving some green top still attached. Trim the roots, but leave the root end intact (this will keep the onions in wedges, rather than slices). Cut the onions lengthwise into ¼-inch-thick wedges.

Heat two pans over medium-high heat for 2 minutes. (In order to get nice color on the onions and preserve their beautiful shape, it's best to cook them in two large pans so they are not crowded.) Swirl 2 tablespoons olive oil into each pan, and gently place the onions in the pans, cut side down. Season with the thyme, salt, and pepper, and cook the onion wedges 2 to 3 minutes, until they start to brown slightly. Turn the onions, using tongs, and add the haricots verts. Season each pan with ¼ teaspoon salt and freshly ground black pepper, and cook 3 to 4 minutes, stirring to combine. Add the butter and sage leaves and cook a few more minutes, tossing to glaze the vegetables in the butter and let the sage perfume them. Taste for seasoning.

mustard breadcrumbs

1 cup fresh breadcrumbs

2 tablespoons unsalted butter

1 tablespoon Dijon mustard

1 teaspoon thyme leaves

1 teaspoon chopped flat-leaf parsley

Preheat the oven to 375°F.

Place the breadcrumbs in a medium bowl. Heat a small sauté pan over medium heat for 1 minute. Add the butter, and when it foams, whisk in the mustard, thyme, and parsley. Remove from the heat, let cool a few minutes, and then pour the mustard butter over the breadcrumbs, tossing to coat them well. Transfer the breadcrumbs to a baking sheet, and toast them 10 to 12 minutes, stirring often, until they're golden brown and crispy.

meringues "closerie des lilas" with vanilla ice cream, chocolate sauce, and toasted almonds

When I was growing up, I made on special occasions what my family called "the Hemingway dessert." My father was obsessed with Ernest Hemingway. He was an avid collector of his first-edition books, and, despite his lack of academic credentials, somehow talked his way into the International Hemingway Society. My mom, Jessica, and I would tag along on their "Hemingway trips," whose itineraries inevitably included many stops in remote villages to locate particular taverns, hotels, and cafés that the expatriate writer had at one time visited (drinking and carousing along the way, of course!). Closerie des Lilas, a bohemian café on the Left Bank, was one of Hemingway's Parisian hangouts, and the place where this dessert originated under the name Coupe Hemingway.

Don't be afraid of making the meringue. Just remember, meringues are never good when they're rushed, so be sure to give yourself enough time to bake them in a low oven until they're dry and firm.

NOTE You can make the meringues, ice cream, chocolate sauce, and toasted nuts all ahead of time. Then all you have to do is assemble the dessert right before serving.

4 extra-large egg whites

½ cup granulated sugar

6 ounces bittersweet chocolate, roughly chopped

2 tablespoons unsalted butter

2 tablespoons corn syrup

2 tablespoons honey

⅓ cup whole raw almonds

Vanilla ice cream (see page 113)

Preheat the oven to 200°F.

Whisk the egg whites and sugar together in a medium stainless steel bowl. Place the bowl over a pot of simmering water, and whisk continuously for about 2 minutes until the sugar dissolves and the mixture is lukewarm. Transfer to a stand mixer fitted with the whisk attachment, and whip on high speed 2 to 3 minutes, until the mixture cools and you have soft, shiny peaks.

Using a large spoon, scoop out tennis ball–sized spoonfuls of meringue onto a parchment-lined baking sheet or nonstick baking mat, letting them fall into whimsical shapes. Bake for 2 hours, until the meringues are firm but still chewy in the center. They are done when they release easily from the baking sheet.

While the meringues are baking, melt the chocolate and butter in a stainless steel bowl over a pot of simmering water. When the chocolate has melted, whisk in ⅓ cup boiling water. Stir in the corn syrup and honey, and keep the chocolate sauce warm.

When the meringues are done, turn the oven up to 375°F. Spread the almonds on a baking sheet, and toast 8 to 10 minutes, until they're lightly browned and smell nutty. When the nuts have cooled, chop them coarsely.

Using a serrated knife, cut the meringues in half horizontally. Set the tops aside. Arrange large scoops of vanilla ice cream on each bottom and place them on a large platter. Drizzle the chocolate sauce over the meringues and scatter the almonds on top. Place the meringue "tops" over the ice cream.

yellow tomato gazpacho

This recipe was developed by Julie Robles, longtime Lucques cook, then sous-chef, then chef de cuisine. It's one of those magical recipes in which you combine a few simple ingredients and end up with an unexpectedly dramatic result. It's a foolproof recipe, but, tasting it, you'd never know how easy it is to make. As long as you have a blender (it doesn't work as well in a food processor) and really great tomatoes, this refreshing gazpacho is a guaranteed crowd-pleaser.

2½ pounds ripe yellow tomatoes

3 Persian cucumbers, or 1 hot-house cucumber

½ jalapeño, seeded and cut in half

4 sprigs cilantro, plus 12 cilantro leaves

2 cloves garlic, coarsely chopped

2 tablespoons red wine vinegar

⅓ cup extra-virgin olive oil

3 tablespoons diced red or orange sweet pepper

3 tablespoons diced red onion

18 small cherry tomatoes, cut in half

Super-good extra-virgin olive oil, for drizzling

Kosher salt and freshly ground black pepper

Blanch the yellow tomatoes in boiling water for 30 seconds. Cool the tomatoes in a bowl of ice water a few minutes, and then use your fingers to slip off their skins. Remove the cores, and chop the tomatoes coarsely, saving all the juice. Reserve the ice water.

Seed and dice three tablespoons' worth of unpeeled cucumber, as prettily as you can manage, for the garnish. Set aside. Peel and coarsely chop the remaining cucumbers.

You will need to make the soup in batches. Place half the yellow tomatoes, coarsely chopped cucumber, jalapeño, cilantro sprigs, garlic, vinegar, and olive oil in a blender with 1½ teaspoons salt and some pepper. Process at the lowest speed until broken down. Turn the speed up to high, and purée until the soup is completely smooth. If the soup is too thick, add a little of the reserved ice water. Strain the soup and taste for seasoning. Repeat with the rest of the soup ingredients. Chill the soup in the refrigerator; it should be served very cold.

Toss the diced pepper, diced onion, and diced cucumber together in a small bowl.

Pour the gazpacho into six chilled soup bowls, and scatter the pepper mixture over the soup. Season the cherry tomatoes with salt and pepper and place three cherry tomato halves and two cilantro leaves at the center of each bowl. Finish each soup with a drizzle of super-good olive oil. To serve family-style, place the soup in a chilled tureen or pretty pitcher and garnish with the tomato halves and cilantro; pass the diced vegetables on the side.

grilled halibut à la niçoise
with haricots verts, olives, cherry tomatoes, and anchovy butter

6 halibut fillets, 5 to 6 ounces each

2 lemons

2 tablespoons plus 1 teaspoon thyme leaves

¼ cup sliced flat-leaf parsley

¾ pound tiny fingerlings or other small potatoes

¼ cup plus 3 tablespoons extra-virgin olive oil

⅓ pound haricots verts, stems removed, tails left on

3 extra-large eggs

6 ounces baby spinach, cleaned and dried

½ cup pitted Niçoise olives

½ cup thinly sliced shallots

6 tablespoons unsalted butter

1 teaspoon minced anchovy

1 cup small cherry tomatoes, cut in half

2 tablespoons sliced basil, green and opal if possible

Kosher salt and freshly ground black pepper

This warm salad is pure southern France: tomatoes, olives, anchovies, basil, green beans, and soft-cooked eggs. It's easy to make, but it helps to do some of the steps beforehand. As long as your spinach is cleaned and your haricots verts, potatoes, and eggs are cooked, you won't have to do much until the last minute, when you're pulling it all together. While your potatoes are roasting in the oven, light the grill, have a glass of rosé, and look calm, cool, and collected as you wait to finish the last-minute tasks. Recruit an unsuspecting guest or your significant other to grill the halibut while you brown the anchovy butter and finish the warm salad.

NOTE Season the fish with lemon and herbs early in the day. You can roast the fingerlings, blanch the haricots verts, clean the spinach, cut the cherry tomatoes, clean the anchovies, and cook the eggs ahead of time.

Season the halibut with the zest of one lemon, 1 tablespoon thyme, and 2 tablespoons parsley. Cover, and refrigerate at least 4 hours.

Preheat the oven to 400°F.

Toss the potatoes with 2 tablespoons olive oil, 1 teaspoon thyme, and 1 teaspoon salt. Place the potatoes in a roasting pan, cover with foil, and cook 30 to 40 minutes, until they're tender when pierced. (Depending on their size, age, and variety, the cooking time will vary.)

Light the grill 30 to 40 minutes ahead of time. Take the halibut out of the refrigerator 15 minutes before cooking it, so it comes to room temperature.

Blanch the haricots verts in heavily salted water 2 to 3 minutes, until they're tender but still al dente. Remove to a baking sheet or platter to cool. Bring the water back to a boil, and carefully lower the eggs into the water. Turn the heat down to a very low simmer, and cook the eggs exactly 9 minutes. Remove the eggs to a bowl of ice water to cool completely. Peel the eggs, and cut them in half. Season with salt and pepper.

Place the spinach and olives in a large salad bowl.

Heat a large sauté pan over high heat for 1 minute. Pour in ¼ cup olive oil, and add the sliced shallots and remaining tablespoon thyme to the pan. Cook 1 minute, until the shallots are just wilted. Add the haricots verts and the potatoes, and season with ½ teaspoon salt and freshly ground pepper.

When the vegetables are hot, toss them into the bowl of spinach and olives. Season with another ½ teaspoon salt, pepper, and a generous squeeze of lemon juice. Toss well to dress the spinach and wilt it slightly. Taste for seasoning. Arrange the salad on a large platter. Tuck the eggs among the spinach leaves.

Meanwhile, when the coals are broken down, red, and glowing, brush the halibut with a little olive oil and season with salt and pepper. Place the fish on the grill, and cook 2 minutes. Give the fish a quarter-turn, and cook a minute or two more. Turn over, and cook until it's just barely cooked through; peek inside to check for doneness. When it's done, the halibut will begin to flake and separate a little, and the center will still be slightly translucent. Remember, the fish will continue to cook a little more once you take it off the grill. Arrange the fish on top of the salad.

Return the vegetable pan to the stove, and heat over medium-high. Add the butter, and cook a few minutes, until it starts to brown and smells nutty. Add the anchovy, cherry tomatoes, ¾ teaspoon salt, and a few grindings of black pepper. Cook for 30 seconds, shaking the pan often, until the tomatoes release some of their juice. Squeeze some lemon juice into the butter, and taste for balance and seasoning. Stir in the basil and remaining 2 tablespoons parsley. Spoon the sauce over the fish and around the salad.

lamb skewers with lima bean purée and french feta salsa verde

Please try this recipe if you're a lima bean hater. I used to be one, too. I detested those dried-out, mealy, frozen beans from childhood. They fell into the "dreaded vegetables" category, along with beets and Brussels sprouts. But oddly enough those very vegetables are the ones I have grown to love the most. Fresh lima beans are a revelation, and especially delicious in this purée.

Remove all the rosemary leaves from the branches except 2 inches' worth at the top of each. Cut the leafless end of the branch at an angle with a sharp knife to make a point (this will make it easier to skewer the lamb). Coarsely chop the rosemary leaves you removed from the branches.

Cut the lamb into 1-to-1½-inch-thick 2-ounce pieces.

Season the lamb with 2 tablespoons chopped rosemary leaves, the smashed garlic, thyme, and cracked black pepper. Cover, and refrigerate at least 4 hours, preferably overnight.

Light the grill 30 to 40 minutes before cooking, and take the lamb out of the refrigerator so it comes to room temperature.

Skewer three pieces of lamb onto each rosemary branch. The pieces on each skewer should be of similar thickness and not skewered too tightly or they will not cook evenly.

Stir the feta into the salsa verde. Taste for seasoning. It does not usually need salt but might need lemon and a pinch of pepper. Set aside.

When the coals are broken down, red, and glowing, brush the lamb skewers with olive oil, and season generously with salt. Place the lamb on the grill, and cook 3 minutes on each side, rotating the skewers a few times to get nice color, until they're medium-rare.

Spoon the warm lima bean purée onto a large warm platter. Scatter the dandelion greens over it, and arrange the skewers on top. Spoon some of the French feta salsa verde over the lamb, and serve the rest on the side.

6 branches rosemary, about 7 to 8 inches long

2½ pounds lamb sirloin

3 cloves garlic, smashed

1 tablespoon thyme leaves

2 teaspoons cracked black pepper

¼ pound French feta cheese, crumbled

1 recipe salsa verde (see page 132)

½ lemon, for juicing

2 tablespoons extra-virgin olive oil

Lima bean purée (recipe follows)

1 bunch dandelion or arugula, cleaned

Kosher salt and freshly ground black pepper

lima bean purée

½ cup extra-virgin olive oil

1 small sprig rosemary

1 dried chile de árbol, crumbled

2 teaspoons minced garlic

2 cups cooked fresh lima beans, well drained (see page 128)

½ lemon, for juicing

Kosher salt and freshly ground black pepper

Heat a medium saucepan over medium heat for 1 minute. Pour in the olive oil and turn the heat down to low. Add the rosemary sprig and the crumbled chile. When the rosemary begins to sizzle, add the garlic. Cook a minute or so, then add the lima beans and ½ teaspoon salt. Stew gently 5 to 7 minutes, until the beans are soft but not mushy. Strain the beans, reserving the oil. Discard the rosemary sprig and chile.

Place the beans in a food processor and purée. With the motor running, slowly pour in some of the reserved oil until the mixture has a smooth consistency. You may not need all the oil. Season with salt, pepper, and a squeeze of lemon to taste.

raspberry gratin

Everyone has had berries in cobblers and pies, but when people see this gratinéed dessert, their eyebrows rise in curious anticipation. The raspberries and custard are cooked briefly under the broiler, creating a delicious warm crust that only partially hides the tart berries and warm cream beneath. Once you learn this technique, you can use it with other berries, or even peaches and nectarines. In the winter, a gratin made with sautéed apples or pears with dried fruit is delicious, too. Choose an attractive dish that can go from oven to table.

1½ cups whole milk

3 extra-large egg yolks

½ cup plus 1 tablespoon granulated sugar

2 tablespoons plus 1 teaspoon cornstarch, sifted

2 tablespoons unsalted butter, cut into small pieces

A pinch of kosher salt

1 cup crème fraîche

1 pint raspberries (2 baskets)

1 tablespoon confectioners' sugar

In a medium heavy-bottomed pot, bring the milk to a boil, and then turn off the heat. Whisk the egg yolks together in a medium bowl, and then whisk in ½ cup sugar and the cornstarch. Continue whisking until the mixture thickens and is a pale yellow color. Slowly whisk in the hot milk, at first a few tablespoons at a time, and then more quickly. Return the mixture to the stove, and cook over medium heat, alternating between a whisk and a rubber spatula, until the pastry cream thickens to a puddinglike consistency.

Remove from the stove, and stir in the butter and salt.

Transfer the mixture to a bowl. Place a piece of plastic wrap on the surface to keep it from forming a skin. Poke a few holes in the plastic to let the heat escape. Cool in the refrigerator.

When the custard has cooled, fold in the crème fraîche.

Preheat the broiler.

Toss the raspberries with 1 tablespoon granulated sugar, and scatter half of them on the bottom of a 9-by-9-inch (or equivalent) gratin dish. Spoon the custard into the dish, and scatter the rest of the berries on top. Sift the confectioners' sugar over the top, and pass under the broiler for about 7 minutes, until bubbling and gratinéed on top.

Serve the gratin at the table with a big serving spoon.

summer fruit salad with arugula and marcona almonds

This recipe is a way to show off the best summer fruit you can find. If possible, use an assortment of fruits, such as plums, peaches, figs, and berries, but make sure that all the fruit is up to snuff. Rather than striving for variety and ending up with less-than-ideal examples of each fruit, you're better off with a simpler salad composed of only the most perfect nectarines or gorgeous peaches all alone.

The dressing is made by pounding some of the fruit into a juicy vinaigrette. Figs are my favorite for this purpose. They mellow the vinegar and give the dressing body and chunkiness. If you've never had a Marcona almond, you may not forgive me for introducing you to them. Rich and dense, this Spanish almond variety is outrageously addictive. If you can't find Marcona almonds, use toasted regular almonds or pecans.

Combine the shallot, vinegar, and ½ teaspoon salt in a bowl, and let sit 5 minutes.

Using a mortar and pestle, pound three fig halves to a coarse purée. Transfer the fig purée to the shallot mixture, and whisk in the olive oil. Taste for balance and seasoning.

Cut the nectarine, peach, and plums in half and remove the pits, and cut them into ¼-inch-thick slices. Place the sliced fruit, remaining figs, and berries in a large bowl. Drizzle half of the vinaigrette over the fruit, and season with salt and pepper. Gently toss in the arugula, sprinkle in some more salt and pepper, and taste for seasoning, adding more vinaigrette and a squeeze of lemon if needed.

Arrange on a large chilled platter, and sprinkle the nuts on top.

2 tablespoons finely diced shallot

3 tablespoons sherry vinegar

12 fresh figs, stems removed and cut in half

7 tablespoons extra-virgin olive oil

1 ripe nectarine

1 ripe peach

2 ripe plums

½ basket (about 1 cup) blackberries or Persian mulberries

8 ounces arugula, cleaned and dried

½ lemon, for juicing

⅔ cup Marcona almonds (see Sources)

Kosher salt and freshly ground black pepper

ricotta gnocchi with chanterelles, sweet corn, and sage brown butter

Gnocchi is one of those dishes that many home cooks shy away from. Whether they're made of potatoes or cheese, the process seems mysterious—until, of course, you finally take the plunge and make a batch yourself at home. These ricotta gnocchi are quick and easy and the perfect launch into your gnocchi-making career. Once you get the hang of rolling them off the tines of the fork, there's nothing to it. And when you've become the accomplished gnocchi-maker you never thought you'd be, you'll find all sorts of ways to serve them. Try them with a fresh tomato sauce, or simply toss them in this sage brown butter.

NOTE You can make and blanch the gnocchi ahead of time.

1½ cups fresh breadcrumbs

¼ cup extra-virgin olive oil

7 tablespoons unsalted butter

¾ pound chanterelles, cleaned

1 tablespoon thyme leaves

1 tablespoon sliced sage leaves

3 cups fresh corn kernels (from about 4 ears)

⅔ cup diced shallots

1 recipe ricotta gnocchi, blanched (recipe follows)

½ cup chopped flat-leaf parsley

Kosher salt and freshly ground black pepper

Preheat the oven to 375°F.

Toss the breadcrumbs with 2 tablespoons olive oil. Spread them on a baking sheet, and toast 8 to 10 minutes, stirring once or twice, until golden brown.

If the mushrooms are big, tear them into bite-size pieces.

Heat a large sauté pan over high heat for 2 minutes. Add the remaining 2 tablespoons olive oil, and heat another minute. Swirl in 1 tablespoon butter, and when it foams, add the mushrooms, half the thyme, ½ teaspoon salt, and a healthy pinch of pepper. Sauté the mushrooms about 5 minutes, stirring occasionally, until they're tender and a little crispy. Don't be tempted to move them around in the pan too much in the beginning: let them sear a little before stirring. Transfer the cooked mushrooms to a platter.

Return the pan to the stove, and heat on high for 1 minute. Add the remaining 6 tablespoons butter to the pan, and cook a minute or two, until the butter starts to brown. Add the sage, let it sizzle, and then add the corn, shallots, remaining ½ tablespoon thyme, 1½ teaspoons salt, and some freshly ground black pepper. Sauté quickly, tossing the corn in the hot butter for about 2 minutes, until the corn is just tender. Add the gnocchi and toss well to coat with the corn and brown butter. Season with 1 teaspoon salt, and add the mushrooms. Toss to combine, and heat the mushrooms through. Add the parsley. Arrange the gnocchi on a large platter, and shower the breadcrumbs over the top.

ricotta gnocchi

2 extra-large eggs

2 cups all-purpose flour, plus extra for rolling

1 pound whole milk ricotta, drained if wet

3 tablespoons extra-virgin olive oil

Kosher salt and freshly ground black pepper

Beat the eggs together in a small bowl.

Place 2 cups flour, 1¾ teaspoons salt, ¼ teaspoon freshly ground black pepper, and the ricotta in a large mixing bowl. With a dinner knife in each hand, cut the ricotta into the flour. When the flour and ricotta are combined, make a well in the center and pour in the eggs. Use a fork and, starting in the middle of the mixture, incorporate the eggs into the flour and ricotta. Knead the dough with your hands briefly, just to bring it together while being careful not to overwork it. Shape the dough into a ball, and place it on a lightly floured cutting board. Cut the ball into four pieces, and cover with a clean kitchen towel.

Bring a large pot of heavily salted water to a boil.

One by one, take each piece of dough out from underneath the towel, cut it in half, and roll it into a ¾-inch-thick rope on a lightly floured cutting board. The amount of flour on the board is very important: if you have too much the dough is difficult to roll, and if you don't use enough, the dough will stick to the board. Cut the ropes into 1-inch-long pieces, and sprinkle a little flour over them. Using your thumb, roll each piece of dough over the back of the tines of a fork, leaving an indentation from your thumb on one side and the markings from the fork on the other.

Plunge the gnocchi into the boiling water in batches. Once they rise to the surface, cook them for 1 minute more. Use a slotted spoon to transfer them to a baking sheet or platter. Drizzle the cooked gnocchi with the olive oil, and toss to coat them well.

california sea bass kabobs with eggplant, peppers, and charmoula

These skewers of sea bass are seasoned with a North African condiment called charmoula and served over marinated eggplant and peppers. Charmoula, like so many Old World recipes, has as many versions as there are cooks. Although the proportions and some ingredients vary, everyone seems to agree that charmoula must have cilantro, garlic, cumin, and paprika and then be finished with olive oil and vinegar.

One Sunday when we were working on this dish, Julie Robles, then sous-chef at Lucques, suggested adding rice wine vinegar to our charmoula experiment. It's certainly not authentic, but we both liked the milder, sweeter nuance it gave the sauce. In fact, the charmoula was so good we decided to use it twice. First we marinated the fish in the spicy condiment (acid-free, so it wouldn't "cook" the fish), and then, as we pulled the kabobs from the grill, we slathered them once again in charmoula.

NOTE The peppers and eggplant can be made the day before. Make the charmoula base and marinate the fish in the morning. Add the vinegar and lemon at the last minute.

2 tablespoons whole cumin seeds

2 cloves garlic

2½ cups coarsely chopped cilantro leaves

1 cup coarsely chopped flat-leaf parsley leaves

1 tablespoon paprika

½ teaspoon cayenne pepper

¾ cup plus 2 tablespoons extra-virgin olive oil

2½ pounds California sea bass, cut into 1½-inch cubes (about 1¼ to 1½ ounces each)

2¼ teaspoons rice wine vinegar

1 tablespoon plus 2 teaspoons lemon juice

1 bunch arugula, cleaned

Marinated peppers and eggplant (recipe follows)

Kosher salt and freshly ground black pepper

Toast the cumin seeds in a small pan over medium-high heat about 2 minutes, until the seeds release their aroma.

Using a mortar and pestle, pound the cumin, garlic, and a pinch of salt to a paste. Transfer to a medium bowl. Pound the cilantro and parsley in batches. As each batch of herbs is pounded to a paste, add it to the garlic mixture. Add the paprika and cayenne, and stir well. Put half the mixture in a large bowl or container for marinating the fish, and stir in ¼ cup olive oil. Gently toss the fish with the herb purée, cover, and refrigerate at least 4 hours.

Stir the remaining ½ cup plus 2 tablespoons olive oil into the remaining herb purée, and refrigerate.

Light the grill about 30 to 40 minutes before cooking.

Remove the fish from the refrigerator 30 minutes before cooking, to bring to room temperature. Skewer the chunks of fish, being careful that the pieces on each skewer are a similar thickness and not pressed together too tightly, so they will cook evenly.

Take the reserved charmoula out of the refrigerator and stir in the rice wine vinegar, lemon juice, and ½ teaspoon salt. Taste for balance and seasoning.

When the coals are broken down, red, and glowing, season the skewers of fish with salt and pepper. Grill the fish 3 to 4 minutes, rotating the skewers once, until you have nice color on the first side. Turn the fish over, and cook a few more minutes, until just cooked through. When it's done, the fish will begin to flake and separate a little; the center will still be slightly translucent. Remember, the fish will continue to cook a little more when you take it off the grill.

Scatter the arugula on a platter. Arrange the marinated peppers and eggplant and all their juices on top. Place the fish kabobs on the peppers and eggplant, and smear some of the charmoula over each kabob. Serve the remaining charmoula on the side.

marinated peppers and eggplant

4 pounds sweet peppers, in a variety of colors, excluding green

2 pounds small eggplants, Italian or Japanese (about 6)

½ to ⅔ cup extra-virgin olive oil

1 cup sliced red onion

1 teaspoon thyme leaves

2 cloves garlic, thinly sliced

3 tablespoons balsamic vinegar

3 tablespoons red wine vinegar

Kosher salt and freshly ground black pepper

Part of what makes these marinated peppers and eggplant so delicious is the involved process they go through to get to their seemingly simple final state. In her book, *The Zuni Cafe Cookbook*, Judy Rodgers suggests that the chef's eternal quest is to make the simplest process more difficult: "Stop, think, there must be a harder way," she writes. There are easier ways to make peppers and eggplant, but once you taste this version, it's hard to go back. If you like, make them the day before and let the vegetables marinate overnight.

Char the peppers on all sides on a medium-hot grill, or on the burners of a gas stove, or in the broiler, until all sides are just blackened (you want to char the skin of the peppers without burning the flesh underneath). Place the peppers in a large paper bag, close it tightly, and let them steam at least 15 minutes. (They sometimes leak, so put the closed bag on a plate.)

Meanwhile, cut the stems from the eggplants and discard. Like many vegetables, eggplants vary widely in size and shape, so you'll need to use your judgment as you cut them. The goal is to achieve pieces that are roughly the same size, around 2 inches long and ¼-inch thick, and that show off the natural curve of the eggplant. To begin, cut ¼-inch slices lengthwise. (Do not cut the eggplant into circles.) If your eggplants are very small, you may be able to stop after this lengthwise slicing. If they're larger, you'll need to cut them again. Place them flat on your cutting board and slice in half across the diagonal. When you're satisfied with your slices, score them shallowly on both sides with a knife (make a crosshatch of very shallow cuts to increase surface area), sprinkle each with ¼ tea-spoon salt, and let them sit 10 minutes. Use paper towels to blot the water that beads on their surfaces.

Heat a large sauté pan over high heat for 2 minutes. Swirl in 2 tablespoons olive oil, and wait 1 minute. Carefully place some of the eggplant in the pan. (The eggplant shouldn't be crowded; do this in batches or in two large pans.) Drizzle another tablespoon or two of olive oil into the pan, and cook 3 to 4 minutes, until golden brown. If the pan is smoking or the eggplant starts to burn, turn the heat down. Turn the eggplant over, and cook another 2 to 3 minutes, on the second side, until tender and golden. Remove the eggplant to a platter or baking sheet lined with paper towels. Continue until all the eggplant is cooked.

Open the bag of roasted peppers, and let them cool slightly. Peel each one carefully. Do not run them under water or you will lose all their delicious juices. Work over a strainer set in a bowl to catch the juices. Tear the peppers in half lengthwise, along their natural seam, and remove the seeds and membranes. Cut or tear the peppers into 1-inch-thick strips. Set them aside in the reserved juices.

Wipe out the eggplant pan, and return it to the stove over high heat for 2 minutes. Add 2 tablespoons olive oil, and sauté the red onion and thyme about 2 minutes. Add the garlic, cook a few more minutes, and then add the peppers and their juices to the pan. Season with 1 teaspoon salt and a pinch of pepper, and cook 6 to 8 minutes, stirring often, until the peppers have caramelized slightly.

Transfer the peppers and onions to a shallow nonaluminum dish. Add the two vinegars to the pan, and reduce by half over low heat. Turn off the heat, and swirl in 2 tablespoons olive oil. Use a rubber spatula to scrape the oil and vinegar over the peppers. Toss well to combine the flavors.

Gently toss the eggplant and peppers together and taste for seasoning.

plum tarte tatin with crème fraîche

3 pounds plums or pluots

8 tablespoons (1 stick) unsalted butter

1 cup plus 2 tablespoons granulated sugar

1 sheet frozen all-butter puff pastry

1 egg, beaten

1 cup crème fraîche

The first tarte Tatin was accidentally invented by the Tatin sisters in France, when their apple tart somehow went into the oven without its bottom crust. The sisters resourcefully placed the forgotten dough on top instead and let the tart finish baking. Once it was out of the oven, they inverted the tart to cover up their mistake. I'm sure they had no idea of the sensation that their sweet mishap would unleash.

Unable to leave well enough alone, pesky chefs like me love to play with variations on the classic caramelized upside-down apple tart. In this summer version, I've replaced the apples with plums. The plums give off more juice than apples, which makes working with them a little trickier. To compensate for this, I toss the plums in sugar to help draw out some of their juices and then cook them on the stove with butter and sugar, creating a delicious "plum caramel."

NOTE It's best to start this dessert early in the day or even a day in advance. It's not too difficult but there are a few steps that require time. The plums are first macerated for 30 minutes, and, since puff pastry is best when baked from very cold, I like to chill the caramelized plums for at least 2 hours before placing the pastry on top. Bake the tart a few hours before serving: I prefer tarte Tatin room temperature rather than right out of the oven.

Cut the plums in half and remove the pits. Toss the fruit with ¼ cup sugar and let sit for 30 minutes.

Heat a 10-inch cast-iron pan (or other heavy-bottomed pan that can go in the oven) over medium heat for 1 minute. Add the butter, and when it foams, add ¾ cup sugar. Cook about 6 minutes, swirling the pan often, until you have a deep brown caramel. Remove the pan from the heat and let it cool for 20 minutes.

Drain the plums and discard the liquid (or make a delicious cocktail!). Carefully arrange the plums, cut side down, in tight concentric circles in the pan (they should overlap slightly). Make sure to pack the plums in well, because they will shrink as they cook. The finished tart should be full of fruit.

Return the pan to the stove over medium-low heat. Cook the plums in the caramel without stirring for 20 minutes—the fruit will stew and simmer in its own juices. Allow to cool completely (for best results refrigerate for at least 2 hours).

When you are ready to bake the tart, preheat the oven to 375°F and take the puff pastry out of the freezer to thaw just enough so that it's malleable.

Cut an 11-inch circle from the pastry, pierce it in a few places with a fork, and place it on top of the plums. Brush the pastry with the beaten egg and sprinkle the remaining 2 tablespoons sugar over the top.

Bake the tart 45 to 55 minutes, until the pastry is deep golden brown and cooked through. Cool the tart on a rack for 30 minutes.

Choose a serving plate that is a few inches larger than the tart. Place the plate on top of the tart and, using two hands and two pot holders, carefully invert the tart onto the plate. You may have to adjust a few pieces of plum if they have fallen out of place.

Serve the tart with a bowl of crème fraîche.

sweet corn soup with avocado cream and cilantro

4 tablespoons unsalted butter

1 cup diced peeled Yukon Gold potato (¼-inch cubes)

1½ cups diced yellow onion

½ chile de árbol

1 tablespoon thyme leaves

4 cups fresh corn (from about 6 ears)

6 sprigs cilantro plus 18 cilantro leaves for garnish

½ jalapeño, seeded

½ large ripe avocado

⅓ cup crème fraîche

½ teaspoon lime juice

Kosher salt and freshly ground black pepper

At Lucques, we search out the heirloom varieties of corn, available all summer long from our local farmers' markets. This soup is spiced with jalapeño and cilantro and topped with avocado cream and lime. The key to its silky texture is blending it long enough at high speed and adding enough liquid to achieve the consistency of heavy cream. Although customers swear this rich soup must have cream in it, the only cream you'll find is in the topping that garnishes the soup: a delicious purée of avocado, crème fraîche, and lime juice.

Heat a large saucepan over medium heat for 1 minute. Add the butter, and when it foams, add the potato, onion, chile, and thyme. Reduce the heat to low, and cook about 10 minutes, until the onion is translucent and the potatoes release their starch and appear creamy.

Turn the heat to high, and add the corn, cilantro sprigs, the jalapeño, 1½ teaspoons salt, and some pepper. Stir to coat the corn in the butter, onion, and potato mixture. Pour 10 cups of water into the pot and bring to a boil, stirring occasionally. Turn the heat down to low, and simmer about 30 minutes, until the corn and potatoes are tender but not mushy.

Meanwhile, purée the avocado and crème fraîche in a food processor until smooth. Season with the lime juice, salt, and pepper to taste.

Strain the soup over a large bowl, and discard the chile de árbol. Put half the corn mixture into the blender with ½ cup of the liquid. (You will need to purée the soup in batches.) Process at the lowest speed until the corn is puréed. Then, pour in 1 cup of liquid. Turn the speed up to high, and pour in more liquid, a little at a time, until the soup has the consistency of heavy cream. Blend at least a minute, until the soup is completely smooth. Transfer to a container, and repeat with the second half of the soup. (You may not need all the liquid.) Taste the soup for balance and seasoning.

To serve family-style, put the soup in a warm tureen and scatter the cilantro leaves over the top. Serve the avocado cream on the side. Or serve in bowls and garnish each with a generous dollop of avocado cream and three cilantro leaves.

santa barbara spot prawns with tomato confit, garlic, and chile

Maine has lobster and Maryland has soft-shell crabs, but the prize shellfish of Southern California is the Santa Barbara spot prawn. Spot prawns have a softer texture than most shrimp and are best when cooked in their shells, heads on. As the shrimp shells caramelize in the pan, they leave behind crispy bits that infuse the sauce with a rich shellfish flavor. Besides, they're fun to eat out of the shell, and they make for a beautiful and dramatic presentation. Serve the spot prawns with salt and lemon and a big hunk of crusty bread. This is a messy feast, so choose guests who will enjoy participating in such a primal feeding frenzy.

NOTE If you can't find spot prawns, make this summer dish with another type of fresh prawn or large gulf shrimp sold in their shells.

You can make the yellow tomato confit in the morning. The rest of the cooking must be done at the last minute, but you can get all the slicing and herb-prepping done ahead, so that when it comes time to cook you'll be ready. The spot prawns should be cleaned right before they're cooked and not any earlier. When it comes to sautéing the prawns, for six people you'll need two or three sauté pans, or you can do them in batches. While cooking the shallots and tomatoes in one pan, you could be sautéing the last batch of prawns in the other.

24 large spot prawns (about 4½ pounds)

¾ cup extra-virgin olive oil

1½ cups sliced shallots

1 tablespoon thyme leaves

1 tablespoon thinly sliced chile de árbol

½ cup sliced garlic

1½ pints cherry tomatoes, cut in half

Yellow tomato confit (recipe follows)

¼ cup sliced flat-leaf parsley

1 tablespoon chopped oregano

2 tablespoons sliced green basil

2 tablespoons sliced opal basil

1 lemon, for juicing

Use kitchen scissors to cut the shells of the spot prawns down their backs, from the base of their heads to the tip of their tails. (Don't remove the shells.) If the prawns are wet, dry them with paper towels.

Heat two heavy-bottomed sauté pans over high heat for 3 to 4 minutes. Swirl 2 tablespoons olive oil into each pan, and carefully place the prawns in the pans, on their sides. (You will need to cook the prawns in batches to avoid overcrowding them.) Season each batch of prawns with ½ teaspoon salt and some pepper. Pour another 2 tablespoons oil into each pan, and cook about 5 minutes, until the shells get some color and the flesh begins to turn opaque on the first side.

Turn the prawns over, drizzle another 2 tablespoons oil into each pan, and season the second side of each batch with ½ teaspoon salt and some pepper. Cook another 3 minutes or so, until the prawns are just cooked. (You can peek inside the cut shell to see that the flesh is completely opaque.)

Remove the prawns to a platter, and turn the heat under both pans down to medium-low. Divide the shallots, thyme, and sliced chiles between the two pans. Season with ¼ teaspoon salt and some pepper. Cook 2 minutes, until the shallots are translucent, scraping the pan with a wooden spoon to release all the flavorful shrimp bits. Divide the garlic between the pans, and cook 3 to 4 minutes, stirring often, until the shallots and garlic are soft and just starting to color. Turn the heat back up to high, and add half the cherry tomatoes, ½ teaspoon salt, and lots of freshly ground black pepper to each pan. Taste for seasoning, and cook a minute, stirring often.

Spoon the hot yellow tomato confit onto a large warm platter.

Add half the prawns, sliced parsley, oregano, and the two basils to each pan, and roll the prawns in the cherry tomatoes to coat well. This final step is a little cumbersome but really helps coat the prawns in the cherry tomato sauce.

Arrange the prawns on the platter, and squeeze a generous amount of lemon juice over them. Spoon the remaining cherry tomato sauce over the top.

Serve with lots of crusty bread for sopping up the sauce and juices. The prawns would also be great with steamed rice or over pasta.

yellow tomato confit

NOTE The tomatoes need to fit snugly in the baking dish in one even layer. If there is too much room in the pan, the sauce will be thin and lose some of its intensity.

½ cup sliced red onion

2 dried chiles de árbol, broken in half with your hands

1 tablespoon sliced garlic

2 sprigs basil

2 sprigs oregano

1½ pounds yellow tomatoes

1 cup extra-virgin olive oil

Kosher salt and freshly ground black pepper

Preheat the oven to 400°F.

Scatter the red onion, chiles, garlic, and basil and oregano sprigs in a baking dish. Core the yellow tomatoes and place them, stem side down, on top of the onions. Sprinkle with 2 teaspoons salt, and pour the olive oil and 1 cup water over the tomatoes.

Cook the tomatoes in the oven about 50 minutes, until they soften and blister. Remove the pan from the oven, and let cool 10 minutes. Strain the tomatoes and onions over a bowl, saving the juice. Discard the herbs and half the chiles.

Transfer half the tomato mixture to a blender with ½ cup of the liquid. (You will need to purée in batches.) Process at the lowest speed until the tomatoes are puréed. Pour in more liquid, a little at a time, until the tomato confit is the consistency of heavy cream. Turn the speed up, and blend about a minute, until completely smooth. Transfer to a container, and repeat with the second half of the tomatoes. (You may not need all the liquid.) Season with ½ teaspoon salt and some pepper. Taste for seasoning.

bistecca california with peperonata, baked ricotta, and lemon

This dish was inspired by one of my favorite Italian meals, *bistecca fiorentina*, a huge, rare grilled steak dressed simply with salt and lemon juice. Instead of the traditional T-bone steak served in a Tuscan *ristorante*, I opted for tri-tip, a less expensive but super-flavorful cut from the triangular end of the sirloin, popular in the central coast region of California.

NOTE You can certainly substitute your favorite steak in this recipe, although the cooking time may be different. Marinate the meat the night before. You can set up the ricotta ahead of time and put it in the oven to bake when you light the grill. You can also make the peperonata ahead of time and heat it up just before serving.

Trim the beef of excess fat, leaving a ¼-inch-thick cap. Season with the rosemary, sliced chile, lemon zest, and cracked black pepper and refrigerate for at least 4 hours, preferably overnight.

Light the grill 30 to 40 minutes before cooking, and remove the tri-tip from the refrigerator to come to room temperature. After 10 minutes, season the meat with the *fleur de sel,* and drizzle it with the olive oil.

When the coals are broken down, red, and glowing, place the tri-tip, fat side down, on a relatively cool part of the grill, away from direct heat. (Because it's a larger piece of meat, you'll need to cook it slowly, so it's not charred on the outside and raw on the inside. Cook the steak over nondirect medium-low heat, to render the fat, get a nice crust, and cook it through evenly.) Cook about 15 minutes, rotating the meat to caramelize it well. Move the meat away from the flames if they flare up. Turn the tri-tip over, and cook another 10 minutes or so, until medium-rare. A meat thermometer inserted into the center of the tri-tip should read 120°F to 125°F.

Rest the steak on a wire rack set on a baking sheet for 8 to 10 minutes.

Spoon the hot peperonata onto a large warm platter and scatter the arugula over the top. Slice the steak against the grain, and arrange it over the peppers. Squeeze a generous amount of lemon juice over the steak, and drizzle it with a few tablespoons of super-good olive oil. Serve the gratin dish of baked ricotta on the side.

3 pounds prime beef tri-tip or steak of your choice

1 tablespoon chopped rosemary

1 teaspoon thinly sliced chiles de árbol

2 lemons, zested

1 tablespoon cracked black pepper

2 scant tablespoons *fleur de sel*

2 tablespoons extra-virgin olive oil

Peperonata (recipe follows)

1 bunch arugula, cleaned

2 to 3 tablespoons super-good extra-virgin olive oil

Baked ricotta (recipe follows)

peperonata

4 large sweet peppers (about 1¾ pounds)

5 tablespoons extra-virgin olive oil

3 cups sliced red onion

1 tablespoon thyme leaves

2 tablespoons salt-packed capers, soaked and drained

3 tablespoons red wine vinegar

2 tablespoons oregano leaves

Kosher salt and freshly ground black pepper

Cut the peppers in half lengthwise and remove the stems, seeds, and membranes. Thinly slice the peppers lengthwise. Heat a very large sauté pan over high heat for 2 minutes. (You may have to use two pans or do this in two batches to avoid overcrowding.) Swirl in 3 tablespoons olive oil and wait 1 minute. Add the onion, peppers, thyme, 1½ teaspoons salt, and ¼ teaspoon pepper. Sauté over high heat 5 to 6 minutes, tossing often, until the peppers soften. (They should still have a little crunch to them but be tender.)

Add the capers and remaining 2 tablespoons olive oil to the pan, cook another minute, and transfer the peppers to a shallow nonreactive dish. Turn the heat off, add the vinegar, and reduce by half. The residual heat should be enough to reduce this small amount of vinegar. Use a rubber spatula to scrape all the vinegar over the peppers. Add the oregano, and toss well to combine. The heat of the peppers will help release the flavor of the oregano. Taste for seasoning.

baked ricotta

3 cups fresh whole milk ricotta cheese (1⅓ pounds)

6 tablespoons extra-virgin olive oil

1½ teaspoons thyme leaves

1 tablespoon chopped flat-leaf parsley

¼ teaspoon diagonally sliced chile de árbol

Kosher salt and freshly ground black pepper

I like this baked ricotta warm and slightly underbaked to a soft, creamy consistency. Avoid the grainy, flavorless, commercial ricottas from the supermarket, and seek out a fresh, artisanal version. Bake the cheese in a Spanish-style cazuela or small attractive casserole and serve it at the table so your guests can help themselves.

Preheat the oven to 400°F.

Place the ricotta in a large bowl, and stir in 5 tablespoons olive oil, 1 teaspoon thyme, the chopped parsley, ½ teaspoon salt, and ¼ teaspoon pepper.

Transfer the ricotta to an 8-inch gratin dish or cazuela. Gently press the top of the cheese with your fingers to make slight indentations, and decorate the ricotta with the remaining ½ teaspoon thyme and the sliced chile. Drizzle the remaining tablespoon olive oil over the top, and bake 30 to 40 minutes, until golden brown on top.

ode to hadley's: date shake with candied walnut wedge

This recipe is in honor of Hadley Fruit Orchards, a legendary stop on the way to Palm Springs where "ice cold date shakes" have been soothing weary and over-heated drivers on Route 10 for years.

10 large Medjool dates
  (¼ pound), pitted

1 cup whole milk

10 ice cubes

1 pint vanilla ice cream
  (see page 113)

Candied walnut wedge
  (recipe follows)

Place the dates in a blender with the milk. Purée 20 seconds or so, until combined. Add the ice cubes, and blend for another 10 seconds. Add the ice cream, and blend until just combined. Don't blend for too long or all the ice cream will melt. Serve in glasses, with slices of walnut wedge. You can keep the shake in the blender in the freezer for up to 15 minutes.

candied walnut wedge

Pastry chef Kimberly Sklar came up with this walnut wedge as the ultimate accompaniment to the thick, creamy date shake. It tastes like the best part of a perfectly made pecan pie—toasty crisp nuts suspended in a chewy, buttery caramel. Since this "pie" doesn't have a crust, make sure to bake it long enough that it holds its shape when you slice it.

3 tablespoons unsalted butter,
  plus more to butter pan

1¼ cups coarsely chopped
  walnuts

1½ cups walnut halves

½ vanilla bean

3 tablespoons brown sugar

3 tablespoons granulated sugar

2 tablespoons dark rum

6 tablespoons light corn syrup

1 extra-large egg yolk

1 extra-large egg

Preheat the oven to 375°F.

Butter the bottom and sides of a 9-inch springform pan, and line the bottom with parchment paper. Close the latch, and place the pan on a large sheet of aluminum foil. Fold the foil up around the sides of the pan to prevent the filling from leaking out while the walnut wedge bakes. Place the pan on a baking sheet.

Toast the chopped walnuts and walnut halves separately on a baking sheet, about 8 minutes, until they've browned slightly and smell nutty.

Place 3 tablespoons butter in a small sauté pan. Split the vanilla bean lengthwise, and use a paring knife to scrape out the pulp and seeds onto the butter. To make sure not to lose any of the precious seeds, run your vanilla-coated knife through the butter. Add the vanilla pod to the pan, and cook the butter and vanilla over medium heat, swirling the pan a few times, until the butter browns and smells nutty.

In a stand mixer fitted with the whisk attachment, beat the sugars, rum, and corn syrup at medium speed 4 to 5 minutes. Add the warm brown butter, and mix another 2 to 3 minutes to incorporate. Add the egg and yolk, and continue to mix at medium speed another minute or two.

Spread the chopped walnuts in an even layer in the prepared pan. Place the walnut halves in concentric circles over the chopped walnuts. Pour the filling evenly over the nuts, and bake about 40 minutes, until the nuts are caramel-colored and the filling is set.

Let cool about 30 minutes. Remove from the pan, and cut into wedges.

tomato tart with capers, anchovies, and caramelized onions

This tart has all the boisterous Mediterranean flavors of pasta puttanesca: tomatoes, anchovies, capers, and olives layered on puff pastry and caramelized onions. Make a tapestry of red, yellow, and orange by layering different-colored heirloom tomato slices over the onions. Though I usually want to put cheese on everything, this tart doesn't need it. The tomatoes are the stars, so let them shine.

NOTE You can caramelize the onions ahead if you like.

Heat a large sauté pan or Dutch oven over high heat for 2 minutes. Swirl in 3 tablespoons olive oil, and add the onions, 2 teaspoons thyme, 1 teaspoon salt, and some pepper. Cook 10 minutes, stirring often. Turn the heat down to medium, add the butter, and cook 15 minutes, stirring often and scraping the bottom of the pan with a wooden spoon, until the onions are a deep golden brown. Let cool completely before you make the tart, so they don't melt the pastry.

Preheat the oven to 400°F.

Place the defrosted puff pastry on a parchment-lined baking sheet. Use a paring knife to score an ⅛-inch-thick border around the edge of the pastry. Whisk together the egg yolk and 1 teaspoon water. Brush the border with the egg wash. Spread the caramelized onions evenly within the border.

Core the heirloom tomatoes. Hold each tomato on its side and slice it into ¼-inch-thick round slices. Place the tomato slices, just touching but not overlapping, on top of the caramelized onions (there will be some onion peeking through). If necessary, cut some of the tomato slices in half so they fit, placing the cut side of the slices flush with the border. Season the tomatoes with ¼ teaspoon salt and a few grindings of black pepper.

Slice the anchovies thinly on the diagonal.

Arrange the anchovies, capers, and olives over the tomatoes and onions. Sprinkle the remaining teaspoon of thyme over the tart.

Bake the tart 10 minutes. Turn the sheet pan, and bake another 10 to 12 minutes, until the crust is deep golden brown.

3 tablespoons extra-virgin olive oil

6 cups thinly sliced onions (about 1½ pounds)

1 tablespoon thyme leaves

1 tablespoon unsalted butter

1 sheet frozen all-butter puff pastry

1 extra-large egg yolk

3 medium heirloom tomatoes (about 1½ pounds), mixed colors

3 or 4 salt-packed anchovy fillets, rinsed, bones removed

2 teaspoons salt-packed capers, soaked and drained

¼ cup Niçoise olives, pitted, cut in half

½ pint cherry tomatoes, cut in half

1 tablespoon finely diced shallot

1 tablespoon super-good extra-virgin olive oil

½ lemon, for juicing

1 bunch arugula, cleaned and dried

½ cup flat-leaf parsley leaves

¼ cup small basil leaves, preferably green and opal

¼ cup ½-inch-snipped chives

Kosher salt and freshly ground black pepper

Just before serving, place the cherry tomatoes and diced shallot in a bowl, and season them with ¼ teaspoon salt and a few grindings of black pepper. Drizzle the super-good olive oil over the tomatoes, squeeze in a little lemon juice, and toss together. Add the arugula and herbs and toss well. Taste for seasoning. Cut the tart into six wedges, and place on six plates. Arrange some of the cherry tomato–herb salad next to each wedge of tart.

spaghetti with heirloom tomatoes, basil, and bottarga breadcrumbs

This is the dish to make in the middle of the summer when heirloom tomatoes are everywhere. I can think of few more satisfying things to eat. Bottarga, considered the caviar of Sicily, is a delicacy made by drying tuna or mullet roe in the sun until it forms a dense, rust-colored block. Here, it's shaved and tossed into the pasta, adding a deep oceany essence and salty-savory contrast to the sweet summer tomatoes.

NOTE I like to cook the noodles in the sauce for at least a few minutes. The pasta gets nicely glazed and coated with the sauce and the flavors have a chance to meld. Also, I have made this dish many times without the bottarga—it's delicious both ways.

Preheat the oven to 375°F.

Put a large pot of heavily salted water on to boil over high heat.

Toss the breadcrumbs with 2 tablespoons olive oil, spread them on a baking sheet, and toast 8 to 10 minutes, stirring once or twice, until golden brown.

Heat a large sauté pan over high heat for 2 minutes. Pour in the remaining ¼ cup olive oil, and add the rosemary and crumbled chiles. Let them sizzle in the oil a minute or so, and then add the sliced onion and thyme. Season with 1 teaspoon salt and some pepper. Turn the heat down to medium, and cook 3 minutes, stirring often. Stir in the garlic, and cook another 3 to 4 minutes, until the onion is translucent and starting to color slightly.

Drop the pasta in the boiling water.

Turn the heat under the onions back up to high, and add the tomatoes to the pan with 1 teaspoon salt and some freshly ground black pepper. Stir the tomatoes often, and cook about 8 minutes, until their juices are released and start to reduce.

When the pasta is al dente, drain it and add it to the tomatoes. Toss well, add the butter, and cook 3 to 4 minutes, to reduce the juices so they coat the noodles well. Season with ½ teaspoon salt and taste. Add the basil, parsley, and half the bottarga to the pan, and toss to combine. Transfer to a large warm pasta bowl or platter. Shower the breadcrumbs over the pasta, and scatter the remaining bottarga shavings on top.

1½ cups fresh breadcrumbs

¼ cup plus 2 tablespoons extra-virgin olive oil

½ sprig rosemary

2 chiles de árbol, crumbled with your hands

2 cups sliced red onion

1 tablespoon thyme leaves

¼ cup sliced garlic

1 pound spaghetti

2 pounds very ripe heirloom tomatoes, chopped

4 tablespoons unsalted butter

½ cup sliced basil

¼ cup sliced flat-leaf parsley

Small chunk bottarga di tonno, shaved or thinly sliced to equal ¼ to ½ cup

Kosher salt and freshly ground black pepper

lamb osso buco with shell bean ragoût, haricots verts, and tapenade

6 pounds lamb osso buco

6 cloves garlic, smashed

Zest of 1 lemon

1 tablespoon thyme leaves plus 4 whole thyme sprigs

2 tablespoons rosemary leaves

1 tablespoon cracked black pepper

5 tablespoons extra-virgin olive oil

1 cup diced onion

½ cup diced fennel

¼ cup diced carrot

2 bay leaves, preferably fresh

2 cups dry white wine

2½ cups chicken stock

2½ cups veal stock

4 flat-leaf parsley sprigs

Haricots verts and fresh shell bean ragoût (recipe follows)

Tapenade (recipe follows)

Kosher salt

This was one of our first Sunday suppers at Lucques. It's a variation on the classic osso buco, which is traditionally made with veal shanks. I use the same technique, but for this lighter summer version I braise the lamb shanks in white wine and a combination of veal and chicken stock (as opposed to straight veal stock). The tender shanks are a rich counterpoint to the freshness of the shell beans and crunch of the haricots verts. Ask your butcher for lamb osso buco, but if you can't find it you can use lamb shanks.

NOTE You can braise the lamb a day or even two before serving. Just remember to marinate it one day before you braise. You can also cook the shell beans and blanch the haricots verts in advance; just wait to sauté them for the ragoût until right before serving. The tapenade can be made a few hours ahead as well.

Toss the lamb osso buco in a large bowl with the crushed garlic, lemon zest, thyme leaves, rosemary leaves, cracked black pepper, and 2 tablespoons olive oil. Cover, and refrigerate overnight.

Remove the lamb from the refrigerator 1 hour before cooking so it comes to room temperature. After 30 minutes, season the meat generously with salt. Reserve the garlic and any excess herbs that fall off the lamb.

Preheat the oven to 325°F.

Heat a large Dutch oven over high heat for 3 minutes. Pour in the remaining 3 tablespoons olive oil and wait a minute or two, until the pan is very hot, almost smoking. Place the osso buco in the pan, and sear on all sides until nicely browned. Depending on the size of your pan, you might have to sear the meat in batches. (Do not crowd the meat or get lazy or rushed at this step. It's very important that the meat sear to a deep golden brown on all sides. This will probably take a good 15 to 20 minutes.) When the shanks are nicely browned, transfer them to a braising pan. They should sit flat, bones standing up, in one layer.

Turn the heat under the Dutch oven down to medium, and add the onion, fennel, carrot, thyme sprigs, bay leaves, and reserved garlic and herbs. Stir often with a wooden spoon, scraping up all the crusty bits in the pan. Cook 6 to 8 minutes, until the vegetables just begin to caramelize. Add the white wine, turn the heat to high, and reduce the liquid by half.

Add the stocks and bring to a boil. Pour the liquid over the shanks, scraping any of the vegetables that have fallen on the meat back into the liquid. The stock mixture should almost cover the meat. Tuck the parsley sprigs into the broth around the lamb. Cover tightly with plastic wrap (yes, it can go in the oven), aluminum foil, and a tight-fitting lid, if you have one. Braise in the oven for 2½ to 3 hours.

To check the lamb for doneness, carefully remove the plastic and foil and pierce a piece of meat with a paring knife. When the meat is done, it will yield easily to the knife. Taste a piece if you're not sure.

Turn the oven up to 400°F.

Carefully transfer the lamb osso buco to a baking sheet and return them to the oven to brown for 10 to 15 minutes.

Strain the broth into a saucepan, pressing down on the vegetables with a ladle to extract all their juices. Skim the fat from the braising juices. If necessary, reduce the broth over medium-high heat to thicken slightly. Taste for seasoning.

Arrange the hot haricots verts and fresh shell bean ragoût on a large warm platter. Place the lamb osso buco over the beans, and spoon lots of the braising juices over them. Spoon some tapenade over each lamb shank, and serve the rest at the table.

haricots verts and fresh shell bean ragoût

I like to use a variety of shell beans for this dish. Because of their different sizes and shapes, cook each type of bean separately, dividing the other ingredients as necessary. You may need a little more oil if you have many varieties of beans. The starchy liquid from cooking the beans is delicious in the ragoût.

¼ to ½ cup extra-virgin olive oil

¼ cup finely diced onion

2 teaspoons minced garlic

1 tablespoon thyme leaves

3 cups fresh shell beans, such as flageolets, black beans, black-eyed peas, limas, or cranberry beans

½ pound haricots verts, stems removed, tails left on

2 tablespoons finely diced shallot

2 tablespoons sliced opal basil

2 tablespoons chopped flat-leaf parsley

Kosher salt and freshly ground black pepper

to cook fresh shell beans For each type of bean, heat a small or medium saucepan over medium heat for 2 minutes. Swirl 2 tablespoons olive oil into each pan and divide the onion, garlic, and 2 teaspoons thyme between them. Sauté over medium heat about 5 minutes, until the onion is translucent. Add the shell beans (again, cooking each variety separately), and cook a few minutes, stirring to coat them in the oil. Add salt and water to cover by 2 inches. Simmer 10 to 15 minutes, until the beans are just tender. (The cooking time will really depend on the beans. Taste one to see if it's done.) Remove from the heat, and cool the beans in the cooking liquid.

to make the ragoût   While the beans are cooking, blanch the haricots verts in a large pot of salted boiling water 2 to 3 minutes, until tender but still al dente. Transfer the haricots verts to a baking sheet to cool.

Drain the shell beans, reserving their cooking liquid.

Heat a large sauté pan over high heat for 1 minute. Swirl in 2 tablespoons olive oil, and add the haricots verts, diced shallot, and remaining 1 teaspoon thyme to the pan. Season with ¼ teaspoon salt and some pepper. Cook 3 to 4 minutes, tossing to coat the haricots verts in the shallot mixture. Add the shell beans, and stir gently, being careful not to crush the beans. Add about ½ cup (or a little more if you like) shell bean liquid to moisten the ragoût. Taste for seasoning, and cook a few minutes, until the beans are hot. Toss in the basil and chopped parsley at the last minute.

tapenade

¾ cup pitted Niçoise olives

1 small clove garlic

1 salt-packed anchovy, rinsed, bones removed

2 teaspoons salt-packed capers, rinsed, drained, and coarsely chopped

1 tablespoon chopped flat-leaf parsley

¼ cup extra-virgin olive oil

½ lemon, for juicing

Chop two-thirds of the olives coarsely, and chop the remaining third finely.

Using a mortar and pestle, pound the garlic, anchovy, and half the capers to a paste. Stir in the olives, remaining capers, parsley, and olive oil. Season with a squeeze of lemon, to taste.

fig-and-almond custard tart

Figs and almonds—a classic pairing. For this tart, I cut the figs into quarters and sauté them with sugar, butter, and vanilla for a jammy texture. Then I pour the super-easy custard base into a baked pâte sucrée crust with the caramelized figs, and bake until the top is slightly browned. Be sure to bake the crust completely before filling it, to ensure it stays crisp. Although this tart is so very French, it reminds me just a little bit of all-American Fig Newtons.

1 recipe pâte sucrée
  (recipe follows)
½ cup raw almonds
24 black mission figs
2 tablespoons unsalted butter
½ vanilla bean
6 tablespoons granulated sugar
2 extra-large eggs
1 cup heavy cream
1 teaspoon pure vanilla extract
1 tablespoon cognac
Kosher salt

Preheat the oven to 400°F.

Line a 10-inch fluted tart pan with the pâte sucrée according to the instructions on page 196. Prick the bottom with a fork, and line it with a few coffee filters opened out or a piece of parchment paper. Fill the lined tart shell with beans or pie weights, and bake 15 minutes, until set. Take the tart out of the oven, and carefully lift out the paper and beans. Return the tart to the oven, and bake another 10 to 15 minutes, until the crust is an even golden brown. Set aside on a rack to cool completely.

Meanwhile, spread the almonds on a baking sheet, and toast 8 to 10 minutes, stirring a couple times, until they are golden brown and smell nutty. When the almonds have cooled, chop them finely.

Remove the stems from the figs, and cut the figs into quarters.

Place the butter on a small plate. Slice the vanilla bean in half lengthwise, and use a paring knife to scrape the seeds and pulp onto the butter. To make sure not to lose any of the precious seeds, run your vanilla-coated knife through the butter. Heat a large sauté pan over high heat for 2 minutes. Add the butter, and when it foams, add 2 tablespoons sugar and the vanilla pod. Swirl the pan, and when the sugar has dissolved, add the figs. Season with a pinch of salt, and cook, tossing often, 2 to 3 minutes, until the figs soften slightly and are coated in the caramelizing sugar and butter. Place the figs and all the caramelized juices in the tart shell (use a rubber spatula to make sure you get all the good stuff).

Whisk together the eggs, remaining ¼ cup sugar, the cream, vanilla extract, cognac, and a pinch of salt. Add the almonds, and pour the mixture over the figs.

Bake about 30 minutes, until the custard puffs up and the tart is golden brown on top.

Serve alone, with whipped cream, vanilla ice cream (see page 113), or almond ice cream (see pages 94–95).

pâte sucrée

¼ cup heavy cream

2 extra-large egg yolks

2¾ cups plus 2 tablespoons all-purpose flour

¼ cup plus 3 tablespoons granulated sugar

¼ teaspoon kosher salt

½ pound unsalted butter

Whisk the cream and egg yolks together in a small bowl.

In a stand mixer fitted with the dough hook, combine the flour, sugar, salt, and butter on medium speed until you have a coarse meal. Gradually add the cream and yolks, and mix until just combined. Do not overwork the dough. Transfer the dough to a large work surface and bring it together with your hands to incorporate completely. Divide the dough in half, shape into 1-inch-thick discs, and wrap one of them to freeze and use later.

If the dough is too soft, put in the refrigerator for 5 to 10 minutes to firm up a little. If the dough is manageable, place it on a lightly floured work surface, sprinkle a little flour over the dough, and roll it out into a ¼-inch-thick circle, flouring as necessary. Starting at one side, roll and wrap the dough around the rolling pin to pick it up. Unroll the dough over a 10-inch tart pan. Gently fit the dough loosely into the pan, lifting the edges and pressing the dough into the corners with your fingers. To remove the excess dough, roll the rolling pin lightly over the top of the tart pan for a nice clean edge, or work your way around the edge pinching off any excess dough with your fingers. Chill for 1 hour.

fall

While living in Providence, Rhode Island, as a college student, I was fortunate to experience an eastern fall, memorable for the spectrum of colors and the gusto with which locals celebrate the season before bearing down for the winter. To this day, even when it's 80 degrees in Los Angeles, I find myself reminiscing about autumn back east and the walks I would take through the streets of Providence, energized by the cold breeze, awestruck by those crazy-colored trees and the earthy smell of leaves all around me.

Here on the West Coast, I get my autumn fix by strolling through the farmers' market. We may not have psychedelic trees dotting our ocean-meets-desert landscape, but we do have at our fingertips the most incredible selection of fall produce.

As the summer crops begin to wane, the curious varieties of winter squash, sugary sweet potatoes, earthy wild mushrooms, and tiny Brussels sprouts take center stage. Stone fruits disappear, making way for heirloom apples, perfumed quince, and juicy pears.

This new assortment of ingredients, and the accompanying change in weather, means it's time to reassess your cooking techniques and presentation as well as the dishes you prepare. In the fall, Sunday suppers transition to robust, hearty menus, with recipes that require longer cooking times. Stewing, braising, and confiting are techniques that come to the forefront this time of year, and stay with us through winter. Though these techniques may seem more complicated in the beginning, the truth is most of your work is done once your pot is in the oven. Give a fatty or tougher cut of meat a long, slow braise and the result is almost always tender and luscious. And the best part of all is that the rich, savory sauce is already in the pan. I don't abandon the grill just yet either: I simply substitute heartier fare like duck, quail, and tuna. Certain fall vegetables also benefit from longer cooking times. I roast root vegetables with olive oil and herbs, and pan-braise Brussels sprouts with pancetta and balsamic vinegar.

Fall salads are more substantial than their spring and summer counterparts, and I often serve them warm. For one, I roast Kabocha squash and toss it with warm bacon and dandelion greens. For another, I sauté pears until they are caramelized and serve them with endive, hazelnuts, and a creamy blue cheese. And for a crunchy, refreshing salad, I slice crisp apples and Asian pears and toss them with radicchio and buttermilk dressing.

I think autumn calls for desserts that are especially indulgent, which means more brown butter, more nuts, and, of course, more chocolate. I also like to play with tradition. I know everyone loves pumpkin pie, but I have a hunch my "Pumpkin" Cake with Pecan Streusel and Maple Ice Cream might just sneak its way onto your Thanksgiving menu. And nothing would please me more.

fall market

apples

The everyday apple, once considered prosaic, is back in vogue. Farmers across the country have revived many heirloom varieties, and suddenly there's an incredible array to choose from. Some of my favorites for eating raw are Ashmead's Kernel, Spitzenberg, Braeburn, and Gernes Red Acre. For cooking, I prefer Smokehouse, Arkansas Black, Calville Blanc, and Pink Pearl. In general, the softer, sweeter varieties are better for cooking and baking, whereas firm, crisp, juicy apples are best for eating out of hand or sliced into salads.

In most places, apple picking begins around Labor Day, ending when the first frost hits. Apples are best stored in a cold place so they don't continue to ripen.

asian pears

Asian pears fall somewhere between an apple and a standard European pear in flavor. The flesh is super-crisp and juicy with a low acid content and an exotic perfume. Some of the types grown by local farmers here in California are Hosui, Shinseiki, Kosui, and Ya Li. Most Asian pears have the shape of an apple with dull, russeted skin. Some are yellow, while others tend toward deep greens and pale browns. I like them best raw, either eaten out of hand or sliced into salads.

To find the sweetest and crunchiest Asian pears, you need to taste them. Unlike regular pears, which should yield to the touch, Asian pears should be very firm.

broccoli and rapini

My favorite broccolis are the sweeter, crunchier Italian varieties sold as baby broccoli, Italian broccoli, or sprouting broccoli. Unlike the familiar head broccoli, these Italian varieties have long, slender, leafy stalks with tiny, compact florets. The recently available hybrid called asparation or broccolini is a good substitute for these Italian varieties.

Rapini, also called broccoli rabe, may look like Italian broccoli but has an assertive, spicy, and bitter flavor. I usually prepare rapini by sautéing it in olive oil with shallots, garlic, and red chile. You can use rapini in recipes that call for Italian broccoli, as long as you realize it will be spicier and a little bitter (in a good way).

Choose bright, perky stalks with unwilted leaves. Before cooking Italian broccoli or rapini, trim the ends if they're tough and fibrous.

brussels sprouts

Brussels sprouts grow on strong, bulky stalks up to 3 feet tall. They are best in fall and winter, when moist, cool air promotes growth. It's no surprise they're a member of the cabbage family; when you cut one in half, the small, compact head reveals layers and layers of leaves that look just like a mini-cabbage. Once cooked, Brussels sprouts have a complex flavor, both sweet and bitter.

As with so many vegetables, Brussels sprouts benefit from the contrast of textures achieved through searing and braising, resulting in a crisp, golden brown exterior and tender interior. Of course, they're fine the old-fashioned way—steamed and served with butter—but once you've tasted them pan-braised with pancetta and balsamic vinegar, it's hard to go back.

Choose firm, tightly closed sprouts that aren't discolored. Try not to store Brussels sprouts for more than a few days in the refrigerator, or they will lose their sweetness and become bitter. Wash them well and trim the stem ends before cooking.

cavolo nero

Cavolo nero won my heart many years back, when a local farmer, Bill Coleman, got his hands on the seeds in Italy and began growing it here in Southern California. A member of the cabbage family, this dark leafy green is also known as Tuscan kale, black kale, lacinato kale, or flat black cabbage. Today, you can find this earthy, crinkly-leafed green at many good markets. Its chewy-textured leaves absorb the flavors of whatever it's cooking in. I love it long-cooked with onions, garlic, and chile, or stir-fried with farro or other grains. It also works well with winter squashes and sweet potatoes.

Choose unwilted, lively bunches, and remove the tough center rib before cooking.

chicories

The chicory family includes a wide variety of greens often used for salads, such as radicchio, endive, and frisée. Belgian endive is a bullet-shaped cluster of pale, almost white, pointed leaves that are grown in the dark to keep them from turning green. It is delicious in salads, grilled, or braised. Its lettucelike sibling escarole has a crunchy texture with a slightly bitter note, which offers a refreshing change when used in place of romaine for a Caesar salad. It's also wonderful added to soups, or simply sautéed with shallots, garlic, and rosemary. Delicate, curly-leafed frisée (think frizzy) is great uncooked or just wilted, adding lift and texture when combined with other salad greens.

The most common red chicory is radicchio, a small cabbagelike head with burgundy-and-white leaves. Treviso is an elongated, slightly more bitter relative of radicchio. Both are delicious torn into a salad or grilled until smoky and rich. When dressing these red chicories, I like to use something sweet such as balsamic vinegar or saba (reduced grape must), or something assertive, like mustard or anchovies, to counter the bitterness.

dates

In the fall, fresh dates come to the Santa Monica Farmers' Market, clinging to their primitive-looking stems. These young, golden dates are firm and crunchy with a nutty flavor, completely different in flavor and texture from their sugary and moist aged incarnation. Aged or dried dates come in a variety of types, each with its own characteristics. Medjool dates are on the larger side, with moist, gooey flesh and a taste reminiscent of brown sugar. The more unusual Barhi dates are small, round, and plump with a super-soft, jellylike texture. Deglet Noor are semi-dried, chewy, and not too sweet. Their firm texture makes them an excellent choice for slicing into salads and relishes.

Even when dates have been dried, their freshness really matters. If you can't buy dates from local farmers, seek out a busy ethnic store, where they're less likely to have been sitting on the shelf too long. Better yet, a

Bill Coleman's stand at the Santa Monica market

couple of our local farmers sell their dates online (see Sources).

grapes

Grapes arrive at the market around mid-to-late summer and continue throughout fall. When shopping for grapes, don't go to the market looking for a specific type, but instead taste what's available and choose the juiciest and most flavorful. Some of my favorites are Autumn Royals and Flame Seedless. Concord grapes have their own appeal, with intense flavor, deep purple color, and thick skin. Besides the obvious—eating them right off the stem—I like to add grapes to a salad of fall fruit, or crush them into a salsa to spoon over grilled fish. As we get deeper into fall, I roast clusters of grapes, still on the stem, to serve with grilled duck or an onion-and-blue-cheese tart.

Look for organically grown grapes that are plump, firm, and succulent.

mustard greens

These peppery cooking greens range in size, color, heat (spiciness), and tenderness. I use the curly-edged mustard greens as well as the more delicate-tasting purple-leafed Japanese variety. Sautéed greens are a welcome addition to many savory dishes, providing a fresh, lively counterpoint to richer ingredients. Think of serving them with braised meats, roasted vegetables, and pasta dishes. The heartier, more mature greens require longer cooking; if the greens seem particularly tough, you'll need to blanch them before sautéing. Sometimes the purple variety is so tender I don't bother cooking it at all. Instead, I place the greens under a piece of grilled fish or meat, letting them wilt slightly from the heat. Tender baby mustard greens are also delicious in salads tossed with a mustard vinaigrette.

As you would with any green, choose unwilted, perky bunches. Discard yellowed leaves, and wash the greens as you would lettuces, letting them soak in a bowl or sink full of water, allowing the sand to fall to the bottom.

pears

Since pears are picked firm and bruise easily, it's hard to come by a perfect ripe pear. Unripe pears require some coddling and attention, so bring them home to ripen on your kitchen counter. Handle them gently, checking them every day, and when they begin to soften slightly and yield to the touch near the stem, eat them right away. To speed up the ripening process, store pears in a brown paper bag until ready to eat.

Bartletts are the most common pear grown in the United States, but, as with apples, there are many varieties in the pear family. I love the buttery Comice, sweet and juicy and balanced with just enough acid. French Butter pears and D'Anjou are also good choices. When perfectly ripe, pears should be eaten out of hand or served very simply, in a salad or with cheese (also perfectly ripe, of course!). Pears are a little more forgiving when cooked, so if they're underripe it's best to sauté, roast, or poach them.

pomegranates

When I was a kid, we used to eat pomegranates with a needle, carefully extracting each tiny kernel out of its hard red skin. Like persimmons, they grew in my neighborhood, dangling off scraggly, leaf-barren trees. Their flavor is intense—the seed adds a subtle bitter counterpoint to the astringent yet sweet juice. Pomegranate juice can be used in salad dressings as a bright alternative to vinegar or lemon juice. A pomegranate vinaigrette is particularly delicious with a salad of arugula, persimmons, and pomegranates. When you get in the habit of using pomegranates, you'll find they're very versatile. Their sweet crunch goes well with many

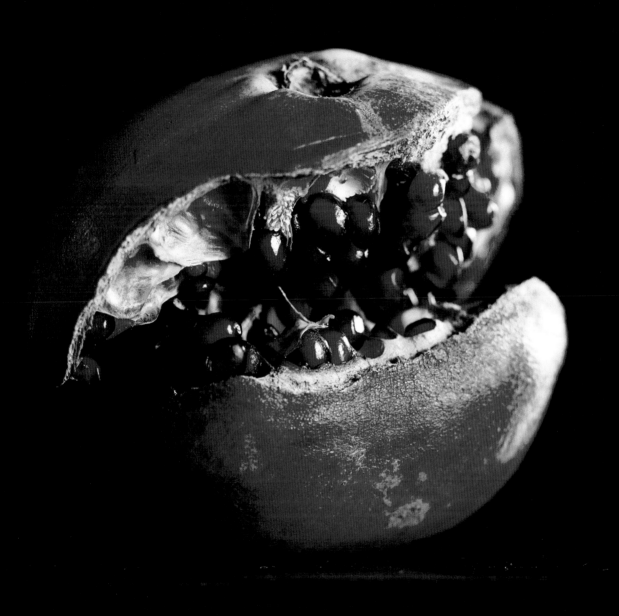

foods, and this time of year I find myself scattering the seeds over salads, antipastos, and even grilled fish. Pomegranate molasses, available in Middle Eastern markets, is a deep burgundy condiment made from concentrated pomegranate juice and sugar. Used sparingly, the sweet-sour syrup is an exotic addition to pomegranate salsas and is also intriguing with braised meats.

Pomegranates aren't an instant-gratification fruit; they take a little work. To juice a pomegranate, use your thumbs to press and soften the skin all the way around the entire fruit. Next, insert a paring knife halfway into the side of the pomegranate to make a small hole. Hold the fruit over a bowl with the hole facing down, and squeeze firmly to extract the juice, which will come running out. To take out the seeds, it's best not to cut the fruit in half or you'll lose precious seeds and juices. Instead, insert a chef's knife about an inch into the top of the pomegranate, and turn the knife slightly to crack the fruit open. Pull the pomegranate apart with your hands, separating it into naturally occurring sections. Then pick the seeds out with your fingers.

Pomegranates are in season starting in early fall and ending in early winter. Look for pomegranates that are heavy in your hand and have supple, not-too-dry skin.

quince

These old-fashioned fruit can fill a room with their tropical aroma. Although closely related to apples and pears, the knobby, fuzzy, and oddly shaped quince must be cooked before it's eaten. A bite of raw quince is extremely astringent and unpleasant.

Quince are delicious poached, roasted, or sautéed and pair well with apples and pears. Before cooking, peel the quince and remove their cores. North African cooks often add quince to their braised meat tagines. The Spanish and Italians cook them into a paste called *membrillo* in Spanish or *cotognata* in Italian. To make this sweet, aromatic condiment, cook the fruit down for hours, until

it thickens and turns a pinkish orange color. When it cools it sets into a dense jellylike consistency.

Quince can be hard to find; sometimes your best option, besides the farmers' market, is to keep an eye out for a tree in your neighborhood. When you do find them, pick extra and store them for up to a month in the refrigerator. Choose firm, golden-colored, fragrant quince.

sweet potatoes

Despite their name, these moist-fleshed, sweet tubers are not related to potatoes. There are many varieties, ranging in color and texture, but when we say "sweet potato" in the United States, we usually mean the orange-fleshed Garnet and Jewel varieties. They are delicious steamed, baked, or roasted. I usually peel them, cut them into chunks, toss them with brown butter and sage, and roast them in the oven to caramelize. The crispy outer texture and soft interior are an irresistible combination. Because of their inherent sweetness, sweet potatoes work well with salty ingredients, like bacon, as well as with spicy elements, such as the Catalan sauce romesco.

Look for sweet potatoes that are firm, avoiding ones that are bruised, scarred, or sprouting. Store them on the counter or in a cool cupboard, not in the refrigerator.

wild mushrooms

Wild mushrooms come in a variety of colors, shapes, and sizes. Some of my favorites are chanterelles, morels, white trumpet, black trumpet, and of course cêpes or porcini. When I come across an especially beautiful crop of wild mushrooms, I sauté them to make a warm salad with soft herbs, or a savory tart with Gruyère and puff pastry. Their earthy flavor and meaty texture give depth and richness to vegetarian pastas and ragoûts as well as poultry, meat, and fish dishes.

Explaining how to cook mushrooms can be tricky,

winter squash

In October, a multitude of winter squash arrive at the markets. Besides the familiar acorn and butternut, you'll find Moroccan, Tahitian, Delicata, and Turban squash, as well as my personal favorite, Kabocha. The velvety deep-orange-fleshed Kabocha is a Japanese variety that has a dense meaty texture and intense flavor. Normally, Kabocha are a deep sea green color on the outside, but if you happen to see an orange-skinned Kabocha, buy it. They're prized by the Japanese and in my experience have always been outstanding. My other favorite squash is the sweet Blue Hubbard. It's never watery or fibrous, and it holds its shape when cooked. Hubbards have an elegant robin's egg blue exterior and are cultivated mostly on the East Coast. Don't think of squash just as a side dish; I love to purée it into soups or serve it in warm salads or even as part of an antipasto. To roast squash, peel it, cut it into wedges, toss it with olive oil or brown butter, and cook in a hot oven until the surface caramelizes, creating a crisp contrast to the soft, sweet flesh.

When choosing squash, pick them up to check that they're very solid and hard and their corklike stems are firmly attached. Store winter squash at room temperature. If a recipe calls for only a portion of the squash, wrap the remainder in plastic and store in the refrigerator for no more than a few days. Winter squash keep for several months on the kitchen counter, or as a fall centerpiece on the table.

because, depending on their condition, even the same variety of mushroom can require different techniques. When mushrooms are very wet, sear them over high heat to help them release their liquid quickly. Be sure not to crowd too many mushrooms into the pan, and don't be tempted to stir them in the beginning. Searing them undisturbed allows them to give off their liquid, which needs to evaporate so they can crisp. Drier mushrooms may cook more quickly and not require such a hot pan. Whether wet or dry, cooked wild mushrooms should be tender and a little crisp on the outside. Instinct and a watchful eye are helpful, but only the mushrooms themselves can tell you exactly how long they need in the pan.

When shopping for wild mushrooms, look at them carefully and smell them. They should be fragrant and smell of the earth, without mustiness or mold. In a perfect world, wild mushrooms should be relatively clean and not too wet. But nature doesn't always oblige, and sometimes they are laden with sand and dirt. Though I hate to immerse them in water, in this case you're better off cleaning them than ending up with gritty mushrooms. If you're not sure whether your mushrooms need to be cleaned, sauté a few, and taste them to see if they are sandy.

chilled red pepper soup with sumac, basil, and lemon yogurt

This refreshing chilled purée wakes up your palate with a jolt of sweet pepper essence, cooling yogurt, and the ubiquitous Middle Eastern spice sumac. Sumac is made from the dried berries of a sumac tree, and in the Middle East it's sprinkled over everything from kabobs to yogurt to rice. The dark-crimson powder lends an acidic, lemony flavor to this soup.

½ cup extra-virgin olive oil

1 small sprig rosemary

1 chile de árbol, crumbled

2 cups diced onion

1 tablespoon thyme leaves

7 large red bell peppers (about 1¾ pounds)

2 teaspoons ground sumac

¼ teaspoon granulated sugar

1 cup whole milk yogurt, Greek-style if possible

1 tablespoon lemon juice

2 tablespoons sliced opal basil

Kosher salt and freshly ground black pepper

Heat a large pot or Dutch oven over high heat for 2 minutes. Add the olive oil, rosemary, and chile. Let them sizzle a minute or so, and then add the onion, thyme, 1 teaspoon salt, and a good amount of pepper. Reduce the heat to medium-high, and cook about 10 minutes, stirring often, until the onion is soft, translucent, and starting to color.

While the onion is cooking, cut the peppers in half lengthwise, through the stems. Use a paring knife to remove the stems, seeds, and membranes. Cut the peppers into rough 1-inch pieces.

Raise the heat back to high, and add the peppers, 1 teaspoon sumac, sugar, 1 tablespoon salt, and more freshly ground black pepper. Sauté for about 5 minutes, stirring often with a wooden spoon, until the peppers start to caramelize slightly.

Add 8 cups water, and bring to a boil. Turn the heat down to low, and simmer about 30 minutes, until the peppers are cooked through and tender but not mushy. You can test by scooping a piece of pepper onto a cutting board and pressing it with your finger or a spoon. When it's done, the flesh will give way easily.

Strain the soup over a large bowl. Put half of the peppers into a blender with ½ cup of the liquid. (You will need to purée the soup in batches.) Blend at the lowest speed until the peppers are puréed. Begin pouring in the liquid, a little at a time, until the soup has the consistency of heavy cream. Turn the speed to high, and blend at least a minute, until the soup is completely smooth. Transfer to a container, and repeat with the second half of the soup. (You may not need all the liquid.) Taste for balance and seasoning, and then chill.

While the soup is chilling, stir the yogurt, lemon juice, and ¼ teaspoon salt together in a small bowl.

When the soup is cold, serve it in chilled bowls and garnish with large dollops of lemon yogurt, a sprinkling of sumac, and the opal basil. Or, to serve family-style, place the soup in a chilled tureen, garnish with the sumac and basil, and serve the lemon yogurt on the side.

warm squid salad with spinach, chorizo, and black olives

Although they might sound like an odd combination, hot crispy squid and spicy chorizo tossed together with spinach, cilantro, and olives make an irresistible warm salad. This salad is a salute to the Portuguese and the Spanish, who have been cooking seafood and meat together for centuries, long before the term "surf and turf" was coined.

2½ pounds small squid, cleaned

2 lemons, zested

2 tablespoons thyme leaves

2 tablespoons sliced flat-leaf parsley leaves

1 cup fresh breadcrumbs

¾ cup plus 2 tablespoons extra-virgin olive oil

¾ pound fresh Mexican chorizo, casing removed

1½ cups finely diced onion

1 tablespoon minced garlic

10 ounces young spinach

1 cup cilantro leaves

½ cup diagonally sliced scallions

1 cup chopped pitted Nyons olives, or other strong-tasting black olives

6 tablespoons sherry vinegar

Cut the squid bodies crosswise into ⅛-inch-thick rings, and leave the tentacles whole. (If you're using larger squid, cut the tentacles into quarters.) Season the tentacles and rings separately with the lemon zest, 1 tablespoon thyme, and the parsley for a few hours.

Preheat the oven to 375°F.

Toss the breadcrumbs with 2 tablespoons olive oil and 1 teaspoon thyme. Spread them on a baking sheet, and toast 8 to 10 minutes, stirring once or twice, until golden brown.

Meanwhile, heat a large sauté pan over high heat for 2 minutes. Swirl in 2 tablespoons olive oil and wait about a minute. Crumble the chorizo into the pan, and cook 1 minute. Add the onion, garlic, and remaining 2 teaspoons thyme. Sauté 5 minutes over medium heat, stirring often with a wooden spoon, until the chorizo is cooked and the onion is translucent and starting to caramelize. Turn off the heat and set aside.

Place the spinach, cilantro, scallions, and olives in a large bowl, and toss to combine. In a small bowl whisk together the sherry vinegar, 2 tablespoons lemon juice, and 6 tablespoons olive oil. Set aside.

Drain the squid in a colander, and blot with paper towels to absorb the excess water.

Heat two large sauté pans over high heat for 3 minutes. Swirl 2 tablespoons olive oil into each pan, and wait 2 more minutes (the pan needs to be very hot to sear the squid). Divide the squid between the pans. Season each batch with 1 teaspoon salt and some freshly ground pepper. Cook 1 to 2 minutes, without stirring, allowing the squid to sear. Then stir with a wooden spoon, and cook another minute or two, until the squid is opaque and just cooked through. Drain the squid. Return the chorizo pan to high heat, and add the squid, stirring well to combine and coat well.

When the mixture is hot, add it to the bowl of spinach. Turn off the heat and add three-quarters of the vinaigrette to the pan and heat quickly, just until hot. Pour the hot vinaigrette over the spinach and squid. Season with ½ teaspoon salt and lots of freshly ground black pepper. Toss with tongs or large spoons to combine the ingredients. Taste for balance and seasoning, and add more vinaigrette if necessary.

Arrange the salad on a large platter, and scatter the breadcrumbs over the top.

grilled pork confit with braised rice soubise and roasted figs

This grilled pork confit evolved one night when I was making a staff meal at Lucques. I salvaged the leftover ends and trimmings from the day's pork confit, crisped them in my favorite cast-iron pan, and ran to the walk-in to see what produce I could find to add to the dish. When I got back to the stove, I noticed half the meat was missing. Looking around, I saw that all the cooks had their heads down, suspiciously quiet. Half of my staff meal had disappeared, but I couldn't be angry. Who can resist succulent pork, hot and crispy, out of the pan? Something so irresistible deserved to be shared with the outside world, so I put this staff meal on the menu!

NOTE Brine the pork 3 days before serving. After 2 days, when the pork comes out of the brine (the day before serving), confit it, and chill overnight. The meat should be very cold, or it will be hard to slice. Start the braised rice soubise 1 hour and 15 minutes or so before serving. It can sit covered and then be rewarmed and finished with the cheese and cream right before serving. Roast the figs while you grill the confit. You could crisp the pork in cast-iron pans rather than grilling it, if you prefer. Heat two large cast-iron pans over high heat 2 minutes. Add 2 tablespoons fat to each pan, and heat another minute. Carefully place the meat in the pan, and cook 4 to 5 minutes on each side, until nicely browned. You can store the leftover fat in the freezer.

2½ to 3 pounds boneless pork shoulder, trimmed of excess fat

Brine (recipe follows)

2 to 3 quarts rendered duck or pork fat

10 fresh figs

2 tablespoons extra-virgin olive oil

1 teaspoon thyme leaves

Braised rice soubise (recipe follows)

1 bunch dandelion greens, cleaned

Kosher salt and freshly ground black pepper

Three days before serving, trim the pork of excess fat and sinew, and place it in the brine. It should be completely submerged. Refrigerate the pork in the brine for 48 hours.

After 48 hours, remove the pork from the brine. Pat it dry with paper towels, and let it sit out 1 hour to come to room temperature.

Preheat the oven to 300°F.

Heat the duck fat in a large Dutch oven over low heat until just warm and melted.

Carefully lower the pork into the fat. It should be completely submerged. Cook 5 to 6 hours, until the meat yields easily to a paring knife when pierced. If at any time the fat starts to boil, turn the oven down to 250°F.

When the pork is done, remove it from the oven and let cool in the fat about

1 hour. Carefully take the pork out of the fat, and refrigerate it overnight. Strain the fat, reserve 4 tablespoons, and store the rest in the freezer.

Light the grill 30 to 40 minutes before you're ready to cook.

Preheat the oven to 400°F.

Slice the figs in half lengthwise. Place the halves in a roasting pan, and drizzle them with the olive oil. Season with the thyme, ¼ teaspoon salt, and a pinch of pepper. Roast in the oven 10 to 12 minutes, until the figs are slightly caramelized and sizzling.

Place the chilled pork confit on a cutting board, and slice it against the grain into ½-to-¾-inch-thick slabs (about 5 to 6 ounces each). Brush the slabs with a little pork fat. Taste a little piece of the pork to make sure it's seasoned correctly. If not, season with salt and pepper.

When the coals are broken down, red, and glowing, place the pork on the grill and let it sear a few minutes without moving it. Cook a few more minutes, rotating the meat, to crisp and caramelize it. Turn the pork over and finish cooking, another 4 to 5 minutes, on the second side. The meat should be very crisp with a deep golden crust.

Spoon the soubise onto a large warm platter, and scatter the dandelion greens over it. Arrange the pork confit and figs (with their juices) over the soubise and greens.

brine

2 tablespoons juniper berries

2 tablespoons allspice berries

1 tablespoon fennel seeds

⅓ cup granulated sugar

½ cup kosher salt

2 cloves

2 bay leaves

2 chiles de árbol

1 onion, sliced

½ bulb fennel, sliced

1 carrot, peeled and sliced
	on the diagonal

4 sprigs thyme

4 sprigs flat-leaf parsley

MAKES ABOUT 4 QUARTS

Crush the juniper berries coarsely in a mortar. Repeat with the allspice and then the fennel seeds.

Dissolve the sugar and salt in 2 cups hot water (just hot enough to dissolve the sugar) in a large, very clean container. Add the juniper berries, allspice berries, fennel seeds, cloves, bay leaves, chiles, onion, fennel, carrot, thyme, and parsley. Add 3 quarts very cold water, and stir to combine all the ingredients.

braised rice soubise

This dish was inspired by an old Julia Child recipe that my mom used to make when I was a kid. Lots of stewed onions are bound with a tiny bit of Arborio rice, like a very loose risotto in which the onion, rather than the rice, is the key player. Finished with Gruyère and a touch of cream, it's great with grilled lamb, rabbit, and even braised beef.

Preheat the oven to 350°F.

Heat a large saucepan or Dutch oven over medium heat for 1 minute. Add the butter, and when it foams, add the diced and sliced onions, thyme, 2 teaspoons salt, and the white pepper. Turn the heat down to medium-low, and cook the onions gently, for about 10 minutes, stirring often. They should soften and wilt but not be allowed to color at all.

While the onions are cooking, bring a small pot of water to a boil. Cook the rice 5 minutes in the boiling water and drain well. Stir the rice into the onions.

Remove the pot from the heat. Cover it with plastic wrap (yes, it can go in the oven), aluminum foil, and a tight-fitting lid, if you have one. Cook in the oven 30 minutes.

Remove from the oven and let the soubise "rest," covered, about 30 minutes.

Just before serving, uncover the soubise (it will emit lots of steam, so be careful). Heat it over medium heat, stirring once or twice. When the soubise is hot, stir in the cheese and cream. Taste for seasoning, and stir in the parsley.

4 tablespoons unsalted butter

1 cup diced white onion, plus 6 cups thinly sliced white onions (about 1½ pounds)

1 tablespoon thyme leaves

¼ teaspoon ground white pepper

¼ cup Arborio rice

¼ cup grated Gruyère cheese

⅓ cup heavy cream

2 tablespoons chopped flat-leaf parsley

Kosher salt

pastel vasco with blackberry compote and poured cream

During my cooking *stage* at Pain, Adour et Fantaisie, a two-star restaurant in southwestern France, days off were few and far between for the *commis* (French for grunt line cooks). Whenever I got the chance, though, I'd round up my fellow workers for a road trip to the Basque country. We always knew when we crossed the border into Spain, because everything looked different—the Spanish hillsides were rugged and less pristine than the green countryside of southwestern France.

We were cooks, so food was the first thing on our agenda. After plates of *jamón* and several bottles of red wine, we headed to the bakeries, where I was charmed by the simple, heartfelt sweets of the Basque bakers.

A few years back, I was reminded of those quick forays into Spain by an excellent cook named Brian Edwards. His training in Spain had left him with fond memories he was eager to share. When he described his favorite Basque dessert, pastel vasco, I knew it was my kind of sweet. A simple pound cake made with rum and layered with fruit compote sounded like the perfect addition to our dessert list. My pastry chef at the time, Kimberly Sklar, did some research and perfected her own version of this rustic Spanish sweet. We put it on the menu, but for some reason it didn't sell. One morning, I toasted a slice of leftover cake in a buttered cast-iron pan and ate it with warm berry compote. Unable to fathom how such deliciousness could be ignored, I put it back on the menu, embellishing the description just a little: "Pastel Vasco, toasted in the wood-burning oven with blackberries and poured cream." The power of words is amazing. We sold out night after night.

2¼ cups plus 1 tablespoon all-purpose flour

1 tablespoon baking powder

½ teaspoon kosher salt

4 extra-large eggs

1 cup plus 1 tablespoon granulated sugar, plus a handful for sprinkling over the cake

14 tablespoons unsalted butter, melted, plus 3 tablespoons unmelted

2 tablespoons dark rum

½ teaspoon pure vanilla extract

¼ teaspoon pure almond extract

¼ cup fresh orange juice

Blackberry compote (recipe follows)

1 cup heavy cream

Sift the flour and baking powder together. Add the salt.

Whisk 3 eggs together in a large bowl. Whisk in the sugar, melted butter, rum, extracts, and orange juice. Fold in the dry ingredients, and let the batter rest in the refrigerator for 30 minutes.

Preheat the oven to 400°F.

Lightly butter a loaf pan. Pour three-quarters of the batter into the pan, and spoon ¾ cup compote over it. Top with the remaining batter, letting some of the berries show through.

Beat the remaining egg, and brush it over the batter. Sprinkle a handful of sugar over the top. Bake about 1 hour, until a toothpick inserted into the center comes out clean.

Let the cake cool completely on a rack. Cut into ¾-inch slices, and butter lightly on both sides.

Warm the remaining compote in a small saucepan over low heat.

Heat a griddle or large cast-iron pan over medium-high heat. Toast each slice of cake lightly for a minute or two on each side, until it's golden brown and crispy. Arrange the slices, slightly overlapping, on a large platter. Spoon the warm compote over the slices of cake, and serve with a small pitcher of cream.

blackberry compote

½ cup granulated sugar
½ vanilla bean
1 tablespoon cornstarch
2 pints blackberries
2 tablespoons brandy

Pour the sugar into a medium pot. Cut the vanilla bean in half lengthwise, and use a paring knife to scrape the seeds and pulp into the sugar. Add ⅓ cup water, and bring to a boil over medium heat, without stirring. Cook about 10 minutes, swirling the pan occasionally, until the mixture is an amber caramel color.

While the sugar is caramelizing, stir 2 tablespoons water into the cornstarch in a small bowl (this is called a "slurry" and will help thicken the fruit juices). Set aside.

When the sugar has reached an amber caramel color, add half the blackberries and the brandy to the pot. The sugar will harden. Continue cooking for another 3 to 5 minutes, without stirring, over medium-low heat, until the berries release their juices and the sugar dissolves.

Strain the berries over a bowl, and pour the liquid back into the pot. Transfer the cooked berries to the bowl, and stir in the remaining uncooked blackberries. Bring the blackberry caramel back to a boil over medium heat, and slowly whisk in the cornstarch slurry, a little at a time. Cook a few more minutes, stirring often, until the sauce thickens. Pour the thickened juices over the berries, and stir to combine.

richard olney's figs
and prosciutto with melon

This early fall medley was made famous by the legendary Richard Olney, whose books brought the south of France to kitchens all over the globe. In his recipe, the prosciutto is julienned, scattered over figs, and drizzled with a crushed-mint cream. In this version, I add melon, and instead of thin strands of prosciutto, I drape whole slices around the fruit to create a layered antipasto. There's no right or wrong type of fig for this dish; as long as they're super-ripe, luscious, and oozing, they'll work beautifully. If you have the luxury of choosing more than one variety of fig, such as Genoa, Adriatic, or Honey, this is a spectacular way to show them off. The same rules apply for the melon: just pick the sweetest, most perfumed one you can find.

12 mint leaves

¾ cup heavy cream

1 teaspoon lemon juice

1 ripe melon, about 2 pounds

16 ripe fresh figs

12 thin slices prosciutto di Parma

20 very pretty arugula leaves, cleaned

Kosher salt and freshly ground black pepper

Using a mortar and pestle, pound six mint leaves to a paste. If your mortar is large enough to accommodate the cream, stir it in, scraping the sides and bottom of the mortar with a rubber spatula to incorporate the cream fully. Or, if not, transfer the paste to a bowl. Add the lemon juice, and season with a heaping ¼ teaspoon salt and a pinch or two of pepper. Taste for balance and seasoning.

Cut the melon in half lengthwise, remove the seeds, and slice the melon into 1-inch-thick wedges. Remove the peel. Cut half the figs in half, and the other half into quarters. (I like to leave some of the stems attached.) Slice the remaining six mint leaves.

Place six wedges of melon randomly on a large platter. Drape six slices of prosciutto over and around them, leaving some of the melon peeking through. Arrange half the figs and arugula over and around the melon and prosciutto, tucking some of them under the prosciutto. Arrange the remaining melon, prosciutto, figs, and arugula in the same way.

Drizzle the mint cream over the prosciutto and fruit. Scatter the sliced mint on top, and grind a little black pepper over the dish.

grilled tuna with potato-tomato gratin and rouille

6 tuna steaks, 5 to 6 ounces each, about 1 inch thick

1 lemon, zested

1 chile de árbol, thinly sliced on the diagonal

1 tablespoon thyme leaves

1 tablespoon sliced flat-leaf parsley

2 tablespoons extra-virgin olive oil

1 tablespoon *fleur de sel*

1 tablespoon freshly cracked black pepper

2 ounces arugula, cleaned

2 tablespoons super-good extra-virgin olive oil

Rouille (recipe follows)

Potato-tomato gratin (recipe follows)

Kosher salt and freshly ground black pepper

This dish takes me back to Pantelleria, a tiny volcanic island in the Mediterranean, situated between North Africa and Sicily. Undeveloped and relatively untouched by the modern world, the island is famous for two things: the caper bushes that dominate the dry, brush-covered hillsides of the rocky coast, and resident Giorgio Armani. My husband and I spent a magical week in that salt-drenched haven, eating grilled, freshly caught tuna; bowls of couscous; and salads of tomatoes, potatoes, and capers.

The grilled tuna and the combination of tomatoes and potatoes in this dish are a tribute to those leisurely days on Pantelleria. And though rouille isn't part of their Moorish-meets-Italian culinary lexicon, I'm sure the Pantellerians would love this saffron-tinted, spicy pepper mayonnaise.

NOTE Season the tuna with the herbs and lemon zest in the morning. The gratin is easy to assemble but takes quite a while in the oven so start early. You can make it in advance and reheat just before serving. The rouille can be made a few hours before serving.

Season the fish with the lemon zest, chile, thyme, and parsley. Cover, and refrigerate at least 4 hours.

Light the grill 30 to 40 minutes before cooking, and remove the fish from the refrigerator to come to room temperature.

When the coals are broken down, red, and glowing, brush the fish with olive oil, and season on both sides with *fleur de sel* and cracked black pepper. Grill the fish 2 to 3 minutes per side, rotating it once or twice. The tuna should be well seared but still rare.

Scatter the arugula onto a large platter and arrange the tuna on top. Squeeze some lemon juice over the fish, and then drizzle the fish with the super-good olive oil. Dollop each piece of fish with rouille, and serve the potato-tomato gratin and the rest of the rouille on the side.

rouille

Char the pepper on a medium-hot grill, on the burner of a gas stove, or in the broiler. Place the pepper in a small paper bag and close tightly. Let steam 15 minutes.

Toast the saffron in a small pan over medium heat until it just dries and becomes brittle. Be careful not to burn it.

Place the egg yolk in a stainless steel bowl. Begin to whisk in the grapeseed oil drop by drop, as slowly as you can bear. Once the mayonnaise has thickened and emulsified, you can add the remaining oils in a slow steady stream, whisking all the time. If the mixture gets too thick, add a drop or two of water.

Using a mortar and pestle, pound the saffron, garlic, and ½ teaspoon salt. Scrape every little bit of the mixture into the mayonnaise with a rubber spatula, and whisk to combine.

Peel the charred and steamed pepper carefully over a strainer. Do not run the pepper under water or you will lose some of the delicious juices. Remove the stem, seeds, and membranes.

Purée the pepper in a food processor until smooth. Fold it into the mayonnaise, and season with a healthy squeeze of lemon juice, a pinch of cayenne, and a pinch of black pepper. Taste for balance and seasoning.

1 red bell pepper
½ teaspoon saffron threads
1 extra-large egg yolk
½ cup grapeseed oil
½ cup extra-virgin olive oil
1 small clove garlic
½ lemon, for juicing
Pinch cayenne pepper
Kosher salt and freshly ground
  black pepper

potato-tomato gratin

Heat a large sauté pan or Dutch oven over high heat for 2 minutes. Swirl in 3 tablespoons olive oil, and add the onions, 1 teaspoon thyme, 1 teaspoon salt, and some pepper. Cook 6 minutes, stirring often, and then turn the heat down to medium. Add the butter, and cook 15 minutes, stirring and scraping with a wooden spoon, until the onions start to caramelize. Turn the heat down to low, and continue cooking for about 10 minutes, stirring often, until the onions are a deep golden brown. Remove the pan from the heat and set aside.

Preheat the oven to 350°F.

Use a mandoline to slice the potatoes into ⅛-inch-thick rounds. Toss them with the cream, 1 teaspoon thyme, 1 teaspoon salt, and some freshly ground black pepper.

Cut the tomatoes into ¼-inch-thick slices, arrange them on a plate, and season them with 1 teaspoon salt and some pepper.

5 tablespoons extra-virgin olive
  oil
6 cups thinly sliced onions
  (about 1½ pounds)
1 tablespoon thyme leaves
1 tablespoon unsalted butter
1¼ pounds Yukon Gold potatoes,
  peeled
½ cup heavy cream
2¼ pounds ripe tomatoes
¼ cup sliced opal basil
Kosher salt and freshly ground
  black pepper

Place half the caramelized onions in an even layer in a 9-by-9-inch (or equivalent) gratin or baking dish. Arrange one layer of alternating potatoes and tomatoes on top of the onion layer. Drizzle with 2 tablespoons of the cream from the potatoes and 1 tablespoon olive oil. Season with ¼ teaspoon salt, a healthy pinch of pepper, ½ teaspoon thyme, and half the basil.

Scatter the rest of the caramelized onions over the potatoes and tomatoes.

Arrange another layer of potatoes and tomatoes on top; make this layer pretty, because it will be the top of your gratin. Pour the remaining cream (from the potatoes) and remaining tablespoon olive oil over the potatoes and tomatoes. Season with ¼ teaspoon salt, a pinch of pepper, the remaining ½ teaspoon thyme, and the remaining basil. Press the vegetables down with your fingers. The cream and oil will come up through the layers and coat the vegetables evenly.

Cover the baking dish tightly with plastic wrap (yes, it can go in the oven) and then foil. Bake about 2 hours, until the potatoes are tender when pierced. Remove the gratin from the oven and uncover it, being careful of the steam.

Turn the oven up to 450°F and return the gratin, uncovered, to the oven. Cook another 25 to 30 minutes, until the juices have thickened and the top is nice and golden brown (as in gratinéed).

tunisian lamb-and-eggplant stew with farro, parsley, and harissa

This dish was inspired by a trip to Tunisia a few years ago. I fell in love with the Tunisian cooks' use of spices and the bowls of harissa served with every meal. What surprised me most was the use of caraway, which I had always thought of as an Eastern European spice.

For this Tunisian-flavored stew, I season the lamb shoulder overnight with caraway, coriander, chiles, cayenne, and paprika, and then braise it in an aromatic broth with cinnamon and allspice. For a traditional braise I usually deglaze with wine, but in keeping with Muslim prohibitions common in Tunisia, I refrain and substitute lemon juice, which also adds a bright, acidic note to the stew.

NOTE The lamb, like all braises, can be made a day or even 2 days ahead of time. Remember to marinate it overnight before braising. The harissa can also can be made ahead, and keeps for a few weeks in the refrigerator. Make the farro within an hour of serving. I like it best just after it's been cooked and tossed with the butter. Hold it in a warm oven for up to 30 minutes, if that's more convenient for you.

Toast the caraway seeds in a small pan for a few minutes, until the seeds release their aroma and darken slightly. Using a mortar and pestle, pound the seeds coarsely. Repeat with the coriander.

Place the lamb in a large bowl with the caraway, coriander, smashed garlic, chiles, paprika, cayenne, and 2 tablespoons olive oil. Using your hands, toss the lamb, spices, and oil together to coat the meat well. Cover, and refrigerate overnight.

Take the meat out of the refrigerator 45 minutes before cooking. After 15 minutes, season it on all sides with 1 tablespoon plus 2 teaspoons salt and lots of pepper. Reserve the garlic.

Preheat the oven to 325°F.

Heat a large Dutch oven over high heat for 3 minutes. Pour in 3 tablespoons olive oil and wait a minute or two, until the pan is very hot, almost smoking. Place the meat in the pan, being careful not to crowd it. (You will most likely need to do this in two batches.) Sear the meat until it's well browned and caramelized on all sides. (This step is very important and should not be rushed; it may take

1 tablespoon caraway seeds

2 tablespoons coriander seeds

3 pounds lamb shoulder, cut into 1½-to-2-inch chunks

6 cloves garlic, smashed

3 chiles de árbol, crumbled

2 teaspoons paprika

1 teaspoon cayenne pepper

½ cup extra-virgin olive oil

2 cups diced onion

2 bay leaves, fresh if possible

¾ cup San Marzano canned tomatoes, crushed

½ cup lemon juice

2½ cups veal stock

2½ cups chicken stock

1 cinnamon stick

1 teaspoon allspice berries, tied in cheesecloth

2 medium eggplants

Farro with parsley and butter (recipe follows)

Harissa (recipe follows)

¼ cup flat-leaf parsley leaves

Kosher salt and freshly ground black pepper

15 to 20 minutes.) As the batches of meat are browned, remove them to a baking sheet or platter.

Turn the heat down to medium and add the onion, bay leaves, and reserved garlic. Stir with a wooden spoon, scraping up all the crusty bits left in the pan. Cook about 5 minutes, until the onions are caramelized. Add the crushed tomatoes and lemon juice and cook 2 minutes, stirring continuously to coat the onions.

Add the stocks, cinnamon, and allspice. Bring to a boil.

Turn off the heat and add the lamb and its juices to the pot. Cover the pan with plastic wrap (yes, it can go in the oven), aluminum foil, and a tightly fitting lid, if you have one. Braise the lamb in the oven about 3 hours.

While the lamb is braising, cut the eggplant into 1-inch cubes. Toss them with salt, and place them in a colander for 10 minutes to drain. Pat the eggplant cubes dry with paper towels. Heat a large sauté pan over high heat for 2 minutes. Swirl in 3 tablespoons olive oil, and wait 1 minute. Add the eggplant to the pan, and let sear a minute or two. (Do not crowd the pan; you may need to do this in batches.) Once it starts to color, turn the eggplant cubes to achieve a nice color on all sides. Cook 3 to 4 minutes, until tender and golden. Transfer to a paper-towel-lined baking sheet.

To check the meat for doneness, carefully remove the plastic and foil, being mindful of the hot steam. Spoon a piece of meat out of the pan and press it with your thumb or a spoon. If it's done, it will yield easily and almost fall apart. If it's not super-tender, cover again and return the pot to the oven.

When the meat is done, remove from the oven and turn the temperature up to 400°F.

Ladle most of the braising juices into a strainer set over a saucepan, leaving an inch or two of juices in the pan with the lamb. Press down on the vegetables with the ladle to extract all the juices. Discard the cinnamon stick and allspice.

Return the lamb to the oven for about 15 minutes, to caramelize it.

Skim the fat from the braising juices. Reduce the broth over medium-high heat to thicken it slightly, if necessary. Taste for seasoning.

Stir the eggplant in with the browned lamb, and pour the hot broth over the top, stirring to coat well.

Transfer the farro onto a large warm platter. Spoon the braised lamb, along with the eggplant and cooking juices, over the farro. Dollop the harissa over the meat, scatter the parsley on top, and serve the remaining harissa and braising juices on the side.

farro with parsley and butter

Heat a medium saucepan over high heat for 1 minute. Swirl in the olive oil, and add the diced onion, thyme, cinnamon stick, chiles, and bay leaf. Cook 3 to 4 minutes, stirring often, until the onion is translucent.

Add the farro, stirring to coat it with the oil, and toast it slightly. Add 8 cups water and 2 teaspoons salt. Bring to a boil, turn the heat to low, and simmer about 30 minutes, until the farro is tender and just cooked through. Drain the farro and discard the cinnamon stick, chiles, and bay leaf. Toss the hot farro with the butter. When all the butter has melted, stir in the parsley and a few grindings of black pepper. Taste for seasoning.

2 tablespoons extra-virgin olive oil

½ cup diced onion

1 tablespoon thyme leaves

1 cinnamon stick

2 chiles de árbol, crumbled

1 bay leaf, preferably fresh

1½ cups farro (spelt)

4 tablespoons unsalted butter, cut into cubes

¼ cup chopped flat-leaf parsley

Kosher salt and freshly ground black pepper

harissa

This fiery North African condiment is a Lucques favorite.

Heat a large sauté pan over high heat for 1 minute. Add the chiles to the pan and dry-toast them for a few minutes until they are blistered and slightly darkened. Place the chiles in a bowl and cover with very hot water. Let them sit, covered, 15 minutes.

Return the pan to the stove and add the tomato. Cook over medium heat for a few minutes until the juices reduce and the tomato is slightly darkened.

Meanwhile, toast the cumin in a small pan over medium heat 2 to 3 minutes, until the seeds release their aroma and darken slightly. Pound them coarsely in a mortar.

Drain the chiles well and place them in a food processor with the garlic, tomatoes, paprika, cumin, cayenne, vinegar, 1 teaspoon salt, and a pinch of pepper. Purée until well combined. With the motor running, slowly pour in the olive oil and blend until incorporated. Season with a healthy squeeze of lemon juice, and more salt if you like.

6 dried ancho chiles, seeded, membranes removed

⅓ cup San Marzano canned tomatoes

¼ teaspoon cumin seeds

1 clove garlic, chopped

1 teaspoon smoked paprika

A healthy pinch cayenne pepper

½ teaspoon sherry vinegar

½ cup extra-virgin olive oil

½ lemon, for juicing

Kosher salt and freshly ground black pepper

date butter tart
with vanilla ice cream

1 recipe pâte sucrée
  (see page 196)

35 to 40 Deglet Noor dates

½ vanilla bean

9 tablespoons unsalted butter

2 extra-large eggs

⅔ cup plus 1 tablespoon
  granulated sugar

⅓ cup all-purpose flour

¼ teaspoon kosher salt

1 recipe vanilla ice cream
  (see page 113)

Dates were always part of the December onslaught of gifts for my father from his patients. Packages of dried fruit would arrive with bottles of booze, crates of Hickory Farms smoked meats and cheeses, and boxes of C. C. Brown's pecan turtles. Once my sister and I had made our way through all the other edible gifts, our sugar-dazed eyes would turn toward that untouched wicker tray of shrink-wrapped dried fruit. After one bite of those rock-hard dates covered in shredded coconut, we were convinced that dates were inedible.

It wasn't until my late twenties, when I moved back to Los Angeles, that I gave dates another chance. It didn't seem right that something so prominent in the local landscape was absent from my culinary landscape. With date farmers at every turn, I broke down and tried a date. Soft, chewy, and rich, this was definitely not the date of my childhood. I embraced my newfound love with a vengeance, sampling all the different varieties. Now I can't imagine life without dates. For this tart I like Deglet Noors, which have a pleasing chewiness without the cloying sweetness of some other varieties. If you can't find Deglet Noors, you can use another variety; just make sure the dates are plump and supple. (See Sources for my favorite date farmers who ship across the country.)

NOTE This tart is equally delicious served warm or cold.

Preheat the oven to 350°F.

Line a tart pan with the pâte sucrée, according to page 196. Prick the bottom with a fork, and line it with a few coffee filters opened out, or a piece of parchment paper. Fill the lined tart shell with beans or pie weights, and bake 15 minutes, until set. Take the tart out of the oven, and gently lift out the paper and beans. Return the tart to the oven and bake another 10 to 15 minutes, until the crust is an even golden brown. Set aside on a rack to cool completely.

Make a vertical slit in each date, and carefully remove the pit. Use your fingers to press the dates back into their natural shape. Place the dates, slit side down, in concentric circles in the tart shell, leaving ½ inch between each.

Slice the vanilla bean in half lengthwise, and use a paring knife to scrape the seeds and pulp onto the butter. To make sure not to lose any of the seeds, run your vanilla-coated knife through the butter. Heat a medium sauté pan over medium heat for 1 minute. Add the vanilla-streaked butter and the vanilla pod to the pan, and cook 6 to 8 minutes, until the butter browns and smells nutty. Discard the vanilla pod.

Whisk the eggs and ⅔ cup sugar together in a bowl. Whisk in the flour and salt, and stir in the warm butter to incorporate.

Pour the batter over the dates in the tart shell. Sprinkle the top with the remaining tablespoon sugar. Bake 30 minutes, until the filling puffs up, browns, and is set.

Cool the tart at least 20 minutes, then cut the tart into wedges and serve with scoops of vanilla ice cream.

roasted pear salad with endive, hazelnuts, and st. agur

¾ cup blanched hazelnuts

¼ cup plus 1 teaspoon hazelnut oil

½ cup plus 2 tablespoons grapeseed oil

5 Comice or Bartlett pears, peeled, cored, and cut into eighths

4 tablespoons unsalted butter

2 teaspoons thyme leaves

1 tablespoon finely diced shallot, plus 2 tablespoons thinly sliced shallot

2½ tablespoons sherry vinegar

2 tablespoons rice vinegar

6 heads Belgian endive, core removed, separated into spears

1 ounce arugula, cleaned and dried

¼ pound St. Agur blue cheese

Kosher salt and freshly ground black pepper

A variety of cheeses work in this salad, but I particularly love St. Agur, a triple-crème French cow's milk blue cheese. Its pungent and intense blue flavor is balanced by an unusually creamy and sensuous texture. When shaved into long thin ribbons, the cheese is elegant on the plate and delicate on the palate. To make thin ribbons, I use an old-fashioned cheese pull, a wide metal spatula-shaped utensil with a slotted blade in the center. Pears and cheese are always happy companions, so if you can't find St. Agur choose another blue, or seek out a good sheep's milk cheese, such as a Roncal, Manchego, or pecorino. We've had more than one customer order this salad as dessert, so you decide where it falls in the meal.

NOTE *If you don't have a cheese pull, you can run your knife under hot water and then cut thin, pristine slices.*

Preheat the oven to 375°F.

Toast the hazelnuts on a baking sheet 8 to 10 minutes, until they smell nutty and are a light golden brown. Remove them from the oven, and toss with 1 teaspoon hazelnut oil and a healthy pinch of salt. When they have cooled, chop the nuts coarsely.

Heat two large sauté pans over high heat for 2 minutes. Swirl 1 tablespoon grapeseed oil into each pan, and then carefully place the pears in the pan, cut side down. Add 2 tablespoons butter to each pan, and season each batch with 1 teaspoon salt and 1 teaspoon thyme. Reduce the heat to medium-high, and cook the pears about 6 minutes, until they're golden brown on the first side. Carefully turn the pears over, and cook another 3 to 4 minutes, until the second side is golden brown and the pears are tender but not mushy.

Using a mortar and pestle, or the side of a large chef's knife, pound or mash six of the pear wedges to a chunky paste. Combine the diced shallot, sherry vinegar, rice vinegar, and ¾ teaspoon salt in a medium bowl, and let sit for 5 minutes. Whisk in the remaining ¼ cup hazelnut oil and ½ cup grapeseed oil. Stir in the pear purée and taste for balance and seasoning.

Place the remaining roasted pear wedges, the endive, and the sliced shallots in a large salad bowl, and toss with about three-quarters of the vinaigrette. Season with ¼ teaspoon salt and a few grindings of black pepper, and toss gently, being careful not to break up the pears. Toss in the arugula gently, and taste for seasoning, adding more vinaigrette if you like.

Arrange half the salad on a large platter. Use a cheese pull to make long ribbons of the blue cheese, and place half of them in and around the greens. Sprinkle half of the nuts on top. Place the remaining salad on top, and finish with shavings of cheese and the rest of the nuts.

pappardelle with wild mushrooms, shell beans, and parmesan

1½ pounds mixed wild
    mushrooms

5 tablespoons extra-virgin olive
    oil

4 tablespoons unsalted butter

¾ cup fresh breadcrumbs

¾ pound dry pappardelle
    noodles

1 cup sliced shallots

4 cloves garlic, sliced

1 tablespoon thyme leaves

1¼ cups cooked shell beans
    (see page 193)

1 to 1½ cups mushroom,
    vegetable, or chicken stock
    or pasta water

4 ounces young spinach, cleaned
    and dried

¼ cup chopped flat-leaf parsley

¼-pound hunk Parmigiano-
    Reggiano, for shaving

Kosher salt and freshly ground
    black pepper

Chanterelles, porcini, mousserons, and white and black trumpets are some of my favorite mushrooms for this pasta. If you can't find any of those, use shiitake or oyster instead. When you sauté the mushrooms, don't crowd too many in one pan. If your pan isn't large enough, cook them in batches. I love the brightness of fresh shell beans, but in winter, you can make this dish with dried beans, such as cannellini or flageolets, which will be a little more hearty but equally delicious.

Preheat the oven to 375°F.

Put a large pot of heavily salted water on to boil.

If the mushrooms are big, tear them into large bite-sized pieces. (They'll shrink once they're cooked, so don't make them too small.)

Heat a large sauté pan over high heat for 2 minutes. Swirl in 2 tablespoons olive oil, and wait a minute. Add 1 tablespoon butter, and when it foams, scatter half the mushrooms into the pan. Season with ½ teaspoon salt and a healthy pinch of pepper. Sauté the mushrooms about 5 minutes, stirring occasionally, until they are tender and a little crispy. (The cooking time will depend on the particular mushrooms you use.) Transfer the cooked mushrooms to a plate, and repeat with the second half of the mushrooms.

While the mushrooms are cooking, toss the breadcrumbs with 1 tablespoon olive oil, spread them on a baking sheet, and toast 8 to 10 minutes, stirring once or twice, until golden brown.

Drop the pasta in the boiling salted water, and cook the noodles until al dente. (Reserve 1½ cups pasta water if using.)

While the pasta is cooking, return the mushroom pan to the stove over medium-high heat. Swirl in 2 tablespoons butter, and when it foams, add the shallots, garlic, and thyme. Cook a minute or two, and add the cooked mushrooms and shell beans. Cook 3 to 4 minutes, stirring to combine well.

Pour in 1 cup of the stock or pasta water, and add the cooked pasta to the pan. Toss gently, using tongs and a wooden spoon, and cook 3 to 4 minutes to coat the pasta with the juices. Taste for seasoning. Add more stock or pasta water if the noodles seem dry. Remember, the pasta will keep absorbing liquid, so make sure it's juicy enough when you plate it. Quickly toss in the spinach and chopped parsley.

Transfer the pasta to a large warm platter. Using a vegetable peeler, shave some Parmigiano-Reggiano over the top, and shower the dish with the toasted breadcrumbs.

grilled pancetta-wrapped trout with verjus, crushed grapes, and fennel gratin

3 tablespoons unsalted butter

1½ cups thinly sliced red onion

1 teaspoon thyme leaves

1½ cups sliced sorrel

⅓ cup heavy cream

6 trout, 8 ounces each, boned and butterflied

6 slices pancetta, about ⅛-inch thick

1 cup red seedless grapes, picked from the stems

4 tablespoons extra-virgin olive oil

2 tablespoons sliced flat-leaf parsley

1 bunch watercress, cleaned, tough stems removed

Verjus sauce (recipe follows)

Fennel gratin (recipe follows)

Kosher salt and freshly ground black pepper

Rainbow trout is a delicious option for fish-loving home cooks. It's available year-round and won't break the bank even when you want to feed a crowd. Have your fishmonger bone and butterfly the trout for you, leaving the tail intact and keeping the two fillets attached on the fin side.

This preparation is a study in contrasts, a three-way complement to the flaky flesh of the trout. The blushing sweet-tart sauce is made with both crushed grapes and verjus, the juice of unripe wine grapes. (The French used verjus in medieval and Renaissance times in much the same way we use vinegar or lemon juice today.) Less acidic and more complex than most vinegar, the verjus's refreshing fruitiness plays counterpoint to the salty cured Italian bacon wrapped around the trout. And finally, hidden within this lively package: rich, herbaceous sorrel cream, bringing us back to earth.

NOTE You can stuff and wrap the fish the morning before you plan to grill it. Both the fennel gratin and the verjus sauce can also be prepared ahead of time and reheated before serving.

Heat a medium sauté pan over medium heat for 1 minute. Add the butter, and when it foams, stir in the red onion. Add the thyme, a healthy pinch of salt, and a pinch of black pepper. Sauté about 10 minutes, until the onion is translucent and soft. Add the sorrel to the pan, and stir to combine. Turn the heat up to medium-high, add the cream, and cook, stirring continuously, about 3 minutes, as the cream reduces and coats the onions. Taste for seasoning, and transfer to a plate to cool completely.

Lay the trout, skin side down, on a cutting board, open like a book. Season lightly with salt and pepper, and spread the sorrel onions on one side of each fish. Fold the fish back together, and wrap each trout with a piece of pancetta, spiraling the meat around the fish like the stripe on a candy cane. Refrigerate the fish until 15 minutes before cooking.

Light the grill 30 to 40 minutes before cooking.

Meanwhile, using a mortar and pestle, pound the grapes until they're partially crushed. Transfer to a bowl, and stir in 2 tablespoons olive oil, the parsley, a healthy pinch of salt, and a pinch of black pepper.

When the coals are broken down, red, and glowing, brush the trout with the remaining 2 tablespoons olive oil and season with salt and pepper. Grill the trout 3 to 4 minutes on each side, rotating the fish a quarter-turn after a couple of minutes, to get the skin crispy.

Scatter the watercress on a large platter, and place the trout on top. Spoon the warm verjus sauce over the fish, and top with the crushed grapes. Serve the fennel gratin at the table.

verjus sauce

Place the grapes, shallot, and verjus in a small saucepan over medium heat. Add ⅛ teaspoon salt, and simmer until the liquid is reduced by three-quarters. Let the mixture cool until lukewarm.

Transfer to a blender, and, with the motor running, add the cold butter a little at a time, blending until the butter is just incorporated. Taste for seasoning, and add a little lemon juice, a pinch of pepper, and more salt if you like. Return the sauce to the pan, cover, and keep in a warm place. Reheat just before serving.

1½ cups seedless red grapes

1 small shallot, thinly sliced

1 cup verjus

8 tablespoons (1 stick) cold unsalted butter, cut into small pieces

½ lemon, for juicing

Kosher salt and freshly ground black pepper

fennel gratin

Preheat the oven to 425°F.

Toast the fennel seeds in a small saucepan over medium-high heat 2 to 3 minutes, until they release their aroma and are a light gold color. Using a mortar and pestle, pound the seeds coarsely.

Trim the root end of the fennel, cut the stalks off where they meet the bulb, and peel off any outer layers that are brown or bruised. Cut the bulb in half lengthwise, leaving the core intact. Place the halves, cut side down, on a cutting board, and slice the fennel thinly lengthwise. You should have about 6 cups of sliced fennel.

Toss the fennel in a large bowl with the onion, thyme, bay leaves, fennel fronds, fennel seeds, and ⅓ cup olive oil. Season with 1½ teaspoons salt and a pinch of pepper.

Slice the potatoes on a mandoline into ¹⁄₁₆-inch-thick slices. Toss the potatoes in a medium bowl with the cream and 1 teaspoon salt.

1 tablespoon fennel seeds

1½ pounds fennel (4 or 5 bulbs)

1½ cups thinly sliced red onion

1 tablespoon thyme leaves

2 fresh bay leaves, sliced

1 tablespoon chopped fennel fronds or dill

⅓ cup extra-virgin olive oil

¾ pound Yukon Gold potatoes, peeled

⅔ cup heavy cream

2 tablespoons chopped flat-leaf parsley

Kosher salt and freshly ground black pepper

Add the potatoes and parsley to the fennel, scraping all the cream into the bowl. Toss well to combine, and taste for seasoning.

Arrange one layer of potato slices in the pan, overlapping them slightly, on the bottom of a gratin dish. (For this recipe, I like to use a copper or black iron dish, so the potatoes get extra crisp.)

Toss the remaining fennel-potato mixture again, and arrange it over the layer of potatoes. Pour all the remaining creamy juices over the top. Bake about 45 minutes, until the potato is cooked and the fennel is golden and slightly crispy on top.

vanilla pot de crème with chocolate sablés

The vanilla bean is one of the wonders of the culinary world. Cured until nearly shriveled, black as a two-week-old banana, the slender pods have a sweetness that belies their appearance. The rich fragrance of true vanilla is so intense that, after my first encounter with a vanilla pot de crème in France, it seemed to permeate even my dreams.

I have adapted this pot de crème recipe from one of my favorite cookbooks, *Simply French*, by Patricia Wells and Joel Robuchon. The French-inspired chocolate sablés were developed by my pastry chef Roxana Jullapat. Encourage your guests to use them as edible spoons to scoop up the rich, silky custard.

NOTE The pots de crème should be served very cold so make sure to allow 4 hours in the refrigerator.

1½ cups whole milk

1 cup heavy cream

2 vanilla beans

6 extra-large egg yolks

½ cup granulated sugar

Chocolate sablés (recipe follows)

Combine the milk and cream in a medium pot. Split the vanilla beans in half lengthwise, scrape out the seeds and pulp with a paring knife, and add them to the pot. Add the vanilla pods. Bring to a boil over high heat. Turn off the heat, cover, and let the flavors infuse for 30 minutes.

Preheat the oven to 325°F.

Using a stand mixer fitted with the whisk attachment, beat the egg yolks and sugar at high speed for about 3 minutes, until the mixture is thick and pale yellow. When you lift the whisk attachment, the mixture should form ribbons as it falls from the whisk. Bring the milk and cream back to a boil, and then turn off the heat. With the mixer at low speed, add the hot cream slowly, ¼ cup at a time, to temper the eggs. When half the cream has been incorporated, you can add the rest more quickly. Strain the mixture, and let sit for 20 minutes. Skim all traces of foam from the cream.

Pour the mixture into six coffee cups or ramekins. Place in a roasting pan, and pour hot water into the pan to come halfway up the outsides of the cups. Cover completely with foil, and bake in the oven about 30 minutes, until the custard is just set.

Chill at least 4 hours. Serve the pots de crème on pretty napkins set on dessert plates with the cookies next to them.

chocolate sablés

¾ cup all-purpose flour

¼ cup unsweetened cocoa
  powder

¼ teaspoon kosher salt

8 tablespoons (1 stick) unsalted
  butter

6 tablespoons confectioners'
  sugar

1 extra-large egg yolk

1 teaspoon coffee extract
  (optional)

½ cup bittersweet chocolate
  shards

1 to 2 tablespoons granulated
  sugar

Sift the flour and cocoa powder together. Add the salt.

In the stand mixer fitted with the paddle attachment, cream the butter and confectioners' sugar at medium-high speed 3 to 4 minutes, until the mixture is light and fluffy. Add the yolk and coffee extract, and beat until fluffy again. Add the dry ingredients slowly, and mix at low speed. The dough should be crumbly and not quite bound together. Right before the dough comes together, add the chocolate shards and mix for a second, just to incorporate.

Shape the dough into logs about 1½ inches in diameter. Roll the logs in the granulated sugar, and wrap each one in plastic. Refrigerate until very cold and firm.

Preheat the oven to 350°F.

Slice the dough into ¼-inch-thick rounds, and place them ½ inch apart on a parchment-lined baking sheet. Bake 12 to 15 minutes, until set. (They will seem a little underbaked because of the chocolate shards.)

warm kabocha squash salad with dandelion, bacon, roncal, and pecans

This warm salad came about, like many of my dishes, as a way to show off one of my favorite ingredients—in this case, the lovely Kabocha squash.

I roast the wedges of squash until they're practically caramelized and then weave them into a salad of dandelion greens with a tart sherry vinaigrette. Tucked into the greens and squash you'll find bacon *lardons*. Not to be confused with bacon bits, *lardons* are oversized rectangles of chewy, slightly crisped bacon, meaty and satisfying to bite into. Also hiding in the mix are salty toasted pecans and elegant shards of Roncal, an earthy sheep's milk cheese from Spain.

½ cup pecan halves (see Sources)

6 tablespoons plus 1 teaspoon extra-virgin olive oil

2 pounds Kabocha squash

1 tablespoon thyme leaves

⅔-pound slab applewood-smoked bacon

3 tablespoons sherry vinegar

8 ounces young dandelion greens, cleaned

¼ cup sliced shallots

¼-pound hunk Roncal, Manchego, or pecorino

Kosher salt and freshly ground black pepper

Preheat the oven to 375°F.

Spread the pecans on a baking sheet and toast about 10 minutes, stirring once or twice, until they smell nutty. Toss with 1 teaspoon olive oil and a pinch of salt.

While the pecans are toasting, cut the squash in half lengthwise and remove the seeds. Place the squash, cut side down, on a cutting board, and use a sharp knife to remove the peel. Slice the squash lengthwise into ¾-inch-thick wedges.

When the pecans are done, turn the oven up to 425°F.

Toss the squash wedges with ¼ cup olive oil, 2 teaspoons salt, some pepper, and the thyme. Place the squash flat on a baking sheet, and roast in the oven about 30 minutes, until tender when pierced.

Meanwhile cut the bacon into ⅜-inch-thick slices and stack them in two piles, then cut the bacon crosswise into ⅜-inch even-sided rectangular shapes or *lardons*.

In a small bowl, whisk together the sherry vinegar, 2 tablespoons olive oil, and ¼ teaspoon salt.

Place the dandelion greens in a large salad bowl.

Heat a large sauté pan over high heat for 1 minute. Add the bacon, and cook, stirring occasionally, about 5 minutes, until the bacon just begins to brown but is

still tender and chewy. Lower the heat to medium, add the shallots, and toss to combine. Remove the pan from the heat, and swirl in the vinaigrette to warm it. Add the warm squash and the contents of the pan to the dandelion greens. Season with ¼ teaspoon salt and a pinch of pepper, and toss gently to dress the salad. Taste for seasoning.

Arrange half the salad on a large platter. Use a vegetable peeler to shave some Roncal over the salad, and sprinkle half the nuts over that. Top with the remaining salad, more shavings of cheese, and the rest of the nuts.

california sea bass with shell bean risotto and gremolata butter

6 California sea bass fillets,
    5 to 6 ounces each

2 lemons, zested

1 tablespoon thyme leaves

½ cup chopped flat-leaf parsley,
    plus ¼ cup whole parsley
    leaves

1 heaping teaspoon minced
    garlic

6 tablespoons unsalted butter,
    softened

2 tablespoons extra-virgin olive
    oil

Shell bean risotto
    (recipe follows)

Kosher salt and freshly ground
    black pepper

Shell beans are a big part of late summer and early fall in our kitchen. If you happen to come by Lucques on a slow night when they're in season, you'll see runners, cooks, and dishwashers gathered around huge piles of shell beans, shucking, shucking, shucking. For me, shucking provides a much-needed period when my hands can do the work and my brain takes a little time off. Don't worry, shell beans for six won't require a crew of shuckers.

NOTE Season the fish with the lemon zest and herbs in the morning. You can cook the shell beans ahead of time, but the risotto must be cooked "to order." To time this well, start cooking the fish when the risotto is just about done. (The risotto can "rest" for a moment while you pull everything together.)

Season the fish with the thyme, half the lemon zest, and 2 tablespoons parsley. Cover and refrigerate at least 4 hours.

To make the gremolata butter, mince the remaining lemon zest and combine with the minced garlic and remaining 6 tablespoons chopped parsley on a cutting board. Chop the mixture together until very fine. Scrape the gremolata into a small bowl and mash together with 6 tablespoons butter and 1 teaspoon lemon juice. Season with a heaping ¼ teaspoon salt and some pepper.

Heat a large sauté pan over high heat for 2 minutes. (Depending on the size of your pan, you may need to cook the fish in batches.) Season the fish with salt and pepper on both sides. Swirl in the olive oil and wait 1 minute. Carefully lay the fish in the pan, skin side down, and cook 3 to 4 minutes, until the skin is crisp. Turn the fish over, lower the heat to medium-low, and cook a few more minutes, until it's almost cooked through. When it's done, the fish will begin to flake and separate a little and the center will still be slightly translucent. Remember, the fish will continue to cook a little more once you take it out of the pan.

Spoon the hot risotto onto a large platter. Arrange the fish on top, and smear each fillet with some of the gremolata butter. Squeeze lemon juice over the fish and risotto, and scatter the whole parsley leaves on top.

shell bean risotto

Bring the chicken stock and 3½ cups water to a boil over high heat. Then turn off the heat.

Heat a medium pot over medium-high heat for 2 minutes. Swirl in 3 tablespoons butter, and when it foams, add the onion, thyme, chile, ½ teaspoon salt, and a few grindings of black pepper. Sauté about 5 minutes, stirring often, until the onion is translucent. Stir in the rice, 1½ teaspoons salt, and a pinch of pepper. Cook 2 minutes, stirring continuously, until the rice just begins to toast and the grains of rice have a white dot at their center.

Pour in the white wine, and once it has evaporated, quickly add 1 cup of the hot stock, stirring continuously. When the stock is completely absorbed, begin adding the liquid in 1-cup batches, stirring all the time with a wooden spoon in a rhythmic back-and-forth motion. Wait for each batch of liquid to be absorbed before adding the next. The rice should be bubbling and quickly absorbing the stock. After about 15 minutes, taste the rice for doneness. It should be slightly but not too al dente. The risotto may need more liquid and more time, so keep cooking until it's done. It should be neither soupy nor dry; each grain of rice should be coated in a flavorful, starchy "sauce."

When the rice is almost done, turn off the heat and stir in the shell beans. Let the risotto "rest" for a minute or two and then quickly stir in the remaining tablespoon butter, the spinach, parsley, and basil. Taste for seasoning. The rice will keep absorbing liquid so add a little more stock if it seems dry.

3½ cups chicken stock

4 tablespoons unsalted butter

1 cup diced white onion

2 teaspoons thyme leaves

1 chile de árbol, crumbled

1½ cups high-quality Arborio rice (see Sources)

¼ cup white wine

1 cup cooked mixed shell beans (see page 193)

2 ounces young spinach, sliced

2 tablespoons sliced flat-leaf parsley

2 tablespoons sliced opal basil

Kosher salt and freshly ground black pepper

pork porterhouse with sautéed quince, apples, and potatoes

6 pork porterhouse, 8 to 10
    ounces each, about
    1¼ inches thick

1 recipe brine (page 214)

4 ounces quince paste (*membrillo*
    or *cotognata*) (see Sources)

2 tablespoons extra-virgin
    olive oil

Sautéed quince, apples, and
    potatoes (recipe follows)

1 bunch small dandelion greens,
    cleaned

This is not your mild-mannered pork chop! The pork porterhouse is two cuts of meat in one—just like its better-known cousin the beef porterhouse. From the short loin of the pig, the pork porterhouse (porkerhouse?) consists of the soft, luscious tenderloin on one side of the bone and the meatier loin on the other.

The classic American accompaniment to pork is, of course, apples. But in place of the traditional applesauce, I like to serve these hefty chops with the time-honored duo of apples and potatoes. Called *deux pommes*, or two apples—one from a tree and one from the earth—the two are sautéed together until crispy and golden brown. To show off more of fall's cornucopia, I've added quince, "Eve's apple," to the mix. Slathering the chops with quince jam (*membrillo* in Spanish cuisine, *cotognata* in Italian) is a sophisticated nod back to that applesauce.

Be sure to cut the quince, apples, and potatoes into similar-sized pieces, so when they're cooked they all look the same. The mystery is part of the fun; there's no telling which bite will be which *pomme*.

NOTE Brine the pork chops a day or two before serving. You can roast the potatoes and sauté the apples and quince in advance. Sauté the potatoes right before you grill the pork; you can keep them warm in the oven.

Submerge the pork chops in the brine and refrigerate for 24 hours.

Light the grill 30 to 40 minutes before cooking, and remove the pork chops from the refrigerator. If they're still wet from the brine, pat them dry with paper towels. Take the quince paste out of the refrigerator and put in a warm spot to soften to a spreadable consistency.

When the coals are broken down, red, and glowing, brush the pork chops with the olive oil and place them on the grill. Cook them on the first side about 5 minutes, rotating them a couple of times. When they have nice color, turn them over and cook another 4 to 5 minutes, rotating them once or twice. The pork chops should be cooked to just under medium. Peek inside at the bone; they should still be a little pink, and when you press them with your thumb, they should be springy.

Arrange the hot sautéed quince, apples, and potatoes on a large warm platter. Scatter the dandelion greens over them. Slather the chops with the quince paste, and place them on top.

sautéed quince, apples, and potatoes

Preheat the oven to 400°F.

Toss the potatoes with 1 tablespoon olive oil, the garlic, thyme sprigs, bay leaf, and 1 teaspoon salt. Place in a roasting pan, cover with aluminum foil, and cook about 45 minutes, until tender when pierced. (Depending on the size, age, and variety of potatoes, cooking time will vary.)

When the potatoes have cooled, peel them. Cut the potatoes in half lengthwise, and then place them, cut side down, on a cutting board. Cut each half crosswise into four or five wedges.

While the potatoes are cooking, heat a large sauté pan over high heat for 2 minutes. Swirl in 1 tablespoon olive oil and wait 1 minute. Carefully place the apples in the pan, flat side down. Add 2 tablespoons butter, and season with 1 teaspoon thyme leaves, 1 teaspoon salt, and a pinch of black pepper. Turn the heat down to medium, and cook about 5 minutes, until the apples are a beautiful deep golden brown. Turn the apples over, and continue cooking until they're golden on the second side. They should be tender and cooked through. Transfer them to a plate to cool.

Repeat this process with the quince. (They will take a little longer to cook.)

Heat a large sauté pan over high heat for 2 minutes. Swirl in 2 tablespoons olive oil and wait 1 minute. Place the potato wedges carefully in the pan, and season with the remaining teaspoon thyme leaves, ¼ teaspoon salt, and some freshly ground black pepper. Cook the potatoes about 8 minutes, until they are crispy on one side. (Don't try to move them or turn them if they are stuck to the pan; they will eventually release themselves if you're patient.)

Turn the potatoes over, add another tablespoon olive oil to the pan, and season the second side with ¼ teaspoon salt. Cook another 3 to 4 minutes, and then add the apples and quince. Cook a few more minutes, tossing well to combine. Taste for seasoning, and add the parsley.

1 pound medium Yukon Gold potatoes, ideally the size of the apples

6 tablespoons extra-virgin olive oil

3 cloves garlic, unpeeled, smashed

4 sprigs thyme, plus 1 tablespoon fresh thyme leaves

1 bay leaf

3 apples, peeled, cored, and cut into 8 wedges each

4 tablespoons unsalted butter

2 quince, peeled, cored, and cut into 12 wedges each

¼ cup chopped flat-leaf parsley

Kosher salt and freshly ground black pepper

cranberry-walnut clafoutis with bourbon whipped cream

The clafoutis was invented in Limousin, France, to showcase that region's famous cherries. Some compare the eggy consistency of clafoutis to flan, as it's neither cake nor custard. To me, it's more like an extra-thick crêpe dotted with fruit. Clafoutis puffs beautifully as it bakes, and hot out of the oven, it's crisp on the outside and airy in the middle. When chilled, however, it collapses, becoming dense and custardlike. I love it both ways.

One of the great aspects of clafoutis is its versatility. Once you know how to make the batter, you can make great desserts with it year-round. At Lucques, we've made clafoutis with sautéed apples in the winter and with berries in the summer. For the fall, I like a clafoutis featuring that indigenous American jewel, the cranberry. This dessert is delicious as is, but if you want to gild the lily, serve it with a dollop of bourbon-spiked whipped cream.

1 cup plus 2 tablespoons whole milk

2 tablespoons plus 1 teaspoon unsalted butter

3 extra-large eggs

½ cup plus 2 teaspoons granulated sugar

¾ cup all-purpose flour, sifted

½ teaspoon kosher salt

¾ cup walnuts

½ cup dried cranberries

1 cup heavy cream

1½ teaspoons bourbon

Heat the milk and 2 tablespoons butter in a small saucepan over medium heat until warm but not hot.

In a large bowl, whisk the eggs together. Whisk in ½ cup sugar, the flour, and the salt. Add the warm milk, whisking well to incorporate completely. Let the batter rest 1 hour at room temperature.

Preheat the oven to 375°F.

Spread the walnuts on a baking sheet, and toast about 10 minutes, until they're golden brown and smell nutty. When the nuts have cooled, chop them coarsely.

Butter a 10-inch round or oval baking dish with the 1 teaspoon butter. (You could also make six individual clafoutis if you like.) Sprinkle the remaining 2 teaspoons sugar in the dish, and tip it to coat the bottom and sides. Pour the batter into the dish. Scatter the walnuts and cranberries on top (most of them will sink). Bake about 45 minutes, until the clafoutis puffs up and is golden brown.

While the clafoutis finishes baking, whip the cream and bourbon to soft peaks.

Serve the clafoutis directly from the baking dish with the whipped cream on the side.

coleman farm's treviso with gorgonzola, walnuts, and saba

⅔ cup walnuts

2 tablespoons plus 1 teaspoon extra-virgin olive oil

3 heads Treviso

1 shallot, thinly sliced

1 tablespoon lemon juice

⅓ cup flat-leaf parsley leaves

½ pound Gorgonzola, at room temperature

About 2 teaspoons or more saba (see Sources)

¼ teaspoon freshly cracked black pepper

Kosher salt and freshly ground black pepper

Local farmer Bill Coleman specializes in all sorts of exotic herbs and greens, such as curry leaf, epazote, purslane, and fenugreek. When he can, Bill travels to faraway places to source unusual herbs and spices and little-known fruits and vegetables. He carries home the precious seeds and plants them at his farm near Santa Barbara, providing a wonderful source of inspiration for us lucky local chefs. It's always exciting to see what he will, literally, unearth next. A few years back, Treviso, a beautiful elongated relative of radicchio from the north of Italy, was his plant of the moment. Bill Coleman's Treviso practically dared me to come up with a dish that would show off its striking magenta leaves and complex, slightly bitter flavor. I paired the Treviso with pungent Gorgonzola and drizzled both with sweet saba, a syrup made by reducing grape must with sugar. This salad-meets-cheese course is the perfect beginning (or ending) to an autumn meal.

Preheat the oven to 375°F.

Spread the walnuts on a baking sheet and toast about 10 minutes, until they're golden brown and smell nutty. When the nuts have cooled, break them up with your hands and toss them with 1 teaspoon olive oil and a pinch of salt.

Cut the root ends off the Treviso, and remove any tough or damaged outer leaves. Set the delicate center leaves aside, and then stack the larger spears into piles of about six. Cut these lengthwise, into long ½-inch-thick ribbons.

Place all the Treviso and the sliced shallot in a large bowl. Drizzle with the remaining 2 tablespoons olive oil, the lemon juice, ¼ teaspoon salt, and freshly ground black pepper. Toss gently and taste for seasoning. Toss in the walnuts and the parsley leaves. Gently transfer the salad to a large platter.

Cut the cheese into ¼-inch-thick slabs. Tuck the cheese around the salad leaves (some of the slabs will crumble a little; this is fine).

Dip the tines of a dinner fork into the saba, and then, with swift, purposeful movements, whip the fork over the salad, leaving thin lines of saba across the white cheese. Top each piece of cheese with a little pinch of cracked black pepper. Serve more saba at the table if you like.

spiced snapper with carrot purée and gingered beets

This exotic spiced snapper dish evolved from the most mundane ingredient in the mix: the everyday carrot. But the carrots that inspired it, grown by local farmer Jerry Rutiz, are by no means ordinary. His funky-shaped, dirt-encrusted carrots are the sweetest and most delicious of any I've tasted.

One week at Lucques, we found ourselves with an abundance of Jerry's carrots. I ended up making a big batch of carrot soup for the staff, just to get the carrots out of the walk-in refrigerator. The result was so delicious that I had to find more ways to show off these remarkable roots. Caramelized and puréed with onion and cilantro, they are the perfect foil for this harissa-spiced snapper topped with gingered beets and lime salsa.

6 snapper fillets, 5 to 6 ounces each, skin on

¾ cup harissa (see page 225)

3 bunches baby beets

½ cup extra-virgin olive oil

2 teaspoons finely diced shallot

1 teaspoon finely diced jalapeño

½ teaspoon minced garlic

2 teaspoon grated fresh ginger

¼ cup minced mint

¼ cup minced cilantro

2 teaspoons lime juice

Carrot purée (recipe follows)

1 bunch watercress, cleaned, tough stems removed

½ lemon, for juicing

Kosher salt and freshly ground black pepper

Marinate the fish with the harissa, coating it well. Cover, and refrigerate at least 4 hours.

Preheat the oven to 400°F.

Cut the stems off the beets, leaving about ½-inch stem still attached. (Save the greens for sautéing later—they are delicious, so don't throw them away!) Clean the beets well, and toss them with 2 tablespoons olive oil and 1 teaspoon salt. Place the beets in a roasting pan with a splash of water in the bottom. Cover tightly with foil, and roast about 40 minutes, until tender when pierced. (The roasting time will depend on the size and type of beet.) When the beets are done, carefully remove the foil. Let cool, and peel the beets by slipping the skins off with your fingers. Cut them into ½-inch wedges.

Combine the shallot, jalapeño, garlic, ginger, mint, and cilantro in a large bowl, and stir in the remaining 6 tablespoons olive oil. Toss in the beets, and season with ¼ teaspoon salt, a few grindings of black pepper, and the lime juice. Taste for balance and seasoning.

Light the grill 30 to 40 minutes before you're ready to cook the snapper. Take the snapper out of the refrigerator 15 minutes before grilling.

When the coals are broken down, red, and glowing, season the snapper lightly with salt and pepper. (You don't need too much, because the harissa is salty and spicy.) Place the fish on the grill, skin side down, and cook 3 to 4 minutes, rotating the fish once after a couple of minutes to get the skin crispy. (The fish will stick to the grill initially, but it will eventually release. Don't try to move it too soon or force it if it seems stuck.) Turn the fish over, and cook a few minutes on the other side. Be careful not to overcook the snapper. When it's done, the fish will begin to flake and separate a little and the center will still be slightly translucent. Remember, the snapper will continue to cook a little more once you take it off the grill.

Spoon the hot carrot purée onto a large warm platter. Scatter the watercress over the purée and arrange the fish on top. Season the fish with a squeeze of lemon juice, and spoon the gingered beets and their vinaigrette over and around the fish.

carrot purée

2 pounds carrots, peeled and cut into ¼-inch rounds

A handful of cilantro stems, plus ¼ cup leaves

¾ cup extra-virgin olive oil

1 cup diced white onion

Kosher salt and freshly ground black pepper

Steam the carrots with the cilantro stems about 20 minutes, until tender. When the carrots are almost done, heat a Dutch oven over high heat for 1 minute. Pour in ½ cup olive oil, and add the onion. Season with 2 teaspoons salt and ¼ teaspoon freshly ground black pepper, and cook the onion about 5 minutes, stirring often, until it's translucent. Add the steamed carrots and cilantro leaves and cook another 8 minutes, stirring and scraping the pan with a wooden spoon, until the carrots are lightly caramelized. Purée the mixture in a food processor until it's smooth. With the motor running, slowly pour in the remaining ¼ cup olive oil, and process until the oil is incorporated and the purée is very smooth. Taste for seasoning.

braised chicken with saffron onions, italian couscous, and dates

While I'm not a fusion person, I do often find myself melding different cultures into a single dish. This chicken dish is a great example, drawing paprika and sherry from Spain, and dates, saffron, and couscous from Morocco. In place of Morrocan couscous in this dish I use *fregola sarda,* Sardinia's answer to traditional couscous. *Fregola sarda* is made from hand-rolled balls of coarsely ground semolina. Although often called "Italian couscous," its larger size and slightly toasted flavor distinguish it from its North African counterpart. It lends the dish a nutty flavor and chewy texture, and is the perfect accompaniment to soak up all the spiced broth and fragrant saffron onions. The final addition of sliced dates and fresh herbs gives this Mediterranean tagine a sweet finish.

NOTE The chicken is even better when it's braised the day before. Remember, it needs to marinate a day ahead.

Toast the cumin seeds in a small pan for a few minutes, until the seeds release their aroma and are lightly browned. Using a mortar and pestle, pound them coarsely. Repeat with the coriander seeds.

Place the chicken in a large bowl with the smashed garlic, thyme, parsley, crumbled chile, cumin, coriander, and paprika. Using your hands, toss the chicken and spices together to coat the chicken well. Cover, and refrigerate at least 4 hours, preferably overnight.

Remove the chicken from the refrigerator 30 minutes before cooking, to allow it to come to room temperature. After 15 minutes, season the chicken on all sides with 1 tablespoon and 1 teaspoon salt and lots of pepper.

Preheat the oven to 325°F.

Heat a large sauté pan over high heat for 2 minutes. Swirl in the olive oil and wait 1 minute. Place the chicken legs, skin side down, in the pan, and cook 8 to 10 minutes, until golden brown and crispy. (If your pan is too small for all of the legs to fit, brown them in batches so you don't crowd them.) Every so often, swirl the oil and rendered fat around the pan. Turn the legs over, and reduce the heat to medium. Cook 2 minutes on the second side. Arrange the chicken (in one layer) in a braising dish. The chicken legs should just fit in the pan.

1 tablespoon plus 1 teaspoon cumin seeds

2 tablespoons coriander seeds

6 chicken legs with thighs attached

3 cloves garlic, smashed

1 tablespoon thyme leaves

2 tablespoons sliced flat-leaf parsley

1 chile de árbol, crumbled

2 teaspoons bittersweet paprika

2 tablespoons extra-virgin olive oil

1 cup sliced onion

1 cup sliced fennel

2 bay leaves

¼ cup chopped San Marzano canned tomatoes

2 tablespoons sherry vinegar

½ cup white wine

½ cup sherry

4 cups chicken stock

¼ cup cilantro leaves

Italian couscous (recipe follows)

Saffron onions (recipe follows)

Date relish (recipe follows)

Kosher salt and freshly ground black pepper

Pour off some of the fat and return the sauté pan to medium heat. Add the onion, fennel, and bay leaves. Cook 6 to 7 minutes, stirring often, until the vegetables are lightly caramelized. Add the tomatoes and cook another 5 minutes, stirring and scraping with a wooden spoon. Add the sherry vinegar, white wine, and sherry. Turn the heat up to high and reduce by half. Add the chicken stock and bring to a boil.

Add the cilantro and pour the broth and vegetables over the chicken, scraping off any of the vegetables that have fallen on the chicken back into the liquid. The liquid should not quite cover the chicken. Cover the pan very tightly with plastic wrap (yes, it can go in the oven) and then aluminum foil. Braise in the oven 1½ to 2 hours.

To check the chicken for doneness, remove the plastic and foil, being careful of the steam. Pierce a piece of the chicken with a paring knife. If the meat is done, it will yield easily and be tender but not quite falling off the bone.

Turn the oven up to 400°F.

Transfer the chicken to a baking sheet, and return it to the oven to brown for about 10 minutes.

Strain the broth into a saucepan, pressing down on the vegetables with a ladle to extract all the juices. If necessary, reduce the broth over medium-high heat for about 5 minutes, to thicken it slightly.

Place the hot couscous on a large warm platter. Spoon the saffron onions over it, and arrange the chicken on top. Ladle some of the juices over the chicken, and top each leg with a spoonful of date relish. Serve the extra broth and date relish on the side.

italian couscous

Bring a large pot of heavily salted water to a boil over high heat.

Add the couscous and cook 8 to 10 minutes, until tender but still al dente.

Drain the couscous, return it to the pot, and toss with the butter, parsley, and a pinch of pepper. Taste for seasoning.

2½ cups Italian couscous, or *fregola sarda*

2 tablespoons unsalted butter

2 tablespoons chopped flat-leaf parsley

Kosher salt and freshly ground black pepper

saffron onions

1 teaspoon saffron threads

3 tablespoons unsalted butter

3 tablespoons extra-virgin olive oil

5 cups sliced onions (about 1¼ pounds)

1 bay leaf

1 chile de árbol, crumbled

1 teaspoon thyme leaves

Kosher salt and freshly ground black pepper

Toast the saffron threads in a small pan over medium heat until they just dry and become brittle. Be careful not to burn the precious saffron. Pound the saffron in a mortar to a fine powder. Dab a tablespoon of the butter into the powder, using the butter to pick up the saffron.

Heat a large sauté pan or Dutch oven over medium heat for 2 minutes. Add the olive oil, remaining butter, and saffron. When the butter foams, add the onions, bay leaf, chile, thyme, 1½ teaspoons salt, and some pepper. Cook 8 to 10 minutes, stirring often, as the onions wilt. Turn the heat down to low, and cook another 20 minutes, stirring every now and then, until the onions are soft and sweet. Taste for seasoning.

date relish

½ cup Deglet Noor dates

2 tablespoons super-good extra-virgin olive oil

1 tablespoon lemon juice

2 tablespoons sliced flat-leaf parsley

1 tablespoon sliced cilantro

Kosher salt and freshly ground black pepper

Pit the dates, and slice them thinly lengthwise.

Toss the dates with the olive oil, lemon juice, parsley, and cilantro. Season with ½ teaspoon salt and some pepper.

olive oil cake with crème fraîche and candied tangerines

I have a well-deserved reputation as an olive oil junkie. I use olive oil in most dishes, and not with a light hand. When my regular customers saw this dessert on the menu, they thought I'd gone too far—until they tasted it. The oil takes the place of butter and makes for an incredibly moist crumb. It's delicious with candied oranges and whipped cream, or by itself in the afternoon with a cup of tea. Or if you're a chocolate lover, try a slice drizzled with the chocolate sauce from the meringues recipe on pages 159–160.

1 cup extra-virgin olive oil, plus
    extra for greasing the pan
¾ cup all-purpose flour
2½ teaspoons baking powder
½ cup semolina
½ teaspoon kosher salt
¼ cup brandy
3 extra-large eggs
6 extra-large egg yolks
1 cup granulated sugar
1 cup heavy cream
¼ cup crème fraîche
Candied tangerines
    (recipe follows)

Preheat the oven to 375°F.

Brush a 9-inch round cake pan with a little olive oil.

Sift the flour and baking powder together and then stir in the semolina and salt. Combine 1 cup olive oil and the brandy in a small bowl.

Using a stand mixer fitted with the whisk attachment, beat the eggs, yolks, and sugar at high speed for 7 minutes until full volume. Remove the bowl from the mixer and transfer the egg mixture to a large bowl. Alternate folding in the dry and wet ingredients, a third at a time. Pour the batter into the prepared cake pan. Tap the pan three times to remove any air bubbles.

Bake about 40 minutes until the cake begins to pull away from the sides of the pan and a toothpick inserted into the center comes out clean. The cake should be golden brown and spring back slightly when you touch the center. Cool the cake on a rack for at least 15 minutes.

Using a stand mixer fitted with the whisk attachment, whip the cream and crème fraîche together to soft peaks.

Cut six slices from the cake and place them on six dessert plates. Spoon some of the candied tangerines and syrup over each piece and dollop with the whipped cream.

candied tangerines

½ vanilla bean

1 cup granulated sugar

1 cup water

6 tangerines, peeled and
separated into segments

Slice the vanilla bean in half lengthwise, and use a paring knife to scrape the seeds and pulp into a medium saucepan. Add the vanilla pod, the sugar, and the water and bring to a boil over medium-high heat.

Meanwhile, remove all the white veins, or pith, from the tangerine segments.

Turn the heat down to low and add the tangerines to the syrup. Simmer the fruit 3 to 5 minutes, until the tangerines look a little puffy and shiny.

Strain the mixture over a bowl and discard the vanilla pod. Return the liquid to the pan and reduce over medium-high heat until it's slightly thickened and coats the back of a spoon.

Allow the syrup to cool completely and gently stir in the tangerines.

warm wild mushroom salad with soft herbs, pecorino, and hazelnuts

In this indulgent salad, wild mushrooms are sautéed until tender and crisp, then tossed in a warm sherry vinaigrette with bitter greens and herbs. There are so many different herbs in this salad that each forkful tastes different, depending on which herb you bite into. Chervil contributes a mild anise nuance, while chives add a peppery, oniony note. Tarragon has a pungent licorice bite, and parsley a bright grassiness. Ribbons of pecorino and a sprinkling of toasted hazelnuts are the final layer of luxury in this delicious warm salad.

All Italian sheep's milk cheeses are called pecorino. They are usually named after their place of origin, as in Pecorino Romano or Pecorino Toscano. However, my favorite pecorino, Pecorino di Grotta, for this salad is from the Emilia-Romagna region. The story goes that the local housewives would hide a wheel or two of this aged cheese in the basement (*grotta*), storing it for later, when they would sneak out of the house and sell it for pocket money. Let's hope that times have changed for the ladies in Emilia-Romagna!

½ cup blanched hazelnuts

2 tablespoons finely diced shallots

3 tablespoons sherry vinegar

9 tablespoons extra-virgin olive oil

2 pounds wild mushrooms, such as chanterelles, black trumpets, or hedgehogs, cleaned

2 tablespoons unsalted butter

2 teaspoons thyme leaves

6 ounces mixed salad of Treviso, dandelion greens, and frisée, cleaned and dried

¼ cup tarragon leaves

¼ cup chervil sprigs

½ cup flat-leaf parsley leaves

¼ cup ½-inch chive *bâtonnets*

¼ cup sliced shallots

¼-pound hunk Pecorino di Grotta or other pecorino

Kosher salt and freshly ground black pepper

Preheat the oven to 375°F.

Toast the hazelnuts on a baking sheet 8 to 10 minutes, tossing them once or twice, until they smell nutty and are a light golden brown. Let them cool, then chop the hazelnuts coarsely.

Place the diced shallots, sherry vinegar, and ½ teaspoon salt in a bowl, and let sit for 5 minutes. Whisk in 5 tablespoons olive oil and set aside.

If the mushrooms are large, tear them into large (1½- to 2-inch) pieces. (They'll shrink once they're cooked, so don't make them too small.)

Heat a large sauté pan over high heat for 2 minutes. Add 2 tablespoons olive oil and heat another minute. Swirl in 1 tablespoon butter, and when it foams, scatter half the mushrooms in the pan. Season with 1 teaspoon thyme, ¾ teaspoon salt, and a healthy pinch of pepper. Sauté the mushrooms about 5 minutes, stirring occasionally, until they're tender and a little crispy. (The cooking time will depend on the particular mushrooms you use.) Transfer the cooked mushrooms to a plate, and repeat with the second batch.

Meanwhile, place the salad and herbs in a large salad bowl.

When the second batch of mushrooms is done, add the first batch back to the pan. Cook for another minute or two to heat thoroughly, then toss in the sliced shallots. Spoon the hot mushrooms over the salad. Return the pan to the stove and add three-quarters of the vinaigrette, swirling the pan to heat it. When the dressing is very warm, pour it over the salad. Season with ¼ teaspoon salt and freshly ground black pepper. Toss carefully to dress the salad and mushrooms, and taste for seasoning. You may need a little more salt, pepper, vinaigrette, or straight sherry vinegar.

Arrange half the salad on a large platter. Use a vegetable peeler to shave some pecorino over the salad, and sprinkle half the hazelnuts over that. Place the remaining salad on top, and finish with shavings of cheese and the rest of the nuts.

grilled quail with pancetta, ricotta pudding, and sicilian breadcrumbs

I hope this quail recipe tempts you to venture away from the usual poultry mainstays. These smaller birds don't have as much meat as others, but they make up for their size in flavor. On this platter, you'll find all of my favorite Sicilian ingredients. Ricotta is the favored soft cheese of the south, and here I've blended it into a hearty, savory pudding. Pancetta, the essential flavoring of so many things Italian, gives the wilted spinach its salty punch. Olive oil–toasted breadcrumbs are the crunchy finish, a tasty result of the Sicilians' thrifty mentality. And last but not least, currants and pine nuts are a classic Sicilian combination, bringing sweetness and earthiness to the dish.

Grilling the quail gives them a smokiness you can't achieve in the oven. Build a large fire, and spread the coals to heat the entire surface of the grill. If your barbecue is too small to accommodate all twelve birds at once, grill them in batches and reheat in a very hot oven just before serving. Watch the birds carefully as they grill, so they don't overcook and dry out.

> NOTE If you can't find boneless quail, butterfly whole ones: Use scissors to cut through the cavity down one side of their backbones, and then place them on a cutting board and gently press down with the heel of your hand to flatten them slightly. Prep and marinate the quail the night before. You can also make the currant–pine nut relish a day ahead.

12 boneless quail (see note)

2 tablespoons coarsely chopped rosemary, plus 2 small sprigs rosemary

2 tablespoons plus 2 teaspoons thyme leaves

2 chiles de árbol, thinly sliced on the diagonal

7 tablespoons extra-virgin olive oil

1 cup fresh breadcrumbs

Six ⅛-inch-thick slices pancetta, about 6 ounces total

1 cup sliced shallots

½ cup currant–pine nut relish (see page 58)

10 to 12 ounces young spinach, cleaned, large stems removed

½ lemon, for juicing

Ricotta pudding (recipe follows)

Kosher salt and freshly ground black pepper

Season the quail with the chopped rosemary, 2 tablespoons thyme, half the sliced chiles, and 2 tablespoons olive oil. Cover and refrigerate at least 4 hours, preferably overnight.

Preheat the oven to 375°F.

Toss the breadcrumbs with 2 tablespoons olive oil. Spread them on a baking sheet, and toast 8 to 10 minutes, stirring once or twice, until golden brown.

Light the grill 30 to 40 minutes before you're ready to cook. (Remember to use extra coals, spreading them out, so the heat is evenly dispersed over the entire area of the grill.) Take the quail out of the refrigerator to come to room temperature.

Stack the pancetta slices and cut them into quarters. Heat a large, deep sauté

pan or Dutch oven over high heat for 2 minutes. Add 2 tablespoons olive oil, swirl, and place the pieces of pancetta in the pan. Cook 2 to 3 minutes, until the pancetta is crisp, and turn the pieces over. Add the rosemary sprigs to the pan, and cook another 2 to 3 minutes, until the pancetta is crispy on the second side. Turn the heat down to medium and add the shallots, 2 teaspoons thyme, and the remaining sliced chile. Sauté 3 to 4 minutes, stirring often, until the shallots are translucent and starting to caramelize. Turn off the heat.

When the coals are broken down, red, and glowing, season the quail with salt and pepper. Tuck the wing tips behind the wing joints. Place the quail, breast side down if you're using boneless or skin side down if you're using butterflied, on the grill. Cook 3 to 4 minutes, rotating the birds a few times, until the skin crisps. Turn the quail over and cook them another 2 to 3 minutes or so, until the meat is just rosy. I like to peek inside the legs (a rather obscene gesture, I know, but it works!) to check for doneness.

Toss the currant–pine nut relish with the breadcrumbs. Season with a pinch of salt and pepper and taste. (These are the Sicilian breadcrumbs.)

Reheat the shallots and pancetta over medium-high heat for 1 to 2 minutes, until hot. Turn off the heat, and add half the spinach. Toss quickly with tongs to combine the ingredients. As the spinach just begins to wilt (this will happen very quickly), add the rest of the spinach, tossing to coat well with the pancetta and shallots. Season with ½ teaspoon salt, a pinch of freshly ground black pepper, and some lemon juice. Taste for seasoning, and arrange on a large warm platter.

Place the quail over the spinach, and sprinkle the Sicilian breadcrumbs on top. Serve the warm ricotta pudding on the side.

ricotta pudding

Preheat the oven to 350°F.

Whisk the eggs, egg yolk, and ricotta together in a large mixing bowl. Add the cream, milk, 1 teaspoon thyme, 2 teaspoons salt, and ¼ teaspoon pepper. Whisk to combine. The mixture will be a little lumpy.

Taste for seasoning, and pour into a buttered 9-inch baking dish. Decorate the top of the pudding with the chile and remaining ½ teaspoon thyme. Cover the dish with foil, place it in a water bath, and bake about 1 hour, until the custard is just set.

2 extra-large eggs

1 extra-large egg yolk

2 cups fresh whole milk ricotta, drained if wet

1 cup heavy cream

1 cup whole milk

1½ teaspoons thyme leaves

1 chile de árbol, thinly sliced on the diagonal

Kosher salt and freshly ground black pepper

pan-roasted rib eye steak "marchand de vins" with watercress and grossi's potatoes

6 rib eye steaks, 10 ounces each, about 1½ inches thick

2 to 3 tablespoons *fleur de sel*

1 to 2 tablespoons freshly cracked black pepper

2 tablespoons extra-virgin olive oil

8 tablespoons (1 stick) unsalted butter

2 bunches watercress, cleaned, tough stems removed

2 tablespoons super-good extra-virgin olive oil

½ lemon, for juicing

½ cup finely diced shallots

1 cup red wine

2 tablespoons chopped flat-leaf parsley

Grossi's potatoes (recipe follows)

Kosher salt and freshly ground black pepper

My mother's version of this juicy pan-fried steak came from her grease-marked kitchen bible, *Mastering the Art of French Cooking*, by Julia Child. The classic bistro sauce is made by sautéing minced shallots in the same pan as the steak, adding a generous amount of red wine, and finishing it with butter and parsley.

Although I love the smoky flavor of the grill, nothing gives the meat a better crust than a very hot cast-iron pan. And if you're planning on making a pan sauce, those crispy bits left behind by the steak will give it a deep, meaty flavor. But remember to get the pan super-hot and smoking before cooking the steaks. You might have to disconnect your smoke alarm temporarily, but it's worth it.

NOTE You can roast the potatoes for Grossi's potatoes ahead of time and sauté them while you cook the steaks (or do them a little ahead and hold them in a warm oven). If you don't have two cast-iron pans, cook the steaks in batches. After they're sautéed, let the first steaks rest on a wire rack set on a baking sheet while the other steaks finish cooking. You can reheat them by putting the entire baking sheet (leaving the meat on the rack) in a 425°F oven.

Remove the steaks from the refrigerator 30 minutes before cooking to let them come to room temperature. Season them on both sides with *fleur de sel* and cracked black pepper.

Heat two large cast-iron pans over high heat for 8 minutes. Drizzle 2 table-spoons olive oil over the steaks, and place them in the hot pans. Sear them 2 min-utes, and then add a tablespoon of butter to each pan. Cook another 2 minutes or so, until the steaks are well browned and caramelized. Turn the steaks over, and cook them about 3 to 4 minutes more for medium-rare. Baste the steaks often with the butter by carefully tipping the pan, scooping up the butter with a spoon, and pouring it over the tops of the steaks. When the steaks have reached the desired degree of doneness, remove them from the pan and rest them on a wire rack (so they don't steam and continue cooking).

Toss the watercress with the super-good extra-virgin olive oil, salt, pepper, and a squeeze of lemon juice. Taste for balance and seasoning.

Pour the fat out of the pans and return one pan to the stove over medium heat. (You will need only one pan to make the sauce.) Add 1 tablespoon butter and the diced shallots. Sauté the shallots 2 minutes, scraping the pan constantly with a wooden spoon. When the shallots are just starting to caramelize and have picked up lots of crispy bits, pour the wine into the pan. Turn the heat up to high and cook about 4 minutes, scraping the bottom of the pan constantly with a wooden spoon, until the wine has reduced by two-thirds. Swirl in the remaining 5 tablespoons butter, and cook another minute, until the butter is incorporated. Turn off the heat, taste for seasoning, and add the chopped parsley.

Place the watercress at one side of a platter with a few watercress leaves scattered over the rest of the platter. Lay the steaks on the platter, and spoon the hot sauce over them. Serve Grossi's potatoes on the side.

grossi's potatoes

In the early days at Lucques, Corina Weibel, my opening sous-chef, and I were the only two cooks in the kitchen on Sundays. After a hectic Saturday night, both of us looked forward to cooking in a tranquil kitchen on Sunday. During those afternoons, Corina loved to tell stories about her Swiss heritage and to reminisce about her grandmother's cooking. When she described her *grossi's* potatoes, a combination of crisp sautéed potatoes with a coating of crunchy breadcrumbs, I knew I would love them (starch plus starch!).

2 pounds Yukon Gold potatoes (about 4 medium-sized)

7 tablespoons extra-virgin olive oil

3 cloves garlic, unpeeled and smashed

4 thyme sprigs, plus 1 tablespoon thyme leaves

1 bay leaf

1 cup fresh breadcrumbs

4 tablespoons unsalted butter

2 tablespoons sliced flat-leaf parsley

Kosher salt and freshly ground black pepper

Preheat the oven to 400°F.

Toss the potatoes with 2 tablespoons olive oil, the garlic, thyme sprigs, bay leaf, and 2 teaspoons salt. Place in a roasting pan, cover with aluminum foil, and roast about 50 minutes, until tender when pierced.

Toss the breadcrumbs with 2 tablespoons olive oil. Spread them on a baking sheet and toast 8 to 10 minutes, stirring once or twice, until light golden brown.

When the potatoes have cooled, peel them and cut them in half lengthwise. Place each half, cut side down, on a cutting board, and cut crosswise into five wedges.

Heat a large sauté pan over high heat for 2 minutes. Pour in 2 tablespoons olive oil, swirl the pan, and wait 1 minute. Place the potato wedges carefully in the pan, cut side down. (It's okay if they won't all fit; you can add the stragglers later.) Season with ½ teaspoon salt, the thyme leaves, and some pepper. Cook them about 8 minutes, until they are crispy on one side. Don't try to move them or turn them if they are stuck to the pan; they will eventually release themselves if you're patient!

Now turn the potatoes over, and add any remaining potatoes to the pan with a tablespoon olive oil and ½ teaspoon salt. Cook another 8 minutes, scraping and tossing vigorously with a metal spatula (they don't need to lie perfectly flat this time). Add the butter, and when it foams, sprinkle the breadcrumbs into the pan. Sauté, stirring continuously, 2 to 3 minutes, until the potatoes are deep golden brown and completely coated in the crumbs. You want to cook the potatoes and crumbs together as long as possible without letting the crumbs burn. Toss in the parsley, and taste for seasoning.

caramel-nut tart with milk chocolate and cognac cream

This nut tart is my dream dessert: sticky caramel poured into a buttery crust and studded with salty nuts. It's a chewy, gooey delight, and whenever it's on the menu at Lucques I can't stop myself from sneaking over to the pastry station and cutting paper-thin slices to snack on. It's also an addictive finger food, so encourage your guests to pick it up and eat it with their hands instead of struggling with a knife and fork. To turn it into a decadent, highbrow candy bar, drizzle some milk chocolate over each slice and dollop with cognac cream.

NOTE The tricky part to this dessert is making the caramel filling. If it cooks too long, it will taste bitter; and if it doesn't cook long enough, it won't achieve that chewy consistency.

1 recipe pâte sucrée (see page 196)

1¾ cups whole nuts (I like a combination of almonds, walnuts, macadamia, pine nuts, pecans, and hazelnuts)

2½ cups granulated sugar

1⅔ cup heavy cream

2 teaspoons mild honey, such as orange blossom

½ teaspoon kosher salt

6 ounces milk chocolate

1½ teaspoons cognac

Preheat the oven to 375°F.

Line the tart pan with the pâte sucrée according to page 196. Prick the bottom with a fork and line it with a few open and fanned out coffee filters or a piece of parchment paper. Fill the lined tart shell with beans or pie weights, and bake 15 minutes, until set. Take the tart out of the oven, and carefully lift out the paper and beans. Return the tart to the oven, and bake another 10 to 15 minutes, until the crust is an even golden brown. Set the tart on a rack to cool completely.

Spread the nuts on a baking sheet (keep each type separate) and toast 8 to 12 minutes, until they're golden brown and smell nutty. Some will toast more quickly than others, so watch them carefully and remove the toasted nuts as needed.

Place the sugar and 1 cup water in a very clean medium-sized heavy-bottomed saucepan. Over medium-high heat, cook the sugar, shaking the pan often to stir—don't use a utensil to stir, as it could cause the sugar to crystallize. Continue cooking and swirling the pan until the caramel is a deep golden brown, just beyond the soft-crack stage (about 310°F on a candy thermometer). It should be a nice dark color, but not burned.

Remove from the heat, and slowly whisk in ⅔ cup cream, stirring with the whisk the entire time, until the caramel is smooth and the cream is fully incorporated. (Be aware that the caramel will foam up as you add the cream. It's very hot, so be careful and pour slowly.) Allow to cool a few minutes. Place the nuts and honey in a bowl. Pour the caramel over them, and stir to combine well. Season with ¼ teaspoon salt, and pour the mixture into the baked tart shell, to just below the rim. It's important not to overfill the crust. Refrigerate the tart at least 2 hours.

Melt the milk chocolate in a small saucepan over very low heat, and stir in ⅓ cup water. Just before serving, whip 1 cup cream and the cognac to soft peaks in a stand mixer fitted with the whisk attachment.

Slice the tart in half, and cut one half into twelve thin slices. Refrigerate the rest for leftover snacking. Place one slice at the center of each of six plates. Prop up a second slice on top of the first, setting it at an angle and letting the pointed end of the slice rest on the plate. Continue with the remaining slices. Garnish each with three dollops of the cognac cream, and drizzle the milk chocolate across the tart.

roasted beet salad with fried chickpeas, nyons olives, and ricotta salata

I was raised by a beet-hating mother, so we never ate them when I was grow-
ing up. But when I left the nest and actually tasted a "forbidden" fresh beet, I was
smitten with its sweet earthiness and beautiful color. For years, my mother and I
battled back and forth: I relentlessly tried to convince her of beets' many virtues,
and she adamantly hung on to her contempt for them. One Sunday, she called
Lucques to ask me what we were serving for supper that night. And then I did it—
I lied to my mother. I couldn't help myself, and made up the name of a beetless
dish that I knew would tempt her. I told myself it was all for a good cause. When
Mom came in that night and tasted roasted beets, bathed in toasty cumin vinai-
grette and arranged on the plate with so many delicious treats, like Nyons olives,
fried chickpeas, and slivers of dried ricotta, I knew I had cured her of her beet-
hating ways.

3 bunches beets, mixed colors
    if possible

¾ cup extra-virgin olive oil

1½ teaspoons cumin seeds

2 tablespoons plus 2 teaspoons
    red wine vinegar

1 tablespoon lemon juice, plus
    more for seasoning

1 cup cooked chickpeas, drained
    (recipe follows)

¼ cup thinly sliced shallots

½ cup Nyons olives or other
    strong-tasting oil-cured black
    olives

½ cup flat-leaf parsley leaves

¼ pound ricotta salata cheese

Kosher salt and freshly ground
    black pepper

Preheat the oven to 400°F.

Cut the greens off the beets, leaving about ½ inch of the stem still attached. (Save the leaves for sautéing later—they are delicious!) Clean the beets well, and toss them with 2 tablespoons olive oil and 1 teaspoon salt. Place the beets in a roasting pan with a splash of water in the bottom. Cover the pan tightly with foil, and roast the beets about 40 minutes, until they're tender when pierced. (The roasting time will depend on the size and type of beet, so it's best to check them earlier.) When the beets are done, carefully remove the foil. Let cool, and peel the beets by slipping off the skins with your fingers. Slice the beets into wedges and place in a large bowl. (If the beets are small, just cut them in half.)

While the beets are roasting, toast the cumin seeds in a medium pan over medium heat 2 to 3 minutes, until the seeds release their aroma and darken slightly. Pound half the cumin seeds to a fine powder in a mortar.

Transfer this powder to a bowl with the remaining cumin seeds, ¼ teaspoon salt, red wine vinegar, and 1 tablespoon lemon juice. Whisk in ½ cup olive oil. Taste for balance and seasoning.

Add the remaining 2 tablespoons olive oil to the cumin pan, and heat 2 minutes, until the oil is very hot. Add the chickpeas, and fry them 4 to 5 minutes, shaking the pan often, until they are crispy. Drain on paper towels, and season with a few pinches of salt and some pepper.

Add the shallots to the beets, season with ¼ teaspoon salt and a few grindings of black pepper, and gently toss them with three-quarters of the vinaigrette. Season to taste, and add more lemon, salt, or freshly ground black pepper if you like.

Gently toss in the olives and parsley leaves. Add a little more vinaigrette if necessary.

Cut the ricotta salata into ¼-inch-thick slabs.

Arrange half the salad on a platter. Tuck half the cheese in and around the beets and scatter half the chickpeas on top. Place the rest of the salad on top and nestle the remaining ricotta salata and chickpeas into the salad.

chickpeas

¼ cup extra-virgin olive oil

½ cup diced onion

3 cloves garlic, smashed

1 chile de árbol, crumbled

1 teaspoon thyme

1 bay leaf

1½ cups dried chickpeas (see Sources)

1 teaspoon paprika

A healthy pinch cayenne pepper

1 cinnamon stick

Heat a medium pot over high heat for 2 minutes. Pour in the olive oil, wait a minute, and then add the onion, garlic, chile, thyme, and bay leaf. Cook for a minute or two until the onion is wilted and then add the chickpeas, paprika, cayenne, and cinnamon stick. Stir for a few minutes, coating the chickpeas with the oil and spices.

Cover with water by 3 inches, and bring to a boil over high heat. Turn the heat down to low, and place a paper towel on top of the chickpeas to keep them under the surface.

Simmer for 30 minutes, and then add 2½ teaspoons salt. Continue cooking on a low simmer about 1 hour, until the chickpeas are tender. As they cook, add water as necessary. When they are done, taste for seasoning and cool the chickpeas in their juices.

mussels and clams with vermouth, cannellini beans, and cavolo nero

1 pound cavolo nero or other hearty greens, center ribs removed

½ cup extra-virgin olive oil

1 cup diced red onion

1 cup diced fennel

¼ cup sliced garlic

2 chiles de árbol, crumbled

1 sprig rosemary

1 tablespoon thyme leaves

Cannellini beans (recipe follows)

2 pounds Manila clams, well scrubbed

2 pounds small- to medium-sized mussels, well scrubbed

1 cup dry vermouth

4 tablespoons unsalted butter

Super-good extra-virgin olive oil, for drizzling

Kosher salt and freshly ground black pepper

Shellfish and beans are a classic Italian combination. In the tradition of frugal and resourceful peasant cooking, nothing goes to waste in this dish. As the beans simmer away with the thyme, rosemary, and chile, they create another invaluable ingredient: a delicious stock. Starchy and flavorful, it's added to the steaming shellfish, thickening their juices into a complex broth. The cavolo nero adds an earthy note and a chewy texture to the seafood stew. This is a rustic family meal in which everyone should take part, serving themselves from the bountiful platter at the center of the table. And don't forget to serve big hunks of crusty bread for sopping up all those juices.

NOTE I like to use a wide pan, ideally 14 inches across, as opposed to a deep pan for this dish. That way all of the shellfish get coated and cook evenly. With a deeper pot, it's difficult to stir, and inevitably some of the mussels and clams end up on the top, brothless and dried out. If you don't have a lid for that wide pan, use a piece of tinfoil or two to fake a lid for steaming. And if you don't have a really wide pan, use two of your widest pans and split the recipe between them.

You can make the beans the day before.

Blanch the cavolo nero in heavily salted boiling water for 5 minutes. Drain, let cool, and squeeze out the excess water with your hands. Cut the greens into 1-inch ribbons.

Heat a very large sauté pan over high heat for 2 minutes. Pour in the ½ cup olive oil and wait a minute. Add the onion, fennel, garlic, crumbled chiles, rosemary, and thyme to the pan. Season with 1½ teaspoons salt and lots of pepper. Cook over medium heat 3 to 4 minutes, until the onion starts to wilt. Add the greens, and stir them to coat with the oil and onions. Cook about 10 minutes, until the vegetables are translucent and tender and the greens start to break down.

Drain the beans and reserve the liquid. Add the beans to the vegetables, and cook a minute or two. Turn the heat up to high and add the clams. Cook 2 minutes, stirring occasionally, then add the mussels, and stir well to combine. Pour in the vermouth and cover the pan. Let the shellfish steam a few minutes, until they open. Remove the lid and add 1 cup of the bean-cooking liquid. If the dish doesn't seem brothy enough, add a little more. Bring to a boil, stirring well to combine the flavors, and swirl in the butter. Taste for seasoning.

Serve in a large shallow bowl with a large serving spoon. Pass the super-good extra-virgin olive oil and hunks of crusty bread at the table. Remember to provide small bowls for shells.

cannellini beans

Toast the fennel seeds in a small pan over medium heat for 2 to 3 minutes, until they release their aroma and are golden brown. Pound the fennel seeds coarsely in a mortar.

Heat a medium pot over high heat for 2 minutes. Pour in the olive oil, and add the rosemary sprig and the crumbled chile. Let them sizzle in the oil about 1 minute. Add the onion, thyme, and fennel seeds, and sauté about 2 minutes, until the onion is wilted.

Add the beans to the pan and cook another minute, stirring to coat well. Cover with water by 3 inches, and bring to a boil over high heat. Turn the heat down to low, and place a paper towel over the beans to keep them underwater. Simmer, stirring once in a while. After 30 minutes, add the salt to the beans, and continue cooking at a low simmer until the beans are tender, about an hour. Remove the beans from the heat, and let them cool in their juices. As the beans cook, add water as necessary, but not too much. You want the bean liquid to be rich and a little starchy, because it will be an important part of the finished broth.

2 teaspoons fennel seeds
¼ cup extra-virgin olive oil
1 sprig rosemary
1 chile de árbol, crumbled
½ cup diced onion
1 tablespoon thyme leaves
1½ cups dried cannellini beans
2½ teaspoons kosher salt

grilled duck breasts with crème fraîche, roasted grapes, and potato-bacon gratin

If you've never had grilled duck breasts, you're in for a revelatory surprise. The contrasts are striking: the smoke of the grill against the richness of the duck fat, the juicy meat capped by crispy skin. At the restaurant, we buy Liberty Farms breasts (see Sources), which I have found superior to others in taste and texture. They raise a variety of duck called Pekin, a smaller, more compact bird (a single breast is perfect for one person) with a brighter, more delicate flavor and feel. You may have more luck finding Muscovy duck breasts, which are heftier, more steak-like. If you use Muscovy, you'll only need four breasts to feed six people.

Grilling duck breasts requires some attention. The fat from under the skin will inevitably drip into the fire, causing flare-ups, which can blacken the breasts if you're not careful. If a flare-up occurs, use tongs to snatch the breasts off the grill for a few seconds, then return them once the flames have subsided. You may need to move them around the grill almost continuously as the fat renders out. The reward for this vigilance, however, is perfection—crisp golden brown skin and plump, succulent meat. An easier option is to sauté them in a cast-iron pan over medium-low heat, still skin side down, taking your time to render the fat from under the skin. Once the skin is crisp, which can take longer than you might expect, turn the breast over and cook a few more minutes, until medium-rare.

NOTE Marinate the duck overnight and make the gratin in the morning, then reheat the gratin (giving it that beautiful gratinée color) while the ducks are on the grill.

1 tablespoon juniper berries

6 single Pekin duck breasts, 6 to 8 ounces each (or 4 larger Muscovy breasts)

1 tablespoon thyme leaves

½ pound seedless red or purple grapes, in bunches

2 teaspoons extra-virgin olive oil

1 bunch dandelion greens or arugula, cleaned

6 tablespoons crème fraîche

Potato-bacon gratin (recipe follows)

Kosher salt and freshly ground black pepper

Pound the juniper berries in a mortar until coarsely ground. Score the skin of the duck breasts with a sharp knife, and season with the juniper berries and the thyme. Cover, and refrigerate at least 4 hours, preferably overnight.

Light the grill 30 to 40 minutes before cooking, and remove the duck from the refrigerator and allow it to come to room temperature.

Preheat the oven to 450°F.

Using scissors, snip the grapes into six clusters. Toss the clusters gently with the olive oil, and season with salt and pepper. Roast the grapes on a baking sheet 12 to 15 minutes, until the skin is slightly crispy and starting to blister.

When the coals are broken down, red, and glowing, push the embers to one side of the grill. Season the duck with salt and pepper. Place the duck breasts, skin side down, on the cooler half of the grill. As they cook, rotate the breasts in a quarter-turn pattern every 2 minutes or so, to allow the fat to render and the skin to crisp. Turn the breasts over, and cook a few more minutes, until the duck is medium-rare and still springy to the touch. Remove from the heat, and rest 5 minutes, on a wire rack set over a baking sheet.

Scatter the greens onto a large warm platter. Slice the duck breasts, and place them over the greens. Spoon a little crème fraîche over each duck breast, and arrange the clusters of roasted grapes around the platter. Serve the potato-bacon gratin at the table.

potato-bacon gratin

½ pound slab applewood-smoked bacon

1 tablespoon extra-virgin olive oil

4 cups thinly sliced onions (about 1 pound)

1 tablespoon plus 2 teaspoons thyme leaves

2¼ pounds Yukon Gold potatoes, peeled

About 2 cups heavy cream

Kosher salt and freshly ground black pepper

This potato and bacon gratin was created by Rob Chalmers, a chef de cuisine at Lucques who had a great love of food and a big Boston attitude to go along with it. When he first told me about this gratin, I thought he was joking. That much fat in one pan might put even *me* over the edge. But lo and behold, bacon, potatoes, and cream really do taste good together!

Preheat the oven to 350°F.

Cut the bacon into ⅜-inch-thick slices, and stack them in two piles, then cut the bacon crosswise into ⅜-inch even-sided rectangular shapes, or *lardons*.

Heat a large sauté pan or Dutch oven over medium-high heat for a minute. Swirl in the olive oil and add the bacon. Cook the bacon about 5 minutes, stirring often, until tender and lightly crisped. Remove to a plate with a slotted spoon, reserving the bacon fat in the pan.

Add the onions, 2 teaspoons thyme, 1 teaspoon salt, and some pepper to the pan. Cook 15 minutes, stirring and scraping with a wooden spoon, until the onions start to caramelize. Turn the heat down to low, and continue to cook, about 10 minutes, stirring often, until the onions are a deep golden brown. Remove from the heat and set aside.

Use a mandoline to slice the potatoes into 1/16-inch-thick rounds. Pour ½ cup cream evenly onto the bottom of a 9-by-9-inch (or equivalent) gratin dish. Place one layer of potatoes side by side, slightly overlapping, on the bottom of the dish. Spread a third of the onions over them and scatter a third of the bacon on top. Arrange a second layer of potatoes, drizzle ¼ cup cream over it, and season with ¼ teaspoon salt, a healthy pinch of pepper, and 1 teaspoon thyme. Press the potatoes down with your fingers, letting the cream soak up through the layers. This will ensure that the cream is evenly distributed and coats the potatoes well.

Arrange another layer of potatoes on top, followed by another third of the caramelized onions and the bacon. Drizzle over another ¼ cup cream, and continue with two more layers of potatoes. Drizzle with ½ cup cream and season with ¼ teaspoon salt and a pinch of pepper. Press the potatoes down with your fingers again. Scatter the rest of the onions and bacon over the potatoes, and drizzle with ⅓ cup cream. Season one last time with ¼ teaspoon salt, 1 teaspoon thyme, and a pinch of pepper. The cream should cover the potatoes but not be "soupy." Add more cream if the gratin seems dry.

Cover tightly with plastic wrap (yes, it can go in the oven) and then foil. Bake 1½ hours, until the potatoes are tender when pierced. Remove from the oven, and carefully uncover. Turn the oven up to 425°F and return the gratin to the oven. Cook another 20 minutes or so, until the top is nice and golden brown, as in gratinéed.

sbrisolona with moscato d'asti zabaglione

¾ cup raw almonds

1 cup plus 2 tablespoons all-purpose flour

6 tablespoons finely ground cornmeal

½ teaspoon kosher salt

7 tablespoons cold unsalted butter, cut into small cubes, plus butter for the pan

3 tablespoons lightly packed brown sugar

⅓ cup granulated sugar

1 extra-large egg yolk

¼ teaspoon pure almond extract

¼ teaspoon pure vanilla extract

1 tablespoon finely grated orange zest

Moscato d'Asti zabaglione (recipe follows)

My ongoing quest to find new ways to eat butter, sugar, and nuts together resulted in this happy discovery: sbrisolona. A regional specialty of Mantova, Italy, this cookie gets its name from its crumbly texture. The dough is worked together by hand into a dry, coarse meal, pressed into a cake pan, and baked until it's very firm. I follow the Italian tradition and break the giant cookie into rough, jagged pieces. Like biscotti, its dense, nutty quality makes it the perfect vehicle for scooping up zabaglione. This old-fashioned Italian custard is traditionally made by whisking egg yolks, sugar, and Marsala wine over simmering water. In this festive version I've substituted slightly sweet sparkling Moscato d'Asti for the Marsala.

NOTE The zabaglione needs to cool for 2 hours before serving.

Preheat the oven to 350°F.

Spread the almonds on a baking sheet, and toast 8 to 10 minutes, tossing a couple of times, until they're golden brown and smell nutty. When they have cooled, chop the nuts coarsely.

Place the flour, cornmeal, and salt in a large bowl. Add the butter, and work it into the flour with your fingers until you have a coarse meal. Stir in the sugars and almonds. Make a well in the center of the dry ingredients.

Combine the egg yolk, extracts, and zest together in a small bowl. Pour into the well at the center of the dry ingredients. Mix gently with your hands. The dough will look dry and crumbly, similar to a streusel.

Transfer the dough into a buttered 8-inch springform pan. Very lightly, press the dough into the pan, being careful not to pack it too tightly; the top should be somewhat uneven.

Bake 30 to 40 minutes, until set and deep golden brown.

When it has cooled completely, break the sbrisolona into "rustic" pieces, and serve with a bowl of the zabaglione. Invite your guests to scoop up dollops of zabaglione onto the sbrisolona and eat with their hands. Serve with glasses of Moscato d'Asti, of course!

moscato d'asti zabaglione

Split the vanilla bean in half lengthwise and, using a paring knife, scrape the seeds and pulp into a medium saucepan. Add the vanilla pod, sugar, and ⅓ cup water. Bring to a boil over high heat, then reduce the heat to medium and cook, without stirring, to a light caramel. Add the Moscato (don't worry when the caramel seizes up; it will remelt). Reduce the mixture to 1 cup and remove the vanilla pod.

Whisk the egg yolks together in a large mixing bowl. Whisk a few table-spoons of the Moscato caramel into the egg yolks to temper them. Slowly, add another quarter or so of the mixture, whisking constantly. At this point, you can add the rest of the Moscato caramel in a slow steady stream, whisking all the time.

Place the mixture in a double boiler, and cook over low heat about 6 min-utes, whisking continuously, until it's thick and light in color and forms ribbons when it falls from the whisk. Cool in a stainless steel bowl in the refrigerator for at least 30 minutes.

When you're ready to serve, whip the cream in a stand mixer fitted with the whisk attachment at high speed until it holds stiff peaks. Fold the whipped cream carefully into the custard base. Serve the zabaglione in a beautiful bowl.

½ vanilla bean
⅓ cup granulated sugar
2 cups Moscato d'Asti
5 extra-large egg yolks
1 cup heavy cream

barbara's apples and asian pears with radicchio, mint, and buttermilk dressing

1 extra-large egg yolk

½ cup plus 2 tablespoons
  grapeseed oil

2 tablespoons finely diced shallot

1 to 2 lemons, for juicing

¼ cup crème fraîche

¼ cup buttermilk

2 apples, firm, crisp, and juicy

2 Asian pears

2 heads radicchio

2 tablespoons sliced mint

1 tablespoon chopped flat-leaf
  parsley

Kosher salt and freshly ground
  black pepper

When I was growing up, apples seemed *so* bland and boring—I could never get excited about a mushy Red Delicious the way I could a summer peach. But today, thanks to small farmers around the country like Barbara and Bill Spencer of Windrose Farms, we have a lot more choices where apples are concerned, and a lot more to get excited about.

Determined to revive the disappearing heirlooms, the Spencers painstakingly planted more than forty varieties of apple trees on their farm in Paso Robles, California. It took 6 years for the trees to produce, and that glorious fall, when Barbara turned up at the back door of Lucques with boxes and boxes of their impressive crop, I was blown away. The apples looked dazzlingly beautiful and tasted even better. From russeted emerald greens to mottled pinks to deep burgundy-blacks, we sampled our way through them all, picking our favorites and taking note of which were better raw and which were better cooked. Some of our favorites for eating out of hand were Braeburn, Arkansas Black, and Gernes Red Acre. Crisp, sweet, and tart, these revelatory fruits were the inspiration for this fall salad.

And if it's not enough that they're growing all these beautiful heirloom apples, Barbara and Bill also grow some of the best Asian pears I've ever tasted. Juicy and delicately perfumed, they're a fun surprise, sliced and tossed with the apples, buttermilk, mint, and radicchio in this thirst-quenching salad.

Place the egg yolk in a stainless steel bowl. Begin whisking in the grapeseed oil drop by drop, as slowly as you can bear. Continue in this manner until the mixture begins to thicken. Once the mayonnaise has emulsified, you can add the rest of the oil in a slow steady stream, whisking all the time.

Combine the shallot, 1 tablespoon lemon juice, and ½ teaspoon salt in a small bowl, and let sit 5 minutes. Whisk in the crème fraîche and buttermilk. Gently whisk this mixture into the mayonnaise, and taste for balance and seasoning.

Slice the apples and Asian pears away from the core. Cut into ⅛-inch thick slices and place them in a large salad bowl. Tear the radicchio into large bite-sized pieces and add to the bowl. Toss the salad with three-quarters of the dressing, and season with salt and pepper. Add a squeeze of lemon and a little more of the dressing if necessary.

Transfer to a large chilled platter and scatter the mint and parsley over the top.

sautéed skate with parsnip purée, brussels sprouts, pancetta, and balsamic brown butter

¾ cup Wondra flour

2 pounds boneless skate

¼ cup extra-virgin olive oil

6 tablespoons unsalted butter

2 tablespoons balsamic vinegar

Parsnip purée (recipe follows)

Balsamic-braised Brussels
sprouts with pancetta
(recipe follows)

2 tablespoons chopped flat-leaf
parsley

Kosher salt and freshly ground
black pepper

Kite-shaped rays, or skate, coast along the ocean floor foraging for mollusks. Eating clams, shrimp, and periwinkles gives skate a sweet, rich flavor. Its oddly ridged and finely textured flesh is unique in the fish world. In France, the classic preparation pairs skate with a nutty brown butter called *beurre noir*, usually garnished with lemon and capers.

Here I dredge the skate in ultra-fine Wondra flour, then quickly sauté it until golden brown. For a play on the classic, I finish the brown butter with sweet balsamic vinegar. The creamy parsnip purée and Brussels sprouts sautéed with pancetta harmonize nicely with the crisp, glistening skate and sweet, nutty butter.

NOTE You can make the parsnip purée and balsamic-braised Brussels sprouts ahead of time and then gently rewarm them right before serving.

Wondra flour, a finely milled flour available at most supermarkets, gives a delicate crust. But if you can't find it, all-purpose flour will do.

Preheat the oven to 225°F.

Place the flour on a large plate or pie pan for dredging. Season the fish lightly with salt and pepper (skate can sometimes be salty, so go easy on the seasoning). Dredge the fish in the flour, coating both sides well.

Heat a large sauté pan over high heat for 2 minutes. Swirl in 2 tablespoons olive oil and wait a minute. (You will probably need to cook the fish in two batches or two pans.) Place the fish in the pan and cook about 3 minutes, until the skate is nicely browned. Turn the fish over, turn the heat down to medium, and cook another minute or so. Transfer to a rack set on a baking sheet and keep warm in the oven.

Pour the oil from the pan and discard it. Wipe the pan clean, and return it to the stove over medium heat. Swirl in the butter and cook 3 to 4 minutes, until it browns and smells nutty. Turn off the heat and add the balsamic vinegar. Swirl the pan to combine the vinegar with the butter, and season with salt and pepper to taste. (Be careful not to burn your tongue!)

Spoon the hot parsnip purée onto a large warm platter. Place half of the hot Brussels sprouts over the purée, and arrange the fish on top. Scatter the remaining Brussels sprouts over and around the fish. Stir the parsley into the balsamic brown butter, and spoon the sauce over the fish.

parsnip purée

NOTE At the restaurant, we pass this mixture twice through a fine-mesh *tamis* or strainer, using a rubber spatula to push it through. This makes an extremely smooth purée. You can skip this step if you want a more rustic-style parsnip purée.

1½ pounds russet potatoes, peeled and cut into chunks

1½ pounds parsnips, peeled and cut into chunks

¾ cup heavy cream

¾ cup whole milk

8 ounces unsalted butter, cut into chunks

Kosher salt

Place the potatoes and parsnips in two medium sauce pots. Add 1 tablespoon salt to each pot, and then fill the pots with cold water. Bring both pots to a boil over high heat, then turn down the heat and simmer until tender.

When the potatoes and parsnips are cooked through, strain them and set them aside to cool for a moment. In a small saucepan, heat the cream and milk together, and then turn off the heat. Pass the potatoes and parsnips through a food mill or potato ricer, and transfer to a heavy-bottomed pot. Stir over medium heat with a wooden spoon to dry them out. Then, slowly, add in the chunks of butter, stirring all the while with the wooden spoon. Season with 2 teaspoons kosher salt.

When all the butter has been incorporated, slowly stir in the warm cream mixture until you have a smooth purée. Taste for seasoning and pass through a fine-mesh tamis if you like.

balsamic-braised brussels sprouts with pancetta

2 tablespoons extra-virgin olive oil

2 tablespoons unsalted butter

1 pound small Brussels sprouts, washed and trimmed

¼ pound pancetta, finely diced

2 tablespoons finely diced shallots

1 tablespoon minced garlic

¼ cup balsamic vinegar

1 cup veal stock

Kosher salt and freshly ground black pepper

It's funny when some of your biggest enemies turn out years later to be your best friends. As a child, I dreaded nothing more than those mushy, boiled-to-death, off-color Brussels sprouts. But once I discovered fresh Brussels sprouts and learned how to cook them, I became a full-fledged devotée! Here, in my favorite preparation, they're sautéed with pancetta, shallots, and garlic and then braised in the pan with balsamic vinegar and veal stock until they're shiny and glazed.

Heat a large sauté pan over high heat for 2 minutes. Swirl in the olive oil and butter, and wait another minute. Add the Brussels sprouts, and season them with 1 teaspoon salt and some pepper. Shake the pan, rolling the Brussels sprouts around to help them brown evenly. After a few minutes, turn the heat to medium, and cook another 3 to 4 minutes, until the sprouts soften slightly.

Add the diced pancetta to the pan and cook a minute or two, until it starts to crisp. Stir in the shallots and garlic, and cook another minute or so, until they're translucent. Pour in the balsamic vinegar and reduce by half. Add the veal stock and reduce to about ¼ cup, stirring and shaking the pan often to glaze the Brussels sprouts. If you start to run low on liquid before the sprouts are cooked, add a little water to the pan. Serve immediately, or transfer to a baking sheet to cool.

spiced pork stew with polenta, root vegetables, and gremolata

When you live in Southern California it's hard not to be influenced by the spicy, vibrant flavors of Mexican food. People might imagine chefs spending their few and precious nights out wining and dining on five-course meals, but in reality you're far more likely to find me at the sushi bar, Korean barbecue house, or my favorite *taqueria*. This spiced pork stew satisfies my cravings for the spicy, robust flavors of ethnic food.

I start with some of the Mexican spices I love so much—cumin, cayenne, coriander, and chile—tossing them with chunks of fatty and flavorful pork shoulder and braising it into this succulent pork stew. Pork shoulder is one of my favorite cuts to cook with. As an added bonus, it's one of the few meats that are still pretty inexpensive. People go crazy for this tender, slow-cooked pork bathed in its own spicy sauce, but don't worry—it's so impressive, they'll never know you did it on the cheap.

NOTE You can make the polenta a little ahead of time; cover the pot with plastic wrap to keep it from drying out. Right before serving, stir in a little more water if necessary. Roast the vegetables and make the gremolata in the afternoon if you like. The pork, of course, can be braised a day or even two ahead.

Toast the cumin seeds a few minutes in a small pan over medium heat, until they release their aroma and are lightly browned. Pound them coarsely in a mortar. Repeat (separately) with the coriander and fennel seeds.

Place the pork in a large bowl with the cumin, coriander, fennel seeds, cayenne, smashed garlic, oregano leaves, and thyme. Using your hands, toss the pork and spices together to coat well. Cover and refrigerate overnight.

Take the meat out of the refrigerator 45 minutes before cooking. After 15 minutes, season it on all sides with 1 tablespoon plus 2 teaspoons salt and some black pepper. Reserve the garlic and any excess herbs and spices.

Preheat the oven to 325°F.

Heat a large Dutch oven over high heat for 3 minutes. Pour in the olive oil and wait a minute or two, until the pan is very hot and almost smoking. Place the meat in the pan, being careful not to crowd it. (You will most likely need to cook

1 tablespoon cumin seeds

2 tablespoons coriander seeds

2 tablespoons fennel seeds

3 pounds pork shoulder, cut into 1½-to-2-inch chunks

1 teaspoon cayenne pepper

6 cloves garlic, smashed

1 tablespoon oregano leaves, plus 3 whole sprigs

1 tablespoon thyme leaves

3 tablespoons extra-virgin olive oil

1 cup diced onion

¼ cup diced carrot

¼ cup diced fennel

2 bay leaves, fresh if possible

1 chile de árbol, crumbled

1 cup white wine

2 cups veal stock

2 cups chicken stock

1 lemon

4 sprigs cilantro

Roasted root vegetables with gremolata (recipe follows)

1 recipe polenta (see page 97)

Kosher salt and freshly ground black pepper

the meat in batches.) Sear the meat until well browned and caramelized on all sides; this will probably take at least 15 minutes. As the batches of meat brown, transfer them to a baking sheet.

Turn the heat down to medium, and add the onion, carrot, and fennel. Stir with a wooden spoon, scraping up all the tasty crusty bits left in the pan. Stir in the bay leaves, crumbled chile, and reserved garlic and spices. Cook 6 to 8 minutes, until the vegetables start to caramelize.

Pour in the white wine and reduce by half, about 5 minutes. Add the stocks and bring to a boil.

Use a vegetable peeler to pull long strips of zest from the lemon.

Turn off the heat, and add the pork to the pot. Tuck the cilantro, oregano sprigs, and lemon zest around the meat. Cover the pan with plastic wrap (yes, it can go in the oven), aluminum foil, and a tightly fitting lid if you have one. Braise in the oven about 2½ hours.

To check the meat for doneness, remove the plastic and foil, being careful of the hot steam. Spoon a piece of meat out of the pan, and press it with your thumb or a spoon. If it's ready, it will yield easily to a knife and almost fall apart. Taste it!

Turn the oven up to 400°F.

Ladle most of the braising juices and vegetables into a strainer set over a saucepan, pressing down on the vegetables with the ladle to extract all the juices. Discard any remaining herb sprigs from the braising pan.

Return the pork to the oven for about 15 minutes to caramelize the meat.

Skim the fat from the braising juices. If necessary, reduce the broth over medium-high heat about 5 minutes, to thicken it slightly. Taste for seasoning.

Pour the hot broth over the browned meat, and stir to coat well. Transfer the stew to a large warm platter. Scatter the warm gremolata-coated root vegetables over the stew. Serve with the bowl of hot polenta. Tell your guests to spoon the polenta onto their plates and top with the pork and vegetables, making sure to get lots of the delicious braising juices. (You may need to serve more braising juices on the side if your platter is too shallow to hold them all.)

roasted root vegetables with gremolata

Look for young root vegetables that are small enough that you can leave a little of their stems on and preserve their natural shape. If you're using larger root vegetables, cut them in half lengthwise, place them cut side down on a cutting board, and slice on the diagonal. It's important to cut all the vegetables approximately the same size, so they cook evenly. I like to divide the root vegetables between two pans so they aren't too crowded.

Place the lemon zest on a cutting board and chop it coarsely. Place the garlic and parsley on top, and chop the whole mixture together until very fine. This mixture is called gremolata.

Slice the carrots and parsnips in half lengthwise, leaving the stems attached. If they are on the bigger side then slice each half lengthwise again, into long quarters. Clean the turnips, cut off the tails, and trim the stems, leaving ¼ inch of the stems. Cut small turnips in halves or quarters; if they're larger, cut them in half and then into ½-inch wedges.

Heat 2 large sauté pans over high heat for 2 minutes. Swirl in the olive oil and wait 1 minute. Divide the carrots, parsnips, and turnips between the pans and season with 1 teaspoon salt, ¼ teaspoon pepper, and the thyme. Cook 10 minutes, stirring often, until the vegetables just start to caramelize.

Add the butter and sauté another 5 minutes, tossing them often. Add the shallots and ½ teaspoon salt, and cook another 5 minutes or so, until the shallots and all the vegetables are tender and nicely caramelized. If you're serving dinner soon, turn off the heat and hold them in the pan. Rewarm if necessary. Toss with the gremolata just before serving.

Zest of 1 lemon

1 teaspoon minced garlic

½ cup chopped flat-leaf parsley

9 small or 3 medium carrots, peeled

9 small or 3 medium parsnips, peeled

9 small or 3 medium turnips

3 tablespoons extra-virgin olive oil

1 tablespoon fresh thyme leaves

2 tablespoons unsalted butter

1 cup ¼-inch-thick slices shallot

Kosher salt and freshly ground black pepper

"pumpkin" cake with pecan streusel and maple ice cream

1 Kabocha or butternut squash

8 tablespoons (1 stick) unsalted butter, plus a little for the pan

½ vanilla bean

2 cups all-purpose flour

¾ teaspoon baking soda

¾ teaspoon baking powder

¾ cup granulated sugar

½ teaspoon ground cloves

1 teaspoon ground cinnamon

½ teaspoon freshly grated nutmeg

¼ teaspoon kosher salt

1½ cups whole milk

1¼ cups heavy cream

3 extra-large eggs

1 tablespoon honey

Pecan streusel topping (recipe follows)

Maple ice cream (recipe follows)

Sometimes, in the middle of fall, usually just before Thanksgiving, it hits me: a desperate craving for pumpkin pie. One year, after a few days of my whining and hinting, pastry chef Roxana Jullapat came up with this delicious cake to shut me up. As comforting as that classic American pie but even better, Roxana's pumpkin cake was super moist and infused with the spicy flavors of fall. And, knowing my love of all things crunchy, nutty, and salty, Roxana topped the cake with a generous layer of crispy pecan streusel.

Though pumpkins have an esteemed place in our childhood memories, they actually aren't very good to cook with—they're often watery and usually lacking in flavor and sweetness—so we make our "pumpkin" cake with Kabocha or butternut squash instead. "Winter squash cake" just doesn't have the same ring to it.

NOTE You can roast the squash and make the streusel a day ahead of time. Be sure to drain the squash after it's roasted and just before using it; it often continues to give off water. I've been told you can substitute canned pumpkin in this recipe.

Preheat the oven to 400°F.

Cut the squash in half lengthwise and place on a baking sheet, cut side up. (Don't remove the seeds yet; they give extra flavor.) Cover with foil, and roast about 1 hour, until very tender. Let cool 10 minutes, and then scoop out the seeds and discard them. Purée the warm squash through a ricer or food mill and measure out 1½ cups. (You can reheat any leftover purée, season it with salt, pepper, and butter, and eat it for dinner!)

Turn the oven down to 350°F.

Cut a circle of parchment paper to fit the bottom of a 10-inch round cake pan. Brush the bottom of the pan with a little butter, and then line it with the paper.

Place the 8 tablespoons butter in a medium saucepan. Slice the vanilla bean lengthwise down the center, and use a paring knife to scrape the seeds and pulp onto the butter. To make sure not to lose any of the seeds, run your vanilla-coated knife through the butter (don't use your fingers, because the seeds will stick to them). Add the vanilla pod to the pan, and cook the butter over medium heat

6 to 8 minutes, shaking the pan occasionally, until the butter browns and smells nutty. Remove the vanilla pod and discard.

Sift together the flour, baking soda, baking powder, sugar, cloves, cinnamon, and nutmeg into a large bowl. Add the salt. Make a well in the center.

In another large bowl, whisk the reserved 1½ cups squash purée, milk, ¼ cup cream, eggs, and honey to combine. Pour the liquid into the well in the dry ingredients, and whisk until incorporated. Stir in the brown butter, scraping with a rubber spatula to make sure you get all the brown bits from the pan.

Pour the batter into the prepared pan and bake 25 minutes, then remove the cake from the oven and sprinkle the streusel evenly over the top. Bake the cake another 45 minutes, until the topping is crisp and the cake has set. (The center of the cake will still be somewhat soft and won't pass the toothpick test.) Cool the cake on a rack for at least 15 minutes.

In a stand mixer fitted with the whisk attachment, whip 1 cup cream to soft peaks.

Cut six slices from the cake and serve with scoops of maple ice cream and dollops of whipped cream.

pecan streusel topping

Preheat the oven to 375°F.

Spread the pecans on a baking sheet, and toast them 8 to 10 minutes, until they darken slightly and smell nutty. When the nuts have cooled, chop them coarsely. Toss the nuts with the oil and salt.

In a food processor, pulse the butter, sugars, flour, cinnamon, and nutmeg until just combined. Remove to a bowl, stir in the salted pecans, and chill until ready to use.

¼ cup pecans
1 teaspoon grapeseed oil
¼ teaspoon kosher salt
4 tablespoons cold unsalted butter, cut into cubes
¼ cup granulated sugar
1 tablespoon brown sugar
¼ cup plus 2 tablespoons all-purpose flour
¼ teaspoon ground cinnamon
⅛ teaspoon freshly grated nutmeg

maple ice cream

MAKES 1 QUART

Bring the milk and cream to a boil over medium heat. Turn off the heat and cover.

Whisk the egg yolks and maple sugar together in a bowl. Whisk a few tablespoons of the warm cream mixture into the yolks to temper them. Slowly, add

2 cups whole milk
2 cups heavy cream
4 extra-large egg yolks
⅓ cup maple sugar
2 tablespoons maple syrup

another ¼ cup or so of the warm cream, whisking continuously. At this point you can add the rest of the cream mixture in a slow steady stream, whisking all the time. Pour the mixture back into the pot, and return it to the stove.

Cook the custard over medium heat 6 to 8 minutes, stirring frequently and using a rubber spatula to scrape the bottom and sides of the pan. The custard will thicken, and when it's done will coat the back of the spatula. Strain the mixture, stir in the maple syrup, and chill at least 2 hours in the refrigerator. Process in an ice cream maker according to the manufacturer's instructions.

winter

Cold weather calls for serious changes in the kitchen. Robust stews, potent sauces, and buttery side dishes satisfy our cold-weather cravings. Red wine, herbs, butter, breadcrumbs, citrus zest, spices, grains, beans, nuts, and dried fruits are some of the key ingredients that make up my winter palette.

Winter is a time for cooking rustic, peasant-style dishes. I dig out my Dutch oven to braise rugged cuts of meat such as brisket or short ribs, simmering them in full-bodied wine and stock for hours, until they're so tender you could eat them with a spoon. When I was growing up, my father referred to these brothy, soothing bowls of comfort as "tuck-in" food. Made ahead of time, these one-pot meals are ideal for a relaxing Sunday supper.

Winter wouldn't be winter without rich, creamy gratins, crispy stuffings, and cheesy savory tarts. Some favorite accompaniments in my winter lineup include Turnip-Parsnip Gratin with Prunes; Sweet Potatoes with Bacon and Spinach; Romesco; and Chestnut Stuffing seasoned with pancetta and fennel—in my world these are considerably more than side dishes. Served together with a salad of winter chicories, say, they constitute a nurturing winter feast.

Just because it's cold doesn't mean that things stop growing in the fields. Take advantage of the season's underrated array of produce like leeks, root vegetables, and cavolo nero. They may not seem as sexy and glamorous as tomatoes and asparagus, but when prepared well they are surprisingly seductive. Stewed with olive oil, braised with white wine, roasted in the oven, or flavored with bacon, these oft-ignored members of the vegetable family truly stand out.

Winter fruits offer more variety and versatility than they get credit for, too. They add color to the muted tones of the season and provide a refreshing counterpoint to the hearty dishes of winter. Meyer lemons diced into a relish, pomegranates stirred into a salsa, and grapefruits cut into a salad invigorate many of the upcoming savory winter recipes.

On the sweet side of the kitchen, I turn to old-fashioned desserts like roasted apples or chocolate bread pudding. Without being too fussy or complex, they're shamelessly decadent and comforting. I use brown butter, vanilla, and assertive spices like cloves, nutmeg, and cinnamon with abandon, filling the kitchen with holiday aromas. These desserts are the ultimate send-off to a winter meal.

winter market

cauliflower

Like its siblings—broccoli, cabbage, kale, and Brussels sprouts—the best cauliflower arrives in the fall, winter, and early spring, when the growing climate is cooler. While I would happily eat a plate of plain steamed broccoli, for me cauliflower calls for a more involved preparation. I like to cook it in an Italian style, sautéed with anchovies, currants, and pine nuts and tossed with pasta. Or, for a spicier Indian-inspired dish, I roast it with curry, cumin, and red wine vinegar.

Look for compact, dense heads, preferably with fresh, unwilted leaves.

citrus

Citrus are the essential fruits of winter, uplifting and refreshing. Eat them out of hand or make them into curds or sorbet for dessert. They're also terrific in salads, paired with Parmesan, olives, arugula, or avocado. In the heart of the season, when many citrus varieties are available, I like to show them off in a kaleidoscopic salad of pink and white grapefruit, burgundy blood oranges, and vivid orange tangerines and tangelos.

When preparing citrus, don't forget about the zest. I use it to season all sorts of things, from vinaigrettes to marinades. Use a zester to make long strands, or, if you don't have a zester, use a vegetable peeler to remove the outer layer of peel, being careful to avoid the white pith. Chop the zest finely.

When buying citrus, look for fruit that's heavy for its size with supple, tight skin. If leaves are still attached and fresh, that's a guarantee that the fruit was picked recently.

blood oranges   These ruby jewels show up in markets around late winter. They originated in southern Italy and were brought to California in the thirties by Italian immigrants. Sometimes their skin is orange with a little burgundy pigmentation; others are almost completely deep red in color.

To prepare blood oranges, remove the peel and pith with a knife and then slice the flesh into pinwheels or, to make segments, use your knife to cut in between the membranes to release the fruit. Blood-orange juice is a dramatic alternative to your regular morning orange juice, and is also great for cocktails, in vinaigrettes, or reduced to a glaze as a sauce for poultry.

grapefruits and pomelos   Few people are aware of the wide variety of grapefruits available. White-fleshed Oro Blancos and hot pink Ruby Reds are two of my favorites. Pomelos are the largest citrus fruit of all. An Asian ancestor of the grapefruit, this oversized fruit has a slightly spicy, exotic taste.

meyer lemons   Meyer lemons are a seasonal, sweet variety of lemons that usually come to market in January and stay through spring. Though they're a specialty item to many people, in California they're considered a backyard fruit, easy to grow and very common. Meyer lemons have a distinct sweet fragrance and smooth, shiny peel. They are less acidic than other lemons, with a background flavor of orange, making them more palatable to eat, peel and all.

I like to cut them into segments and pinwheels for salads, or dice their sweet flesh into salsas to spoon over fish. Their juice can be used in place of that of regular lemons for vinaigrettes, ice cream, and tarts.

Unlike regular lemons, Meyer lemons are sometimes on the soft side. Look for unblemished skin and fragrant fruit. In a perfect world, the leaves and stems would still be attached.

tangerines   There are many varieties of tangerines—Clementines, Pixies, and Satsumas tend to be less seedy, more juicy, and both tart and sweet. Tangelos, a cross between a mandarin tangerine and a pomelo, are one of my childhood favorites. Distinguished by their knoblike stem ends and deep orange color, tangelos are easy to peel and have a bright, almost tropical flavor.

parsnips

This lesser-known root vegetable resembles a white carrot. Peeled, cut into wedges, and roasted, parsnips caramelize on the outside but become soft in the center. They have a starchy sweetness, and they combine well with other root vegetables, like carrots, turnips, and rutabagas. They also provide a sweet counterpoint to more savory, bitter vegetables, like Brussels sprouts or radicchio. I purée them with potatoes, layer them into gratins, and blend them into creamy winter soups.

Choose firm, medium-sized parsnips. If you happen to find the more elusive baby parsnips, buy them.

persimmons

I use two types of persimmons at Lucques: Hachiya and Fuyu. Hachiyas are picked when firm and left to ripen until they're very soft. Don't eat this variety before it ripens; its astringent quality makes it practically inedible. Hachiyas are distinguished from other varieties by their acornlike shape. You can make "instant persimmon sorbet" by freezing ripe, squishy Hachiyas. Once they are frozen, cut them in half and scoop out the ice-cold pulp. Hachiyas are best for baking cookies, puddings, and cakes. Fuyu persimmons are rounder and resemble squat tomatoes. These persimmons are meant to be eaten when firm; I love their crisp, juicy texture and eat them out of hand like apples or slice them into salads. Fuyu persimmons brighten up a fall antipasto of *jamón serrano,* Manchego, and almonds. Some varieties have seeds that need to be removed as you slice. Look for persimmons October through December. Buy Hachiyas very, very soft, or ripen them at home. Be patient; it can take a while. For Fuyus, choose deep orange, firm, unblemished fruit.

turnips

Turnips vary in flavor and texture, depending on their size. Precious baby turnips are elegant and delicately flavored, while large, mature turnips are earthy and robust. I like to use turnips both raw and cooked. Their spicy flavor mellows and becomes sweet when they're roasted or sautéed. In a more unusual preparation, thinly sliced raw turnips add a crunchy, peppery bite to winter slaws and salads.

When preparing turnips, consider their size and condition. For smaller baby turnips, I like to leave a little of the green stem attached and cut them in halves or quarters, maintaining their natural shape. I don't peel baby turnips unless they're bruised. Larger turnips should be peeled and can be sliced and layered into a turnip-potato gratin, or cut into wedges and roasted with olive oil and thyme. Equal to the turnip itself are its greens. Tossed into a sauté of winter vegetables or grains, the greens add a fresh, bright note. Choose very firm turnips, and look for perky green tops.

Beets, available mainly in winter, are a favorite of mine.

young onion tart with cantal, applewood-smoked bacon, and herb salad

Lucques had been open only a few months when we were asked to host an Alsatian wine dinner. Working on the menu reminded me of a road trip I had taken many years before through that northeastern region of France. With a corkscrew in the glove compartment and a stinky wheel of Muenster tucked away in the backseat, my boyfriend and I tooled around the picturesque Alsatian countryside. We lived for a few days on tall glasses of *Hefeweizen*—golden, unfiltered wheat beer always served with a slice of lemon—and on wedges of *Flammeküche*, warm, cheesy bacon-onion tarts. I made this version of that traditional tart for our wine dinner.

NOTE Assemble the tart in the morning, cover, and refrigerate. Bake just before you're ready to serve.

Preheat the oven to 400°F.

Defrost the puff pastry slightly and unroll it onto a parchment-lined baking sheet. Use a paring knife to score a ¼-inch border around the edge of the pastry. Make an egg wash by whisking one egg yolk with ½ teaspoon water, and brush the egg wash along the border. (You will not need all of the egg wash.) Return the puff pastry to the freezer until you're ready to use it.

Slice the bacon into ⅜-inch-thick slices. Stack the slices in two piles, then cut the bacon crosswise into ⅜-inch even-sided rectangles or *lardons*.

Heat a large sauté pan over high heat for 2 minutes. Add 1 tablespoon olive oil, and allow to heat another minute. Add the bacon, and sauté over medium-high heat 4 to 5 minutes, until slightly crisp but still tender. Reduce the heat to low, and toss in the young onions, thyme, and ½ teaspoon salt. Stir together a minute or two, until the onions are just wilted. Toss in the onion tops, and remove to a baking sheet or platter to cool.

Place the ricotta, remaining egg yolk, and remaining tablespoon olive oil in the bowl of a food processor. Purée until smooth, and transfer to a medium bowl.

1 sheet frozen all-butter puff pastry

2 extra-large egg yolks

½-pound slab applewood-smoked bacon

2 tablespoons extra-virgin olive oil

2 cups sliced young onions, red and white if possible

1 tablespoon thyme leaves

½ cup diagonally sliced young onion tops

½ cup whole milk ricotta, drained if wet

¼ cup crème fraîche

⅓ pound Cantal, Gruyère, or Comté cheese, thinly sliced

½ cup flat-leaf parsley leaves

¼ cup tarragon leaves

¼ cup chervil sprigs

¼ cup ½-inch-snipped chives

A drizzle super-good extra-virgin olive oil

½ lemon, for juicing

Kosher salt and freshly ground black pepper

Gently fold in the crème fraîche and season with ⅛ teaspoon salt and a pinch of pepper.

Spread the ricotta mixture on the puff pastry within the scored border. Lay the Cantal over the ricotta, and arrange the bacon-onion mixture on top.

Bake the tart 20 to 25 minutes, rotating the baking sheet once, until the cheese is bubbling and the crust is golden brown. Lift up the edge of the tart and peek underneath to make sure the crust is cooked through. (If you underbake the tart, it will be soggy.)

Toss the herbs in a small bowl with salt, pepper, a drizzle of super-good olive oil, and a squeeze of lemon juice.

Let the tart cool a few minutes, and serve it on a cutting board at the table. Serve the herb salad in a small, pretty bowl.

To serve individual portions, cut six wedges from the tart and garnish each one with a little herb salad.

taylor bay scallops with chanterelles, sherry, and parsley breadcrumbs

Taylor Bay Scallops are named for fisherman Rod Taylor, who farm-raises them and harvests them by hand in the icy waters off Cape Cod. Unlike diver scallops, which are larger and have a meaty texture, the small, delicate Taylor Bays are sold live in their beautiful pink shells. Their size and sweetness make them perfect for steaming, which releases the juices trapped in the scallop shells, giving an oceany, scallopy flavor to the broth.

NOTE You can toast the breadcrumbs, slice your onions and herbs, and clean the chanterelles and scallops ahead of time, but most of the work for this dish is done at the last minute. It goes very quickly and isn't too complicated. To cook this many scallops, use two pans, preferably cooking both batches at the same time. (The scallops taste best right after they open.)

1 cup fresh breadcrumbs

1 tablespoon extra-virgin olive oil

3 tablespoons chopped flat-leaf parsley

8 tablespoons (1 stick) unsalted butter

¾ pound chanterelle mushrooms, cleaned

2 teaspoons thyme leaves

1 cup sliced young onions

48 Taylor Bay Scallops (3 pounds in the shell) (see Sources)

1 cup Amontillado sherry

1 cup vegetable, mushroom, or chicken stock

½ cup heavy cream

Kosher salt and freshly ground black pepper

Preheat the oven to 375°F.

Toss the breadcrumbs with the olive oil and 1 tablespoon chopped parsley. Spread on a baking sheet, and toast 8 to 10 minutes, stirring often, until they're golden brown and crispy.

Heat two large sauté pans or Dutch ovens over high heat for 2 minutes. Add 3 tablespoons butter to each pan, and when it foams, add half the chanterelles, half the thyme, 1 teaspoon salt, and a pinch of pepper to each pan. Sauté the mushrooms, stirring occasionally with a wooden spoon, 6 to 8 minutes, until they're tender and start to crisp slightly.

Turn the heat down to medium and add 1 tablespoon butter to each pan. Divide the spring onions between the pans, season them lightly with salt and pepper, and cook 2 to 3 minutes, stirring often, until translucent.

Divide the scallops between the two pans, and toss to coat them with the mushrooms and onions. After 2 minutes, add half the sherry to each pan, and let reduce 20 seconds. Add half the stock to each pan, turn the heat back up to high, cover, and let the scallops steam open, about 5 minutes. When they have opened, add the cream, stir to incorporate, and turn off the heat. Taste the broth for seasoning and discard any unopened scallops. Toss in the remaining 2 tablespoons sliced parsley, and transfer to a large warm shallow bowl. Scatter the breadcrumbs over the top.

braised beef short ribs with potato purée, swiss chard, and horseradish cream

Every chef has a love-hate dish, the dish that made it into the first review, the one that customers call ahead for, the dish, therefore, the chef will never be able to take off the menu. Short ribs are mine. I used to be tortured by them, but I've come to accept that they're a permanent member of the Lucques family.

The short-rib saga began one cool and rainy weekend when, inspired by the weather, I made them for a Sunday supper. The response was so overwhelming that I added them to our daily menu. When spring arrived and the city began to warm up, I replaced the short ribs with something lighter. That week, I went out to the dining room to say hello to a friend and was assaulted by diners at three different tables, who waved me over to find out (you guessed it) where the short ribs had gone. At first I was stubborn and refused to serve them in 90-degree weather. But I had a change of heart when I realized how much people loved them and how easily I could satisfy their craving. The short ribs went back on the menu and will probably remain there for all eternity.

NOTE Short ribs, like most braised dishes, taste even better the next day. Remember you will need to marinate them a day before braising.

Season the short ribs with 1 tablespoon thyme and the cracked black pepper. Use your hands to coat the meat well. Cover, and refrigerate overnight.

Take the short ribs out of the refrigerator an hour before cooking, to come to room temperature. After 30 minutes, season them generously on all sides with salt.

When you take the ribs out of the refrigerator, preheat the oven to 425°F.

Toss the pearl onions with 2 tablespoons olive oil, 1 teaspoon thyme, ¾ teaspoon salt, and a pinch of pepper. Spread them on a baking sheet and roast them about 15 minutes, until tender. When they have cooled, slip off the skins with your fingers and set aside. Turn the oven down to 325°F.

When it's time to cook the short ribs, heat a large sauté pan over high heat for 3 minutes. Pour in 3 tablespoons olive oil, and wait a minute or two, until the pan is very hot and almost smoking. Place the short ribs in the pan, and sear until they are nicely browned on all three meaty sides. Depending on the size of your

6 beef short ribs, 14 to 16 ounces each (ask for 3 bone center-cut)

1 tablespoon plus 1 teaspoon thyme leaves, and 4 whole sprigs thyme

1 tablespoon freshly cracked black pepper

3 dozen small pearl onions

½ cup extra-virgin olive oil

1 cup diced onion

⅓ cup diced carrot

⅓ cup diced celery

2 bay leaves

2 tablespoons balsamic vinegar

1½ cups port

2½ cups hearty red wine

6 cups beef or veal stock

4 sprigs flat-leaf parsley

2 bunches Swiss chard, cleaned, center ribs removed

Potato purée (recipe follows)

Horseradish cream (recipe follows)

Kosher salt and freshly ground black pepper

pan, you might have to sear the meat in batches. Do not crowd the meat or get lazy or rushed at this step; it will take at least 15 minutes. When the ribs are nicely browned, transfer them to a braising pan. They should lie flat, bones standing up, in one layer.

Turn the heat down to medium, and add the onion, carrot, celery, thyme sprigs, and bay leaves. Stir with a wooden spoon, scraping up all the crusty bits in the pan. Cook 6 to 8 minutes, until the vegetables just begin to caramelize. Add the balsamic vinegar, port, and red wine. Turn the heat up to high, and reduce the liquid by half.

Add the stock and bring to a boil. Pour the liquid over the short ribs, scraping any vegetables that have fallen on the ribs back into the liquid. The stock mixture should almost cover the ribs. Tuck the parsley sprigs in and around the meat. Cover tightly with plastic wrap (yes, it can go in the oven) and then aluminum foil. Braise in the oven for about 3 hours.

To check the meat for doneness, remove the plastic and foil, being careful of the escaping steam, and pierce a short rib with a paring knife. When the meat is done, it will yield easily to a knife. Taste a piece if you are not sure.

Let the ribs rest 10 minutes in their juices, and then transfer them to a baking sheet.

Turn the oven up to 400°F.

Place the short ribs in the oven for 10 to 15 minutes, to brown.

Strain the broth into a saucepan, pressing down on the vegetables with a ladle to extract all the juices. Skim the fat from the sauce and, if the broth seems thin, reduce it over medium-high heat to thicken slightly. Taste for seasoning.

Heat a large sauté pan over high heat for 2 minutes. Tear the Swiss chard into large pieces. Add 3 tablespoons olive oil to the pan, and stir in the cooked pearl onions. Add half the Swiss chard, and cook a minute or two, stirring the greens in the oil to help them wilt. Add a splash of water and the second half of the greens. Season with a heaping ¼ teaspoon salt and a pinch of ground black pepper. Cook for a few more minutes, stirring frequently, until the greens are tender.

Place the Swiss chard on a large warm platter, and arrange the short ribs on top. Spoon lots of braising juices over the ribs. Serve the hot potato purée and horseradish cream on the side.

potato purée

NOTE At the restaurant, we press the mixture twice through a fine-mesh *tamis* with a rubber spatula. This makes an extremely smooth purée. You can skip this step if you want a more rustic-style potato purée. If you are going to serve the purée immediately after cooking, you can hold the potatoes in a double boiler or in a warm oven. Otherwise, let them cool, then refrigerate them and reheat the potatoes gently over medium-low heat, stirring often, and adding more cream if necessary.

1½ pounds russet potatoes

1½ pounds Yukon Gold potatoes

¾ cup heavy cream

¾ cup whole milk

8 ounces (2 sticks) unsalted butter, cut into chunks

Kosher salt

Place the two types of potato, whole and unpeeled, in two medium sauce pots. Add 1 tablespoon salt to each pot and fill the pots with cold water. Bring the potatoes to a boil over high heat, turn down the heat to low, and simmer about 45 minutes, until tender.

When the potatoes are cooked through, strain them, and set them aside to cool for 10 minutes or so. Heat the cream and milk together in a small saucepan, then turn off the heat. When the potatoes have cooled, peel them and pass them through a food mill or potato ricer. Put the riced potatoes in a heavy-bottomed pan. Heat them over medium heat a few minutes, stirring continuously with a wooden spoon, to dry them out a little. Add the butter slowly, stirring constantly. Season with 2½ teaspoons salt.

When all the butter has been incorporated, slowly stir in the warm cream mixture until you have a smooth purée. Taste for seasoning.

horseradish cream

Combine the crème fraîche and horseradish in a small bowl. Season with ¼ teaspoon salt and pepper. Taste for balance and seasoning.

¾ cup crème fraîche

1 tablespoon prepared horseradish

Kosher salt and freshly ground black pepper

warm crêpes with lemon zest and hazelnut brown butter

2 extra-large eggs

1½ cups whole milk

½ cup heavy cream

About 5 tablespoons unsalted butter, melted

1 teaspoon finely grated lemon zest

2 tablespoons Frangelico liqueur

1 cup all-purpose flour

2 tablespoons granulated sugar

¼ teaspoon kosher salt

Hazelnut cream (recipe follows)

Hazelnut brown butter (recipe follows)

Many people associate particular years of their childhood with the television shows they watched or the sports they played. In my family, intervals of time were marked by food. The break between third and fourth grade was the summer of crepes. My parents had just returned from a trip to Brittany, and my mother was determined to re-create the handiwork of their famous *crêperies*.

I got on the crêpe bandwagon, too, and borrowed her Teflon-coated electric skillet on the weekends. While my sister entertained all the neighborhood kids in the pool, I set up my backyard crêpe stand and spent the afternoon flipping and filling to the sounds of "Marco . . . Polo . . . Marco. . . ."

These lemon-hazelnut crêpes are a little more refined than those childhood concoctions (banana-chocolate was my specialty in those days!), but they still remind me of those joyful afternoons in my makeshift *crêperie*.

NOTE Two things about your crêpe pan are extremely important: temperature and "seasoning." The pan needs to be hot enough that the batter starts cooking immediately but not so hot that the crêpes burn. A thin film of butter will season the pan so the crêpes cook evenly and don't stick. Often one or two practice crêpes are needed; the fat in the batter will create the seasoning while letting you see if the pan's temperature needs adjustment.

You can make the crêpe batter and the hazelnut cream a day ahead. (You must make the batter at least 2 hours ahead.) Fill the crêpes an hour or so ahead, and then pop them in the oven just before serving.

Whisk the eggs, milk, cream, 2 tablespoons melted butter, lemon zest, and Frangelico together in a medium bowl.

Sift the flour and sugar into a large bowl, and stir in the salt. Make a well in the center of the dry ingredients. Slowly pour the liquid into the well, whisking all the time at the center. Once the batter starts to incorporate, slowly bring in more dry ingredients, working from the center out.

Cover the bowl, and let the batter rest in the refrigerator at least 2 hours or overnight.

Preheat the oven to 400°F.

Heat two black iron crêpe pans or 6-inch nonstick pans over medium heat. Swirl about ½ teaspoon butter in each pan, and when it foams, swirl in 2 tablespoons crêpe batter, moving the pan to coat the bottom with a thin layer of batter. Cook the crêpe 30 seconds or so, until the edges are golden brown. Flip the crêpe over and cook another 30 seconds on the second side. The crêpes should be thin and lacy.

Remove the crêpes from the pans onto a warm plate. Stack the crêpes as you go, keeping them covered with a towel. Repeat until you have twelve crêpes.

Lightly butter a baking sheet. Place the crêpes on a work surface with the pretty, brown lacy sides down. Spoon 1 tablespoon hazelnut cream onto the lower-right quadrant of each crêpe. Fold the crêpes loosely in half over the hazelnut cream, and then fold them again, loosely into quarters (with the unfilled quarter on top). Top each crêpe with a teaspoon of hazelnut cream, and place them all on the buttered baking sheet.

Bake the crêpes in the oven 6 to 8 minutes, until they start to crisp around the edges.

Arrange the crêpes on a large warm platter, and spoon the hazelnut–brown butter sauce over them.

hazelnut cream

Place the hazelnuts, sugar, and salt in a food processor, and pulse until finely ground. Add the flour, butter, egg, egg yolk, and Frangelico. Pulse until completely combined.

4 ounces blanched hazelnuts

½ cup confectioners' sugar

Healthy pinch of kosher salt

2 tablespoons all-purpose flour

6 tablespoons unsalted butter, softened

1 extra-large egg

1 extra-large egg yolk

1 tablespoon Frangelico liqueur

hazelnut brown butter

Preheat the oven to 375°F.

Spread the hazelnuts on a baking sheet, and toast 8 to 10 minutes, until they're golden brown and smell nutty. When the nuts have cooled, chop them coarsely.

Dissolve the sugar in the Frangelico in a small bowl.

Cook the butter in a medium saucepan over medium heat about 5 minutes, shaking the pan occasionally, until the butter browns and smells nutty. Once the butter has browned, remove the pan from the heat and wait a minute or two. Add the nuts, salt, and the Frangelico mixture, making sure to scrape all the Frangelico and sugar into the pan. (Be careful, the butter might foam up a little, and it's very hot.)

2 ounces blanched hazelnuts

1½ teaspoons granulated sugar

2 tablespoons Frangelico liqueur

8 tablespoons (1 stick) unsalted butter

¼ teaspoon kosher salt

james's broccoli with burrata, pine nuts, and warm anchovy vinaigrette

¾ cup fresh breadcrumbs

½ cup extra-virgin olive oil

½ cup pine nuts

1 tablespoon sliced flat-leaf parsley

1 pound Italian broccoli, sprouting broccoli, or broccolini, trimmed

6 tablespoons unsalted butter

2 teaspoons minced salt-packed anchovy

½ chile de árbol, sliced thinly on the diagonal

2 teaspoons minced garlic

1 teaspoon thyme leaves

1 pound burrata or fresh mozzarella (see Sources)

¼ cup sliced shallots

1 lemon, for juicing

Kosher salt and freshly ground black pepper

If you leaned against your sink, closed your eyes, and focused on conjuring up the quintessential organic farmer, James Birch would appear in your kitchen. He looks like a cross between a grizzly bear and an overgrown Little Prince. And he is, in fact, the king of broccoli.

I'd guess that most people don't walk into Lucques with a hankering for broccoli, but this appetizer might just change that. Tossed with a garlicky anchovy butter, topped with pine nut breadcrumbs, and served with slices of creamy burrata cheese, this broccoli is how addictions get started.

Burrata literally translates as "bag." Cream is beaten into mozzarella, creating a skin of cheese that's filled with creamy curd. Burrata's silky, soft texture and rich flavor make it feel like a mozzarella that died and went to heaven.

We get our burrata from Caseificio Gioia, which, although it sounds like a quaint Italian village, is actually a family-owned cheese company in the decidedly unromantic industrial township of South El Monte, just outside Los Angeles. For many years, they've been providing L.A. chefs with the most delicious fresh mozzarella, ricotta, and burrata this side of the Atlantic. Burrata has a shelf life of about 3 to 4 days, so eat it quickly. (If you can't find burrata, substitute a soft, fresh handmade mozzarella.)

Preheat the oven to 375°F.

Bring a large pot of heavily salted water to a boil over high heat.

Toss the breadcrumbs with 1 tablespoon olive oil. Spread them on a baking sheet, and toast 8 to 10 minutes, stirring once or twice, until golden brown and crispy.

Spread the pine nuts on another baking sheet, and toast them 4 to 5 minutes, until they're golden brown and smell nutty. Crush half the pine nuts, and combine them with the whole pine nuts, breadcrumbs, and parsley in a small bowl. Season with salt and pepper.

Blanch the broccoli in the rapidly boiling water 2 to 3 minutes, until just tender. Drain, and cool on a baking sheet.

Meanwhile, heat the remaining 7 tablespoons olive oil and the butter in a small saucepan over low heat. Add the anchovy and chile and cook 5 minutes, stirring with a wooden spoon as the anchovy melts into the sauce. Add the garlic and thyme and turn off the heat. The garlic will finish cooking in the hot oil. Season with ½ teaspoon salt.

Cut the burrata into six slices, and then cut each slice in half.

Heat a large sauté pan over high heat for 1 minute. Add the anchovy butter, shallots, and broccoli, and season with salt, pepper, and a squeeze of lemon juice. Toss well to warm the broccoli and coat it with the anchovy butter. Taste for seasoning.

Arrange half the broccoli on a large platter in one layer. Tuck half the burrata slices among the broccoli, and continue layering the remaining broccoli and burrata. Shower the pine nut breadcrumbs over the top.

torchio with cauliflower, cavolo nero, currants, and pine nuts

1 pound cavolo nero, cleaned, center ribs removed

1 cup extra-virgin olive oil

½ sprig rosemary

2 chiles de árbol, crumbled

1 cup sliced onion, plus 1 cup diced onion

¼ cup sliced garlic

1½ cups fresh breadcrumbs

1 medium head cauliflower (about 2½ pounds), broken into bite-sized florets

1 pound torchio, orecchiette, or penne pasta (see Sources)

1 tablespoon thyme leaves

2 teaspoons minced salt-packed anchovy

¼ cup (½ recipe) currant–pine nut relish (see page 58)

Kosher salt and freshly ground black pepper

This pasta might sound unsubstantial, but I promise you won't leave the table wishing you'd made a roast instead. The caramelized cauliflower, rich cavolo nero, and chewy pasta, sautéed with rosemary, chile, garlic, anchovy, and onion, meld together into a filling, savory whole. Although sautéing the pasta isn't traditional, I love the integration of flavors and the slightly crisped noodles.

NOTE If you can't find torchio, choose a pasta with lots of nooks and crannies to capture all those delicious ingredients. You can stew the cavolo, blanch the cauliflower, and toast the breadcrumbs in advance.

Put two large pots of heavily salted water on to boil.

Blanch the cavolo nero in rapidly boiling water for 2 minutes. Drain, and cool the greens on a baking sheet. When they have cooled, squeeze out the excess water with your hands.

Heat a large pot or Dutch oven over medium heat for 2 minutes. Pour in ¼ cup olive oil. Add the rosemary sprig and 1 crumbled chile, and let them sizzle in the oil about a minute. Turn the heat down to medium-low and add the sliced onion. Season with ½ teaspoon salt and a few grindings of black pepper. Cook a couple of minutes, then stir in half the sliced garlic. Continue cooking gently until the onion is soft and starting to color slightly, another 5 to 7 minutes.

Add the cavolo nero and 2 more tablespoons olive oil, stirring with a wooden spoon to coat the greens with the oil. Season with a heaping ¼ teaspoon salt, and cook the cavolo nero slowly, over low heat, about 30 minutes, stirring often, until the greens turn a dark, almost black color and get slightly crispy around the edges. (I usually alternate turning the heat up a little bit, so the cavolo sizzles, and then turning it back down to low, so it stews.) Turn off the heat and set aside. When it's cooled, remove the rosemary and chile.

Preheat the oven to 375°F.

While the greens are cooking, toss the breadcrumbs with 2 tablespoons olive oil. Spread them on a baking sheet and toast 8 to 10 minutes, stirring once or twice, until golden brown and crispy.

Blanch the cauliflower in rapidly boiling water for 4 to 5 minutes, until just tender and not too crunchy. Using a slotted spoon, transfer to a baking sheet to cool. Bring the water back to a boil and drop in the pasta.

Heat a large sauté pan or Dutch oven over high heat for 2 minutes. Pour in ¼ cup olive oil and wait a minute. Add the diced onion, the remaining crumbled chile, and the thyme. Sauté over medium heat 2 minutes, and then add the anchovy. Stir well with a wooden spoon to break up the anchovy and dissolve it into the onion. Turn the heat up to high and add the cauliflower. Stir well, to coat the cauliflower with the oil. Add the remaining sliced garlic, and season with ½ teaspoon salt and a few grindings of black pepper. Add the remaining ¼ cup olive oil, and sauté the cauliflower 8 to 10 minutes, until it's caramelized, scraping the pan continuously with a wooden spoon, and smashing the cauliflower a little to make small pieces. Add the cavolo nero to the pot, and stir well to combine.

When the pasta is al dente, set aside 1 cup of the cooking water.

Drain the pasta and add it to the vegetables, stirring and tossing well to combine and coat the noodles. The pasta will fry a little in the oil and stick to the pan; this is good, so keep scraping and tossing with the wooden spoon.

After a few minutes, when the pasta is well coated and has a little color on it, add ½ cup of the reserved pasta water to the pan. Stir to combine, and add more water if necessary. Taste for seasoning. Add the currant–pine nut relish and stir to combine. Transfer the pasta to a large warm platter and shower the toasted breadcrumbs over the entire dish.

My beloved cavolo nero!

chicken paillards with parmesan breadcrumbs, escarole, capers, and rosemary

6 boneless, skinless chicken breasts

¾ cup all-purpose flour

2 extra-large eggs

4½ cups fresh breadcrumbs

1 cup grated Parmigiano-Reggiano

6 tablespoons chopped flat-leaf parsley

6 tablespoons extra-virgin olive oil

8 tablespoons (1 stick) unsalted butter

1 sprig rosemary, broken in half

1 chile de árbol, broken in half

2 cloves garlic, sliced

2 heads escarole, core removed, leaves separated and cleaned

1 lemon, zest finely grated

2 tablespoons chopped capers

Kosher salt and freshly ground black pepper

Chicken breasts probably wouldn't make the list of my favorite foods. But these chicken paillards are a different story. Pounded thin, dredged in Parmesan breadcrumbs, and sautéed until golden and crispy, these chicken breasts are a synthesis of a few retro classics: chicken Parmesan meets chicken Milanese meets fried chicken. Whatever you want to call it, it's a true crowd-pleaser, for everyone from the most sophisticated diner to the pasta-with-butter-eating child.

Place the chicken breasts between two pieces of plastic wrap, and pound them with a mallet to an even ⅓-inch thickness.

Place the flour on a plate or in a pie pan. Beat the eggs in a shallow bowl. Combine the breadcrumbs, Parmigiano, and 3 tablespoons chopped parsley in a shallow dish. Line the three dishes up in a row.

Season the chicken breasts with salt and pepper. Dredge the chicken in the flour, then the egg, and then the breadcrumb mixture, using your hands to pat the breadcrumbs onto the chicken. Transfer the prepared chicken breasts to a large plate or baking sheet.

Heat two sauté pans over high heat for 2 minutes. Swirl 2 tablespoons olive oil into each pan, and wait a minute. Place three chicken breasts in each pan. Cook 3 minutes, and then add 1 tablespoon butter to each pan. Cook another minute, and when the crumbs are golden brown, carefully turn the chicken over. Turn the heat down to medium, and cook a few more minutes, until the second side is golden brown and the chicken is just cooked through. Remove the chicken to a baking sheet.

Return the pans to medium heat and swirl 1 tablespoon olive oil into each pan. Divide the rosemary and chile between the two pans, and let sizzle 30 seconds. Add half the garlic to each pan, stir a few seconds, and then add the escarole to the pans. Season with salt and pepper, and sauté gently 2 to 3 minutes, until the greens have just wilted. Season the escarole with a squeeze of lemon juice, and transfer to a large platter. Place the chicken on top.

Wipe out one of the pans, and return it to the stove over medium heat. Add the remaining 6 tablespoons butter, and cook until it's brown and smells nutty. Remove from the heat and wait a few seconds. (It is very hot and will foam up and overflow if you add something to it right away.) Add the capers, lemon zest, a generous squeeze of lemon juice, and the remaining 3 tablespoons parsley. Carefully taste for balance and seasoning.

Spoon the caper brown butter over the chicken and around the escarole.

jessica's favorite meyer lemon tart with a layer of chocolate

During my last year in high school, we were given 2 weeks off from classes for "senior projects." While my peers pursued scuba diving, rock climbing, sailing, and photography, I headed to Ma Maison, the culinary pinnacle of Los Angeles, circa 1984.

Being a girl in a French restaurant in 1984, I was led straight to the pastry kitchen. When I arrived, my fear of being in the way was quickly put to rest; the pastry chef had just been fired, and the sous-chef, Aisha, was running the show all alone. In no time at all, she had me making doughs, whipping mousses, and filling tart shells. Thrilled with my newfound pastry skills, I rushed home every day after work to re-create those desserts for my family.

One of the first things I learned to make that spring was a classic lemon tart with a pâte sucrée crust. The first time I tried it at home, my chocoholic sister begged me to add some chocolate. I refused and stuck to the classic French recipe. But one day, when her birthday rolled around, I gave in to her suggestion. I melted some bittersweet chocolate, spread it over the baked crust, and waited for it to solidify. Nervously, I poured the warm lemon curd over and waited to see if it would work. It was the first time I'd ever deviated from a pastry recipe, and I was terrified I might ruin it. To Jessica's delight (and mine, too), it was even better than the original. To this day, whenever this tart is on the Lucques menu, Jessica gloats, proud of our lemon-chocolate collaboration.

1 recipe pâte sucrée (see page 196)

2 ounces bittersweet chocolate

4 extra-large eggs

3 extra-large egg yolks

1 cup plus 1 tablespoon granulated sugar

1 cup Meyer lemon juice

10 tablespoons cold unsalted butter, cut into small pieces

A pinch of kosher salt

1 cup heavy cream

NOTE This tart should be served cold, so make it at least a few hours before serving. When you make the lemon curd, you need to stir it the entire time. For an ultra-smooth curd, I use both a whisk and a rubber spatula, alternating between the two as I stir. Start with the whisk, and as the mixture begins to get frothy, switch to the spatula (which helps get rid of the froth), scraping the bottom and sides continuously. Remove the curd from the heat and let it cool slightly before pouring it over the hardened chocolate layer. Don't cool the curd completely before pouring or it will lose its nice sheen. You can also make this tart with regular lemon juice.

Preheat the oven to 375°F.

Line the tart pan with the pâte sucrée according to the instructions on page 196. Prick the bottom with a fork, and line it with a few opened and fanned-out coffee filters or a piece of parchment paper. Fill the lined tart shell with beans or pie weights, and bake 15 minutes, until set. Take the tart out of the oven, and carefully lift out the paper and beans. Return the tart to the oven, and bake another 10 to 15 minutes, until the crust is an even golden brown. Set aside on a rack to cool completely.

Melt the chocolate in a double boiler over medium-low heat. Spread the chocolate evenly on the crust, and chill in the refrigerator for at least 15 minutes, until the chocolate has solidified completely.

While the crust is chilling, make the curd. Whisk the eggs, egg yolks, sugar, and lemon juice together in a heavy-bottomed saucepan. Cook over medium heat, stirring continuously, alternating between a whisk and rubber spatula (see note), until the lemon curd has thickened to the consistency of pastry cream and coats the back of the spatula.

Remove the lemon curd from the heat. Add the butter a little at a time, stirring to incorporate completely. Season with the salt.

Let the curd cool about 8 minutes, and then strain it into the prepared tart shell. Chill the tart in the refrigerator.

Just before serving, whip the cream in a stand mixer fitted with the whisk attachment (or by hand) until it holds soft peaks. Cut six wedges from the tart, plate them, and serve with dollops of whipped cream.

persimmon and pomegranate salad with arugula and hazelnuts

This is one of those salads that I can't stop eating once I start. It's thirst-quenching, crunchy, and downright addictive. The juice from the pomegranate binds with the olive and hazelnut oils to make a bright, acidic dressing for the peppery arugula and sweet persimmons. Juicing your own pomegranates is easy, but if you're not careful, it can result in some embarrassing mishaps. One night at Lucques, a customer asked for a pomegranate martini. Bartender Soren Banks, having seen a bowl of pomegranates in the kitchen, happily agreed to make her one. He rushed back to the kitchen for a quick juicing lesson, and then back to the bar. Following what he interpreted to be my instructions, he proceeded to spray himself and all the customers at the bar with the bright-red juice. Fortunately, everyone was more amused than angry, especially after a free round of pomegranate martinis (juiced this time in the kitchen).

See Fall Market Report (page 206) for the best way to juice a pomegranate.

⅔ cup blanched hazelnuts

1 tablespoon plus 1 teaspoon hazelnut oil

1 tablespoon finely diced shallot; plus 2 small shallots, thinly sliced

3 tablespoons fresh pomegranate juice (from 1 to 2 pomegranates), plus ⅓ cup pomegranate seeds

1 tablespoon sherry vinegar

2 teaspoons rice vinegar

3 tablespoons extra-virgin olive oil

2 small Fuyu persimmons, thinly sliced

½ lemon, for juicing

½ pound arugula

Kosher salt and freshly ground black pepper

Preheat the oven to 375°F.

Spread the hazelnuts on a baking sheet, and toast 8 to 10 minutes, stirring once or twice, until they smell nutty and are lightly browned. When the nuts have cooled, chop them coarsely and toss them with 1 teaspoon hazelnut oil and a generous pinch of salt.

Place the diced shallot, pomegranate juice, both vinegars, and ½ teaspoon salt in a bowl, and let sit 5 minutes. Whisk in the olive oil and the remaining 1 tablespoon hazelnut oil. Taste for balance and seasoning.

In a large salad bowl, toss the persimmons, sliced shallots, and pomegranate seeds with the dressing, and season with salt, pepper, and a squeeze of lemon. Gently toss in the arugula and taste for seasoning. Arrange the salad on a platter, and scatter the hazelnuts over the top.

grilled halibut with herb salad and meyer lemon–green olive salsa

6 fillets Alaskan halibut,
    5 to 6 ounces each

1 Meyer lemon, zested

1 tablespoon thyme leaves

1 tablespoon sliced flat-leaf
    parsley, plus ½ cup packed
    flat-leaf parsley leaves

1 small fennel bulb, sliced

½ teaspoon *fleur de sel*

3 tablespoons super-good
    extra-virgin olive oil

2 tablespoons extra-virgin
    olive oil

1½ cups small arugula or small
    watercress sprigs

¼ cup fresh tarragon leaves

¼ cup chervil sprigs

¼ cup ½-inch-snipped chives

¼ cup small mint leaves

¼ cup small opal and green basil
    leaves

Meyer lemon–green olive salsa
    (recipe follows)

Kosher salt and freshly ground
    black pepper

This invigorating dish is a refreshing change from the hearty comfort foods of winter. The herbs here aren't relegated to the sidelines; tossed with arugula, they become the main attractions of this bright salad. Meyer lemons are diced with their peels on and combined with green olives, champagne vinegar, honey, and olive oil for a bracing sweet-tart salsa to accompany the grilled halibut.

NOTE The halibut needs to be seasoned with lemon and herbs at least 4 hours ahead of time. You can pick the herbs and make the salsa a few hours ahead.

Season the fish with the lemon zest, thyme, and sliced parsley. Cover, and refrigerate at least 4 hours or overnight.

Remove the fish from the refrigerator 15 minutes before cooking, to let it come to room temperature.

Light the grill 30 to 40 minutes before you're ready to cook.

Just before you grill the fish, toss the sliced fennel with the *fleur de sel,* the super-good olive oil, and 1 tablespoon Meyer lemon juice in a large bowl.

When the coals are broken down, red, and glowing, brush the fish with the regular extra-virgin olive oil and season with salt and pepper on both sides. Place the fish on the grill, and cook 2 to 3 minutes, rotating the fish once, until it's nicely colored on the first side. Turn the fish over, and cook a few more minutes, until it's almost cooked through. Be careful not to overcook the fish. When it's done, it will begin to flake and separate a little, but the center will still be slightly translucent. Remember, the halibut will continue to cook a bit more once you take it off the grill.

While the fish is cooking, very gently toss the arugula and herbs with the fennel. Season with salt and freshly ground black pepper and taste. Arrange the salad on a large platter, place the fish on top, and spoon some of the Meyer lemon–green olive salsa over the halibut. Serve the remaining salsa on the side.

meyer lemon–green olive salsa

Place the shallot, champagne vinegar, and a healthy pinch of salt in a small bowl, and let sit 5 minutes.

Slice the stem and blossom ends from the Meyer lemons. Stand the lemons on one end, and cut them vertically into ⅛-inch slices. Stack the slices in small piles on a cutting board, and cut them lengthwise into ⅛-inch-thick matchsticks. Line up the matchsticks, and cut them into ⅛-inch cubes.

Add the diced lemon to the shallot. Stir in the honey, olives, parsley, a pinch of pepper, and the olive oil. Taste for balance and seasoning.

2 tablespoons finely diced shallot

1 tablespoon plus 1 teaspoon champagne vinegar

2 Meyer lemons

1 teaspoon honey

¾ cup pitted Lucques olives, chopped

2 tablespoons sliced flat-leaf parsley

½ cup extra-virgin olive oil

Kosher salt and freshly ground black pepper

cured pork chops with sweet potatoes, bacon, and romesco

6 pork rib chops, 10 ounces each

1 recipe brine (see page 214)

2 tablespoons extra-virgin olive oil

Sweet potatoes with bacon and spinach (recipe follows)

1 recipe romesco (see page 44)

Kosher salt and freshly ground black pepper

In my opinion there is no better accompaniment to pork than pork. I'm shamelessly infatuated with this versatile meat and use it often, not only as the key player but also as a seasoning. In this dish it's both—the chop is the star and the bacon supports it, echoing the great pork flavor. Brining adds an additional layer of flavor, both sweet and salty, while also tenderizing the meat, making for an extra-juicy chop.

Catalan romesco is one of my favorite condiments. Made from roasted tomatoes, ancho chiles, nuts, garlic, olive oil, and fried bread, this spicy sauce is delicious on grilled fish, fried tetilla cheese, roasted leeks and onions—I don't know where to stop. . . .

NOTE The chops need to soak in the brine for 24 hours, so plan ahead. You can make the romesco the day before. And you can cook the sweet potatoes in the morning and reheat them just before serving.

Submerge the pork chops completely in the brine, and refrigerate for 24 hours.

Light the grill 30 to 40 minutes before you're ready to cook, and take the pork chops out of the refrigerator to bring them to room temperature. If they're wet from the brine, pat them dry with paper towels.

When the coals are broken down, red, and glowing, brush the pork chops with the olive oil, and place them on the grill. Cook the pork chops 5 to 7 minutes on the first side (depending on how thick they are), rotating them a couple of times, until they're seared and have a nice color. Turn them over and cook another 4 to 5 minutes or so, rotating them often, until medium-rare to medium. You can peek inside, near the bone; they should be a little pink.

Arrange the sweet potatoes on a large warm platter, and drizzle about ¼ cup romesco over them. Place the grilled pork chops on top, and slather each one with a generous spoonful of romesco. Serve the rest of the romesco on the side.

sweet potatoes with bacon and spinach

Preheat the oven to 400°F.

Peel the sweet potatoes, and cut them into 1½-inch cubes. Place them in a large bowl and toss with the sugar.

In a medium sauté pan, cook the butter over medium heat 6 to 8 minutes, until it's brown and smells nutty. Remove from the heat and let cool a few minutes. Add the sage and thyme to the butter, and pour it over the sweet potatoes, scraping the pan with a rubber spatula to get all the brown bits. Toss with a large spoon, being careful of the hot butter. Season with 1 tablespoon salt and ¼ teaspoon pepper. Transfer the sweet potatoes to a large roasting pan and bake in the oven 50 minutes to 1 hour, until the potatoes are caramelized and tender. Stir with a metal spatula every so often, to coat the potatoes evenly with the butter and sugar.

While the potatoes are cooking, slice the bacon lengthwise into ⅜-inch-thick slices. Stack them in two piles, then cut the strips crosswise into ⅜-inch even-sided rectangles, or *lardons*. Heat a large sauté pan over medium heat for 1 minute. Add the bacon, and cook about 5 minutes, until it's tender and lightly crisped. Using a slotted spoon, transfer it to a plate.

When the sweet potatoes are done, remove the pan from the oven and toss in the bacon and spinach. Taste for seasoning.

4 pounds sweet potatoes, Jewel or Garnet

⅓ cup brown sugar

8 ounces (2 sticks) unsalted butter

1 tablespoon sliced sage leaves

2 teaspoons thyme leaves

¾-pound slab bacon

½ pound young spinach, cleaned

Kosher salt and freshly ground black pepper

churros y chocolate

Churros and chocolate have a long history at Lucques, and an even longer one in Spain, where they dominate the dessert scene in late-night cafés. The hot chocolate is made thick and syrupy sweet, meant for dipping the piping-hot crullers.

In preparation for one Spanish-themed Sunday supper, my former pastry chef Kimberly Sklar experimented with traditional churro recipes from Spanish cookbooks. Though the flavors were good, the Spanish versions seemed a little too heavy and not tender enough for our liking. Then Kim tried a batch of *pâte à choux*, the traditional French dough used to make such pastries as cream puffs and éclairs. It was the perfect solution.

Next we set out to conquer the chocolate. Again, in my opinion, the traditional Spanish hot chocolate was better in theory than in reality. Spaniards love sugar, and their version is just too sweet for my taste. Still thick and rich in the vein of the traditional *chocolate,* ours is super-chocolaty but not as cloyingly sweet. I like to add a generous pinch of salt, to play up the bittersweet notes of the chocolate.

This is a festive, interactive dessert that requires some last-minute attention when it's time to fry the churros. Make the batter and hot chocolate ahead, and just before you serve dessert, invite your friends into the kitchen to help you fry. It's fun to watch the dough transform into deep golden brown snakes and then to roll them in the glittery cinnamon-sugar.

> NOTE The batter for the churros can be made up to 8 hours in advance but *must* be made at least 2 hours ahead. You will need a pastry bag fitted with a number-4 star tip to pipe the churros into the hot oil.

1 cup plus 1 tablespoon whole milk

2 teaspoons kosher salt

½ cup plus 1½ teaspoons granulated sugar

8 ounces (2 sticks) unsalted butter

1 cup plus 2 tablespoons all-purpose flour, sifted

3 extra-large eggs

1 extra-large egg yolk

2 to 3 quarts vegetable oil, for frying

¾ teaspoon ground cinnamon

Hot chocolate (recipe follows)

Bring the milk, 1 cup plus 1 tablespoon water, salt, 1½ teaspoons sugar, and the butter to a boil in a medium saucepan over medium heat. Remove the pan from the heat, and add all the flour at once. Stir together with a wooden spoon, and return the pan to the stove over low heat. Work the batter back and forth, stirring with a wooden spoon, to dry the batter. When the dough begins to roll away from the sides of the pan, cook another 5 minutes.

Transfer the batter to the bowl of a stand mixer fitted with the paddle attachment. With the mixer running at low speed, drop the eggs and egg yolk in one by one, waiting for each to be incorporated before adding the next. Let the batter rest at least 2 hours in the refrigerator before using.

Heat the oil to 350°F on a deep-frying thermometer, over medium heat, in a heavy wide-bottomed pan.

Place the dough in a pastry bag fitted with a number-4 star tip. (You may have to do this in batches.)

Combine the cinnamon and remaining ½ cup sugar in a bowl.

Squeeze 4-inch-long pieces of dough into the oil. Don't overcrowd the pan; the churros shouldn't be touching. Fry the churros 2 to 3 minutes, turning them gently with tongs once or twice to brown all sides. Test one to make sure the center is done. It should be cooked all the way through and have a crisp exterior and soft center.

Drain the churros on paper towels, and pat to remove any excess oil. While they're still hot, roll each churro in the cinnamon sugar, and serve right away with cups of the hot chocolate for dipping.

hot chocolate

4 ounces bittersweet chocolate, coarsely chopped

2 tablespoons unsweetened cocoa powder

1 cup whole milk

1 cup heavy cream

2 teaspoons pure vanilla extract

¼ teaspoon kosher salt

Place the chocolate in a double boiler and melt over medium heat. Whisk in ¼ cup hot water to incorporate.

Sift the cocoa powder into a large mixing bowl. Whisk in about 2 tablespoons milk, to form a paste. Whisk in the rest of the milk, the cream, vanilla, and salt.

Whisk the milk-and-cocoa mixture into the melted chocolate, and transfer to a medium saucepan. Bring to a boil over low heat, whisking continuously.

kabocha squash and fennel soup with crème fraîche and candied pumpkin seeds

Of all winter squash, Kabocha holds a special place in my heart. Rich and sweet, its dense orange flesh is one of my favorite winter flavors. For this soup, instead of sautéing the squash and fennel, I roast them in the oven to bring out their natural sweetness. If you can't find Kabocha, use another winter squash, such as butternut or Hubbard. The pumpkin seeds, or pepitas, are coated in sugar, paprika, cumin, cinnamon, and cayenne; I think of them as adult Halloween candy. Sprinkled over the top, they give this delicious winter soup a feisty coronation.

2 pounds Kabocha squash

2 medium bulbs fennel

4 tablespoons extra-virgin olive oil

2 teapoons fennel seeds

4 tablespoons unsalted butter

2 cups sliced onions

1 tablespoon thyme leaves

2 chiles de árbol

1 bay leaf

¾ cup sherry

10 cups chicken or vegetable stock or water

¼ cup crème fraîche

Candied pumpkin seeds (recipe follows)

Kosher salt and freshly ground black pepper

Preheat the oven to 400°F.

Cut the squash in half lengthwise, and remove the seeds. Place the squash cut side down on a cutting board, and use a sharp knife to remove the peel. Slice the squash into 1-inch-thick wedges. Cut the fennel in half lengthwise and then into ½-inch-thick wedges.

Toss the squash and fennel with the olive oil, 1 teaspoon salt, and some freshly ground black pepper. Place the vegetables flat on a baking sheet and roast about 35 minutes, until tender and slightly caramelized.

Meanwhile, toast the fennel seeds in a small pan over medium heat 2 to 3 minutes, until the seeds release their aroma and are lightly browned. Pound them coarsely in a mortar.

Heat a Dutch oven or soup pot over high heat for 2 minutes. Add the butter, and when it foams, add the onions, fennel seeds, thyme, chiles, bay leaf, 1 tea-spoon salt, and a good amount of freshly ground black pepper. Reduce the heat to medium-high, and cook about 10 minutes, stirring often, until the onions are soft, translucent, and starting to color.

Add the squash and fennel, and stir to coat with the onions for a minute. Turn the heat back up to high and pour in the sherry. Let it reduce for a minute or two, and then add the stock and 1 tablespoon salt. Bring to a boil, turn down the heat, and simmer 20 minutes.

Strain the soup in a colander set in a pot. Put a third of the solids into a blender with ½ cup of the broth. (You will need to purée the soup in batches.)

Process at the lowest speed until the squash mixture is puréed. Add another ½ cup broth and then turn the speed up to high and pour in more liquid, a little at a time, until the soup has the consistency of heavy cream. Blend at least a minute on high speed, until the soup is completely smooth and very creamy. Transfer to a container, and repeat with the rest of the ingredients. You may not need all the liquid. Taste for balance and seasoning.

Pour the soup into six bowls, spoon some crème fraîche in the center of each, and scatter the pumpkin seeds over the top. Or serve family-style in a tureen with the crème fraîche and pumpkin seeds on the side.

candied pumpkin seeds

Toast the cumin seeds in a small pan over medium heat 2 to 3 minutes, until the seeds release their aroma and are lightly browned. Pound them coarsely in a mortar.

Melt the butter in the cumin pan over medium heat. Add the pumpkin seeds and sugar, then sprinkle the spices and a healthy pinch of salt over them. Toss the pumpkin seeds to coat them well with the butter, and cook a few minutes, until just after they begin to pop and color slightly.

Turn off the heat, and wait 30 seconds. Add the honey, tossing well to coat the pumpkin seeds. Spread on a plate and let them cool.

¼ teaspoon cumin seeds

2 teaspoons unsalted butter

½ cup raw pumpkin seeds

1 tablespoon granulated sugar

Generous pinch each of ground cinnamon, paprika, and cayenne pepper

1 teaspoon honey

Kosher salt

devil's chicken thighs with braised leeks and dijon mustard

12 chicken thighs, trimmed of excess skin and fat

1 cup thinly sliced onion

3 tablespoons plus 1 teaspoon thyme leaves

2 chiles de árbol, thinly sliced on the diagonal

2 fresh bay leaves, thinly sliced, or 2 dried leaves, crumbled

¾ cup dry vermouth

2 cups fresh breadcrumbs

5 tablespoons unsalted butter

2 tablespoons chopped flat-leaf parsley

½ cup finely diced shallots

½ cup Dijon mustard

1 extra-large egg

2 teaspoons chopped tarragon

2 tablespoons extra-virgin olive oil

¾ cup chicken stock

Braised leeks (recipe follows)

Kosher salt and freshly ground black pepper

I'm not sure which parent I'm indebted to for this recipe. Probably both. When my mother met my father, she was neither a practiced diner nor an experienced cook. To rectify the situation and satisfy his own culinary demands, my father gave my mother a copy of Julia Child's *Mastering the Art of French Cooking* as soon as they were married. When I was growing up, this was one of my favorite recipes from that book.

I served my own interpretation of the dish at one of our first Sunday suppers at Lucques. First I browned the chicken thighs and slathered them in a quick-to-make mustard-and-breadcrumb combo and then roasted them on a bed of braised leeks. The chicken emerges from the oven crisp and brown, while the leeks become tender, and permeated with the flavors of the chicken.

NOTE The chicken is best when it marinates overnight. The leeks need to be braised ahead; you could even braise them the day before. You can also sear the chicken thighs, grind the breadcrumbs, and make the mustard mixture a few hours in advance. Then the only thing left to do is assemble the thighs over the braised leeks and bake.

Place the chicken thighs in a large bowl with the sliced onion, 2 tablespoons thyme, chiles, bay leaves, and ¼ cup vermouth. Using your hands, toss to coat the chicken well. Cover, and refrigerate at least 4 hours, preferably overnight.

Place the breadcrumbs in a medium bowl. Heat a large sauté pan over medium heat for 1 minute. Add 3 tablespoons butter, and cook until it's brown and smells nutty. Use a rubber spatula to scrape the brown butter over the breadcrumbs. Wait 1 minute, and then toss well with the parsley and 1 tablespoon thyme.

Preheat the oven to 375°F.

Return the sauté pan to medium heat for 1 minute. Swirl in the remaining 2 tablespoons butter, and when it foams, add the shallots and remaining 1 teaspoon thyme. Sauté about 2 minutes, until the shallots are translucent. Add the remaining ½ cup vermouth and reduce by half. Transfer to a bowl and let cool a few minutes. Whisk in the mustard, egg, chopped tarragon, and a pinch of black pepper.

Remove the chicken from the refrigerator 30 minutes before cooking, to bring it to room temperature. Discard the seasonings, and pat the chicken dry with paper towels. After 15 minutes, season the thighs well on both sides with salt and pepper.

Return the same sauté pan to high heat for about 2 minutes. Swirl in the olive oil, and wait 1 minute. Place the chicken thighs in the pan, skin side down, and cook 8 to 10 minutes, until the skin is a deep golden brown. Turn the thighs over, and cook a minute or two on the other side. Place the chicken on the braised leeks. Turn off the heat and discard the fat. Add the chicken stock to the pan, and scrape with a wooden spoon to release the crispy bits stuck to the bottom. Pour the chicken stock over the braised leeks.

Toss the chicken thighs in the bowl with the mustard mixture, slathering them completely, and then rearrange them over the braised leeks. Spoon any remaining mustard mixture over the chicken thighs. Top each thigh with bread-crumbs, patting with your hands to make sure they get nicely coated. (You want lots of mustard mixture and lots of breadcrumbs.) Bake about 40 minutes, until the chicken is just cooked through. To check for doneness, pierce the meat near the bone with a paring knife; when ready, the juices from the chicken will run clear.

Turn the oven up to 475°F and cook the chicken thighs another 10 minutes, until the breadcrumbs are golden brown.

Serve in the baking dish, or transfer to a large warm platter.

braised leeks

These leeks are also delicious cold, dressed with a mustard vinaigrette and served with sliced prosciutto and chopped egg.

6 large leeks

About ¾ cup extra-virgin olive oil

1 cup sliced shallots

1 tablespoon thyme leaves

½ cup dry white wine

1½ to 2 cups chicken or vegetable stock or water

Kosher salt and freshly ground black pepper

Preheat the oven to 400°F.

Remove any bruised outer layers from the leeks. Trim off to the roots, leaving the root end intact. Trim the tops of the leeks on the diagonal, leaving 2 inches of the green part attached. Cut the leeks in half lengthwise, and submerge in a large bowl of cold water to clean them. Shake the leeks well to dislodge the dirt stuck inside. Let them sit a few minutes, to allow any grit inside the layers to fall to the bottom of the bowl. Repeat the process until the water is clean. Place the leeks, cut side down, on a towel and pat dry completely.

Turn the leeks over so their cut sides are facing up, and season with 2 teaspoons salt and a few grindings of black pepper.

Heat a large sauté pan over medium-high heat for 2 minutes. Pour in ¼ cup olive oil, and wait 1 minute. Place the leeks in the pan, cut side down, being careful not to crowd them. (You will probably need to sauté them in batches or in two pans. Add more olive oil to the pan as needed, for each batch.) Sear them 4 to 5 minutes, until they are golden brown. Season the backs of the leeks with salt and pepper, and turn them over to cook another 3 to 4 minutes. Transfer them to a large gratin dish, lining them up, cut sides facing up. (Choose a baking dish or gratin dish that can go from oven to table and that will accommodate all the leeks and chicken thighs, or use two smaller dishes.)

Pour ¼ cup olive oil into the pan and heat over medium heat. Add the shallots, thyme, ¼ teaspoon salt, and a pinch of pepper. Cook about 5 minutes, until the shallots are just beginning to color. Add the white wine and reduce by half. Add 1½ cups stock, and bring to a boil over high heat.

Pour the liquid over the leeks. The stock should not quite cover them; add more stock if necessary.

Braise in the oven 30 minutes, until the leeks are tender when pierced.

braised beef brisket with beluga lentils, horseradish cream, and salsa verde

When I was chef de cuisine at Campanile, I had to make brisket every Friday for the weekend brunch menu. Pounds and pounds of it passed through the hot ovens and sat resting on the counter before it was put away in the refrigerator. Sometimes I'd hear someone whisper, "Hide the brisket, she's coming." Nancy Silverton, the owner, would suddenly appear from around the corner, fingers poised to pilfer the fatty top layer from the roast. It was so rich and addictive, we couldn't blame her. When you buy your brisket, don't let your butcher cut away that top fatty layer; it adds essential flavor and keeps the brisket from drying out. Look for a brisket sold "point-on"—that triangular end is the most tender and flavorful part of the meat.

You don't have to serve both sauces with the brisket, but I think it's super delicious that way. One bite gets an herby, acidic note of salsa verde and the next one rewards you with a fiesty horseradish cream. When I made this dish at home, my husband, brother-in-law, and best friend managed to polish off the entire 6-pound brisket by themselves while watching a single basketball game. I was shocked. It's always better to make more brisket rather than less. And even if your friends don't have as big appetites as mine do, you'll be happy to have the leftovers for sandwiches or hash the next day.

> **NOTE** I find that the easiest (and most delicious) way to prepare brisket is to braise it a day or two ahead. Then slice it and reheat it in its juices. The increased surface area of exposed meat means more chance for crispy caramelization!

Ingredients

6 pounds whole beef brisket, with ½-inch top layer of fat

3 tablespoons thyme leaves

2 fresh bay leaves, thinly sliced, or 2 dry, crumbled

10 cloves garlic, smashed

3 chiles de árbol, crumbled with your hands

1 tablespoon plus 2 teaspoons cracked black pepper

3 tablespoons extra-virgin olive oil

2 medium onions

3 medium carrots, peeled

1 stalk celery

¼ cup balsamic vinegar

3 cups dark beer, such as Guinness or Samuel Smith

4 cups beef stock, or more if needed

Beluga lentils (recipe follows)

Salsa verde (see page 132)

Sautéed rapini with garlic and chile (recipe follows)

1 recipe horseradish cream (see page 303)

Kosher salt

Place the brisket in a large shallow dish, and rub the thyme, bay leaves, garlic, chiles, and cracked black pepper onto both sides of it, coating the meat well. Cover, and refrigerate overnight.

Take the brisket out of the refrigerator 1 hour before cooking to bring it to room temperature. After 30 minutes, season the meat with 2 tablespoons salt.

Preheat the oven to 325°F.

Heat a large heavy-bottomed sauté pan over high heat for 2 minutes. Add 3 tablespoons olive oil and wait 1 minute. Place the brisket in the pan (reserving the garlic and chile). Sear the meat on both sides, about 8 minutes per side, until it's deep golden brown. You will need to sear a portion of the meat at a time, because the entire brisket probably won't fit in your pan. To do this, leave one end of the brisket hanging off the edge of the pan, and then move that end into the pan when the other part is well seared. Once both sides are well browned, transfer the brisket to a roasting pan or Dutch oven that's big enough to accommodate the entire piece of meat.

Cut the onions in half through the root end and peel them. Cut them into 1-inch-thick wedges, leaving the root end intact. Cut the carrots and celery into thirds. Return the original brisket pan to the stove over medium-high heat. Add the vegetables to the pan, and cook 8 to 10 minutes, until they're caramelized. Stir often with a wooden spoon, scraping up all the crusty bits. Add the reserved garlic and chiles and cook a few more minutes.

Turn off the heat (so that the liquids won't evaporate immediately), and add the balsamic vinegar, then the beer. Turn the heat back up to medium-high and reduce the beer by a quarter. Add the beef stock and bring the stock to a boil over high heat. Use a slotted spoon to scoop out most of the vegetables and place them under and around the brisket. Pour the hot stock over the meat. It should come just to the top of the brisket. Add more stock if necessary. Cover the pan tightly with plastic wrap (yes, it can go in the oven) and then aluminum foil. Braise in the oven 5 to 6 hours.

To check for doneness, carefully remove the foil and plastic, watching out for the hot steam. Test the meat by inserting a fork into it; if the fork slides in easily, then the brisket is done.

Let the brisket cool in its juices for 30 minutes. Carefully transfer it to a baking sheet, and chill completely.

Strain the braising juices into a saucepan, pressing down on the vegetables with a ladle to extract all the liquid. Skim the fat from the braising juices and chill.

When you are ready to serve, preheat the oven to 400°F. Cut the cold brisket against the grain into ¼-inch-thick slices. Lay the slices in two large roasting pans (or equivalent). Heat the braising juices and pour some over the meat, just to cover. Cook about 20 minutes until the meat is hot and caramelized and crispy on top.

Spoon the hot beluga lentils onto a large warm platter, and arrange the brisket on top. Spoon some of the braising juices over the meat, and drizzle some of the salsa verde on top. Serve the remaining salsa verde, the sautéed rapini, horseradish cream, and any extra braising juices on the side.

beluga lentils

These tiny black lentils are named for their resemblance to caviar.

Rinse the lentils, and pick through them to remove any small stones.

Heat a medium saucepan over medium heat for 2 minutes. Swirl in 2 tablespoons olive oil and wait a minute. Add the onion, thyme, chile, 1 teaspoon salt, and a pinch of pepper. Cook the onion, stirring often, until soft and translucent, about 5 minutes.

Add the lentils and 1 teaspoon salt. Cook about 2 minutes, stirring to coat the lentils in the oil and vegetables. Reduce the heat to low, and add the wine. Quickly add 6 cups water, and bring to a boil over high heat. Turn down the heat, and simmer 25 to 30 minutes, until the lentils are tender.

Strain the lentils over a bowl. Toss them with the remaining 6 tablespoons olive oil, the basil sprigs, ½ teaspoon salt, and ⅓ cup of the cooking liquid. (Add more of the liquid if the lentils seem dry.) Taste for seasoning.

1½ cups beluga lentils (see Sources)

½ cup extra-virgin olive oil

½ cup diced white onion

1 teaspoon thyme leaves

1 chile de árbol

¼ cup red wine

3 sprigs basil

Kosher salt and freshly ground black pepper

sautéed rapini with garlic and chile

The amount of oil called for in this recipe might shock you, but to get the rapini nicely sautéed and coated in all the flavors of the chile, shallot, and thyme, it really is necessary. If you don't want to end up eating all that oil, you can remove the rapini from the pan with tongs, leaving the oil behind. Or you can serve it all together, and let the olive oil pool beneath the rapini on the plate. Of course, I can never resist sopping up the oil with a crusty hunk of bread!

Bring a large pot of heavily salted water to a boil.

Blanch the rapini a couple of minutes in the rapidly boiling water, until just tender and al dente. Drain, and cool on a platter or baking sheet.

Heat a large sauté pan over high heat for 2 minutes. Pour in ¼ cup olive oil, and add the garlic, shallots, thyme, and chile. Cook a few minutes, until the shallots are translucent. Add the rapini and 1 teaspoon salt. Stir well, coating the rapini with the other ingredients and bathing it in the oil. Drizzle the remaining ¼ cup oil over the rapini, and sauté 2 minutes, tossing often. Sprinkle another teaspoon salt and a pinch of black pepper over the rapini, toss, and taste for seasoning.

1½ pounds rapini, ends trimmed

½ cup extra-virgin olive oil

3 cloves garlic, thinly sliced

2 shallots, thinly sliced

1 teaspoon thyme leaves

1 chile de árbol, thinly sliced on the diagonal

Kosher salt and freshly ground black pepper

toasted pain d'épice with kumquat marmalade butter

3 tablespoons unsalted butter, softened, plus more for the pan

¾ cup honey

½ cup brown sugar

2 cups all-purpose flour

1½ teaspoons baking powder

1 teaspoon baking soda

1½ teaspoons ground cinnamon

1½ teaspoons freshly grated nutmeg

½ teaspoon ground cloves

2 extra-large eggs

1 extra-large egg yolk

1 tablespoon grated fresh ginger, juice reserved

Kumquat marmalade butter (recipe follows)

When we were opening Lucques, we had very little money for the renovation. The space had a decent kitchen but lacked a great oven. Fritz León, one of our purveyors, was hanging out with us one long day of construction and happened to mention a "huge, fantastic" deck oven that one of his other clients downtown was selling for (and this was the key) "cheap." What more could I ask for? I bought it on the spot.

I began to doubt myself when we went to pick it up and found it was so huge and heavy that we had to take it apart just to get it through the kitchen door. It was a monster, and when we finally did get it installed it seemed as if the old dinosaur had a mind of its own. Each deck ran at a specific, apparently predetermined temperature, no matter what setting we mere mortals put it at. The lower deck was at a constant 350°F, the middle at 400°F, and the top at a raging 500°F plus.

It wasn't long before the top deck was christened "the Terminator," and now I can't imagine life at Lucques without it. It was even instrumental in the evolution of our pain d'épice, developed by former pastry chef Kimberly Sklar. For a crispy exterior, she sliced the classic Alsatian spice bread and toasted it on the floor of the Terminator before slathering it with butter and kumquat marmalade. At home, you can simulate the "Terminator effect" in a hot cast-iron pan.

Preheat the oven to 350°F.

Lightly butter a loaf pan.

In a large saucepan, bring the honey, brown sugar, and ¾ cup water to a boil, stirring frequently. As soon as it comes to a boil, take the mixture off the heat. Sift in 1 cup of the flour, whisking continuously. Set aside.

Sift together the remaining cup of flour, the baking powder, baking soda, cinnamon, nutmeg, and cloves.

Whisk together the eggs, egg yolk, ginger, and ginger juice. Whisk the honey mixture into the eggs. Slowly fold the remaining dry ingredients into the batter in three parts (if you add too much or too quickly, your batter will be lumpy).

Pour the batter into the prepared loaf pan, and bake 35 to 40 minutes, until the loaf is firm to the touch. Let cool completely before slicing.

Heat one or two cast-iron pans over medium-high heat for 2 minutes. (You can toast the pain d'épice in two pans or in batches.)

Cut six ½-inch-thick slices of pain d'épice, and butter them on both sides. Place the slices in the pan, and toast a few minutes on each side, until golden brown and crisp. Slather each slice with kumquat marmalade butter, and fan them out on a platter, overlapping them slightly. Top with the reserved candied kumquats.

kumquat marmalade butter

In a medium saucepan, bring the granulated sugar and 2 cups water to a boil over medium-high heat, stirring to make sure the sugar is completely dissolved. Add the kumquats, and cover the fruit with a piece of parchment or a small plate to keep them submerged. Turn the heat to low, and cook about 25 minutes, until the kumquats are translucent. Drain the fruit, reserving the sugar syrup. When the kumquats have cooled, cut them in half lengthwise and remove the seeds. Cut halves lengthwise into ⅛-inch-thick slices.

Cream the butter and confectioners' sugar at medium-low speed in the bowl of a stand mixer fitted with the paddle attachment until it's light and fluffy, about 3 minutes. Add all but 3 tablespoons of the candied kumquats. Add a tablespoon or two of the reserved syrup and a pinch of salt. Mix to combine, taste, and add more syrup if you like.

1 cup granulated sugar

½ pound kumquats

½ pound (2 sticks) unsalted butter, at room temperature

¼ cup confectioners' sugar

Kosher salt

beets and tangerines with mint and orange-flower water

3 bunches small to medium beets

6 tablespoons extra-virgin olive oil

2 pounds tangerines (6 large tangerines or 8 smaller ones; larger ones are easier to work with)

2 tablespoons finely diced shallot

1 teaspoon red wine vinegar

1 tablespoon lemon juice

A few drops orange-flower water (see Sources)

12 mint leaves, sliced thinly on the diagonal

Kosher salt and freshly cracked black pepper

Earthy, sweet beets and tangy, juicy tangerines were meant for each other. I'm just the hungry matchmaker. I set them up on an exotic date with a splash of fragrant orange-flower water and ribbons of mint. Not only do they taste delicious together, they also make quite a stunning couple.

Preheat the oven to 400°F.

Cut the greens off the beets, leaving about ½ inch of the stems still attached. (Save the leaves for sautéing later—they are delicious!) Clean the beets well, and toss them with 2 tablespoons olive oil and 1 teaspoon salt.

Place the beets in a roasting pan with a splash of water in the bottom. Cover tightly with foil, and roast about 40 minutes, until tender when pierced. (The roasting time will depend on the size and type of beet.) When the beets are done, carefully remove the foil. Let them cool, and then peel them by slipping off the skins with your fingers. Cut them into ½-inch wedges.

Slice the stem and bottom ends from the tangerines. Stand the tangerines on one end and, following the contour of the fruit with your knife, remove the peel and cottony white pith. Work from top to bottom, rotating the fruit as you go. Then hold each tangerine over a bowl and carefully slice between the membranes and the fruit to release the segments in between. Discard the seeds and reserve the juice.

Combine the diced shallot, vinegar, lemon juice, ¼ cup tangerine juice (from segmenting the citrus), and ½ teaspoon salt in a small bowl, and let sit 5 minutes. Whisk in the remaining ½ cup olive oil, and a drop or two of orange-flower water (be careful, it can be overpowering; a little goes a long way). Taste for balance and seasoning.

Toss the beets in a bowl with half the vinaigrette and a sprinkling of salt and pepper. Taste for seasoning.

Arrange half the beets on a large chilled platter, and place half the tangerines among the beets. Scatter half the mint over the salad. Follow with the rest of the beets, tangerines, and mint. Sprinkle a few drops of orange-flower water over the salad.

australian barramundi with winter vegetables bagna cauda and toasted breadcrumbs

This dish is the Italian equivalent of the French *grand aïoli*. In France, a colorful assortment of vegetable crudités is accompanied by a large bowl of garlicky homemade mayonnaise. In Italy, instead of dipping the vegetables into aïoli, they dunk them into a bowl of bagna cauda, a "warm bath" of garlic and anchovy simmering in butter and olive oil. In this dish, I toss my favorite winter vegetables with the bagna cauda and pair them with a meaty Australian bass, barramundi.

Feel free to adapt the recipe to your location, season, and cravings. If you're in the mood for asparagus or potatoes, add them to the mix. And if you can't find barramundi, this dish is delicious when made with another bass, snapper, or halibut.

NOTE Season the fish with lemon zest and herbs in the morning or night before. You can make the bagna cauda and prep all the vegetables in advance, sautéing the vegetables in the bagna cauda while you cook the fish.

6 fillets barramundi, 5 or 6 ounces each

1 lemon, zested

1 tablespoon thyme leaves

3 tablespoons sliced flat-leaf parsley

1 cup fresh breadcrumbs

3 tablespoons extra-virgin olive oil

Winter vegetables bagna cauda (recipe follows)

Kosher salt and freshly ground pepper

Season the fish with the lemon zest, thyme, and 2 tablespoons parsley. Cover, and refrigerate at least 4 hours.

Preheat the oven to 375°F.

Toss the breadcrumbs with 1 tablespoon olive oil. Spread them on a baking sheet, and toast 8 to 10 minutes, stirring once or twice, until they're golden brown and crispy. Toss in the remaining tablespoon parsley.

Heat a large sauté pan over high heat for 2 minutes. (Depending on the size of your pan, you may need to cook the fish in batches.) Season the fish with salt and pepper on both sides. Swirl in the remaining 2 tablespoons olive oil and wait 1 minute. Carefully lay the fish in the pan, skin side down, and cook 3 to 4 minutes, until the skin is crisp. Turn the fish over, lower the heat to medium-low, and cook a few more minutes, until it's almost cooked through. Be careful not to overcook the fish. When it's done, the fish will begin to flake and separate a little, and the center will still be slightly translucent. Remember, the fish will continue to cook a bit more once you take it out of the pan.

Arrange the winter vegetables bagna cauda on a large warm platter. Nestle the fish among the vegetables, and squeeze lemon juice over the top. Spoon the

4 tablespoons of reserved *bagna cauda* over the fish, and shower the breadcrumbs on top.

winter vegetables bagna cauda

3 heads baby cauliflower,
   or 1 small head cauliflower

6 bulbs baby fennel, or 1 large
   bulb fennel

1 bunch radishes

15 baby carrots, or 3 medium
   carrots

¼ pound baby broccoli,
   or 1 small head broccoli

¾ cup extra-virgin olive oil

8 tablespoons (1 stick) unsalted
   butter

2 teaspoons chopped salt-packed
   anchovies

1 chile de árbol, thinly sliced

4 cloves garlic, thinly sliced

2 teaspoons thyme leaves

1 head Belgian endive, separated
   into spears

1 head Treviso, separated into
   spears

1 lemon, for juicing

Kosher salt and freshly ground
   black pepper

Bring a large pot of heavily salted water to a boil.

Cut the cauliflower into florets each the size of one large bite. Cut the baby fennel in half lengthwise, or cut the large bulb into twelve wedges, keeping the root end intact. Trim the radish stems to ¼ inch, and cut each radish in half lengthwise. Peel the baby carrots, leaving ¼-inch stems, and cut them in half lengthwise. For larger carrots, peel them and cut on the diagonal into ¼-inch-thick slices. Trim the ends of the baby broccoli, or cut the larger head into large bite-sized florets.

Starting with the lighter-colored vegetables first, blanch each vegetable separately until tender, and cool on a baking sheet. (You'll need to taste for doneness; the vegetables should be tender yet still somewhat firm, since they will continue to cook a little after you remove them from the water.) Remember to bring the water back to a boil before each new batch of vegetables.

Heat the olive oil and butter in a medium saucepan over very low heat. Add the anchovies and chile and cook 3 to 4 minutes, stirring with a wooden spoon, until the anchovy melts into the sauce. Add the garlic and thyme. Turn off the heat, and let the garlic finish cooking in the hot oil. Season with a heaping ½ teaspoon salt. Taste for seasoning.

Place the endive and Treviso in a large salad bowl.

Heat a large sauté pan over medium heat for 1 minute. Without stirring, spoon 6 tablespoons of the oil from the top of the bagna cauda and add it to the pan. Add the cauliflower, fennel, radishes, carrots, and broccoli. Season with salt and pepper. Cook 4 to 5 minutes, stirring often, to coat the vegetables well and heat them through.

Stir the bagna cauda well, and set aside 4 tablespoons of it. Pour the rest of the bagna cauda over the vegetables. Toss well to coat, and transfer the vegetables to the salad bowl. Toss with the Treviso and endive, and season generously with lemon juice. Taste for seasoning.

herb-roasted rack of lamb with flageolet gratin, roasted radicchio, and tapenade

3 racks of lamb, trimmed

2 tablespoons thyme leaves, plus 6 whole sprigs thyme

2 tablespoons rosemary leaves, plus 6 whole sprigs rosemary

6 cloves garlic, smashed

1 tablespoon freshly cracked black pepper

3 tablespoons extra-virgin olive oil

Roasted radicchio (recipe follows)

¼ cup flat-leaf parsley leaves

1 recipe tapenade (see page 194)

Flageolet bean gratin (recipe follows)

Kosher salt

This lamb dish is saturated with the bold flavors of Provence—rosemary, thyme, garlic, olives, and capers. First the lamb is seared with broken sprigs of rosemary and thyme to infuse the meat with smoky, eucalyptus notes. Then it's buried under plenty of garlic and herbs, roasted in the oven until medium-rare, and served with a sweet and creamy flageolet gratin, roasted radicchio, and black olive tapenade.

NOTE Season the lamb with the herbs, pepper, and garlic the night before. For extra smoky flavor, you could sear the lamb on the grill instead of in a pan. Either way, remember to let the meat rest before slicing it into chops. If you like, set up the gratin and bake it ahead of time. You can also roast the radicchio and make the tapenade in advance.

Season the lamb with the thyme leaves and sprigs, rosemary leaves and sprigs, garlic, and cracked black pepper. Cover, and refrigerate at least 4 hours, preferably overnight.

Take the lamb out of the refrigerator 1 hour before cooking, to bring it to room temperature. After 30 minutes, season the lamb generously on all sides with salt. Reserve the garlic and herb sprigs.

Preheat the oven to 325°F.

Heat a large sauté pan over high heat for 3 minutes. Swirl in 2 tablespoons olive oil and wait a minute or two, until the pan is very hot and almost smoking. Place the lamb racks in the pan, and sear them on all sides until they're well browned and caramelized. (You will need to do this in batches.) As the meat sears, break up the rosemary and thyme sprigs and add them to the pan. They will sizzle and flavor the lamb as it cooks.

Transfer the seared lamb to a roasting rack set in a roasting pan. Top with the seared herbs and reserved garlic. Roast in the oven 20 to 25 minutes, until the lamb is medium-rare; a meat thermometer inserted into the center of the eye will register 120°F. Let the lamb rest at least 8 minutes. Slice the lamb between the bones into chops.

Arrange the roasted radicchio on a large warm platter, scatter the parsley leaves over the radicchio, and place the lamb chops on top. Spoon some tapenade over the lamb, and serve the flageolet gratin and remaining tapenade on the side.

roasted radicchio

Preheat the oven to 350°F.

Cut the radicchio in half lengthwise through the core. Place the halves on a cutting board, cut side down, and cut each half into four wedges, leaving the root end intact to hold the wedges together.

Carefully toss the radicchio with the olive oil, vinegar, rosemary leaves, 1 teaspoon salt, and lots of pepper. Let sit 15 minutes.

Place the wedges snugly, cut side down, in a gratin dish. (Choose a dish in which the radicchio just fits; it won't cook properly if there is too much empty space.) Roast 30 to 40 minutes, until the radicchio is tender, slightly crisp, and caramelized on top.

2 heads radicchio

3 tablespoons extra-virgin olive oil

1 tablespoon balsamic vinegar

2 teaspoons rosemary leaves

Kosher salt and freshly ground black pepper

flageolet gratin

Every time I make this flageolet gratin, I think about my first days at Chez Panisse.

Everything went smoothly the first week. It seemed my studying—I had read *La Varenne Pratique* cover to cover and was working my way through *Larousse Gastronomique*—had paid off, until one of the cooks asked me to go and get a bag of "flageolets" from the storeroom. All of the blood rushed to my face. Too embarrassed to admit I didn't know what he was talking about, I scurried away, hoping for divine intervention. In my panic, I spotted a French cookbook and quickly read that flageolets were dried kidney-shaped French beans. I found the beans in the pantry, wiped the sweat from my brow, and rushed back to my station. Saved—until the next time!

Heat a medium pot over high heat for 2 minutes. Pour in ¼ cup olive oil, and add the rosemary sprig and crumbled chile. Let them sizzle in the oil a minute. Add the diced onion, fennel, garlic, 1 tablespoon thyme, and the bay leaf, stirring a minute or two, until the onion is wilted. Add the flageolets, and cook a few more minutes, stirring to coat the beans with the oil.

7 tablespoons extra-virgin olive oil

1 small sprig rosemary

1 chile de árbol, crumbled

½ cup diced onion, plus 5 cups thinly sliced onions

½ cup diced fennel

3 cloves garlic, smashed

2 tablespoons thyme leaves

1 bay leaf

1½ cups dried flageolets (see Sources)

5 tablespoons unsalted butter

2 cups fresh breadcrumbs

2 teaspoons chopped flat-leaf parsley

Kosher salt and freshly ground black pepper

Cover with water by 3 inches, and bring to a boil over high heat. Turn the heat down to low, and place a paper towel over the beans to keep them under the surface.

Simmer for 30 minutes, and then add 2½ teaspoons salt to the beans. Continue cooking on a low simmer about 1 hour, until the beans are tender. As the beans cook, add water as necessary (but don't add too much—you want these juices to be rich and a little starchy, since they will be an important part of the finished gratin). Remove the beans from the heat, and let them cool in their juices. Taste for seasoning.

While the beans cook, caramelize the sliced onions. Heat a large sauté pan or Dutch oven over high heat for a minute. Swirl in the remaining 3 tablespoons olive oil, and add the sliced onions, 2 teaspoons thyme, 1 teaspoon salt, and some freshly ground black pepper. Cook 6 minutes, stirring often. Turn the heat down to medium, and stir in 1 tablespoon butter. Cook 15 minutes, stirring often and scraping with a wooden spoon, until the onions start to caramelize. Turn the heat down to low, and continue to cook about 10 minutes, stirring often, until the onions are a deep golden brown. Spread the onions on the bottom of a 9-by-9-inch (or equivalent) gratin dish. Spoon the flageolets into the gratin dish with a good amount of their cooking juices. The beans will expand a little as they bake, so fill the gratin dish only three-quarters full (reserve any extra beans for use in another dish).

Preheat the oven to 425°F.

Toss the breadcrumbs in a medium bowl with the remaining teaspoon thyme and the chopped parsley. Melt the remaining 4 tablespoons butter in a small saucepan over medium heat. Cook about 3 minutes, swirling the pan occasionally, until the butter browns and smells nutty. Pour the brown butter over the breadcrumbs (make sure to scrape up all the brown bits), let cool a minute or two, and toss to combine.

Sprinkle the brown butter breadcrumbs over the beans, and bake 1½ hours, until the gratin is bubbling, nicely browned, and crispy on top.

gâteau basque with armagnac prunes

The first time I had gâteau basque, I was living in the southwest of France and trying, in my little spare time, to sample as many of the local treats as possible. Gâteau basque, a very moist, buttery cake with a certain *je ne sais quoi,* was by far my favorite.

Despite its name, it's not really a *gâteau,* or cake, but rather two layers of buttery, crumbly crust filled with pastry cream. As it bakes, the crust and filling meld into one delicious whole. This rural dessert has many interpretations, with fillings that vary from almonds to raisins to fruit jams.

For this version our first pastry chef, Sara Lauren, came up with a pastry cream spiked with an unusual combination of Armagnac, rum, orange-flower water, and almond extract. The cake doesn't taste like any one of those flavorings, but together they somehow evoke that unforgettable flavor of the Basque country.

NOTE The pastry dough must be made at least 2 hours before assembling the *gâteau.* It's a good idea to make the pastry cream in advance as well, as it must be chilled before using.

2 cups all-purpose flour

¼ almond meal

2 teaspoons baking powder

1 teaspoon kosher salt

1 cup granulated sugar

8 ounces (2 sticks) unsalted butter, softened, plus more for the pan

1 extra-large egg

3 extra-large egg yolks

1 tablespoon finely grated lemon zest

2 tablespoons Pernod

Basque pastry cream, cooled (recipe follows)

1 cup heavy cream

¼ cup crème fraîche

Armagnac prunes (recipe follows)

Combine the dry ingredients in the bowl of a stand mixer fitted with the paddle attachment. With the mixer running at low, add the butter. When the butter has been incorporated, add the egg, 2 egg yolks, the lemon zest, and the Pernod. Mix at low speed until the dough just comes together. Divide the dough into two-thirds and one-third portions. Wrap each portion in plastic and refrigerate at least 2 hours.

Lightly butter a 9-inch ring mold (1 inch high) and set it on a baking sheet.

Roll out the larger piece of dough on a lightly floured board into an 11-inch circle, ⅓ inch thick. (The dough may be a little hard to work with. Don't worry if you have to patch it together—when it bakes, the mistakes will disappear.) Roll the dough around the rolling pin, and then unroll over the ring and gently tuck the dough into the corners, letting the excess fall over the edges. Fill the shell with the cooled Basque pastry cream. Roll out the remaining piece of dough into a circle slightly larger than the pan. Place the dough over the pastry cream. Roll the rolling pin over the top of the ring to seal the bottom and top layers of dough together. Chill for 30 minutes.

Preheat the oven to 425°F.

Whisk the remaining egg yolk with a little water, and brush the *gâteau* with this egg wash. Score the top of the cake with a paring knife in a crisscross or harlequin pattern.

Bake about 35 minutes, until golden brown.

Whip the cream and crème fraîche until it holds soft peaks.

Cut six wedges from the *gâteau*. Spoon some Armagnac prunes and their syrup over each piece, and finish with a dollop of whipped cream.

basque pastry cream

1½ cups whole milk
3 extra-large egg yolks
6 tablespoons granulated sugar
2 tablespoons cornstarch, sifted
¾ teaspoon kosher salt
2 teaspoons dark rum
2 teaspoons Armagnac
1 teaspoon orange-flower water
1 teaspoon pure almond extract

In a medium heavy-bottomed pot, bring the milk to a boil, and then turn off the heat. Whisk the egg yolks together in a medium bowl, and then whisk in the sugar, cornstarch, and salt. Continue whisking until the mixture thickens and is a pale yellow color. Whisk in the hot milk a few tablespoons at a time, progressing to a slow steady stream. Return the mixture to the stove, and cook over medium heat, whisking until thickened.

Strain into a baking dish or bowl, and place a piece of plastic wrap on the surface of the custard to keep it from forming a skin. Poke a few holes in the plastic to let the heat escape. Cool it in the refrigerator. When the pastry cream has cooled, stir in the rum, Armagnac, orange-flower water, and almond extract.

armagnac prunes

½ pound pitted prunes
1½ cups hot black tea
½ cup granulated sugar
¼ cup Armagnac

Place the prunes in a bowl and pour the hot tea over them. Cover and steep 1 hour. Strain the prunes, reserving ¼ cup tea. Place the tea and sugar in a small sauce pot, bring to a boil, and cook 2 minutes. Pour the syrup over the prunes. Add the Armagnac to the pot, bring it just to a boil, and pour it over the prunes. Cover and steep at least 30 minutes. Cool the prunes and store them in the refrigerator.

blood oranges, dates, parmesan, and almonds

Every winter, when the first blood oranges appear at the market, I'm as impressed as I was the first time I saw one, while visiting Rome my junior year abroad. One morning, at the local café where I had my daily cappuccino and pretended to read the paper, I heard a loud racket coming from behind me. When I turned and looked, I got my first glimpse of that blood-red juice spewing from the juicers lined up on the bar. I had to order a glass. When I got the bill, I was shocked by the steep price. But even back then, I knew it was something very special and worth every lira.

This salad is my homage to those blood oranges that won my heart so many years ago. Layered with sweet dates, Parmesan, almonds, and a few leaves of peppery arugula, the blood-orange slices burst with sweet, tart juice. Because this salad has so few ingredients and nothing to "hide behind," now is truly a time to seek out the very best ingredients. Once you've gathered your perfect components, the only difficult part is arranging them on the plate. Thoughtfully weave the ingredients together, layering them into "hills and valleys," rather than piling them up into a "mountain." Think of this as a tapestry, rather than a tossed salad.

½ cup raw almonds

15 Deglet Noor dates

4 large blood oranges

¼-pound hunk Parmigiano-Reggiano

2 ounces arugula

3 tablespoons pure almond oil

Fleur de sel and freshly ground black pepper

NOTE Use an artisanal unfiltered almond oil, such as Huilerie Leblanc (see Sources). The best nut oils are stone-ground and pressed into a pale brown full-flavored oil. If it's clear and looks like vegetable oil, it won't have the intense, toasted nut flavor we're looking for. If you can't find a good pressed nut oil, drizzle with your favorite extra-virgin olive oil instead. If blood oranges are out of season, you can use another delicious orange. The dish won't be as visually stunning, but it will still taste good.

Preheat the oven to 375°F.

Spread the almonds on a baking sheet, and toast 8 to 10 minutes, until they're slightly darkened and smell nutty.

Cut the dates in half lengthwise and remove the pits.

Slice the stem and blossom ends from the blood oranges. Stand the blood oranges on one end and, following the contour of the fruit with your knife, remove the peel and white cottony pith. Work from top to bottom, rotating the fruit as you go.

Slice each orange thinly, into 8 to 10 pinwheels.

Place the Parmigiano-Reggiano, flat side down, on a cutting board. Using a chef's knife, shave eighteen large thin slices of cheese from the hunk.

Scatter one-third of the arugula on a large platter. Arrange one-third of the oranges, dates, cheese, and nuts. Scatter another layer of arugula, and continue layering in the same manner, letting the ingredients intertwine together but not pile up on one another. Drizzle the almond oil over the salad, and season lightly with *fleur de sel,* pepper, and a squeeze of blood orange juice.

grilled squab with farro, kabocha squash, cavolo nero, and pomegranate salsa

6 bay leaves

3 tablespoons coriander seeds

½ teaspoon white peppercorns

⅓ cup honey

⅓ cup sherry

1 tablespoon extra-virgin olive oil

1 tablespoon thyme leaves

6 squab, broken down into
   breasts and whole legs

Farro with Kabocha squash and
   cavolo nero (recipe follows)

Pomegranate salsa
   (recipe follows)

Kosher salt and freshly ground
   black pepper

I stole the marinade in this recipe from my husband. That strange combination of ingredients—toasted bay leaves, coriander, white pepper, honey, and sherry—lends an exotic and aromatic quality to the squab. Farro, Kabocha squash, and cavolo nero are three of my favorite things on earth, so in this dish, I just give in, sautéing them all together into a slightly labor-intensive but super-delicious "stir-fry." I could eat it for lunch (or dinner!) every day. Embellished with a jewellike pomegranate salsa, this dish is a foray into the Near East.

NOTE Ask your butcher to break down the birds into quarters: breasts with wing tip attached, and whole legs (legs and thighs attached). Or, if you know how to butcher a chicken, this is simply a miniature version of that process.
   Marinate the squab overnight.
   To save time, you can make all the elements for the farro with Kabocha squash and cavolo nero the day before. Right before you grill the squab, "stir-fry" the farro and vegetables together, and keep them warm in the oven. You can make the pomegranate salsa an hour or so before serving.

Toast the bay leaves a minute or so in a small pan over medium heat, until they release their aroma. Repeat with the coriander seeds.

Using a mortar and pestle, crush the coriander and white pepper coarsely. Crumble the bay leaves with your hands.

Transfer the spices to a medium bowl, and add the honey, sherry, olive oil, and thyme. Toss the squab breasts and legs in the marinade to coat well. Cover, and refrigerate at least 4 hours, preferably overnight.

Light the grill 30 to 40 minutes before you're ready to cook, and remove the squab from the refrigerator to allow it to come to room temperature. Take the squab out of the marinade, and pat the legs and breasts lightly with paper towels.

When the coals are broken down, red, and glowing, season the squab on both sides with salt and pepper. Place the legs, skin side down, on the grill. (They will take a little longer than the breasts to cook.) After a few minutes, place the breasts on the grill, skin side down, and cook the legs and breasts about 5 minutes more, rotating them once or twice, until the skin is crisp. (If the flames flare up, move the squab so they don't get charred. The skin should render and crisp up, but not be blackened or burned.) Turn the squab over and move them to a cooler part of the grill. Cook about 3 more minutes, until the legs are just cooked through and the breasts are medium-rare.

Arrange the farro with Kabocha squash and cavolo nero on a large warm platter. Place the squab on top, and spoon over the pomegranate salsa.

farro with kabocha squash and cavolo nero

Preheat the oven to 425°F.

Bring a large pot of heavily salted water to a boil over high heat.

Toss the squash with 2 tablespoons olive oil, 1 teaspoon thyme, ¾ teaspoon salt, and a healthy pinch of pepper. Spread the squash out on a baking sheet, and roast about 15 to 20 minutes, tossing once or twice, until it's tender.

Blanch the cavolo nero in the rapidly boiling water for 2 minutes. Drain, let cool, and squeeze out the excess water with your hands.

Heat a large pot or Dutch oven over medium heat for 2 minutes. Pour in ¼ cup olive oil, and add the rosemary sprig and one of the crumbled chiles. Let them sizzle in the oil about a minute. Turn the heat down to medium-low, and add the sliced onion. Season with ½ teaspoon salt and a pinch of freshly ground black pepper. Cook 2 minutes and stir in the sliced garlic. Continue cooking another 5 to 7 minutes, stirring often with a wooden spoon, until the onion is soft and starting to color.

Add the cavolo nero and 2 more tablespoons olive oil, stirring to coat the greens in the oil and onion. Season with a heaping ¼ teaspoon salt, and cook the greens slowly over low heat for about 30 minutes, stirring often, until they turn a dark, almost black color and get slightly crispy on the edges. Turn off the heat, and set the pot aside. When the ingredients have cooled, remove the rosemary and chile.

While the cavolo nero is cooking, heat another medium saucepan over medium heat for 2 minutes. Pour in the remaining ¼ cup olive oil and add the onion wedges, carrot, celery, remaining crumbled chile, and the bay leaf. Cook the vegetables about 5 minutes, until they're golden brown and softened.

Add the farro, 1 tablespoon thyme, and 2 teaspoons salt to the pan, stirring with a wooden spoon to coat the farro with the oil. Add the sherry and 6 cups water. Bring to a boil over high heat. Turn down the heat to low, and simmer the farro about 30 minutes, until it's tender. Drain the farro, and spread it out on a baking sheet to cool. Discard the vegetables.

2½ cups ½-inch-diced Kabocha squash

¾ cup extra-virgin olive oil

1 tablespoon plus 2 teaspoons thyme leaves

1 pound cavolo nero, cleaned, center ribs removed

½ sprig rosemary

2 chiles de árbol, crumbled

1 cup sliced onion; plus ½ onion, cut into 3 wedges, root end attached

2 cloves garlic, thinly sliced

1 small carrot, peeled, cut into 3 pieces

1 stalk celery, cut into 3 pieces

1 bay leaf

1¼ cups farro (spelt)

¼ cup sherry

2 tablespoons unsalted butter

¾ cup ¼-inch-sliced shallots

Kosher salt and freshly ground black pepper

Heat a large sauté pan over high heat for 2 minutes. Swirl in the butter, and when it foams, add the shallots, remaining teaspoon thyme, and ¼ teaspoon salt. Stir continuously with a wooden spoon as the shallots soften and brown in the butter, 3 to 4 minutes. Add the farro, and sauté, stirring continuously, for another 3 to 4 minutes, until it's slightly crispy. Add the squash and greens, and stir well to combine. Taste for seasoning. Serve immediately, or keep warm in the oven.

pomegranate salsa

3 tablespoons finely diced shallots

1 teaspoon lemon juice

1 tablespoon pomegranate molasses

¼ cup extra-virgin olive oil

½ cup pomegranate seeds

1 tablespoon sliced flat-leaf parsley

Kosher salt and freshly ground black pepper

This time of year, with pomegranates in season, I find myself spooning this salsa over all sorts of things, from duck to turkey and even grilled fish.

Place the shallots, lemon juice, and ¼ teaspoon salt in a small bowl, and let sit 5 minutes.

Whisk in the pomegranate molasses and then the olive oil. Stir in the pomegranate seeds and the parsley. Taste for balance and seasoning.

portuguese-style pork and clams with chorizo and fried potatoes

My first real chef position was at Alloro, a small Italian restaurant in Boston's North End. In this all-Italian neighborhood, the owner was not Italian, but rather a Portuguese guy named Armando. Some cultures care more about food than others, and, like the Italians, the Portuguese are definitely devoted to their cuisine. Armando loved to tell me about the Old Country and the dishes his mother made for him when he was growing up.

This dish is traditionally made with pork loin, but when I tried it, the loin was dry and didn't seem to marry well with the flavors of the clams. So I decided to try it with pork confit, which would get crispy on the outside but stay meltingly tender on the inside. To give more pork flavor to the broth, I added chorizo and came up with my own version of pork (and pork!) and clams. In honor of Armando, I always make my pork and clams with fried potatoes. If he had his way, *everything* would come with fried potatoes.

NOTE This is one of the more involved recipes in this book, but if you plan ahead and prep well, it's actually simple the evening of the dinner. Confit the pork a day or two in advance (remember, it will need to sit in the brine for 2 days before that!). Roast the tomatoes and potatoes in the morning, and then, closer to dinnertime, fry the potatoes and set them aside. The sautéing of the pork and steaming of the clams should be done at the last minute.

2 tablespoons pork fat (from the confit)

1¼ pounds pork confit (see pages 213–214), cut into 1-inch cubes

Fried potatoes (recipe follows)

2 tablespoons extra-virgin olive oil

¾ pound fresh Mexican chorizo, casings removed

½ cup sliced shallots

1 tablespoon thyme leaves

3 pounds Manila clams, well scrubbed

Roasted tomatoes (recipe follows)

1½ cups vermouth

1 cup chicken stock

4 tablespoons unsalted butter, cut into pieces

2 tablespoons minced garlic

¼ cup chopped flat-leaf parsley

Kosher salt and freshly ground black pepper

Preheat the oven to 200°F.

Heat a large sauté pan over high heat for 2 minutes. Swirl in the pork fat and wait 1 minute. Taste a piece of the pork confit to see if it needs more seasoning. Season with salt and pepper, if necessary. Place the pork confit in the pan, being careful not to crowd it. (You may need to do this in two pans or two batches.) Sear the pork 4 to 5 minutes on the first side. When the first side is nicely caramelized, turn the pork cubes over, and brown them on all sides. Stir in the fried potatoes, heat them through, and coat them well with the pork fat. Transfer the pan to the oven to keep it warm.

Heat a Dutch oven over high heat for 2 minutes. Swirl in the olive oil and wait 1 minute. Crumble the chorizo into the pan, and sauté about 4 minutes, until the sausage is crisped on one side but not fully cooked. Add the shallots and thyme, stirring to coat them with the chorizo oil. Add the clams and the roasted tomatoes, stirring for about 2 minutes to combine all the ingredients and coat the clams. Pour in the vermouth and cover the pan. Let the clams steam a few minutes, until they open. Remove the lid and add the stock. Discard any unopened clams. Bring to a simmer, stirring well to combine the flavors, and swirl in the butter. Taste for seasoning. Spoon the clams and chorizo into a large, warm, shallow bowl.

Meanwhile, take the pork out of the oven and return it to the stove, over medium heat. Add the garlic and stir well, so that it coats the meat and potatoes. After a minute or two, when the garlic is translucent and just starting to color, stir in the parsley. Arrange the pork and potatoes over the clams and chorizo.

Serve with a large serving spoon and lots of crusty bread. If you are feeling over the top, a bowl of aïoli would really gild the lily (see page 148).

fried potatoes

1½ pounds Yukon Gold potatoes

¼ cup extra-virgin olive oil

1 head garlic, cut in half horizontally and smashed

2 bay leaves

6 sprigs thyme, plus 2 teaspoons fresh thyme leaves

Kosher salt and freshly ground black pepper

Preheat the oven to 400°F.

Place the potatoes in a roasting pan, and toss well with 2 tablespoons olive oil, the garlic, bay leaves, thyme sprigs, and 1 heaping teaspoon salt. Cover tightly with aluminum foil, and roast the potatoes about 50 minutes, until they're tender. (The time will really depend on size, age, and variety of potatoes.) When the potatoes have cooled, peel them, discard the bay leaves and thyme, and crumble the potatoes into chunky pieces with your hands.

Heat a large sauté pan over high heat for 2 minutes. (To get the potatoes nicely browned and crisp, don't overcrowd them. You may have to use two pans or brown them in batches.) Swirl in the remaining 2 tablespoons olive oil and wait 1 more minute. Add the crumbled potatoes, and season with the thyme leaves, salt, and pepper. Sauté the potatoes until they are crispy on one side. (Don't try to move them or turn them if they are stuck to the pan; they will eventually release themselves, just be patient.) After about 8 minutes, when they've browned nicely on the first side, stir them to let them color on all sides. Serve immediately, or set aside on a baking sheet.

roasted tomatoes

6 Roma or other roasting
  tomatoes

2 tablespoons extra-virgin olive
  oil

2 teaspoons thyme leaves

Kosher salt and freshly ground
  black pepper

Preheat the oven to 400°F.

Slice the tomatoes in half lengthwise, toss them with the olive oil, thyme, 1 teaspoon salt, and a pinch of pepper. Place the tomatoes, cut side down, on a baking sheet, and roast in the oven 30 to 40 minutes, until their skins blister and shrivel. When the tomatoes have cooled, pull off their skins and crush them gently with your hands.

caramelized bread pudding with chocolate and cinnamon

This recipe is a lifer. I've been making it for more than 20 years, and every time I try to file it away, someone inevitably comes along asking for it. I brought it to my first staff get-together when I was working at Chez Panisse and, from then on, for all of the parties that followed, when I would even *think* of making something different, my friends and coworkers would cry out for this caramelized chocolate bread pudding. A few years later, the bread pudding gained an East Coast fan club, too. I was working at Alloro, a tiny restaurant in Boston's Italian district. Back then, the Mafia owned all the local cafés and had a monopoly on the dessert-and-coffee crowd. Whereas the other (probably wiser) restaurants on the street obeyed the unspoken law of not selling dessert, at Alloro we broke the rule and secretly served this bread pudding to our in-the-know customers. We worked hard to keep the highly requested dessert under cover, and it seems we succeeded: both the recipe and I are still around.

A few things make this bread pudding better than most. I love custards and am often disappointed by bread puddings with too much bread and not enough pudding. So be careful to use just a single layer of brioche, which creates a crispy crust but won't absorb all the rich, silky custard underneath. Once you break through the caramelized, toasty top layer and dig down through the luscious custard, a treasure of melted chocolate awaits you at the bottom.

2 tablespoons unsalted butter, softened

4 or 5 slices brioche, or good-quality white bread (I like Pepperidge Farm), ¼ inch thick, crusts removed

3 extra-large eggs

2 extra-large egg yolks

¼ cup brown sugar

1½ cups heavy cream

1¼ cups whole milk

1 teaspoon pure vanilla extract

½ teaspoon ground cinnamon

¼ teaspoon freshly grated nutmeg

¼ teaspoon kosher salt

¾ cup chopped bittersweet chocolate

1 tablespoon granulated sugar, for caramelizing the top

Preheat the oven to 350°F.

Spread the softened butter on one side of the brioche. Cut each slice in half on the diagonal and then again into quarters.

Whisk together the eggs, egg yolks, and brown sugar in a large bowl. Add the cream, milk, vanilla, cinnamon, nutmeg, and salt, whisking to combine well.

Sprinkle the chocolate over the bottom of a 9-by-9-inch (or equivalent) baking dish. Arrange the brioche, buttered side up, with slices overlapping just slightly, on the chocolate (there should be just a single layer of bread). Pour the custard over the bread, pressing down with your fingers to make sure the bread soaks it up. Place the bread pudding in a roasting pan, and pour warm water into the pan to come halfway up the sides of the pudding dish. Bake about 1 hour and

15 minutes, until the custard is set and the bread puffs up slightly. The pudding will be springy to the touch.

Let the bread pudding cool at least 10 minutes.

If you have a kitchen blowtorch, sprinkle the sugar over the top, and torch to brown and caramelize. You could run the pudding under the broiler to caramelize if you don't have a torch, but be careful not to curdle the custard underneath.

Serve the bread pudding from the baking dish at the table, using a big spoon.

wild mushroom tart with gruyère, young onions, and herb salad

Give me almost any combination of toppings, and I'll turn them into a delicious savory tart. The formula is always the same: the crispy, buttery puff pastry crust; a creamy base of ricotta and crème fraîche; a layer of oozing, usually pungent cheese; and then, of course, the topping. In this case, I sauté an array of winter wild mushrooms until they're tender, chewy, and still a little crisp. Since they seem to make everything taste better, I can't resist tossing in a few handfuls of sweet young onions with their spicy green tops. As they all bake together, their flavors unite into this decadent and sophisticated "pizza."

NOTE Assemble the tart in the morning, cover, and refrigerate. Bake just before you're ready to serve.

Preheat the oven to 400°F.

Defrost the puff pastry slightly and unroll it onto a parchment-lined baking sheet. Use a paring knife to score a ¼-inch border around the edge of the pastry. Make an egg wash by whisking 1 egg yolk with ¼ teaspoon water, and brush the egg wash along the border. (You will not need all of the egg wash.) Return the puff pastry to the freezer until you're ready to use it.

If the mushrooms are big, tear them into large bite-sized pieces. (Not too small, as they will shrink when they're cooked.)

Heat a large sauté pan over high heat for 2 minutes. Swirl in 2 tablespoons olive oil and wait 1 minute. Add 1 tablespoon butter, and when it foams, scatter half the mushrooms into the pan. Season with ½ teaspoon salt and a healthy pinch of pepper. Sauté the mushrooms about 5 minutes, stirring occasionally, until they are tender and a little crispy. (The cooking time will depend on the particular mushrooms you use.) Transfer the cooked mushrooms to a baking sheet, and repeat with the second half of the mushrooms.

When the second batch of mushrooms are just cooked, reduce the heat to low and toss in the spring onions, thyme, and ½ teaspoon salt. Stir gently 1 to 2

1 sheet frozen all-butter puff pastry

2 extra-large egg yolks

1¼ pounds wild mushrooms, cleaned

5 tablespoons extra-virgin olive oil

2 tablespoons unsalted butter

1½ cups sliced young onions, plus ¼ cup diagonally sliced young onion tops

1 teaspoon thyme leaves

½ cup whole milk ricotta, drained if wet

¼ cup crème fraîche

¼ pound Gruyère, thinly sliced

½ cup flat-leaf parsley leaves

¼ cup tarragon leaves

¼ cup chervil sprigs

¼ cup ½-inch-snipped chives

A drizzle of super-good extra-virgin olive oil

½ lemon, for juicing

Kosher salt and freshly ground black pepper

minutes, until the onions are just wilted. Stir in the onion tops. Transfer to the baking sheet, and stir to combine with the first batch of mushrooms.

Place the ricotta, remaining egg yolk, and remaining tablespoon olive oil in the bowl of a food processor. Purée until smooth, and remove to a mixing bowl. Gently fold in the crème fraîche, and season with a healthy pinch of salt and a few grindings of black pepper.

Spread the ricotta mixture on the puff pastry within the scored border. Place the Gruyère over the ricotta. Arrange the mushrooms and spring onions on top. If you aren't ready to bake it yet, cover the tart with plastic and chill.

Bake the tart 20 to 25 minutes, rotating the baking sheet after 10 minutes, until the cheese is bubbling and the crust is golden brown. Lift the crust to peek underneath the tart to make sure the crust is really cooked through. (If you underbake the tart, it will be soggy.)

Toss the herbs in a small bowl with salt, pepper, a drizzle of super-good olive oil, and a squeeze of lemon juice.

Let the tart cool a few minutes, and serve it on a cutting board at the table. Serve the herb salad on the side in a small bowl or scatter it over the tart.

winter squash risotto with radicchio and parmesan

People think risotto is a super-rich dish, made with tons of butter. But when it is made properly, the richness comes from the starchy rice and the stock. To make perfect risotto, really pay attention to what's happening in the pan. As the risotto cooks, stir it with a wooden spoon in rhythmic movements that go across the bottom and around the sides of the pan. The rice should be constantly bubbling, drinking up the liquid as it cooks.

Preheat the oven to 425°F.

Toss the squash with 2 tablespoons olive oil, 1 teaspoon thyme, ¾ teaspoon salt, and a healthy pinch of pepper. Roast the squash on a baking sheet 15 to 20 minutes, stirring occasionally, until it's tender when pierced.

Bring the chicken stock plus 4 cups water to a boil, and turn off the heat.

Heat a medium-sized heavy-bottomed pot over medium-high heat for 2 minutes. Add the 3 tablespoons butter, and when it foams, add the onion, remaining 2 teaspoons thyme, chile, ½ teaspoon salt, and a pinch of pepper. Sauté 5 to 7 minutes, stirring often, until the onion is translucent.

Stir in half the roasted squash, the rice, and 1½ teaspoons salt. Cook about 2 minutes, stirring continuously, until the rice just begins to toast and the grains of the rice have a white dot at their center. Pour in the white wine, and once it has evaporated, quickly add 1 cup of the hot stock and stir continuously. When the stock is completely absorbed, begin adding the liquid in 1-cup batches, stirring all the time with a wooden spoon in a rhythmic back-and-forth motion. Wait for each batch of liquid to be absorbed before adding the next. The rice should be bubbling and absorbing the stock quickly. After about 15 minutes, taste the rice. It should be slightly al dente. The risotto may need more liquid and more time, so keep cooking until it's done. It should be neither soupy nor dry; each grain of rice should be coated in a flavorful, starchy "sauce."

When the rice is almost done, turn off the heat and stir in the remaining squash. Let the risotto "rest" for a minute or two and then quickly stir in the radicchio, half the Parmigiano-Reggiano, and ½ teaspoon salt. Taste for seasoning. The rice will keep absorbing liquid, so add a little more stock if it seems dry. Stir in the remaining 2 tablespoons butter and the parsley. Spoon the risotto into a large shallow bowl and sprinkle the rest of the cheese on top.

2 cups ½-inch-diced Kabocha squash

2 tablespoons extra-virgin olive oil

1 tablespoon thyme leaves

4 cups chicken stock

5 tablespoons unsalted butter

1 cup diced white onion

1 chile de árbol, crumbled

2 cups high-quality Arborio rice (see Sources)

¼ cup dry white wine

1 cup thinly sliced radicchio

½ cup grated Parmigiano-Reggiano

¼ cup sliced flat-leaf parsley

Kosher salt and freshly ground black pepper

duck braised in banyuls and
turnip-parsnip gratin with prunes

6 large duck legs, 8 to 10 ounces
    each

1 tablespoon thyme leaves, plus
    6 whole sprigs thyme

Zest of 1 orange

1 tablespoon freshly cracked
    black pepper

2 tablespoons extra-virgin olive
    oil

1½ cups diced onion

½ cup diced fennel

½ cup diced carrot

1 bay leaf, preferably fresh

2 tablespoons balsamic vinegar

2 cups Banyuls

3 to 4 cups chicken stock

¼ cup flat-leaf parsley leaves

Turnip-parsnip gratin with
    prunes (recipe follows)

Kosher salt and freshly ground
    black pepper

One particularly chilly weekend (yes, we have those here every once in a while), I needed a dish that would be opulent and soul-satisfying. At first, duck braised in red wine came to mind. But, I wanted something even more intense and a little bit sweet, and I arrived at Banyuls, a fortified wine from the south of France. Extracted from grenache grapes grown on the rocky, terraced vineyards that overlook the sea, Banyuls is classically paired with chocolate and has deep notes of chestnut, mocha, and dried fruit.

As the duck and Banyuls cooked together slowly in the oven, the deeply concentrated wine permeated the meat and produced a rich ruby broth. A gratin of turnips and potatoes dotted with prunes and baked with cream proved the perfect companion for the tender, falling-apart duck bathed in crimson juices.

NOTE You can braise the duck a day ahead, just remember it has to marinate at least 4 hours first. Make the gratin in the morning, then reheat and gratinée just before serving.

Trim the excess fat from the duck legs. Season them with the thyme leaves, orange zest, and cracked black pepper. Cover, and refrigerate overnight.

Preheat the oven to 325°F.

Take the duck out of the refrigerator 45 minutes before cooking. After 15 minutes, season the legs on all sides with 1 tablespoon plus 1 teaspoon salt.

Heat a large sauté pan over high heat for 2 minutes. Swirl in the olive oil and wait 1 minute. Place the duck legs in the pan, skin side down, and cook 8 to 10 minutes, until the skin is deep golden brown and crispy. (If your pan is too small to fit all of the legs, brown them in batches or in two pans, so you don't crowd them.) Turn the duck legs over, reduce the heat to medium, and cook 2 minutes on the other side. Move the duck, skin side up, to a braising pan. (The duck legs should just fit in the pan.)

Discard half the fat, and return the pan to the stove over medium heat. Add the onion, fennel, carrot, thyme sprigs, bay leaf, and a pinch of pepper. Cook about 10 minutes, stirring often with a wooden spoon to scrape up all the crusty bits.

When the vegetables are nicely browned and caramelized, add the balsamic vinegar and Banyuls. Turn the heat up to high, bring the liquid to a boil, and cook 6 to 8 minutes, until it has reduced by half. Add 3 cups stock and bring to a boil. Turn the heat down to low and simmer 5 minutes.

Pour the broth and vegetables over the duck, then scrape the vegetables that have fallen on top of the duck back into the broth. The liquid should not quite cover the duck (add more stock if necessary). Cover the pan very tightly with plastic wrap (yes, it can go in the oven) and then aluminum foil. Braise in the oven about 2½ hours, until the duck is very tender.

To check the duck for doneness, carefully remove the plastic and foil, and pierce a piece of the duck with a paring knife. If the meat is done, it will yield easily and be tender but not quite falling off the bone.

Turn the oven up to 400°F.

Carefully transfer the duck to a baking sheet and return it to the oven to brown for 10 to 15 minutes.

Strain the broth into a saucepan, pressing down on the vegetables with a ladle to extract all the juices. Skim the top layer of fat from the sauce. If necessary, reduce the broth over medium-high heat about 5 minutes, to thicken it slightly. Taste the juices for seasoning.

Transfer the duck legs to a serving platter. Spoon the juices over the duck, and scatter the parsley leaves over the top. Serve with the turnip-parsnip gratin with prunes.

turnip-parsnip gratin with prunes

NOTE For a nice-looking gratin, look for parsnips and turnips that are about the same size.

Preheat the oven to 350°F.

Use a mandoline to slice the turnips and parsnips into ¹⁄₁₆-inch-thick rounds, and put them into two separate bowls.

Pour ½ cup cream onto the bottom of a 9-by-9-inch (or equivalent) gratin dish. Place one layer of turnips on the bottom of the dish. (The turnips should overlap by about half.) Season with ¼ teaspoon salt and a pinch of pepper. Scatter a third of the prunes on top. Arrange a layer of parsnips over the turnips and prunes. Press the parsnips down with your fingers, letting the cream soak up through the layers. This will ensure that the cream is evenly distributed and coats

1½ pounds turnips, peeled

1½ pounds parsnips, peeled

About 2 cups heavy cream

1 tablespoon thyme leaves

⅓ pound pitted prunes, quartered

Kosher salt and freshly ground black pepper

the vegetables well. Drizzle with ½ cup cream and season with ¼ teaspoon salt, a healthy pinch of pepper, and 1 teaspoon thyme.

Arrange another layer of turnips and drizzle another ¼ cup cream over them. Season with ¼ teaspoon salt, a pinch of pepper, and 1 teaspoon thyme. Scatter a third of the prunes on top and continue with another layer of parsnips. Drizzle on ½ cup cream and season with ¼ teaspoon salt and a pinch of pepper. Press the vegetables down with your fingers, allowing the cream to come up through the layers and coat the vegetables evenly.

Finish the gratin with one more layer, this time of both parsnip and turnip slices, arranging this layer nicely, since it will be the top of your gratin. Scatter the remaining prunes over the top. Drizzle with ¼ to ½ cup cream and season with ¼ teaspoon salt, freshly ground black pepper, and the remaining teaspoon thyme. Press the gratin down with your fingers again. The cream should cover the potatoes but not be too soupy. Add more cream if the gratin seems dry.

Cover tightly with plastic wrap (yes, it can go in the oven) and then foil. Bake about 1½ hours, until the vegetables are tender when pierced. Remove from the oven and carefully uncover. Turn the oven to 425°F and return the gratin to the oven. Cook another 15 to 20 minutes, until the top is nice and golden brown, as in "gratinéed."

roasted apples with calvados and cinnamon ice cream

During my college years, I'd return home to Los Angeles every summer and promptly—you guessed it—look for a restaurant job. One summer, I did a *stage* at L.A.'s premier French restaurant, L'Orangerie. I started my *stage* in the pastry kitchen with Chef Yves. He taught me the classic techniques of crème brûlée, chocolate puff pastry, and soufflés made to order. But my favorite of his desserts was sautéed apples with caramel sauce and crème anglaise. A little less formal and traditional than the rest of his repertoire, that dish was simple, straightforward, and all about the apples.

To make our own version of Chef Yves's apples at Lucques, we cut the apples in half, toss them with lots of butter, cinnamon, brown sugar, and Calvados, and roast them, basting all the time, until they are a deep golden brown and glistening with spicy juices. With a scoop of cinnamon ice cream melting over the apples, this easy-to-make dessert is an elegant way to finish a winter feast.

> NOTE I like to leave some of the cores and stems intact—the apples are a little harder to eat, but so beautiful that way.

1 vanilla bean

8 tablespoons (1 stick) unsalted butter

6 small baking apples, such as Pink Lady or Macintosh

2 tablespoons granulated sugar

2 tablespoons brown sugar

½ teaspoon ground cinnamon

¼ teaspoon freshly grated nutmeg

2 tablespoons Calvados

¼ teaspoon kosher salt

Cinnamon ice cream (recipe follows)

Preheat the oven to 425°F.

Slice the vanilla bean lengthwise down the center, and use a paring knife to scrape the seeds and pulp into the butter. To make sure not to lose any of the seeds, run your vanilla-coated knife through the butter. Add the vanilla pod to the pan, and cook the butter and vanilla over medium heat 6 to 8 minutes, shaking the pan occasionally, until the butter browns and smells nutty. Remove from the heat, and discard the vanilla pod.

Cut the apples in half through the core, and carefully remove the core and seeds with a paring knife (or, for a more dramatic presentation, leave the core and stems intact). Toss the apples in a large bowl with the sugars, brown butter, cinnamon, nutmeg, Calvados, and salt. Arrange the apples, cut side up, in a roasting pan. Top each half with the remaining sugar mixture from the mixing bowl.

Bake the apples about 40 minutes, basting them with the pan juices every 10 minutes, until the flesh has pulled away from the skin and the apples are tender and carmelized.

Arrange the warm apples on a large platter, and pour all the remaining juices over them. Serve with cinnamon ice cream and glasses of Calvados.

cinnamon ice cream

MAKES I QUART

Place the milk, cream, cinnamon sticks, and ground cinnamon in a medium pot. Bring to a boil over medium heat. Turn off the heat, cover, and let the flavors infuse about 30 minutes.

Bring the mixture back to a boil over medium heat, stirring occasionally. Turn off the heat.

Whisk the egg yolks and sugar together in a bowl. Whisk a few tablespoons of the warm cream mixture into the yolks to temper them. Slowly, add another ¼ cup or so of the warm cream, whisking to incorporate. At this point, you can add the rest of the cream mixture in a slow steady stream, whisking constantly. Pour the mixture back into the pot and return to the stove.

Cook the custard over medium heat 6 to 8 minutes, stirring with a rubber spatula, scraping the bottom and sides of the pan. The custard will thicken, and when it's done will coat the back of the spatula. Strain it and chill at least 2 hours in the refrigerator. The base should be very cold before you churn it. Process in an ice cream maker according to the manufacturer's instructions.

2 cups whole milk

2 cups heavy cream

2 cinnamon sticks

½ teaspoon ground cinnamon

4 extra-large egg yolks

½ cup granulated sugar

schaner farm's avocado and citrus salad with green olives

4 pounds mixed citrus fruit
(about ½ cup citrus
segments per person)

2 tablespoons finely diced
shallot

1 teaspoon red wine vinegar

1 tablespoon lemon juice

¼ cup extra-virgin olive oil

2 ripe but not too soft avocados

½ cup pitted Lucques, Picholine,
or other green olives

1 bunch watercress, cleaned,
tough stems removed

1 bunch frisée (about 2 ounces),
cleaned

Kosher salt and freshly ground
black pepper

This dish offers an opportunity to showcase the great variety of citrus that farmer Peter Schaner grows for us this time of year: pomelos, Oro Blancos, grapefruits, mandelos, tangelos, clementines, and blood oranges.

When making the vinaigrette, choose the juice from the oranges and tangerines rather than that of the grapefruits (too bitter) or blood oranges (too dark in color). You'll have more juice than you need for the vinaigrette, so you can pour the leftovers into a chilled glass and sip it as you finish making dinner. (Vodka is optional.) As for the avocados, look for Reed, Hass, Fuerte, Pinkerton, or Bacon varieties. The olives may seem like an odd addition to this dish, but their brininess contrasts wonderfully with the fresh, juicy citrus and the buttery avocado.

Zest some of the citrus to get 1 teaspoon fine zest. Using a sharp knife, cut the stem and blossom ends from the fruit. One by one, place each of the fruits, cut side down, on a cutting board. Following the contour of the fruit with your knife, remove the peel and cottony white pith, working from top to bottom, and rotating the fruit as you go. When the fruits are all peeled, hold them in your hand one by one, and carefully slice between the membranes and the fruit to release the segments in between. Discard all the seeds. If you're using blood oranges, don't cut them into segments; after removing the peel and pith, slice them into pinwheels and set aside in a separate bowl. (Otherwise, they will "bleed" on the other fruit.) You should have about 2½ cups of segments in addition to your blood-orange slices.

Combine the shallot, ¼ cup citrus juice (from segmenting the fruit), the vinegar, lemon juice, and ½ teaspoon salt in a small bowl. Let sit 5 minutes, then whisk in the olive oil and the zest. Taste for balance and seasoning.

Cut the avocados in half lengthwise. Remove the pits and peel. Cut the avocados into ¼-inch slices and place on a plate. Season with ½ teaspoon salt and freshly ground pepper.

Place the citrus and olives in a large bowl, and spoon three quarters of the

the vinaigrette over them. Sprinkle with ¼ teaspoon salt. Gently toss in the water-cress and frisée. Taste for balance and seasoning. Add more vinaigrette if you like.

Plate half the salad on a large chilled platter. Nestle half the avocado slices in the salad, being careful not to flatten the greens. Arrange the rest of the salad on top, and tuck the remaining avocado slices into the salad, so you have a tapestry of colors. Place the blood-orange slices among the greens.

Peter Schaner with those famous Reed avocados

sautéed halibut with arugula, roasted beets, and horseradish crème fraîche

6 halibut fillets, 5 to 6 ounces each

1 lemon, zested

1 tablespoon thyme leaves

2 tablespoons coarsely chopped flat-leaf parsley

2 tablespoons extra-virgin olive oil

4 ounces arugula, cleaned

Roasted beets with horseradish crème fraîche (recipe follows)

2 tablespoons super-good extra-virgin olive oil, for drizzling

Kosher salt and freshly ground black pepper

The colored beets and bright green arugula in this dish make for a visually stunning presentation. The sweet roasted beets marinated in lemon vinaigrette play off the pure white fish and horseradish cream. Look for a few different types of beets, such as golden beets and Chioggia beets, and dress them separately, so the dark ones don't bleed their juices onto the lighter ones. In the spring, you could make this dish with wild salmon. And to make a more hearty meal, serve some beluga lentils on the side (see page 331).

NOTE Season the fish with lemon zest and herbs, roast the beets, and make the vinaigrette and horseradish cream in advance. When it's time for dinner, all you'll have to do is sauté the fish and dress the beets.

Season the fish with the lemon zest, thyme, and parsley. Cover, and refrigerate at least 4 hours or overnight.

Remove the fish from the refrigerator 15 minutes before cooking, to bring it to room temperature.

Heat a large sauté pan over high heat for 2 minutes. (Depending on the size of your pan, you may need to cook the fish in batches or in two pans.) Season the fish on both sides with salt and pepper. Swirl the regular extra-virgin olive oil into the pan and wait 1 minute. Carefully lay the fish in the pan, and cook 3 to 4 minutes, until it's lightly browned. Turn the fish over, lower the heat to medium-low, and cook a few more minutes, until it's almost cooked through. Be careful not to overcook the fish. When it's done, the fish will begin to flake and separate a little, and the center will still be slightly translucent. Remember, the halibut will continue to cook for a bit once you take it out of the pan.

Scatter half of the arugula over a large platter. Arrange the beets on top, and drizzle with half the horseradish cream. Tuck the rest of the arugula among the beets, so you can see the beets peeking through. Nestle the fish in the salad, and spoon a little horseradish cream over each piece. Drizzle the whole dish with the super-good olive oil and a big squeeze of lemon.

roasted beets with horseradish crème fraîche

Preheat the oven to 400°F.

Cut off the beet greens, leaving ½ inch of the stems still attached. (You can save the leaves for sautéing later—they are delicious!) Clean the beets well, and toss them with 2 tablespoons olive oil and 1 teaspoon salt.

Place the beets in a roasting pan with a splash of water in the bottom. Cover the pan tightly with foil, and roast for about 40 minutes, until they're tender when pierced. (The roasting time will depend on the size and type of beet.) When the beets are done, carefully remove the foil. Let cool, and peel the beets by slipping off the skins with your fingers. Cut them into ½-inch-thick wedges.

While the beets are in the oven, combine the diced shallot, both vinegars, 2 teaspoons lemon juice, and ¼ teaspoon salt in a small bowl, and let sit 5 minutes. Whisk in the ½ cup olive oil. Taste for balance and seasoning.

Whisk the crème fraîche and horseradish together in a small bowl. Stir in the heavy cream, remaining ½ teaspoon lemon juice, ⅛ teaspoon salt, and a pinch of pepper.

Toss the beets and sliced shallots with the vinaigrette. (If you're using different-colored beets, dress each color in a separate bowl so the colors don't bleed.) Season with ¼ teaspoon salt and a pinch of freshly ground black pepper, and toss well. Taste for balance and seasoning.

4 bunches different-colored beets

½ cup plus 2 tablespoons extra-virgin olive oil

1 tablespoon diced shallot, plus ¼ cup sliced shallots

1 tablespoon plus 1 teaspoon balsamic vinegar

2 tablespoons red wine vinegar

2½ teaspoons lemon juice

½ cup crème fraîche

1 tablespoon prepared horseradish

¼ cup heavy cream

Kosher salt and freshly ground black pepper

grilled veal chops with chestnut stuffing and pickled golden raisins

I associate chestnuts with winter scenes that while I live in Southern California exist only in my imagination: snuggling up by the fireplace while the snow falls lightly and chestnuts roast on that proverbial open fire. One Christmas Eve, after a few hot toddies and with visions of chestnuts dancing in my head, I revisited my family's traditional stuffing, determined to make my winter chestnut obsession a reality.

For me, the stuffing, not the turkey or roast beef, has always been the highlight of holiday feasts. In fact, when I was a kid, one of my big culinary promotions was when I finally got to take charge of the stuffing. For the first time, my mom gave me carte blanche with the spice cabinet. I pillaged her Spice Island jars and doctored up the Pepperidge Farm box mix, experimenting with how to make things taste better.

Now, as a chef, I've learned that seasoning is one of the keys to making all things, stuffing included, taste their best. Good stuffing starts with a great loaf of bread, torn into croutons, tossed with a generous amount of olive oil, and baked until crispy on the outside and soft in the center. Then I add lots of onion, pancetta, rosemary, fennel, chile, thyme, lemon zest—and chestnuts, of course. The biggest mistake people make at home is underseasoning their stuffing. Don't be afraid to spice it up with plenty of vegetables, herbs, and seasonings. And remember to taste as you go.

NOTE You can bake the stuffing the day before. Reheat covered with aluminum foil, and then uncover and top with little pats of butter. Return to the oven, and bake until nice and crispy on top. The pickled raisins can be made long in advance.

The notion of roasting chestnuts over an open fire is picturesque and romantic, but in reality it's a tedious and very time-consuming chore to peel them once they're roasted. Instead, I use steamed chestnuts sold in a jar, available at quality supermarkets and gourmet shops.

6 free-range veal chops, about 10 ounces each

1 tablespoon rosemary leaves

2 tablespoons thyme leaves

2 cloves garlic, smashed

2 tablespoons extra-virgin olive oil

2 tablespoons *fleur de sel*

1 scant tablespoon freshly cracked black pepper

2 ounces arugula, cleaned

Brian's pickled golden raisins (recipe follows)

Chestnut stuffing (recipe follows)

Kosher salt

Season the veal chops with the rosemary, thyme, garlic, and olive oil. Cover, and refrigerate at least 4 hours, preferably overnight.

Light the grill 30 to 40 minutes before cooking, and remove the veal chops from the refrigerator to come to room temperature.

When the coals are broken down, red, and glowing, season both sides of the veal chops generously with *fleur de sel* and cracked black pepper. Place the chops on the grill, and cook 4 to 5 minutes per side, rotating once or twice, to sear nicely. Cook until medium-rare to medium—you can peek inside at the bone to check that the meat is still a little pink.

Scatter the arugula leaves over a large platter. Place the chops on top, and spoon the golden raisins over. Pass the stuffing at the table.

brian's pickled golden raisins

2 teaspoons yellow mustard seeds

½ cup granulated sugar

3 tablespoons champagne vinegar

1 chile de árbol, crumbled

1 bay leaf

⅓ pound golden raisins

1 teaspoon thyme leaves

1-inch sprig rosemary

1 teaspoon kosher salt

Brian Wolff is the chef de cuisine and resident pickler at Lucques. Every time I turn around, he's got something in the vinegar, like shell beans, cherries, or tiny onions. His pickled raisins are delicious and make a great last-minute condiment. Keep a jar in the refrigerator; if you have a terrine or leftover roast chicken or pork, these raisins make a wonderful sweet-and-sour topping.

Place the mustard seeds in a small pan over medium heat, and toast a few minutes, shaking the pan often, until the seeds just start to pop.

Combine the mustard seeds with 1 cup water and the rest of the ingredients in a small nonaluminum pot. Bring to a boil, and turn the heat down to a low simmer. Cook 6 to 8 minutes, until the liquid has reduced by half. Let the raisins cool, and store them in the liquid in the refrigerator.

chestnut stuffing

Preheat the oven to 400°F.

Cut the crust off the bread and tear the remaining loaf into 1-inch pieces. Using your hands, toss with 6 tablespoons olive oil, squeezing the bread with your hands to help it absorb the olive oil. Toast on a baking sheet 12 to 15 minutes, tossing often, until the croutons are golden brown and crispy on the outside but still a little soft and tender inside. When the croutons have cooled, place them in a large bowl.

Meanwhile, toast the fennel seeds in a small pan over medium heat 2 to 3 minutes, shaking the pan often, until the seeds release their aroma and turn a light golden brown. Coarsely grind the seeds with a mortar and pestle or spice grinder.

Heat a large sauté pan over high heat for 2 minutes. Add the remaining 2 tablespoons olive oil and the pancetta. Sauté 1 to 2 minutes, stirring with a wooden spoon. Turn the heat down to medium, add the rosemary sprig and the chile, and let them sizzle in the pan a minute. Add the onion, fennel, fennel seeds, and thyme. Season with ¼ teaspoon salt and a few grindings of pepper. Sauté about 8 minutes, until the vegetables are lightly caramelized. Stir in the lemon zest, and add the entire mixture to the croutons.

Return the pan to high heat and pour in the white wine. Bring the wine to a boil, and reduce by three-quarters. Add the chicken stock and bring to a boil. Pour the hot liquid over the croutons and vegetables, and toss well to combine.

Wipe the pan out with paper towels, and return it to the stove over medium heat. Swirl in 2 tablespoons butter, and when it foams, add the chestnuts. Sauté 4 to 5 minutes, until the chestnuts are golden and sizzling in the butter. Season with a pinch of salt and pepper, and add to the stuffing. Stir to combine, and taste for seasoning. Add the egg and parsley. Toss well, and put the stuffing in a ceramic baking dish or casserole. Cover with foil, and bake 40 minutes. Remove the foil, and top the stuffing with the remaining 2 tablespoons butter, cut into small cubes. Return the stuffing to the oven, and cook about 20 minutes, until crispy on top.

1 pound country-style bread

½ cup extra-virgin olive oil

1 tablespoon fennel seeds

½ cup finely diced pancetta

1 small sprig rosemary

1 chile de árbol, broken in half

1 cup finely diced onion

1 cup finely diced fennel

1 tablespoon thyme leaves

2 teaspoons finely chopped lemon zest

½ cup white wine

1½ cups chicken stock

4 tablespoons unsalted butter

2 cups steamed chestnuts, crumbled with your hands

1 extra-large egg, beaten

2 tablespoons chopped flat-leaf parsley

Kosher salt and freshly ground black pepper

hazelnut–brown butter cake
with sautéed pears

5 ounces (about 1 heaping cup)
   blanched hazelnuts

½ pound unsalted butter, plus
   1 tablespoon melted butter
   for the pan

½ vanilla bean

1⅓ cups confectioners' sugar

⅓ cup all-purpose flour

5 extra-large egg whites

3 tablespoons granulated sugar

1 cup heavy cream

Sautéed pears (recipe follows)

This cake was a collaboration of sorts between my husband and my pastry chef Roxana Jullapat (don't ask!). I love this cake so much that, when it came time to think about my wedding cake, I wasn't concerned with the flowers on top or the color of the icing; all I knew was that I wanted to serve this incredible hazelnut–brown butter cake. A simple recipe of ground hazelnuts, egg whites, and sugar combined with brown butter results in a moist, rich cake with a delicate, slightly chewy crust. Little did I know, it would take 25 pounds of hazelnuts, 25 pounds of brown butter, and 150 eggs to make a cake big enough to feed our 140 friends and family.

NOTE Trufflebert Farm in Oregon grows the most amazing hazelnuts (see Sources). They're as big as macadamia nuts and have a deep, intensely fresh nutty flavor.

Preheat the oven to 350°F.

Spread the hazelnuts on a baking sheet, and toast 12 to 15 minutes, until they're golden brown and smell nutty.

Cut out a circle of parchment paper to fit in the bottom of a round 10-inch cake pan. Brush the pan with a little melted butter, and line the bottom with the paper.

Place the rest of the butter in a medium saucepan. Slice the vanilla bean lengthwise down the center, and use a paring knife to scrape the seeds and pulp onto the butter. To make sure not to lose any of the seeds, run your vanilla-coated knife through the butter. Add the vanilla pod to the pan, and cook the butter and vanilla over medium heat 6 to 8 minutes, shaking the pan occasionally, until the butter browns and smells nutty. Set aside to cool. Remove the vanilla pod and discard.

Grind the hazelnuts with the confectioners' sugar in a food processor until they're finely ground. Add the flour and pulse to combine. Transfer to a large bowl.

Place the egg whites in the bowl of a stand mixer fitted with the whisk attachment. Add the granulated sugar, and mix on high speed 4 to 5 minutes, until the mixture forms very stiff peaks. When you turn the whisk upside down, the peaks should hold. Transfer the whites to a large mixing bowl.

Alternate folding the dry ingredients and the brown butter into the egg whites, a third at a time. Remember to scrape the bottom of the brown butter pan with a rubber spatula to get all the little brown bits.

Pour the batter into the prepared cake pan, and bake 1 hour. Cool on a rack 30 minutes. Run a knife around the inside edge of the pan, and invert the cake onto a plate. Peel off the paper, and turn the cake back over onto a serving platter.

Whip the cream until it holds soft peaks.

Cut six wedges from the cake and place them on six plates. Spoon the pears and their caramel juices over the cake. Top with dollops of whipped cream.

sautéed pears

Cut the pears in half lengthwise, leaving the stem intact. Cut each half into 1-inch wedges. (Don't remove the core.)

Slice the vanilla bean lengthwise down the center, and use a paring knife to scrape the seeds and pulp onto the butter. To make sure not to lose any of the seeds, run your vanilla-coated knife through the butter.

Heat a large sauté pan over high heat for 2 minutes. Add the butter, vanilla, and vanilla pod to the pan. When the butter foams, place the pear wedges in the pan, cut side down. Season with the salt and cook 2 minutes. Sprinkle the sugar over the pears, and shake the pan to distribute the sugar and help it caramelize in the butter. Cook the pears about 6 minutes, basting them often with the butter, until they're caramelized on the first side. Carefully turn the pears over and cook another 3 to 4 minutes, continuing to baste, until the second side is golden and the pears are tender but not mushy. Transfer them to a platter and keep them in a warm place.

2 pounds Comice or Bartlett pears
½ vanilla bean
2 tablespoons unsalted butter
¼ teaspoon kosher salt
2 tablespoons granulated sugar

sources

almonds (marcona variety)

The Spanish Table
www.spanishtable.com

anchovies, salt-packed

Zingerman's
www.zingermans.com

arborio rice

Surfas
www.surfasonline.com

Zingerman's
www.zingermans.com

bacon

Nueske's
www.nueskes.com

The Grateful Palate
www.gratefulpalate.com
(In addition to bacon, they carry other
goodies like honey, jam, coffee, wine,
and, most important, they have a Bacon
of the Month Club)

beans (flageolet, cannellini, and more)

Zursun, Ltd.
(for dried heirloom beans and lentils, as
well as beluga lentils)
ph: 800-424-8881

Surfas
www.surfasonline.com
(including beluga lentils)

Windrose Farm
www.windrosefarm.org

black rice

Surfas
www.surfasonline.com

bottarga

Zingerman's
www.zingermans.com

cheese

Artisanal Cheese Center
www.artisanalcheese.com

Caseificio Gioia
(for burrata, mascarpone, mozzarella,
ricotta)
ph: 626-444-6015
gioiacheese@hotmail.com

Cheese Store of Beverly Hills
www.cheesestorebh.com

Cowgirl Creamery
www.cowgirlcreamery.com

chestnuts

Lucienne Grunder
ph: 206-848-4816
owl-nuts@ix.netcom.com

chickpeas

Zursun, Ltd.
ph: 800-424-8881

Surfas
www.surfasonline.com

chiles

The Spice House
www.thespicehouse.com
(beware of www.spicehouse.com!)

Windrose Farm
(including dried organic chiles)
www.windrosefarm.org

chocolate

Scharffen Berger
www.scharffenberger.com

dates

Bautista Dates
bautistadates@aol.com
ph: 760-396-2337

Pato's Dream Date Gardens
www.patosdreamdategardens.com

dried fruit

Peacock Family Farms
www.peacockfamilyfarms.com

duck and duck-related products such as duck fat

Sonoma County Poultry
www.libertyducks.com

fleur de sel

Honest Foods.com
www.honestfoods.com

Zingerman's
www.zingermans.com

fregola sarda

ChefShop.com
www.chefshop.com

Surfas
www.surfasonline.com

hazelnuts (oregon organic variety)

Trufflebert Farms
ph: 541-686-6186
truflebert@aol.com

heirloom tomatoes & apples (seasonal)

Windrose Farm
www.windrosefarm.org

kitchen equipment, baking supplies, specialty foods

Surfas
www.surfasonline.com

meat

Niman Ranch
www.nimanranch.com

mushrooms (wild)

Mikuni Wild Harvest
ph: 866-993-9927
www.mikuniwildharvest.com

nut oils from huilerie leblanc

Honest Foods.com
www.honestfoods.com

olive oil

Zingerman's
www.zingermans.com

olives (nyons, niçoise and lucques)

French Feast
www.frenchfeast.com

orange-flower water

French Feast
www.frenchfeast.com

pasta (rustichella brand, including orecchiette and torchio)

Surfas
www.surfasonline.com

pecans

Peacock Family Farms
www.peacockfamilyfarms.com

peppercorns (tellicherry variety)

Zingerman's
www.zingermans.com

polenta

Zingerman's
www.zingermans.com

Bob's Red Mill
www.bobsredmill.com

Anson Mills
www.ansonmills.com

pomegranate molasses

Zingerman's
www.zingermans.com

preserved lemons

ChefShop.com
www.chefshop.com

raisins

Peacock Family Farms
www.peacockfamilyfarms.com

saba

Zingerman's
www.zingermans.com

Surfas
www.surfasonline.com

scallops

Taylor Bay Scallops
ph: 508-990-0591

spanish products (chorizo, membrillo, jamón serrano, olive oil, saffron, paprika, etc.)

La Española
www.laespanolameats.com

The Spanish Table
www.spanishtable.com

spices

The Spice House
www.thespicehouse.com
(beware of www.spicehouse.com!)

sustainable seafood

Monterey Bay Aquarium
www.mbayaq.org
(click on the seafood watch program for Monterey Bay Aquarium's ratings of various kinds of fish)

Seafood Choices Alliance
www.seafoodchoices.com
(another great resource for information and articles on sustainability)

walnuts

Lucienne Grunder
(including the Tulare variety)
ph: 206-848-4816
owl-nuts@ix.netcom.com

Peacock Family Farms
www.peacockfamilyfarms.com

vanilla beans

Surfas
www.surfasonline.com

verjus

French Feast
www.frenchfeast.com

Surfas
www.surfasonline.com

index